VOID

Library of
Davidson College

TOWARD POLITICAL UNION

Planning a Common Foreign and Security Policy in the European Community

edited by
Reinhardt Rummel

Westview Press

Toward Political Union

Toward Political Union

Planning a Common Foreign
and Security Policy in
the European Community

EDITED BY
Reinhardt Rummel

Westview Press
BOULDER • SAN FRANCISCO • OXFORD

This Westview softcover edition is printed on acid-free paper and bound in library-quality, coated covers that carry the highest rating of the National Association of State Textbook Administrators, in consultation with the Association of American Publishers and the Book Manufacturers' Institute.

All rights reserved. No part of this publication may be reproduced or transmitted in any form or by any means, electronic or mechanical, including photocopy, recording, or any information storage and retrieval system, without permission in writing from the publisher.

Copyright © 1992 by Westview Press, Inc., except Chapter 3 © 1989 by Kluwer Academic Publishers. Reprinted by permission of the publisher.

Published in 1992 in the United States of America by Westview Press, Inc., 5500 Central Avenue, Boulder, Colorado 80301-2847, and in the United Kingdom by Westview Press, 36 Lonsdale Road, Summertown, Oxford OX2 7EW

Library of Congress Cataloging-in-Publication Data
Toward political union : planning a common foreign and security policy in the European community / edited by Reinhardt Rummel.
   p. cm.
  ISBN 0-8133-8518-0
  1. European Economic Community countries—Foreign relations.
2. European federation.
KJE5105.T68 1992
321'.04'094—dc20
                                                91-44207
                                                   CIP

Printed and bound in the United States of America

∞   The paper used in this publication meets the requirements of the American National Standard for Permanence of Paper for Printed Library Materials Z39.48-1984.

10   9   8   7   6   5   4   3   2   1

Contents

Preface viii

PART ONE
The Scope of Challenges for a Common Foreign and Security Policy

1 Regional Integration in the Global Test 3
  Reinhardt Rummel

PART TWO
State of the Art of Common Foreign Policy and Security Cooperation:
Internal Organization and External Activity

2 The Community's External Reach 29
  Eberhard Rhein

3 The Constitutional Foundation 41
  Maarten W. J. Lak

4 The Institutional Network and the
  Instruments of Action 55
  Simon Nuttall

5 The Core of Decision-Making 77
  Lawrence L. Hamlet

6 A Test Case of Consistency:
  The San José Dialogue 99
  Veerle Coignez

7 West European Responses to Change in the
  Soviet Union and Eastern Europe 115
  David Allen

8 EPC's Performance in Crises 135
  Christopher Hill

9	Western Europe and the Gulf War *Scott Anderson*	147
10	European Responses to the Yugoslav Crisis: An Interim Assessment *Geoffrey Edwards*	161
11	West European Cooperation on Nuclear Proliferation *Harald Müller*	187

PART THREE
Perceptions and Demands from Outside:
What Kind of Political Union?

12	View from the United States: Common Foreign and Security Policy as a Centerpiece of U.S. Interest in European Political Union *Christopher W. Murray*	211
13	View from the Soviet Union: Integration as a Progressive Concept for the Common European Home *Aleksandr Yakovenko*	219
14	View from Japan: Asymmetries in the Evolving European-Japanese Dialogue *Kensei Hiwaki*	227
15	View from Austria: Preparing for Membership *Manfred Scheich*	239
16	The Hungarian View: An EC Associate's Perspective from Central Europe *Istvàn Körmendy*	243
17	View from Yugoslavia: Political Union to Avoid Nineteenth Century Foreign Policy *Nina Vajic*	253
18	View from Turkey: Political Union as a Contribution to the New Europe *Sermet Atacanli*	259

PART FOUR
Assessing the Concepts for Political Union: CFSP as a Touchstone

19	From the Draft Treaty of 1984 to the Intergovernmental Conferences of 1991 *Rosa Maria Alonso Terme*	267
20	Scope and Structure of the Community's Future Foreign Policy *Giovanni Jannuzzi*	289
21	Beyond Maastricht: Alternative Futures for a Political Union *Reinhardt Rummel*	297

ANNEX
Extracts of Selected Documents on Political Union in 1991

1	European Council	323
2	EC Commission	336
3	European Parliament	349
4	Western European Union	354
5	North Atlantic Treaty Organization	357
6	Bilateral Initiatives	360
7	EC and United States	371

Abbreviations	375
Contributors	376

Preface

The Maastricht European Council meeting of December 1991 has adopted the blueprints for another step toward European Political Union. As a central element of this union, a Common Foreign and Security Policy is expected to turn the Community into a more consistent and more influential international actor. This was a timely initiative: both the international order and the relations on the European continent are in a state of thorough transformation raising many expectations for support and leadership, some of them addressed to the West European countries organized in the European Community. The Community itself cannot opt out of these demands but, as of now, has not been prepared for a qualitatively and quantitatively much wider external reach. Will the Maastricht plans facilitate closing the gap between the Community's internal preparedness and its external ambitions?

This volume attempts to provide the basis for an answer to this question. It draws on the knowledge and the assessment of insiders in the institutional machinery in Brussels as well as on the analysis and the views of experts and diplomats from outside the Community. In its four parts, the book *first* of all maps out the scope and the nature of the external challenges with which a Common Foreign and Security Policy is confronted. It *then* determines the state of the art of present Community external relations by analyzing its internal constitution and its recent performance in international tasks. In the *third* part, perceptions and demands from key countries outside the Community give us an idea of how such a new international actor will be received in the European and international arena. The *final* part is devoted to an assessment of the Maastricht Documents in the perspective of a Community on the road to political union. In preparation for Maastricht, 1991 has been a very busy year for plan designers, rapporteurs and communiqué writers. Extracts of selected documents from major institutions and member states are reprinted in the annex.

The production of the book profited from academic internationalism: on their way from Bologna, Italy, to Washington, D.C., three post-graduate students, Scott Anderson, Sylvia M. Schwaag and Ellen Thalman of the Paul H. Nitze School of Advanced International Studies, The Johns Hopkins University, stayed at the Stiftung Wissenschaft und Politik, Ebenhausen, Germany, for the summer to do most of the editorial work. I also want to thank Ursula Jung and Christine Hammann for assisting with the coordination and documentation of the book as well as Maria Maier and Lorenzo Frau for final composition of the manuscript.

Reinhardt Rummel

PART ONE

The Scope of Challenges for a Common Foreign and Security Policy

1

Regional Integration in the Global Test

Reinhardt Rummel

> *The three days in August were a real watershed. I sometimes say that what happened before the coup was, so to speak, before the new era, and after it was the beginning of a new epoch.*
>
> Mikhail Gorbachev*

After the Confrontation Era: A World in Transition

At present Europe is being driven by two dynamics: integration and disintegration. While Western Europe's Heads of State and Government in Maastricht prepared to erect another pillar of the new "European Union" (EU), leaders in Moscow tried to find a consensus on the construction of a new "Union of Sovereign States" (USS). The contrast and the similarities of the two union building processes in the Western and the Eastern ends of the European continent could not be more dramatic. The failed *putsch* of August 1991 in the Soviet Union had given the final blow to the tumbling communist empire and thus to the postwar world order. In the wake of the *coup*, the Union of Soviet Socialist Republics (USSR) was formally dissolved. The legality of the Communist Party of the Soviet Union on the former territory of the USSR was suspended, and the party was outlawed in some of the republics. The military in the attempted *coup d'état* turned out to be as divided and rife with social and ethnic conflicts as the society at large. While the free fall of the economy was accelerating, the republics and the remnants of the Union were trying to knit a political as well as economic safety net. At the same time, leaders from all parts of the former Soviet Union turned to the Western industrialized countries and especially to the European Community (EC) and its member states for help.

---

* Mikhail Gorbachev, *The August Coup. The Truth and the Lessons*, London: Harper-Collins Publishers, 1991, p. 31.

Brussels had to decide. This was not a decision on emergency measures following a flood, a land slide, an epidemic or some other natural catastrophe; it was a decision to be made after a geostrategic earthquake. The international context for foreign and security policy in Western Europe had fundamentally changed -- and so had the context for regional integration.[1]

The Present Constellation

How does Western Europe's present international environment look at a time when the Community and its member states are asked both to construct their own union and to respond to demands from outside, especially to the disintegration and re-integration process in the wider Europe? Since the early fifties the West European states have been engaged in a process of regional integration, characterized by alternating deepening and widening impulses. Within this process a *rapprochement* of interests has come about in almost all policy areas while at the same time national particularities were reinforced. Within most policy areas a mixture of national, coordinated and communitarian policy instruments has been developed, with the competence of the Community growing significantly. The fundamental change after the end of the Cold War has not yet altered this trend, rather nurtured it.

As a contrast, continuity in transatlantic and especially Pan-European relations has been interrupted on a large scale. North America will remain an essential security partner for Western Europe for specific tasks, but there is no denying the fact that the formerly common monolithic mission of "the West" to check a Warsaw Pact aggression no longer exists.[2] There is no "the East" anymore, and the Bush Administration is trying to reorganize and multiplicate its links with all the actors on the European continent. This includes not only the Community and NATO but also East European countries, the USS and the Conference on Security and Cooperation in Europe (CSCE). All East European countries are in a state of reorientation, internally and externally, with a strong political inclination toward the West. The Yugoslav Federation is dissolving and haunted by civil war. The USS is not yet settled as an entity, the style and content of its foreign and security policy as well as that of its republics are largely unknown.[3]

---

1 Adam Roberts, "A New Age in International Relations?" in: *International Affairs*, Vol 67, No. 3, July 1991, pp. 509-526.
2 Willem F. van Eekelen, *The Changing Environment of Transatlantic Relations*, Paris: European Strategy Group (ESG) Report, 1991.
3 For an analysis of the combination of disintegration and reformation of the former Soviet Union see Hannes Adomeit, "Interaction of Political and Economic Change in the (Soviet) Union: Implications for Foreign Policy," Paper presented to the Defense Academic Research Support Program (DARSP) conference which took

Western Europe is about to transfer more foreign and security policy decision-making power to the Community and to the Western European Union (WEU) as a complement to NATO and CSCE. The neutral and former Warsaw Pact countries are trying to lean on these organizations. The USS remains to a certain extent a co-actor with the US with respect to strategic and global issues. The West Europeans have taken on a new field of responsibility in Eastern Europe and have to deal with new cooperation partners, especially the USS, and therewithin the Russian Republic and the Ukraine. The Council of Europe is likely to count pretty soon almost all European countries among its numbers. The CSCE is undergoing both a further institutionalization and an adaptation of its standards and instruments to the new demands of stability in Europe.

Japan, via the activities of the Economic Summit (G-7), the Organization of Economic Cooperation and Development (OECD) and the World Bank and International Monetary Fund is participating in decisions on how to stabilize Europe. In addition, Tokyo is following a policy of its own in bilateral relations with the USS. Apart from that, Japan presently is no full member of the transatlantic/Pan-European security structure. For the time being, Washington remains Tokyo's exclusive security partner.[4]

Beyond these continuities and changes among the international actors of the northern hemisphere, the structure of the international system has been altered significantly. The shift from a bipolar world to an open system allows and requires new coalition building among states and organizations. It is still an unsettled question as to what extent the countries of the so-called Third World will form an integral part of this extended zone of cooperation in the North. Since the main purpose of confrontation between the former two superpowers has faded, security policy tends to be no longer a separate prime policy area. The international system is determined by economic rather than by military factors, automatically raising the influence as well as the responsibility of the Community and Japan in international conflict prevention as well as management -- whether they like it or not. The fact that the three centers of economic gravity and power, the US, the Community and Japan, have reached a by and large equal level of assertiveness is pushing the Community into a new role as a partial leader in the international system.

This current constellation can turn out to be a stable one, but it is likely that it will undergo further substantial change. The process of transformation as a consequence of the end of the Cold War is by no means finished. Present trends can be reenforced or reversed. Western Europe could well be dragged into the

---

place at USEUCOM on "Military and Political Environment in a Post Cold War Era," Stuttgart, 6-7 November 1991.
4 Zbigniew Brzezinski, "Selective Global Commitment," in: Foreign Affairs, Vol. 70, No. 4, (Fall 1991), pp. 1-20.

turbulences of these shifts or could manage to keep away from them, or could deliberately march into them. By the same token one cannot exclude that within the Community new orientations might also flow from changes in the socio-economic data and the power status of member states or as a consequence of a growing nationalistic behavior. Just like the countries in Eastern Europe the West European societies will have to redefine their values, interests, and goals with respect to a shifting international theater. In this regard, "revolutions" in Western Europe have hardly begun. West European integration and its main strategies might well need adaptation. Community building *must* be different depending on whether the rigidities of a bloc-to-bloc international system or the options of an open global system apply.

External Challenges to the Community

A large part of the debate on West European foreign policy and security cooperation is focusing almost entirely on internal and institutional questions. This is particularly the case in the Community and WEU context, partly also in CSCE and NATO. Institutional preconditions and arrangements do matter, but it seems indispensible, at a juncture of fundamental change in terms of international relations and security demands, to continue all integration efforts in Western Europe, while carefully assessing the nature and scope of challenges to cope with in a new world. The follow-on question then is: What is the specific task which a particular institution such as the Community should cover? Function should drive institution building, not vice versa. A number of outstanding challenges for the future Common Foreign and Security Policy (CFSP) of the Community are in obvious demand of a response. Some of these challenges are briefly characterized below.

How to prevent a military conflict between former Soviet republics? What are the economic, foreign policy and security requirements in the unsettled Balkan conflicts? What is the most relevant risk feature worldwide with regard to the post-Cold War and the post-Iraq War era? It seems that, *first* of all, it is the nature of security shifts from the clearly definable defense issue to the much less definable political issue. Certainly, we will have to continue to cope with military machineries, be it in the former Soviet Union or in the Middle East, but "military solutions" of conflicts are much less ends in themselves than they used to be. Stability in today's Europe is no longer achievable by military balances. Other assets come into being such as economic performance, human rights standards, and freedom of communication. Likewise, the instability caused by Saddam Hussein in the Middle East was not neutralized by fighting a war. Additional, more longterm measures, such as a change in the political culture of the region (see the Madrid International Peace Conference) and a new technology transfer policy from North to South and, indeed, within the

South, have to come into play to control regional conflicts. This means that the foreign and security policy of the new era will be much more political, and will deal with a large range of policies beyond the military one. The conclusion to draw from this observation is that at the heart of future foreign and security policy there must be increasingly more policy coordination than defense coordination. Hence, the importance of a politization of NATO, a much wider role for the European Community, and an obvious need for the two organizations and their member states to develop a joint approach to security, peace and wealth inside and outside Europe.[5]

A *second* important feature of future foreign policy and security challenges is the differentiation of dangers. It would be wrong to aggregate various dangers in an effort to generalize them. Western nations are not in an unspecified situation of a defense *tous azimuts*. Just to introduce one differentiation: The NATO allies have two kinds of neighbors, the East Europeans and the people beyond the southern rim of the Mediterranean.[6] Both groups of neighbors have much in common in terms of dangers they might cause or in terms of responses the Western allies might consider. Any war of significance in Eastern Europe, however, could involve parts of the former Soviet military and could ultimately lead to the destruction of Western societies. By contrast, wars at NATO's southern periphery could be very costly, but (so far) do not have the potential of destroying Western societies. The conclusion here is that in the first category of challenge (aggressive involvement of the former Soviet military),[7] NATO has to be in the forefront of any Western response and any strategic balance concept, while in the second category of challenges (only southern neighbors are involved) Community/WEU could be developed to deal with some of the dangers. Whether in these cases Community/WEU could or should go it alone or rather need to be backed by NATO or the United States is a question to be seriously sorted out.

A *third* feature of challenges in Western Europe's external environment is the change of challenges over time. Thus, the NATO allies are in an uncertain situation as long as the Soviets still remain militarily present in Germany and

---

5 The vast agenda of redefinition of security and institutional reform is analyzed in the volume of Jeffrey Simon (ed.), *European Security Policy After the Revolutions of 1989*, Washington, DC: National Defense University, 1991.

6 Roberto Aliboni, *European Security Across the Mediterranean*, Chaillot Papers No. 2, Paris: Institute for Security Studies, 1991. Maurizio Cremasco, "The Southern Region of Europe, Problems and Perspectives," in: Armand Clesse and Lothar Rühl (eds.), *Beyond East-West Confrontation: Searching for a New Security Structure in Europe*, Baden-Baden: Nomos, 1990, p. 332-341.

7 In November 1991 the Ukraine's parliament accepted central Soviet control over nuclear weapons on its territory but demanded the right to veto their use.

East European countries, while the further course of the USS and its republics remains unpredictable and NATO member countries have already shifted gears.[8] A premature anticipation of complete Soviet withdrawal from Eastern Europe can be very costly. The transition period from now to the end of 1994 holds a set of dangers which is quite different from a post-withdrawal constellation. Western institutional response will have to be prepared for military reconstitution while keeping in mind that at the end of a successful transformation the former Soviet republics could even become NATO members. NATO is absolutely indispensible and should be strengthened during this transition period, but -- because of continuous sensitivity in some parts of the former Soviet Union -- cannot provide much of a direct help to East European countries (see the Liaison Concept as a maximum). Here is a slot for West European organizations, especially the Community and the WEU, even if their response to East European demands for economic assistance, foreign policy consultation and security cooperation remains a modest one. After final Soviet withdrawal, NATO is likely to be in a position to meet some of the security needs of East European countries while West European bodies might well become central players in the economic and political field.

A *fourth* feature is characterized by the new awareness of the importance of international norms and regimes in a new world order which is no longer structured in blocs.[9] Just as Saddam Hussein was not allowed to break vital international rules, the aggressors in Yugoslavia should be denied the right to have it their way. The United Nations (UN) are in a strengthened role in this regard. International regimes and their enforcement will be extended in critical fields such as proliferation of technology for weapons of mass destruction and ecological/cultural damage to mankind. Development of the European code of conduct and its enforcement is on the agenda of the CSCE countries. Some traditional principles such as sovereignty, non-interference in internal affairs, self-determination, minority rights, respect of borders, and veto rights have to be qualified.[10] All of these are at the heart of a new peace order in Europe.[11]

---

8   Ronald D. Asmus, J. F. Brown, Keith Crane, *Soviet Foreign Policy and the Revolutions of 1989 in Eastern Europe,* Santa Monica: RAND, 1991.
9   Alan K. Henrikson, *Defining a New World Order,* A discussion paper for The Fletcher Round Table, 2-3 May 1991, Medford: The Fletcher School of Law and Diplomacy, 1991. According to Henrikson the vision of a new world order can be realized by strengthening regional peace- and security efforts, extending the rule of law to permit internal intervention and creating peace-enforcement and permanent peacekeeping capabilities for future use by the UN.
10 James Mayall, "Non-Intervention, Self-Determination and the 'New World Order'," in: *International Affairs,* Vol. 67, No. 3, July 1991, pp. 421-430.

The demand here is to find a common basis among European countries and societies which come from differing political experiences and civilizations. The difficulty for the CFSP is applying these standards domestically throughout the Community as well.

A *fifth* feature of the future security situation in Europe is determined by the domestic environment of CSCE member countries. Take for example Germany. If Bonn's NATO allies are interested in a German military contribution to out-of-area contingencies (and both Eastern Europe and the Middle East are out of the NATO area), it can only be assured via the multilateral avenue. As long as NATO remains limited to its borders, the Community and/or WEU would have to establish forces of their own to allow the *Bundeswehr* to join multilateral actions beyond the NATO treaty geographical borders. Moreover, Germany has accepted a number of military restraints in the Two-plus-Four Agreement of September 1990 such as no nuclear weapons on the territory of the former German Democratic Republic. As a consequence, the Federal Republic as a whole is likely to refuse the stationing of any future nuclear arsenal on its soil. Domestic particularities in Germany or in almost any other European country (just think of France) will therefore determine the institutional options for West European, transatlantic and all-European foreign policy consultation and security cooperation. [12]

Thus, at the national, regional and global level the main structural problem seems to be identical: the incongruency of dangers and security provisions. Gone are the days when a conflict could be defined institutionally. NATO, even the reformed Alliance, is not *the* solution to all foreign and security problems in Europe. CSCE is a help for some security requirements in Europe, by far not for all of them. WEU, too, was reactivated ten years ago for a different foreign policy and security environment from today's. Likewise, in the case of the Community, its foreign policy agenda and its future security missions have to be redefined in an ideologically and structurally changed international context. Given the underdeveloped policy planning structure of the Community, a crucial question is therefore the evolution of a more powerful and more

---

11 For a comprehensive concept of assuring peace in a post-confrontation era see Dieter Senghaas, "Peace theory and the restructuring of Europe," in: *Alternatives*, Vol. 16, No. 3, Summer 1991, pp. 353-366.

12 See Stephen F. Szabo, *The Changing Politics of German Security*, London: St. Martins Press, 1990. Leon Brittan , "International Security in a Time of Change. Europe within NATO," in: *The RUSI Journal*, Vol. 136, No. 2, Summer 1991, pp. 35-38. Margaret Thatcher, "Unfinished Business, New Challenges," *The Heritage Lectures*, No. 340, 23 September 1991. Edith Cresson, "Défense et l'avenir de l'Europe," in: *Défense Nationale*, Vol. 47, November 1991, pp. 9-2o. Marcel Duval, "Quel avenir pour la dissuasion nucléaire française?" in: *Défense Nationale*, Vol. 47, October 1991, pp. 25-39.

operation oriented foreign policy and security analysis body for the CFSP (see below, chapter 21).

New Tasks for the Community

The East-West power stratification is rapidly dissolving and is causing countless major changes in the international system. The Community which used to develop itself and to operate in a "given" order is now part of the whirlpool of changes and has to take over much more of the responsibility for its own destiny than in the traditional setting. The demands are of a kind and a dimension the Community is hardly prepared to answer, despite the progress which has been made at Maastricht. Successful adaptation would lead the Community into new spheres of action and could turn the foreign policy actor Western Europe into a much stronger and more distinct member of the international system and more specifically of the trans-European and transatlantic realm.

From the large panoply of challenges which are urged on the Community a few stick out because of their unprecedented scope and character. These are the tasks of integrating the new Germany, stabilizing the wider Europe, and modernizing European-American relations. In managing these tasks the Community itself will change its texture as well as its outlook. The concept of regional integration will be put to multiple tests in the sectors of foreign and security policy. Will the Community in this regard prevail and expand or will it fail and disclose more of its limits?

Absorbing United Germany: Nationalism vs. Integrationism

The most outstanding consequence of the breakdown of the "real-socialist" system is demonstrated in the center of Europe. The entire postwar order which was built on the separation of the two Germanys has now become obsolete. The two outposts of the old confrontation order are united since October 1990. This eventually will solve a major part of the perennial central European problem but causes new ones. The absorption of a united Germany into Europe raises the question of size. Germany is now considerably bigger than any other European state except for the Russian Republic. For both states a solution has to be found to integrate them into Europe and into the wider international system in a way which allows for a balance of power and denies any strategic breakout from this system.

It remains to be seen, or better, it has to be studied what the outcome of the unification of the two Germanies will be. What is the potential which the former German Democratic Republic (GDR) is contributing to the political culture of united Germany? How will the body politic in the former Federal

Republic of Germany react to the reality of one large German nation? How will the foreign and security policy of the new Germany be affected? Does Europe have to expect a dangerous reenforcement of German nationalism? Will Germany follow its geographical imperative and -- for the sake of balancing the new power structure in Europe -- cooperate with Russia and the USS member states as much as with its EC partners?

To answer the new German question, the Community has a prominent role to play.[13] The Community has been extremely receptive during the political change in the GDR and the creation of the German economic and monetary union. Brussels has made all efforts to absorb the larger Germany after 3 October, 1990. German size will be accommodated in the European institutions, especially the European Parliament (EP). German economic power will be integrated by further progress in the EC's Economic and Monetary Union (EMU). The efficiency of the German economic system is rather an asset than a challenge for fellow EC-Europeans. German international standing could become an integral part of the future European Political Union (EPU) in Western Europe. Eastern connections of the (former) two German states could be treated as a potential for a more comprehensive approach of the Community's CSFP at large. The strategic position of Germany could be used as an asset of the Community in the cooperative structures of Europe and the Northern zone of cooperation in general.

Most of Germany's EC partners are in a dilemma here. On the one hand they would love to see Bonn/Berlin support their own interests in Eastern Europe while on the other hand nobody seems to like the idea of letting the Germans instrumentalize the Community for their own purposes.[14] There is no easy way out of this dilemma, but neither Germany nor any other West European state should be allowed to go back to 19th century nationalism. The dominant ideology of the outgoing 20th century should be integrationism, at least on the European continent. However, both forces, nationalism and integrationism, should coexist and check each other's extremist developments. In Western Europe, the nation-state will continue to exist, but it will be embedded in an integrationist environment: the process toward European Union, based on the principles of subsidiarity as well as federalism. In this respect, the pledges of Maastricht have to be turned into living reality.

---

13 Rosalind Stevens-Strohmann, "German Unification and Europe's integration," in: *The World Today*, Vol. 47, No. 10, October 1991, pp. 169-171.

14 Michael Lind, "German Fate and Allied Fears," in: *The National Interest*, No. 19 (Spring 1990), pp. 34-44.

Developing Stability on the European Continent: Security via Integration

The concept of integration will also have to be tested as a means to overcome the East-West cleavage and to establish a peaceful all-European order. East European countries are not used to integrationism. Compared to West European countries they lack forty years of experience. They are used to totalitarian oriented regimes. As these socialist dictatures have given way to pluralist democracy, nationalism has become the dominant force of identification among the East European as well as Soviet population. This nationalistic inclination is understandable but rather backward as long as it is not combined with integrationism. The concentration on nationalism disregards the ever growing degree of interdependence, communication and interaction of modern societies. It underestimates the benefits of cooperation and self-restraint.

East European countries can learn about the political system of the Community, but as they did not live it they will need some time to understand it, to evaluate it, and to adopt it, if they so choose. The rules of integrationism are more complicated and demand more political maturity from electorates and more sophisticated skills from policymakers than those of nationalism. The Community's association and cooperation policy with the wider Europe has to take account of this problem which is not only a systemic question but also a question of the mindset.

The *first* major cleavage between East and West on the European continent, therefore, is the difference in political culture. The Community has to demonstrate during the current period of transition in Europe that integrationism works -- especially in times of major demands on the system such as the task of absorbing united Germany which has nationalistic temptations of its own.

The *second* rift to overcome in Europe is of a socio-economic nature. The economic and technological difference between East and West European countries is enormous and will take a long time to be balanced. Social imbalances, already high within the Eastern and South Eastern part of Europe, might even grow during the next years, should some industrializing regions manage to catch up with the West. Social imbalances are likely to provide the environment for turmoil and uncontrollable conflict, perhaps in connection with ethnic and religious claims. These conflicts within Europe cannot be avoided or hedged in by military means. Only economic development can help and, therefore, the Community is well placed to take on as much of this responsibility as possible, using its instruments of external relations with countries of all levels of industrialisation. A paradigmatic case study in this regard is the Mediterranean policy of the Community which, in the early seventies, was designed as a *political* concept of stabilization in the region by *economic* means. The concept of regional integration as an instrument of transferring economic welfare will have to be tested in relation with Eastern Europe as well. The solution cannot be simple and quick enlargement but rather a combination of EC association and autonomous integration within the East.

A *third* feature of separation in Europe is characterized by the military and strategic setup of the postwar period. Major changes are underway concerning the military potential of the former antagonistic camps. Certainly, the reduction of military forces and the alterations of military doctrines will help to change people's mindsets in the former Eastern and Western blocs. Yet, for the time being, it seems that huge military forces and major weapons systems will continue to exist on both sides and will be modernized, even though they might take on a more defensive character. A balance has to be found for the remaining forces and the core problem is how to define the criteria for military stability among the future 40 to 50 states in Europe. The various current negotiation processes are designed to achieve just that and to develop common rules and bodies of verification as well as further confidence building structures (see the March 1992 Helsinki II conference).[15]

The Community's most logical reaction in this new climate of cooperation between Eastern and Western nations cannot be the establishment of a military arm of the European Union. Rather, the Twelve have to contribute to a new approach in the field of security. They have to first reassess the need for such a military arm in a radically changed Europe. A genuine West European assessment of threats, dangers and risks has to precede any further move toward a military component of the West European integration process. In the case of the Community, the argument is too simple that any union of states needs defense forces of its own and that, therefore, a West European defense union has to be created parallel to the Economic, Monetary and Political Union. Rather, policymakers should know more about the specific tasks of those defense forces in a changing domestic, European and international environment before determining size, outfit and missions of these forces and before placing the military instrument in the appropriate proportion to other (costly) instruments of foreign and security policy. Moreover, a certain integration of armed forces could be needed as one of the guarantee factors for the internal stability of the Political Union itself.

One way of overcoming strategic enmities has been demonstrated, in a paradigmatic way, by the ideas of Jean Monnet and Robert Schuman forty years ago. Shouldn't these ideas be reactivated for the creation of an all-European peace order? The principle of their ideas is complementary to the concept of a collective security system which is one of the suggestions in the

---

15 Hans Binnendijk, "The Emerging European Security Order," in: *The Washington Quarterly*, Vol. 14, No. 4, Autumn 1991, pp. 67-81.

present debate. A collective security system is designed to meet a common external threat or challenge. It produces security among participating members only if they perceive a threatening common external enemy. During the Iraq conflict such a danger was looming. However, in the Europe after the Cold War, European nations need first of all internal security, just as the West European nations needed safeguards among themselves after World War II. Monnet's and Schuman's idea to pool national sovereignties in areas of strategic importance for the creation of war industries could be adapted to Europe as a whole. The sectors to be managed by a High Commission would nowadays consist of electronics and communication technology or energy supply (see the Energy Charter of December 1991), rather than coal and steel, but the principle of shifting sectoral sovereignty from individual countries to common policies via an international organisation or community would apply here too.

But just as the West European nations did not stop their cooperation with the inception of the Coal and Steel Community, Europe as a whole as well as its subregions should be put on the tracks of a more comprehensive cooperation process. It is this dynamic of an ever closer cooperation which takes on integration quality and engenders internal security. The goal of an all-European confederation as proposed by François Mitterrand on New Year's Day of 1990 could be the common focus of such a cooperation and integration process. The strategic rift in Europe would be bridged by the dynamics and structures of such a process. Integration serves as a strategic security building concept.

Within an all-European confederation a number of institutions and organisations should take care of reducing major imbalances between regions and states.[16] The Community should be a central player in this regard. In CSCE, the Community should deal specifically with the strategic imbalance and the normative divide of Europe. In the Council of Europe, it should continue its effort to spread democratic values all over Europe. Within the Economic European Area (EEA) and within the OECD, it should try to cope with economic imbalances by stretching cooperative links to East European countries and the former Soviet Republics. Via Eureka (European Research Cooperation Agency), the Community should make sure to include more cooperation partners from the East in order to overcome some of the technological imbalances. These intergovernmental institutions have to be supplemented by a network of nongovernmental and transnational cooperation in Europe.

---

16 Peter Schmidt, "The Development of West European Cooperation in Security and Defence Policy in an All-European Perspective," in: Bo Huldt and Guvilla Herolf (eds.), *Towards a New European Security Order*, Göteborg: MH Publishing, 1991, pp. 238-259.

Before becoming too enthusiastic about the EC-type cooperation as a solution to peace in Europe at large, it should be recalled, however, that the Community has become a peace system itself, also because it was based on the rule of law applying to individual legal persons as well as to states and was largely guided by human rights standards and federal principles -- all this based on relatively strong economies. Circumstances in most parts of the East are not that favorable for now.

Transforming European-American Relations: Integration as an Open System

To the extent that military power and military alliances lose some of their validity, at least in the northern hemisphere of the globe, transatlantic relations are also affected.[17] From one NATO summit to the next, communiqués in the last three years have stressed the political nature of the Atlantic Alliance. The new means to cope with the former enemy in the East are increasingly of a nonmilitary kind. Washington, which used to dominate NATO in an ideologically and militarily confrontational East-West setting, is losing some of its influence. This does not yet seem to be a problem as long as both the United States and the West European allies follow pretty much the same policy toward the East or the Third World. However, some of the traditional transatlantic trade conflicts could well become more visible since NATO and the Soviet threat have ceased playing the disciplining role. The Community and its trade policy will be more exposed to American attempts to make up for its loss of influence, while the West Europeans themselves will have to come forward with substantial solutions for the new sets of dangers which may be small but plenty.

The Community is rapidly developing genuine relations with East European countries and with the republics of the former Soviet Union. This breaks with a tradition of non-relations between the EC/EPC (European Political Cooperation) and Moscow. Most of Western Europe's strategically important connections and negotiations used to be coordinated in NATO and were dealt with in the multilateral framework of the CSCE, in which Washington was an integrated member. It comes as an ambivalent innovation to the American diplomacy that Western Europe is opening up its own dialogues with Moscow and other East European countries and that a network of bilateral treaties is creating a new field of West European prominence: Washington, on the one hand, likes to see the West Europeans take over more of the burdens of assuring stability in Europe. On the other hand, the US Administration suspects a peering of Brussels and Moscow (see the common EPC/USSR declaration on

---

17 Willem F. van Eekelen, *The Changing Environment of Transatlantic Relations*, Paris: ESG Report, 1991.

the Iraq conflict of September 1990) and American business hates to see West European competitors in a more advantageous position. Hence the demand from Washington to coordinate most of the Western policy toward the East within the Western institutions, especially in the G-7 Summit, OECD and NATO. The EC/EPC member states are faced with the need for an extension of the transatlantic dialogue in order to give the U.S. more influence on intra-European relations. Then again, the West Europeans want to develop as much of their own a political union in Western Europe as possible and therefore need a certain amount of autonomy.[18]

Washington's desire to sit in on the Single Market negotiations within the Community has been an example of the United States' interest to remain more immediately involved in structural changes on the European continent. The same attitude emerged when the Twelve worked out the plans for CSFP and more specifically military cooperation. If EMU and the Political Union are installed in the near future, it might well be that Western Europe will be perceived more like a fortress than a system open to enlargement, cooperation and interaction with other states or organizations. Integrationism producing positive results within Europe may lead to a sort of isolationism or extreme "regionalism" on the level of the Community. The United States (having gone through civil wars, before becoming a federated union two centuries ago) may feel like a victim of a federated European Union.

Regional integration in Western Europe should neither lead to the creation of an inward looking power bloc nor to an arrogant or dominant international actor. The Community should develop its relationship with the United States along with the intensification of the West European integration process and the establishment of a cooperative cobweb with Eastern countries. The West Europeans continue to need Washington as a strategic partner to balance both the remnants of former Soviet military power and any other potentially dangerous power concentration in the world which -- like in the Iraq case -- can produce dangerous spillovers. West Europeans also need to maintain close economic and political ties with the Americans in order to preserve and develop the Western values. The quality of their relationship cannot fall beneath a level dictated by the high degree of transatlantic interaction and interdependence. It would thus be foolish as well as backward to ban the US from Europe. However, the kind of American involvement in Europe and the sort of new cooperation with Washington in a post cold-war era should be carefully determined.[19]

---

18 Hugh De Santis, "The Graying of NATO," in: *The Washington Quarterly*, Vol. 14, No. 4, Autumn 1991, pp. 51-66.
19 Helga Haftendorn, *European Security Cooperation and the Atlantic Alliance*, Florence: European University Institute, 1991.

The Community will have to prove to its international partners that regional integration can both unite a group of countries in a viable political entity and keep this entity open for close cooperation and interaction with other international actors. The transformation of US-West European relations is one prominent test case in this regard. Taken together with the task of producing security via integration and of checking nationalism by integrationism, the test will be of a tall order, and it seems unlikely that the Community with its present foundations and institutional provisions can succeed.

EPU as a Way to Adapt to International Change

With the decisions in Maastricht, the Community has set new targets and instruments expected to lead to greater integration of its internal policies and to greater effectiveness in its external action. In other words, a move toward some form of distinct EU which could help deal with the external tasks and challenges as outlined above. After their inception in Rome in December 1990, the IGC (Intergovernmental Conference) on EMU and the IGC on EPU worked parallel during 1991, and their outcome was politically linked. The Maastricht Documents of December 1991 are intended to amend and transcend the Rome Treaties and will have to be ratified in the parliaments of the Twelve by the end of 1992. Thus, by the beginning of 1993, the Community plans to have advanced in three respects: to have completed the Internal Market, to have established the contractual grounds for EMU, and to have set the constitutional stage for EPU.

If all goes well, the perennial plan for a EU will take on a much more elaborate shape. If things go wrong, the Community will not fall apart, but it will have missed a chance for a giant leap forward. In any case, major optional developments are ahead: Is this the reaction to a growing diversity among West European nations or the unavoidable consequence of spillover in the functional approach to West European integration? Is this the final euphoric phase in the creation of the "United States of Europe", or is it simply another desperate move of the West European group of states to adapt to changes in the international system? Is this the birth of a new hegemonic power in Europe or the preparation of an altruistic contributor to the network of all-European cooperation inside and outside the CSCE framework? In answering these questions, the following considerations will be confined to the EPU part of the new *relance européenne* as documented in the reports by the 1991 Luxemburg and Netherlands Presidencies.[20]

---

20 Luxemburg Presidency Report on "Draft Treaty on the Union", reprinted in *Agence Europe* (Documents), No. 1722/1723 (5 July 1991). Dutch Presidency Report on

Deepening and Widening

EPU is meant to intensify the integration process in Western Europe. Deepening the Community means advancing in three respects: develop the political system of the Community, extend its competences, increase the resources for common policies. The political system of the Community is in several respects incomplete and asymmetrical. Its lack of efficiency, its democratic deficit and its intelligibility are well-known and widely identified deficiencies. The EPU-Reports mention a number of areas in which to develop the political system: the (Spanish) idea of a European citizenship, the (German) proposal of a Council of regional representatives, the (British) idea of participation of national parliaments in the European decision-making. Other suggestions are intended to enhance the role of the major Community institutions, especially the European Parliament, the Council of Ministers, the Commission and the European Council. One of the questions here is whether the present balance among these institutions is kept or altered. Most of the decisionmakers claim that the institutional balance should not be changed. It seems, however, almost inevitable, if not wise, to review the traditional status of all institutions on the background of qualitative changes inside and outside the Community.

The EPU-Reports envisage the transfer of more competences to Brussels. This concerns areas of formerly intergovernmental cooperation such as environment, health, energy, research, technology, consumer protection. They also refer to issues which are consequences from the establishment of the Internal Market such as immigration and asylum regulations, the fight against drug abuse and international crime. A third area of extended Community competences is foreign and security policy. New Community policies can not be implemented without an appropriate financial base and the recruitment of skilled personnel. Therefore, the question of more autonomous financial sources for the Community are once again on the agenda including the idea of granting the Community the legal basis to establish a little tax of its own.

Taken together, these proposals form a copious and heterogenious agenda for the Twelve's way beyond Maastricht. If ratifications are successful and the Community is deepened on schedule, enlargement might be reconsidered seriously in early 1993.[21] The dynamics of West Europe's integration has always been an interplay of deepening and widening. Research which has

---

the "Draft Treaty Towards European Union", reprinted in *Agence Europe* (Documents), No. 1734/1735 (3 October 1991).

21   A few weeks before Maastricht, Jacques Delors, EC Commission President, had already suggested a third IGC to be launched on enlargement in order to deal with the political and institutional consequences of a Community with up to 30 member states.

looked into the Northern enlargement in the 1970s and the Southern enlargement in the 1980s has confirmed a positive correlation between widening and deepening.[22] The same may well be expected from the Eastern enlargement of the Community in the 1990s which has already begun with the merging of the German Democratic Republic into the Federal Republic of Germany since 1990 -- even though this was a very particular case. The Eastern enlargement round will be more complicated than the previous ones. It affects five groups of potential candidates of a very diverse nature: the (seven) EFTA countries, the (three) advanced East Central European reform countries, the (three) former Soviet Baltic republics, the (three) less advanced South East European reform countries including the Yugoslav conglomerate (certainly Slovenia and Croatia), and the (twelve) republics of the USR. Each of the first four groups will extend the Community to border the new Union of Sovereign States in the very eastern part of the Continent. Integration dynamics and security considerations will inevitably be intertwined.

Unlike widespread assumption in the European public and, notably, in North America, the Community does not face a dilemma in making a choice between deepening and widening. The Twelve and the Community have made the decision that they would not accept further members before the current round of deepening is successfully concluded by 1993. Policymakers in Brussels regard deepening a precondition and a preparation for widening. It also helps to manage the expected widening process in the second half of the 1990s in an orderly way. Moreover, the Community wanted to make sure that major options for its further development such as a common currency and a common defense policy are not excluded by a premature expansion of the number and the type of new member states. In this regard, the Maastricht deepening effort can be seen as a preemptive move in the perspective of an unavoidable enlargement. If so, the deepening measures will have to anticipate the future size of the Community and will have to shape its internal structure accordingly. This imperative -- the Community functions largely on a structure which dates back to the EC/Six -- placed a heavy burden on the negotiators of the EPU treaty. A further burden was that the Community might not be allowed the luxury of implementing all the deepening decisions before widening: it may well have to do both at the same time. This might occur if enlargement advances to become the most promising answer to evolving critical instabilities in Europe outside the EEA.

---

22 William Wallace, *The Transformation of Western Europe* (London: Pinter, 1990).

A Common Foreign and Security Policy in the Planning

The reason for deepening the Community does not consist of integration strategy alone. More prominent incentives derive from the conviction of the Twelve that they should react in common to the new challenges in external relations, not all of them driven by security concerns. Likewise, the internal rivalry among the Twelve should not be underestimated as either pull or push factor for new initiatives for integration. These internal incentives have become particularly important in a fundamentally changed international environment. The end of the Cold War, German unification, the war against Iraq, as well as Soviet and Yugoslav disintegration have affected each of the Twelve in a particular fashion with a repercussion on individual status and national interests. This is not to say that the wheel of regional integration in Western Europe will be turned back, but the debate over the optimal mix of common, coordinated and unilateral approaches to foreign and security policy has been intensified. This debate and its practical consequences are absolutely vital as a means to stabilize the Community domestically and keep it attractive to outsiders.

The Internal Market, EMU and EEA projects find their roots more in the demands of worldwide competitiveness of European economies than in the mechanics of regional integration strategy. Member states calculate that external strength is generated by common action (politics of scale[23]) and by more internal coherence. Coherence is not achievable via technical harmonization or, simply, the creation of a European Central Bank. It is a policy process, as well, if not predominantly. Major decisions on the transfer of economic welfare within the Community cannot be arranged in an intergovernmental or technocratic way. A full-size policy system is needed to cope efficiently with resource allocation and social conflict. Neither the Internal Market initiative nor the plans for EMU originally included these considerations. After the date and the agenda for an IGC on EMU had been set up at the end of 1989 policymakers increasingly felt that a political component should be added to future economic and monetary competences of the Community.

How to negotiate such a political component? The initial suggestion was to bring the IGC on EMU to an end and then open a second conference on political matters. An alternative idea was to incorporate the political subjects in the IGC on EMU. The plea for a separate and parallel IGC on EPU finally surfaced in April 1990 when Chancellor Helmut Kohl and President François Mitterrand made a respective common proposal. The proposal for a EPU was

---

23 For this term see Roy H. Ginsberg, *Foreign Policy Actions of the European Community. The Politics of Scale* (Boulder: Lynne Rienner, 1989).

triggered by the accelerated process toward German unification and by an increasing demand for a central role of the Community in the transformation process of Eastern Europe and the Soviet Union. Paris feared that the larger and now sovereign Germany would reorient its foreign policy priorities toward the east of Europe and reduce its western ties. Therefore the French supported and partly engaged in the reform process of NATO in order to keep this framework as a strong multilateral structure for the integration and control of the German military power. In addition the French policy wanted to integrate the economic, monetary and political assets of Germany in the Community by speeding up and extending the integration in Western Europe. Decisions on the two IGCs at the European Council meetings in Dublin in April and in June of 1990 reflected this approach.[24]

Apart of the new German question which emerged as a problem of size and orientation for some of the West Europeans, the Twelve were confronted with the demand for help from Eastern countries in order to ease their way to democracy and liberal economy. The Community had not been fully prepared for this task and needed better instruments and more resolve to meet at least a minimum of East European expectations. These and a number of other consequences of the end of the Cold War, such as the reduced influence of both Washington and Moscow in Europe, stimulated the West Europeans to consider the development of a more forceful collective external policy and to play a key role in the formation of a post-cold war order in Europe.

Since August 1990, the project of EPU has been receiving further encouragement from the developments in the Gulf, starting with Iraq's military occupation of Kuwait and reaching its peak with the military countermove of the international alliance between 17 January and 28 February 1991, based on UN Resolution No. 678. The fact that war was once again a living reality had a far-reaching impact on the Community's plans for a common foreign policy. Until the Iraqi aggression, the Community was preparing for an important, yet basically civilian, power role in Europe.[25] To raise now the question of whether the Twelve should have a security policy was to ask whether they should have the capacity to act as a world policeman, and therefore whether they should

---

24 Eckart Arnold, "German Foreign Policy and Unification," in: *International Affairs*, Vol. 67, No. 3, July 1991, pp. 453-472.

25 François Duchêne has introduced the notion of "civilian power" into the European debate, Christopher Hill has developed the concept further. See François Duchêne, Europe's Role in the International System: From Regional to Planetary Interdependence, in Wolfgang Hager, Max Kohnstamm (eds.), *A Nation Writ Large* (London: Macmillan, 1973). Christopher Hill, European Foreign Policy: Power Bloc, Civilian Model - or Flop? in: Reinhardt Rummel (ed.), *The Evolution of an International Actor: West Europe's New Assertiveness* (Boulder: Westview Press, 1990).

have a military capacity as such. This in turn brought up the question of the Twelve's policy toward the Arab-Israeli conflict and their relationship with the United States and the Soviet Union. Consequently, the old debate on a common security policy took on a different dimension. This was expressed by the initiative of Foreign Ministers Roland Dumas and Hans-Dietrich Genscher of February 1991 for a security policy of the Community.

In June 1991, much too early for the Community plans on a security role in Europe to be decided upon and to be implemented, Yugoslavia started to test the new mediating power on the Continent. The Community was *nolens volens* lured into a new role, because nobody else was there to take over the job. In relation to its lack of experience and to its objective constraints as a foreign policy actor, the Community has been doing rather well in this test. Brussels has used all its instruments and even developed new ones while the crisis was going on (observers to a military conflict, a peace conference, an arbitration commission, a mediating peace plan, and consideration of military measures in WEU). By the same token, it demonstrated the domestic and communitarian limits of a coordinated West European foreign policy and the need for a concerted approach of several actors including Washington and Moscow, the CSCE and the UN.

Taken together this makes at least three separate driving forces for EPU: political flanking of economic and monetary integration, preparing for conflict prevention and resolution in Eastern Europe, and preparing for reaction to security challenges beyond Europe. Each of these driving forces aims at elaborating specific ingredients of EPU:

- The flanking of EMU demands an evolution of the political system of the Community, mainly a strengthening of the executive branch ("economic government") and an increase of the participation of political forces in the decision-making process (European Parliament, national parliaments, representatives of the regions).[26]
- The demands for conflict prevention and resolution in Eastern, South Eastern and Southern Europe require the conceptual capacity and the resources for the development of a cooperative network in Europe; in short, a strengthening of the Community as a civilian power.[27]

---

26 Henri Froment-Meurice, Wolfgang Heisenberg, Peter Ludlow, *Governing Europe. Towards a European Foreign and Security Policy* (Brussels: Center for European Policy Studies, 1990).

27 See the joint analysis of six West European research institutes: Forschungsinstitut der Deutschen Gesellschaft für Auswärtige Politik et al., *The Community and the Emerging European Democracies* (London: The Royal Institute of International Affairs 1991).

- New security challenges from inside and outside Europe drag the Community toward a military power: common West European threat assessment, the establishment of a common or coordinated arms export policy as well as the creation of common or coordinated intervention and peace keeping forces.[28]

The Maastricht plans for a Common Foreign and Security Policy are designed to strengthen the civilian power component of the Community and to prepare the option for a common West European military power. After the rapid dissoluton of the postwar order in Europe, new and reliable political and institutional structures are needed. With the United States in a state of partial withdrawal from the European theater and the successor of the former Soviet Union still in a flux and in danger of economic breakdown, including the risk of revisionary military policies, reliable actors in Europe are scarce. The Community might be such a strong actor, but it will have to shoulder a wider range of responsibilities. In Europe, major parts of former defense duties have been transformed into tasks for a new type of security policy, based primarily on nonmilitary instruments. This is the field where the Community has always claimed to have a comparative advantage which it now can bring to bear, just as it has tried to do in the context of its Mediterranean policy since the midseventies. In this respect, the nature of the Community's foreign policy will have to undergo major changes. Its economic foreign policy (EC external relations' style) and its traditional diplomacy (European Political Cooperation style) will be transformed into a foreign policy of a new type (CFSP style), to be developed in detail.

To the extent that the new EPU is planning to develop the Community as a military power, defense matters, for the first time, are not being excluded from activities of the Twelve. As far as the EPU-Reports go, CFSP is supposed to deal with "security" matters only, while "defense" questions remain the prerogative of the individual member state, of WEU and NATO. During their deliberations in the IGC, the twelve foreign ministers did not find convincing criteria for an institutional separation of security and defense matters without denying or distorting the substantial interrelationship of the two policy areas. Moreover, the triangular relationship of the Community, WEU and NATO needs to be sorted out in terms of legal competences, political guidance, operational missions, command structures and financial burden sharing. In this regard the Twelve will need yet another IGC down the road on European Security Union (ESU).

---

28 See for an in-depth study Mathias Jopp, Reinhardt Rummel, Peter Schmidt (eds.), *Integration and Security in Western Europe - Inside the European Pillar*, (Boulder, Colorado: Westview Press, 1991).

In Western Europe, specific preconditions have to be fulfilled before transfering security and defense missions to either the Community or WEU. To set preconditioned objectives is a well-known pattern for both the Economic and the Monetary Union; it should be a guideline for CFSP as well. Moreover, one has to look at the given institutions and states in the foreign policy and security field as a complementary set of actors rather than as competitive or mutually exclusive bodies. This demands a skillful orchestration of institutional evolution.

Congruency of Internal Preparedness and External Risk Taking?

The Maastricht conclusions on CFSP point at a new level of integration in terms of both a bolder risk taking in common external relations as well as a better internal preparedness for such a policy. This new goal does not emerge on the spot. For the time being and especially during 1992 the Community will have to do business within the limits of the present system. Even after a successful ratification of the Maastricht Documents, it will take time until a new level of external action can be reached. What exactly is the scope and the nature of the qualitative leap which the Community is asked to achieve in the field of foreign and security policy? The following sections of this volume will try to give an answer to this question.

Part Two looks at the state of the art of foreign and security policy in the Political Union. Certainly, the Community's achievements to date are quite impressive and also unprecedented for a group of nations on the way to becoming a union, but how can the West Europeans make use of this potential to meet the challenges and tasks in the post-confrontation era? This is first of all a question of making the right choices on where to place emphasis and in what way to reform and complement the existing foreign policy apparatus in the Community and the member states. Key areas in this regard are the legal basis, the institutions, the instruments and the decision-making rules: can the Community continue to develop CFSP on the basis of incomplete constitutional foundations? Can the set of present institutions keep its balance while strengthening efficiency? How should the range of instruments be expanded in harmony with new external ambitions? How should giving up national sovereignty assure that it will not lead to a reduction of international assertiveness?

It is one thing to construct a foreign and security policy on the drawing board, but it is another thing to act in a real given situation. Another set of issues, therefore, derives from the Community's practical experience: the problem of consistency, the ability of crisis management, the capacity to cope with fundamental systemic change in the Community's neighborhood and the question of how to develop and enforce a more appropriate code of conduct for global challenges such as nuclear proliferation. The present performance of the Community in these cases has demonstrated both the limits of the present system and some of the potential limits of the future system of CFSP. It has also shown (see the case of the Yugoslav civil war) that progress can be made without big plans and without comprehensive concepts if the pressure for immediate action of the Community is very high.

Part Three examines perceptions and demands from outside the Community and asks: What kind of a Political Union? A widely unreflected dimension of the process of forming a more forceful external policy of the Community is provided by outside observations. How do Western Europe's main allies, neighbors and partners perceive the establishment of a new collective international actor? In what respect are they affected and do they deserve to have a say in the process? The Community has declared that it does not want to become a "fortress," neither in the economic nor in the political field, but can the European Union be kept open if integration benefits require a particular West European identity? No wonder that the United States feels "threatened" with the possibility of a *fait accompli* policy of the Community, and East European countries might perceive a new demarcation line drawn between East and West in Europe. The architects of CFSP and the Political Union in the Community will have to consider these views and also those from Moscow and Ankara as well as from Vienna and Tokyo. In a zone of intensifying cooperation, the Community has to find a balance between regional integration and multilateral dialogue.

Part Four assesses the concepts for Political Union, looking at the Common Foreign and Security Policy as a touchstone of future integration. Given external as well as internal constraints how far can the concept of CFSP be substantiated during the present round of deepening relations in the Community? The plans for a common foreign and security policy have been an integral part of various initiatives during the last decade, from the Draft Treaty of 1984 via the Single European Act of 1987 to the Maastricht Documents of 1991. The breakthrough has not yet been achieved, but the driving forces have multiplied. While in 1984 it was mainly the European Parliament which wanted to establish a foreign and security policy as an autonomous branch of Community policy, it is now primarily the governments of the member states pushing for a significant progress. The fundamental change in the political and strategic landscape in Europe has convinced most of the leaders in Community capitals that a serious attempt has to be made to pool and federalize their foreign and security policy on the European level. Should this attempt fail because of lack of boldness in the Maastricht plans or because of lacking support from the twelve constituencies, then the entire concept of creating a Political Union in Western Europe will be spoiled for a long time, if not forever. This will lead the Community to the crossroads of alternative futures which are examined here in terms of their merits and possible difficulties.

PART TWO

State of the Art of Common Foreign Policy and Security Cooperation: Internal Organization and External Activity

2

The Community's External Reach

Eberhard Rhein

The Constitutional Bases and Origins

The Rome Treaty does not provide for a common foreign and security policy. The fathers of the treaty did not think in categories of foreign policy, let alone defense policy. After the 1954 European Defense Community (EDC) debacle (the non-ratification of the EDC Treaty by the French Parliament), it was only too natural that the new integration effort was concentrated solely on economic, rather than political, integration: The European Economic Community was to become the instrument of the Continent's political unification!

This economic Community has become involved in external affairs, *au sens large*, from the Treaty's inception in 1958. There are five reasons for this development:

- the Rome Treaty specifically provides for a "common trade policy" (Article 113), the logical consequence of the Community's role as a customs union, or a common market;
- the Community's association with overseas countries and territories, which were still dependent colonies when the Community was established (Article 132);
- the Treaty's provision enabling the Community to conclude "association agreements" with third countries (Article 238);
- the power given to the Community to conclude international treaties (Article 228), to establish relations with the GATT, the UN, the OEEC[1] and other international organizations;
- the power, though limited, to receive and establish diplomatic missions (passive and active right of legation).

---

1   OEEC: Organization for European Economic Cooperation.

In looking back to the first three years of the Community's existence, 1958-1960, one is struck by its early involvement in external relations:

- Among the first nine Directorates General (DG) established in 1958 were two whose jurisdiction rested outside the Community territory, DG I for External Relations and DG VIII for Overseas Territories.
- Within three years of the Community's constitution 17 countries, comprising all the West European neighbors plus the USA, Japan, Canada, New Zealand and Israel had established diplomatic missions in Brussels in order to observe and influence this strange new "animal" of the international order.
- Three countries, Tunisia, Greece and Turkey, asked to be associated with the Community.
- The Community defined its common external tariff (CET), stimulated the first round of international trade negotiations (Dillon Round) by its very constitution, acceded to GATT, and established relations with the OEEC.

These items summarize the essence of the Community's external activities in its early years.

The Community's External Relations at Cruising Speed

What has changed since those early "heroic years"? In essence, only two things:

- the Community's increased internal action in new areas has lent it additional strength on the external front;
- the Community's external role has been broadened since 1969 by the gradual evolution of European Political Cooperation (EPC), which has given a political component to the Community's agreements. These aspects are added to the agreements' economic elements, which remain the Community's actual field of action.

It is the combination and the increasing interaction of these two factors that has turned the Community into a major player on the international scene. In this regard there is virtually no comparison with the modest role played by the Six in the first 15 years of the Community existence: after 1973 a "qualitative leap" occurred: the Nine attained a different, more prominent external stature. This progress coincided with a fundamental change in the industrialized world: the evolution of the USA-EC-Japan triangle which continues to determine the economic destiny of the modern world.[2] The EC has taken its natural place in this relationship, either by itself (in all trade questions) or jointly with the major member states (e.g. world economic summits). Without the constitutional basis (including the enlargements) of the EC, Europe would have been totally eclipsed by the US-Japan-Pacific combination as far as world economic policy matters are concerned. Since this area of international relations is limited to trade and finance, there was no need for any interaction between EC and EPC.

The same is true for the intensification of diplomatic and contractual relations between the Community and the rest of the world. By January 1991, 160 countries had ambassadors accredited to the Community; practically all sovereign countries treat the Community as a sovereign state *sui generis*, despite its restricted internal and international sovereignty. The internal strengthening of the Community and the increased role it plays together with the EPC have dramatically heightened the Community's diplomatic stature: now third countries no longer try to influence just import duties and agricultural prices, but also EPC diplomatic demarches and political resolutions by the European Parliament. Just like in Washington, where Capitol Hill is as important as the administration to foreign diplomats, ambassadors can no longer limit their contacts to the EC Commission, as was previously the case, but they must also cultivate relations with the EC Presidency and influential members of the European Parliament.

The number of bilateral agreements concluded by the Community has grown dramatically during the last 12-15 years. So has their political importance. This is true for the Lomé Convention, the Mediterranean Agreements, the ASEAN Agreement, the agreements with the Central American countries, Argentina, Chile, the six GCC countries, and, of course, the Association Agreements negotiated in 1991 with Hungary, Poland and Czechoslovakia.[3] All these are far from being traditional trade agreements. They all have underlying political motivations or objectives. Many provide specifically for a political dialogue, while others do so informally by creating a suitable platform.

The Lomé Convention I (1975) was the first major foreign policy achievement of the Ten. As a result, the Community has not only established its firm reputation as an advocate of third world interests, but it has -- for the first time -- played its role as a catalyst for other regional groupings in the world.

---

2   From 1958 to 1972 the EC was a Communiy of six member states: Belgium, Federal Republic of Germany, France, Italy, the Netherlands and Luxembourg. From 1973 to 1981 the EC was a Community of nine member states, now including: Denmark, Ireland and Great Britain. In 1982 the EC became a Community of ten member states when Greece joined. Since 1985 the EC has taken on Spain and Portugal as the eleventh and twelfth member states.

3   ASEAN: Association of South East Asian Nations. GCC: Gulf Cooperation Council.

The Mediterranean Agreements (1975-1978) were the first example of a coherent and strategic piece of Community foreign policy. It was the Community that took the initiative, putting its relations with its southern neighbors on a long-term contractual basis: customs union with the northern rim countries (Greece, Turkey, Cyprus, Malta), full or unilateral free trade areas with the southern rim countries (Maghreb, Mashreq, Israel). And the Community managed to do so with a fine-tuned balance of contractual links with Israel on the one hand, and the Arab countries on the other.

After Tito's death in 1980, when Yugoslavia was included in the EC's "global Mediterranean policy," difficult negotiations were concluded in record time. Again the political motivation on the part of the Community was clearly evident, though not at all outspoken. The Cooperation Agreement with the six ASEAN countries (1981) was the first Community agreement with a regional bloc.[4] The Community stressed its interest in a European economic and political presence in Southeast Asia, a dynamic region indeed, via this group-to-group cooperation. The existence of the agreement has given rise to a regular informal political dialogue on issues in Southeast Asia, in particular on Vietnam and Cambodia. It has set the pattern for other agreements, both with regional blocs (Andean Pact, GCC) and with individual countries (India, Pakistan, Mexico, Brazil).

The Cooperation Agreement with the five Central American countries is the first example of an intimate link between the Community and EPC.[5] Indeed, for the first time the Community has formally institutionalized its political weight behind the peace efforts in Central America, and it has substantially increased development assistance to help improve the economic conditions, which had contributed to the political upheavals of the area. It was also the first case in which Community foreign policy visibly deviated from that of the USA; the Community consciously included Nicaragua in the overall cooperation framework. The cooperation with the GCC follows the same fundamental pattern. The Community will affirm its "presence" in a region that is of the highest strategic importance to the Community. It is doing so at the request of these countries who feel "threatened" by their eastern and northern neighbor and who want to emphasize their intimate links with the Community, especially after the war against Iraq in 1991. Again, an institutionalized political dialogue goes along with the agreement.

In all these cases, the most recent being the "Europe Agreements" with East European Countries, the Community is a welcome partner -- it is seen as a balancing force against both the military/political supremacy of the superpowers and the economic dominance of regional powers. There has

---

4   Leaving aside the EFTA agreements (1973).
5   See the article of Veerle Coignez in this volume.

always existed a political element in the external relations of the Community. It would be a mistake to treat the EC's economic measures separately from the EPC's dealing with political issues; because every economic measure taken by the Community is also weighed by its potential political implications. In reality there is no separation between EC and EPC external relations.

This is proven by numerous examples:

- In 1967 the Community suspended all aid and all institutional contacts with Greece as a sanction against the military junta.
- In 1981 the Community undertook the same measures with regard to Turkey. Five years passed before relations were somewhat normalized.
- In 1980/1981 the Community decided to undertake a major food relief operation for Poland, an action clearly designed to express the Community's sympathy with the liberalization of the Polish régime (Solidarity) that had - temporarily - taken place.
- When in the winter 1981/1982 the Soviet Union crushed the Polish "spring" and imposed martial law, the Community responded by imposing - very modest, rather symbolic - restrictions on imports from the Soviet Union.
- One month later the Community took more drastic measures against Argentina: in response to the Argentine invasion of the Falkland Islands, the Community imposed a complete ban on all Argentine imports which lasted for 77 days.
- Deeply concerned with the political developments in Central America, the Community decided in 1982 to triple its financial aid to the region; this decision proved to be politically sensitive because Nicaragua was among the beneficiaries of the aid.
- In 1986 the Community decided to provide exports from the Israeli Occupied Territories (West Bank and Gaza) with the same access to its market that all countries around the Mediterranean enjoy. The measure was essentially politically motivated, with the Community having become increasingly preoccupied with the deterioration of the economic and political situation in the Occupied Territories.
- 18 months later, the European Parliament chose not to ratify two trade protocols and a financial protocol with Israel, in order to "censure" the Israeli attitude in the Occupied Territories and the Israeli refusal to allow Palestinian agricultural exports to Europe without passing through Israeli marketing organizations.
- In 1987, the Council refused to authorize the Commission to negotiate a new 5 year financial protocol with Syria; it also banned all high-level contacts with that country; in response to the involvement of the Syrian government in terrorist activities on Community territory.

- In 1989, the Community cut all aid and all institutional contacts with China, in reaction to the bloody crushing of the "Beijing spring" in May 1989; the freeze lasted until October 1990 when the European Council decided to normalize relations once again.
- In August 1990, the Community imposed a total trade embargo against Iraq and occupied Kuwait in compliance with UN Resolutions. At the same time it joined the US and other countries in a $12 billion economic aid operation in favour of the three hardest hit front-line-states (Turkey, Egypt, Jordan).

This record is a selection from many more cases of joint EC/EPC activity. There is a remarkable interaction between the "political" and the "economic" components of Community external policies, whether in an institutionally organized (and often rather complicated) manner or not.

Through the Community (including EPC), Western Europe has regained part of its traditional influence in international politics. Indeed, whenever the Community takes a position or acts on an international issue, it carries weight. Other nations align their positions with those taken by the Community, in particular European non-member states and Japan. But we are far from a Community foreign policy! Without a common economic and monetary policy on the one hand, and a common defense policy on the other, Community external relations cover only secondary aspects and not the very core of external sovereignty. Leaving aside these fundamental flaws in the present structure of external relations, there are additional weaknesses which affect the efficiency of the Community's external relations. The following three will be briefly addressed:

- the institutional dispersion;
- the weakness of the external instruments;
- the difficulty of designing an active long-term external strategy.

There is no single, dominant actor who has the overall responsibility for the Community's external relations. This is not unusual. Even in individual states, the situation is characterized by a multitude of actors (Foreign, Economic, Trade, Development and Finance Ministries; Parliament). But coordination is, at least in normal situations, relatively easy: there is an identifiable national interest, and a government that finally chooses among divergent views. In the Community things are considerably more complicated. Not so much between the "economic" (Community) and the "political" (EPC) component of external relations, which follow largely parallel patterns. Most issues touch either the one or the other track, seldom both. It is mainly when EPC goes beyond the normal statements, when it wants to engage in substantive action, that the need for coordination arises. Examples are relations with Central America, GCC,

South Africa, Israel and the Israeli Occupied Territories. Past experience proves that - beyond the usual haggling of bureaucrats - the coordination of EC and EPC functions quite satisfactorily.

The institutional dispersion is more of a problem between the EC Commission on the one hand and the various competing and conflicting national bureaucracies and agencies on the other hand. This is essentially due to a weak federal structure: whenever the Community wants to take an action that is considered politically important by the Commission and often even by the majority of Foreign Ministers, the implementation may be blocked for weeks, months or even years by opposition from specific regional (national) interests, for example national Finance, Industry, or Agriculture Ministries. Community foreign policy strategies may be thwarted by often ridiculous sectoral or technical obstacles in one or two member states.

Closely linked to this institutional diffusion at the national and Community levels is the weakness of Community instruments in their ability to implement whatever external policies are adopted. This, too, is a general problem of any external policy, which is exacerbated in the Community because most of the potential instruments of foreign policy are outside the Community's scope. The member states have a large variety of means at their disposal:

- send troops, navies or military advisers to third countries;
- sell arms or refrain from doing so;
- give financial assistance, credits, or grants;
- offer government guarantees for private exports credits;
- send business, cultural and scientific missions, and organize national export fairs (e.g. German industry shows in India and Japan).

The panoply of measures by which member states can express sympathy with or reprobation of a third country has hardly been reduced by the establishment of the Community. Only their relative effectiveness has substantially diminished: who pays attention to the "actions" of individual European states not working in the EC context? The Community possesses only two instruments to lend weight to its external strategies:

- trade measures;
- financial aid.

Both are limited in scope and efficiency. Trade measures, for example, offering better access to the Community market, imposing trade restrictions or even a trade embargo, have to be handled with extreme care. Community action must fully take into account both international obligations (particularly in the GATT) and the Community's own industrial or agricultural interests.

Trade embargoes have persistently proven inefficient, especially if they were intended as long-term measures and if they are not backed and duly enforced by the UN (see the case of Iraq). Aid measures can only be taken within the available EC budgetary resources. These are quite modest compared to those of the member states. Indeed, 80-85% of the overall aid of the EC (taking Community and member states together) continues to be granted by member states individually. The Community does not have a banking institution with an international sphere of action (e.g. Exim Bank). The European Investment Bank (EIB) activity outside the Community is very modest and geographically restricted to the African, Caribbean and Pacific (ACP) and Mediterranean countries.

For these reasons and because of the lack of homogeneity of interests and fundamental positions on external policy issues, the Community has thus far been a rather passive player on the international scene, reacting rather than acting. It has only rarely been able to conceive and implement long-term foreign policy strategies corresponding to its economic and political interests. The relations with the Mediterranean, Central America and perhaps Eastern Europe are exceptions to the rule. This is due fundamentally to the institutional dispersion and weakness, mentioned above. Who is developing long-term political strategy for the European Community? Where in the Community is the foreign policy "think-tank" that defines the Community's external policy agenda for the nineties, let alone the first decades of the 21st century? Where is the Community foreign minister whose ambition pushes him and authorizes him as Council Chairman (!) to use the Community's political and economic weight in order to help solve certain pressing international problems (e.g. Cyprus, Israeli-Arab conflict, Middle East instability, Eastern Europe, Jugoslavia, etc.).

The Community does not, however, seem to have such sweeping ambitions. If it were unhappy with the status of a "secondary power," it would not hesitate to undertake the necessary constitutional and institutional reforms which would allow it to play a much more important role in the international scene. As long as the Community is not determined to transform itself into more of a federal entity, implementing the two essential components of defense and macro-economic policy, there will not be a full-fledged Community foreign policy. Such radical transformation appears unlikely in the next few years. The Intergovernmental Conferences concerning the Political Union and the Economic and Monetary Union will not - yet - create the constitutional and institutional framework necessary for the Community to acquire to all the powers embedded in a nation-state's foreign policy. They will most probably produce further welcomed improvements of the existing set-up, not more.

Future Challenges

Regardless of the future constitutional changes in the Community in the nineties, the Community will have to address two major challenges:

- completing the reunification of the European continent, i.e. integrating Eastern Europe into the Community system;
- playing a greater role in the conduct of world economic affairs.

Historians will judge the Community's political performance in the nineties by its ability to associate Eastern Europe and to establish a cooperative relationship with the Soviet Union. This is the greatest challenge that has ever been put before the European Community. It will require immense efforts in the form of financial and technical assistance, the opening up of the Community market to the industrial and agricultural products from Eastern Europe, and, last but not least, a very intense political dialogue with the Eastern European neighbors.[6] In the longer term, it will require a Community position on the question of if and when to admit those East European countries which want to join the Community and which demonstrate the ability of living up to the commitments of full membership. To put it more boldly, the Community's major responsibility during the nineties is to redefine the governance of the whole of Europe, from the Soviet Union to the Atlantic and from the Mediterranean to the North Cape. Two major questions have to be answered in this regard:

- Is the Community willing and able to accommodate 20-25 member states, without further impairing its internal and external capacity of efficient and speedy action? What constitutional change does this call for, change going probably far beyond what member states presently are prepared to accept, when they set out to define the mission of the Political Union?
- What kind of alternative relationship, short of membership, can be envisaged for those countries who do not want to join the Community?

At present it seems perfectly clear that the Community will come under increasing pressure from those European countries which want to join the "club," a pressure to which, in the end, the Community will have to succumb.[7] It therefore seems likely that by the beginning of the next century, the

---

6 The solution of the nationality problems, especially in the Balkans, will have to be on the agenda of such a dialogue.

7 Five countries have, by July 1991, formally put in their request for accession: Austria, Cyprus, Malta, Sweden and Turkey.

Community will have once again extended its geographical scope, its population, and the number of member states. The Community will have become largely identical with Europe. If this scenario becomes reality, the Community's external policy, which in the past concentrated strongly on Western Europe (even if this seems largely forgotten), will be concerned essentially with the world outside Europe.

With a population and a Gross National Product (GNP) exceeding that of the USA and the Soviet Union, the Community will increasingly have to assume responsibility for the global economy. It has not done so in the past, because macro-economic and monetary policies are not yet a full Community domain. The Community, being affected by economic developments elsewhere in the world and influencing such developments itself, must learn to exert leadership in the world economy, as it has done already for the world trade system. This requires a fundamental change of attitude on the part of the Community's finance and economic ministers, but also on the part of the Commission. The EC member states must learn to define via the Community common positions on the key issues with which the world economy is confronted: the international economic exchange system, the LDC's debt, energy supply, the world's mineral, water, food and fishing resources.[8]

The Community's failure to operate as an entity in the International Monetary Fund (IMF), the World Bank, etc. is in blatant contradiction to the provisions of the Rome Treaty (Article 116). This is bound to change in the second half of the nineties when the European Monetary Union, including the European Central Bank, will be in full swing after 1994. No other single event will have such an overriding impact on the Community's role in the world economy and thus on Europe's involvement in international economic and financial policy as the entry into force of the Treaty on the Economic and Monetary Union (EMU), due to take place on January 1, 1993. One should, therefore, expect the Community to play a substantially greater role in world economic policy, once EMU is in force.

In conclusion, the trend towards more and more Community external involvement will continue, falling short of having a real European foreign policy (i.e. as compared to nation-state foreign policy), shaped by a single European Foreign Office in a federal system. Even if in the next 10-15 years the Community will have to devote continued attention to intra-European affairs (internal market, enlargement, internal cohesion, common macro-economic policies), it will be increasingly drawn into global responsibilities. As one of the few prosperous regions in the world, it cannot shy away from the awful problems of overpopulation, malnutrition, misery, water scarcity, ecological disasters, and energy shortages that almost invisibly creep into the

---

8   LDC: Least Developed Countries.

ecological disasters, and energy shortages that almost invisibly creep into the world around us. It will no longer be sufficient to publish nice resolutions or to set an example of successful regional cooperation. The Community will have to get involved in global issues, because this is what the world expects from it, and because such problems may spill over into the Community, be it AIDS, the population pressure, the depletion of the world's oil reserves or the deforestation of the tropics. The Community's external machinery is not ideally geared to assume such responsibilities. But even within the present cumbersome institutional framework, the Community could do a lot more, provided it has the will to do so and is endowed with courageous leadership.

3

The Constitutional Foundation

Maarten W. J. Lak*

Comparison of EC and EPC: The Two Components of a Common Foreign Policy

European Political Cooperation is the process of information exchange, consultation and common action among the twelve member states of the European Community ("the Twelve") in the field of foreign policy. Its aim is to maximize the Twelve's influence in international affairs through a single, coherent European approach. It is the essential counterpart to progress towards European unity in the Community framework. The key features of EPC are: decision-making by consensus among governments and direct contacts between foreign ministries, allowing speed and flexibility.

It is quite distinct from the work of the Community that follows from legal commitments entered into by the member states in signing the Rome Treaty; substantial parts of national competence were thereby transferred to a supra-national entity, the EC, with unprecedented Community-wide institutions, among them an initiating and managing European Commission, beyond full control of the member states. A wholly new type of Community law has emerged from the developments thus begun, with a Court of Justice to uphold it and a European Parliament to act as guardian of its democratic legitimacy.

European Political Cooperation has none of these characteristics but unites the same member states and the Commission for a "game played by different rules": It started 13 years after the Rome Treaty on the basis of a purely political commitment among Foreign Ministers and was only after 15 years of pragmatic development codified in the Single European Act (SEA), in which the revision of the Rome Treaty on the Community takes pride of place.[1] Still,

---

* The views expressed in this chapter are those of the author personally. A longer version of this article is published in *Common Market Law Review*, No. 26, 1989.
1 *International Legal Materials*, Vol. 25, No. 3, May 1986, pp. 506-518.

the Act does not contain strong legal commitments on EPC, contrary to the legal wording of provisions of Title II on the Community. The wording chosen for its Title III is generally that of a "commitment to endeavor," not of legal obligation. Although it is part of an international treaty, the intrinsic nature of the EPC provisions remains overwhelmingly political and its implementation remains a hostage to the political discretion of each of the twelve member states and the Commission. It must be added, however, that the margins for exercising this discretionary power have, over time, been increasingly defined and narrowed by the cumulation of political constraints produced by a continuous elaboration of common positions: this collective history may well be considered an *acquis politique*.

The three basic reports (Luxembourg 1970, Copenhagen 1973 and London 1981) approved by Ministers provided ground-rules to EPC but were never elevated to treaty rank, nor submitted to parliamentary approval.[2] Over the years, these ground-rules constitute a morally binding non-legal foundation for Political Cooperation. Had the Single European Act not come to codify the essence, the Reports could well have come to form a beginning of customary European law as far as applied in practice, as implementation pursued consistently would have provided validity by precedent.

How do the Twelve organize their collective relations with third countries and international organizations? What are EPC's "external powers"? Various formulas have been employed:

- A political, unilateral positioning towards third parties by issuing a statement. Such statements have no legal value but are mere declarations of political intent, committing partners in EPC to a course they set themselves. They have been adopted on a continuous basis since 1970.
- An informal understanding or agreement to organize relations between the Twelve and a third party, i.e. the 1974 "Gymnich" agreement with the US or transitory arrangements with candidate-members of the Community. Political contacts thus agreed can take the form of meetings with the Presidency or with the Troika (3 successive Presidencies) or yet again with all twelve (i.e. EC-ASEAN).

---

2 First Report of the Foreign Ministers to the Heads of State and Government of the member states of the European Community of 27 October 1970 (Luxembourg Report); Second Report of the Foreign Ministers to the Heads of State and Government of the member states of the European Community of 23 July 1973 (Copenhagen Report); Report on European Political Cooperation issued by the Foreign Ministers of the Ten on 13 October 1981 (London Report) published in: Press and Information Office of the Federal Government (ed.), *European Political Co-operation* (EPC), Bonn, 1988.

- A third type which employs a full formal agreement dealing with both EPC and EC relations can be found in the Act of 12 November 1985 between the Central American states and the EC and its member states.

It is this third category that closely parallels the Community's contractual policy towards third countries and international organizations. The nature of a political dialogue has generally made it possible to organize political contacts in broad terms without legal detail required in the Community's agreements with third parties on trade, aid and financial matters. In this context, the Commission proposes a mandate for negotiations to the Council and conducts these upon approval of the mandate, the Council concluding the final agreement with the European Parliament's authorization. In EPC's "contractual" relations, it is the Presidency that negotiates (assisted by the EPC Secretariat) and all Twelve have by consensus to agree to an agreement for it to become effective.

Interestingly, it is the Single Act title III on political cooperation that contains the basic rules about interaction with EC; there is no corresponding provision in the EC chapters of SEA. These interaction rules also, presumably because of the central role of the Commission in that context, constitute the most 'legal' of the EPC provisions by the language used; it clearly goes beyond the "commitment to endeavor," without however enabling the Court of Justice to hear a case under these provisions (SEA article 31). At the same time, it is no surprise that the Court of Justice is excluded from acting upon EPC, as its intergovernmental nature has not yet in any way been superseded by another quality. The Single Act main provisions relating to consistency run as follows:

- Article 30.3.b: "The Commission is fully associated with the proceedings of EPC."
- Article 30.5: "The external policies of the EC and the policies agreed in EPC must be consistent. The Presidency and the Commission, each within its own sphere of competence, shall have special responsibility for ensuring that such consistency is sought and maintained."
- Article 30.9: "The High Contracting Parties and the Commission, through mutual assistance and information, shall intensify cooperation between their representations accredited to third countries and to international organizations."[3]

EC and EPC are dealt with by different national administrative substructures, generally both situated within ministries of foreign affairs. Only in the United Kingdom, and to a lesser extent in Belgium, are the European

---

3 *International Legal Materials* (note 2), p. 517.

Correspondent-functions integrated into the EC departments; else where, these key positions are firmly within the Political departments, with little or no regular contact with offices dealing with the Community's external relations. The Commission has a special division well established in its General Secretariat, dealing with intergovernmental cooperation among which EPC. The main problem encountered by member states ministries of Foreign Affairs in coordinating EC and EPC is one of providing information to the "neighboring" department, as the spheres of competence are generally kept quite distinct in all capitals. In principle, this can be dealt with in a fairly easy manner by making relevant formal reports and informal information available to the corresponding divisions. However, two types of practical obstacles can prevent this information when available, from being used: the focus of reporting on EC resp. EPC is quite different, so one does often encounter a negative reaction on the part of an officer usually dealing with "the other side" leading to ignoring data relevant to interaction; secondly, there are quite severe time constraints on everyone concerned, which means that attention is generally only given to the material which appears to be of direct operational relevance to the officer concerned. Simply making the information available, is thus generally not sufficient to achieve that it is taken into consideration. Thus, the political level in member states is not always in a position to weigh all aspects involved in arbitration of an issue.

The fact is that the two frameworks use specific rules and apply these to decision making and follow up of conclusions reached; this *per se* does not have to be a negative factor, although the consensus principle of EPC can be a "brake" on speedy decision-making and, consequently, also affect EC's acting upon EPC's impulses.

At the European level, ministers composing the General Affairs Council are also responsible for EPC and the European Council is entrusted with giving a "general political impulse to European Construction" (Stuttgart Declaration 1983).[4] However, the existing EPC-EC interaction regime does not provide for consciously prepared arbitration between the various aspects requiring translation into one European foreign policy.

The Options: 1981-1985

Already right at the beginning of EPC in 1970, the need for interaction with EC was recognized. The Luxembourg Report of that same year noted that the implementation of common EC policies required corresponding developments in the purely political field, in order to hasten the time when Europe could

---

4   Solemn Declaration on European Union (Stuttgart, 19 June 1983); in: *European Political Co-operation* (note 3), pp. 70-78.

speak with one voice (Paragraph 8).[5] This interaction was (and is still) seen as the very *raison d'être* of EPC, and the Commission was invited to give its views when EPC would have an effect on work at hand in the European Communities (Section V). Ministers took it upon themselves to take account, within EPC, of progress of EC in reinforcing its own structures. In this manner the "two-way street" of interaction was firmly established right at the beginning of Political Cooperation.

The 1973 Copenhagen Report went further, especially in regard of practical ways and means. Noting that a "permanent constructive dialogue" with EC had become regular practice at all levels of EPC (ministers, political directors and experts), it reaffirmed that political cooperation was quite distinct from Community activity, which followed from the legal commitments entered into by the member states; both having as their objective to contribute to the process of European unification (Paragraph 12.a).[6] EPC, according to this Report, "must keep in mind implications and consequences of EC common policies and maintain close contact with Community institutions on matters affecting Community activity" (Paragraph 12.b). The following detailed arrangements were to be applied: the Commission was to make known its views; the EC Council would be informed, through the Chairman, about EPC conclusions of interest to work in the Community; Ministers could have EPC study certain political aspects of matters under discussion in the EC framework. Reports were to be communicated through the chairman of COREPER.

An important principle for the Community's common policy towards third countries, related to the subject discussed here, was also set forth at Copenhagen, five months later on 14 December 1973: the member states were to secure that "harmonious and constructive relations" with the outside world would not "compromise, retard or affect their will to progress towards European Union." Also in their bilateral contacts with other countries, they would increasingly base themselves upon common positions established among the member states (Document on European Identity, Paragraph 10).[7]

The London Report of 1981 simply codified the practice of the Commission being fully associated with EPC at all levels, thereby, at least formally putting an end to lingering doubts on the part of some.

The 1983 Stuttgart Solemn Declaration on a European Union stated i.e. that "the European Council ensures consistency between EC and EPC." In between meetings of that Council the General Affairs Council is entrusted with that responsibility. The General Affairs Council deals with Community matters according to the Treaties and, in order to link the EC and EPC institutions, its

---

5   Ibid., pp. 24-31 (26).
6   Ibid., pp. 34-48 (42).
7   Ibid., pp. 48-54 (51).

members also are to deal with EPC, according to its rules. The Declaration emphasizes "the importance of greater consistency and close coordination at all levels in order to allow global and coherent action." The Commission is acknowledged as a force giving impulse to the process of European integration and is once again fully associated with the work of EPC. Significantly, the Stuttgart Declaration, in Paragraph 1.4.2 and Paragraph 3.2 as well as in the statement by the Commission attached to the Solemn Declaration, broadens the scope of EPC beyond the mere political aspects of security recognized by the London Report into its economic aspects. Hereby an additional range of issues came into the EPC-EC interaction orbit, economic aspects generally being considered, until then, exclusively within Community competence.

A completely different approach is taken by the draft-treaty on European Union, prepared by the European Parliament in 1984: here the traditional distinction between EC and EPC is discarded and replaced by a new equilibrium between institutions of the Union on one hand and "common action" (of the Union) and "cooperation" by the member states on the other hand. The latter's field of action applies to foreign policy, when beyond "common action" commercial and development aid policies (the latter after a ten year transition period). This is to be interpreted in a broad sense and meant to leave little room for purely national foreign policy action. Other provisions are that international agreements entered into by the Union are to be approved by absolute majority of Parliament and Council; the Council (of Ministers) of the Union conducts "cooperation"; the Commission may propose policies and actions which shall be implemented either by the Commission or by the member states, at the request of the European Council or the Council of (Ministers) of the Union; the Union is to ensure that international policy guidelines of the member states are consistent. However, there were no provisions in the draft on how interaction between "common action" and "cooperation policies" was to be conducted, although a scheme is proposed for the transfer of matters from one field to the other.

Much more modestly, the 1985 Dooge Report noted that EC-EPC interaction "is both necessary and useful," and "that they must therefore be more closely aligned." Interestingly, this report acknowledges that (all) EC common policies (provided for in the Treaties) have an external dimension; it does not reserve this quality to external EC policies only. The "permanent political cooperation secretariat" envisaged, is to enable Presidencies to ensure greater continuity and cohesiveness of action, and help to strengthen cohesion between political cooperation and the external policies of the Community. EPC working meetings should be regularly organized at the Community place of work. On the decision-making method, the Dooge Report called for "seeking a consensus in keeping with the majority opinions with a view to the prompt adoption of common positions and to facilitating joint measures."

The various drafts on EPC-Treaty provisions, that were put forward in the course of 1985, when the Intergovernmental conference called by the European Council of Milan embarked upon its work, do in varying degrees pay attention to interaction. All drafts assumed that there would be a separate treaty for EPC, distinct from the revision of Community treaties.

The British draft circulated as a first contribution, speaks about "a maximum of consistency." Further more, it leaves open the possibility that, all member states agreeing, the Commission would not participate in all EPC meetings and qualifies the Secretariat's task to advise the Presidency on maintaining consistency by including the explicit proviso "when necessary." In comparison to the Franco-German draft the British proposal preferred to leave things as they were, both as regards consistency, as well as to the -- less then secure -- role of the Commission in EPC. The Franco-German draft has member states ensure "the highest possible degree of consistency" between both fields and expressly states that the Commission participates in EPC to that effect. Also, the Presidency is to see to it that "interaction translates into multiple decisions for common action." This draft envisages a "General Secretariat of the Union," staffed by European officials and not by national personnel on temporary secondment as agreed in the SEA. This "General Secretariat" was to be tasked with EPC's continuity and consistency with EC positions.

The thrust of this draft allows for an *activiste*, even *dirigiste*, approach to consistency. The almost institutional character of the proposed General Secretariat working for the European Council departs from the more evolutionary approach of others and, potentially, puts the distinction between EPC and EC at risk "from the top," so to speak.

The Italian draft wishes for the "greatest possible consistency between EPC and external EC policy," and has the General Affairs Council treat EPC, be it according to EPC rules in order "to return to the unity of the institutional system and pursue one and the same external policy (EPC and EC)." The Presidency, as in the Franco-German draft, has to see to it that EPC-EC interaction translates into common action, also by cooperation between diplomatic missions in third countries. The EPC Secretariat is explicitly called upon to cooperate closely with the Commission, the European Parliament and to closely liaise with the Council General Secretariat. This draft stayed close to the existing institutional situation, but explicitly opens up practical ways to involve the new EPC Secretariat. It also expected the Presidency to take a forward role in translating EC/EPC interaction into common action.

The Netherlands draft opens up the possibility that EC Ministerial Councils treat EPC matters, but leaves the responsibility for ensuring EC-EPC consistency to all member states, without especially tasking the Presidency or the Commission. This draft expressed traditional caution about any risk of modifying the existing institutional balance, which allows the member states and the Commission to play their respective parts, without conceding more than necessary to the Chair.

Only an adoption of the Franco-German draft might have made a considerable difference in the legal framework for EPC-EC interaction. This would have followed from the paramount role this draft forecasted for the European Council seconded by a General Secretary and his staff. Had this approach indeed been adopted, practice would very probably have led to a new regime of EPC-EC interaction with the General Secretary and his staff functioning as a "clearing-house" and potentially even arbitrating -- by delegation -- on consistency of EC external policies with EPC policies.

Other member states did not in 1985 table formal drafts but generally adopted a prudent attitude without expressing themselves clearly on the interaction issue as such. A generally conservative approach to institutional matters and the wish to safeguard freedom of action for national policy-making both militated against most member states showing interest in a progressive formulation of interaction rules.

The Commission, however, early in the negotiations saw great strategic merit in attaching EPC in every practical way feasible at that juncture to the Community Treaties revision under way. It proposed and later achieved that both aspects would be covered in a single act, with a common preamble and separate titles for EC and EPC. Agreement on this unified treaty structure for both pillars of European unification translates the consensus of all concerned to keep open a future option for a single system. Not at any juncture was the Commission seriously considering to propose changing EPC's principle of consensus nor the role of Community institutions regarding EPC. It failed, however, in its attempt to have member states agree to include final provisions -- on revision (in 1992) -- in the Single Act spelling out an ultimate rapprochement between the Community and Political Cooperation. The decision on the structure of the Act can arguably be considered to have left open -- implicitly -- the door for future integration of EPC into the Community.[8]

The Choice Made

The Single European Act, finalized by December 1985, predictably adopts on the principle of consistency between EC and EPC a middle ground between the various drafts, but it does itself not in any way provide practical interaction rules.

In the preamble, the resolve is set forth of member states to implement the "European Union" and "to invest (it) with the necessary means of action."

---

8   Simon Nuttall, *Yearbook of European Law 1986*, p. 208.

The preamble of SEA recalls i.e. the responsibility incumbent upon Europe "to act with consistency in order more effectively to protect its common interest and independence." Article 1 states that EC and EPC "shall contribute together to make concrete progress towards European unity." Clearly, this combined contribution calls for a special quality of interrelationship between the two spheres: action in one needs to support action in the other and both must be interactive. The same article states that the earlier non-treaty EPC provisions (the three Reports and the Solemn Declaration of 1983) as well as the practices gradually established, are confirmed and supplemented by SEA's EPC rules. The pre-existing interaction regime thus remains valid. Practice now must conform to the imperative of Article 30:5. Article 3 draws the traditional boundary between EC and EPC: only the Commission is to exercise its power and jurisdiction in both spheres, but under the conditions and for the purpose of each sphere.

The SEA simply and categorically states in Article 30:5 that policies adopted in EPC and external EC policies must be consistent, and assigns to Presidency and Commission the special responsibility, each within its own sphere of competence, to ensure and maintain that consistency. This per se constitutes an improvement over the Stuttgart Declaration, which gave this task to the European Council and the Council of Ministers. However, matters are not entirely left to practice as the Ministerial Decision of 28 February 1986 does supplement the existing practical interaction rules, that are notably found in the 1973 Copenhagen Report (supra). This Decision governs the practical application of certain aspects of Title III of SEA. In the first place, the Political Committee is to draw Ministers' attention to the positions adopted by the European Parliament on foreign policy matters: these may well go beyond EPC and also pertain to Community competence, thus presenting the challenge that both aspects be considered in relation to each other. On the other hand, the Presidency shall ensure that resolutions of the Parliament are duly taken into consideration in EPC, and reply to resolutions on major importance and general concern on which the Parliament requests the Presidency's comments: those resolutions may well pertain also to Community matters, internal and external, but deal with EPC aspects at the same time. A combined reaction from the EPC and the EC point of view may in these cases well be the only appropriate way to address Parliament's concern.

Secondly, member states' missions and the EC-Commission's delegations are to intensify their existing cooperation in third countries and international organisations.

Thirdly, the EPC Secretariat created by the Single European Act, assists the Presidency "in ensuring the continuity of EPC and its consistency with Community positions." Thus, one of the principal tasks of this body lies in the field of interaction, be it in an ancillary role to the Presidency. This can be particularly relevant when the Secretariat prepares documents and minutes, and assists the Presidency in contact with third countries. As the EPC meetings at expert level take place normally at the Brussels' seat of the EPC Secretariat, informal contacts between EPC experts in various fields with their 'Community' counterparts, be it from the Commission, the Permanent Representations or the General Secretariat of the Council and possibly also the European Parliament's Political Commission, are more feasible then under earlier conditions, when expert working groups routinely would meet in a Presidency's capital. The explicit reference to Brussels as the seat of the EPC secretariat appears per se an important pre-condition for EPC-EC interaction.

If there is one important feature whereby SEA's interaction rules differ from preceding ones, it is in the special responsibility for ensuring consistency explicitly entrusted to the Presidency and to the EPC Secretariat assisting it. Where previous texts only call upon the Commission to give its views and do leave it to each partner in EPC to take into account effects of Community policy, SEA clearly gives primary responsibility in this respect to both the Presidency and the Commission. This has the advantage of laying practical responsibility where it can be taken up. The extent of the potential workload involved in ensuring consistency between EC external policies and EPC is no doubt one of the reasons why the EPC Secretariat was given this as its second main task, together with the maintaining of EPC's continuity. It is of course the Presidency that decides what use is being made in that respect of the Secretariat. It would also appear to be self-evident that continuity and consistency are closely related to each other.

What would have been the situation if EPC would, by the time the SEA was adopted, be based on the same rules as the Community? Assuming that the Community law model would have been its basis and not intergovernmentalism as applied to EPC, it would have implied that member states would have been willing and ready to transfer the greater part of what remains of their sovereignty in international affairs to EC institutions.

The Commission would have had to acquire a new institutional role in EPC, along with other institutions, and propose EPC action to the Council to be enacted in the formal Community format: possibly, a tendency towards majority voting might have developed for EPC, although not within a short period. The Commission would, also in its Community role, have been bound by EPC decisions. There would not be a place for a specific EPC Secretariat, as its functions could have been performed by the Council's General Secretariat, strengthened for that purpose. Also the Commission would have had to increase its capacity to deal with Political Cooperation, possibly drawing in -- on a permanent basis -- expertise from member states. Provided that the traditional Council framework might have come to deal with a number of matters now treated in EPC expert working groups, permanent representations of member states would have come to include political experts.

Also, the Court of Justice would have been competent for EPC matters under litigation and the European Parliament would have quite a different role in political cooperation issues than it can play today.

Challenges and Possible Responses for the 1990s

Given the considerable outside demand for an internationally active community of Twelve, and the decreasing ability of individual member states to attempt and make an impact internationally without the necessary backing, it is inevitable that inconvenient matters will put themselves on the agenda: not dealing with them in an adequate way as in EPC's early years, not bringing to bear the full economic and political potential with the ensuing synergistic effect, will risk disappointing the European population to the point that motivation for continuing the unification will suffer. As a national alternative course of action will most of the time mean inaction, the interaction of EPC and EC will increasingly become an indispensable dimension of foreign policy of each Member State.

The need for continuity and consistency beyond the debilitating rhythm of 6-months Presidencies also points to a framework that would allow better coordination to meet the requirements of circumstances. At the same time, ever closer interaction of EPC and EC will create its own problems: although formally the Commission cannot be bound in the Community sense by consensus in EPC, it will be influenced by it nevertheless and will not, as a rule, await a formal Community decision to make proposals, especially when political will requires translation into Community action. Increased interaction may require active monitoring by the Commission of national implementation of trade and other measures agreed upon collectively. There will also be a host of practical coordination needs to attend to among the various branches of national governments, dealing with EC and EPC respectively. This may well require reorganization and re-allocation of resources in member capitals and between capitals and Brussels. However, although ideally the "ultimate rapprochement" of EPC and EC will necessitate a unified legal basis, at present there is insufficient negative experience with the existing arrangements to conclude that political urgency exists for a unifying approach. Allowing increased perception by experience to show the importance of EPC-EC interaction appears to be a more realistic course.

Having embarked upon completing its Internal Market and in the perspective "beyond 1992," the European Community is perceived by a number of third countries as being distracted by opportunities and challenges within the EC, rather than involving itself sufficiently in trade, aid and investment in third countries. Even if the EC would not succumb to protectionism, this perception may create an appearance of a more inward-looking Community. Its future external policies in trade and aid clearly would need to set off these impressions and effectively counter such arguments. Taking synchronized and parallel "positive action" within EPC, towards third countries, would under these circumstances appear to be a course from which the Twelve and their Community would only at their peril desist. Such positive action would require a well-functioning interaction regime to ensure maximum consistency between EPC and EC policies.

Examples of institutionalized foreign relations with both (potential) EC and EPC aspects as, for instance, in inter-regional relationships like EC-ASEAN, EC-Central-America, EC-Gulf Cooperation Council, Euro-Arab dialogue have proven that the quality of economic and political dialogues generally suffers from insufficiently coordinated European participation. This is manifest especially when better prepared partners are encountered. This is true for the economic aspects, where the Commission is in the lead, but also if not more so for the political aspects, where the Presidency coordinates. Building upon past experience there seems to be a need for far greater and conscious division of tasks among European Ministers and Members of the Commission on a number of issues, when preparing for high level multilateral "bilaterals." This principle once agreed could lead to entrusting the coordinating role on certain (recurrent) issues to one partner for a longer stretch of time then the usual six months term, i.e. to cover at least two Ministerial inter-regional meetings and the interval between them: the handling by EC/EPC of issues of Cambodia, Central America and Israeli-occupied territories would seem to benefit from such an arrangement.

More specifically in the field of EPC/EC interaction the following arrangements could be considered: Firstly, "coordinating task groups" dealing with both economic and political issues could well be set up on the European side for each regional dialogue: these ad hoc task groups might be jointly presided by the Commission and the Presidency and comprise the respective "issue" coordinators from capitals, a member of the EPC Secretariat, a representative from the Council General Secretariat and, if necessary, representatives from other member states drawn from Permanent Representations. Thus an "ad hoc mix" of EC/EPC experts could effectively coordinate Europe's relations with a given regional grouping and report to both COREPER and the Political Committee.

A similar formula could be adopted for relations with individual third countries like for example the United States, Japan, China, India and the Soviet Union and Eastern European states.

In the second place member states may wish to make their own arrangements to ensure that in their policy-making, EC and EPC aspects are adequately coordinated and made inter-active. To that end, an ad hoc participation by officers from Permanent Representations in certain EPC working groups meeting in Brussels might be considered when interactive issues are on the agenda.

Thirdly, for day-to-day business, a special liaison arrangement might well be set up between the EPC Presidency and the Commission, the two principals in interaction between both spheres of Europe's outward projection. In this arrangement, the Presidency could for practical purposes make use of the EPC Secretariat to be able to dispose of the necessary information on work in hand in the Commission. In order to promote efficient use of such an arrangement, the Commission's division responsible for intergovernmental cooperation would have to be kept informed of working level contacts, without necessarily having to actually be at all times a go-between. A gradual evolution in this respect might be facilitated, as more conscious interaction progresses and an "EC-EPC coordination reflex" develops. Some, be it modest, experience has already been built up in this respect, especially in the field of positive measures in favour of victims of apartheid in South Africa. However, to put such an arrangement on a solid basis, it might be advisable to formally agree between Presidency and Commission on a set of ground rules to be followed by those involved in ensuring day-to-day consistency between EC and EPC in Brussels. An arrangement as suggested could well have a positive effect on cooperation between diplomatic missions of the Twelve, including representations of the Commission in third countries and with international organizations.

Finally, in order to promote that due consideration be given to interaction at all levels, it might be considered to have the Presidency with the Commission produce a succinct "Statement of EPC-EC impact" at the occasion of the *colloque* held every three months with the European Parliament's Political Commission. Such an "impact statement" might conceivably address main items where EPC-EC interaction has been at stake in the period under review, assess its possible "synergistic" effect upon third countries and internally upon the Community of Twelve itself and offer a tentative outlook on future developments. The advantage of "accounting for action taken" in the field of interaction would be that forward-thinking at every level of EPC (and EC) could be stimulated, and chairmen at various levels could be brought to take discussions further than they would normally be taken in present, less structured, circumstances. If such a scheme were adopted, the Presidency would possibly want to have the EPC Secretariat's assistance to suggest elements and to liaise with Community institutions. If even this, rather modest, procedural approach would not find favour, one might have to conclude for the present that it is too much to ask that Foreign Ministers in their dialogue with the European Parliament at least relate EPC to EC. The 1988 experience of the Council not taking a political stand in the case of the originally negative vote of the European Parliament on the Community's Financial Protocol with Israel, did not augur too well in this respect. Could Ministers not have undertaken to make efforts -- within EPC -- to at least contribute to a more favorable climate for Parliamentary approval of the Protocol?

When in 1992 either member states' Parliaments vote on the Treaty for Political Union or Ministers determine if EPC provisions in the Single European Act should be reviewed as called for by Article 30:12 of the Single European Act, a modification of the SEA could be considered to reflect the need to draw together in an "interactive mode" both EC external -- and EPC -- policy-making. Article 30:5 SEA could then read as follows:

- The external policies of the European Community and the policies agreed in European Political Cooperation must be consistent (unchanged).
- The Presidency and the Commission, each within its own sphere of competence, shall have special responsibility for ensuring that such consistency is sought and maintained (unchanged).
- The Presidency and the Commission shall make necessary arrangements, including the use of joint steering bodies, to enhance the full effect of EC/EPC consistency in international relations. The High Contracting Parties shall contribute to achieving this objective (suggested addition).

In case such a treaty modification would not be considered opportune, a formula having a comparable effect could be added to the Decision of Ministers of 28 February 1986, which would not require ratification by parliaments, but possibly consolidate an inter-active *modus operandi* between EC and EPC.

A more far reaching addition could be to add a proviso to Article 31 of SEA, to empower the Court of Justice to deal with questions arising from Article 30:5, as amended, without submitting the whole of Title III to its competence; the case law that might be thus engendered could prove to be an important contribution to the ultimate rapprochement of EC and EPC in an European Union.

4

The Institutional Network and the Instruments of Action

Simon Nuttall*

The Interaction of EC and EPC in Common Frameworks

Strictly speaking, the European Council is the only common framework in which both Community and EPC affairs may be officially discussed. Indeed, the need to ensure an overall approach to the internal and external problems facing Europe was given as the reason for establishing it at the Paris Summit of December 1974. The issuing of general political guidelines for the Community and EPC became one of the recognized responsibilities of the European Council, and was acknowledged as such in the Stuttgart Declaration. The Single European Act (SEA) notably forbore from defining the duties and role of the European Council.

In practice, it is difficult to find any examples of the European Council performing this function. The discussion of EPC subjects at European Councils is in fact normally left to Foreign Ministers. They go over the ground generally and look at any drafts which have been prepared for them by the Political Committee. If it is wished that the European Council should adopt conclusions on EPC topics, revised drafts are submitted to Heads of Government. The practice of adopting EPC conclusions is, however, falling into disfavor, as Heads of Government dislike having to rubber stamp run of the mill texts which everyone -- including the press -- knows have not been seriously discussed at the highest level. The procedure followed is an additional reason why European Councils do not in fact issue general guidelines covering both EPC and the Community.

Below the level of the European Council, discussions of EPC and Community affairs take place, at least in theory, in separate frameworks. There

---

* The views expressed in this chapter are those of the author personally. The chapter was essentially completed in 1989.

has, however, been a progressive blurring of the distinction. At the level of Foreign Ministers, the participants' perception of the framework in which they are meeting is sometimes weak. The custom has grown up whereby one of the two formal Ministerial Meetings in each Presidency is held in connection with a meeting of the General Affairs Council in either Brussels or Luxembourg. Attempts were made during the negotiations for both the Stuttgart Declaration and the Single European Act to merge the agendas of the Council and EPC Ministerial Meetings, when these took place consecutively, but they were resisted, no doubt primarily for institutional reasons, but also in consideration of the convenience of the two sets of senior officials who would each only attend a part of a merged meeting.

In addition to meetings of this type, Foreign Ministers almost always take the opportunity of the General Affairs Council to discuss both EPC and Community matters informally. These discussions occasionally result in policy guidelines or procedural decisions which are then taken further in the appropriate framework. The informal nature of the setting makes it possible for genuinely comprehensive discussions covering EPC and Community aspects of a question to take place.

The informal "Gymnich-type" meetings of Foreign Ministers which take place once during each Presidency, also cover both EPC and Community matters. Although these meetings are not supposed to lead to operational conclusions, this increasingly tends to happen. The question then arises how the conclusions are to be recorded and transmitted to those responsible for putting them into effect. The situation is usually clear when it is a question of implementing measures. It is less so when a declaration has to be issued without immediate operational consequences.[1]

---

1 So far, there have only been two significant cases where Ministers have adopted positions covering both EPC and Community aspects of a question in a single genuinely bicephalous text. One was the Declaration on Human Rights of 21 July 1986. It had been drafted with a view to being issued by The Hague European Council, but in the event was adopted a month later by "the Foreign Ministers of the European Community, meeting in the framework of European Political Cooperation and of the Council," on the occasion of an EPC Ministerial Meeting. The EPC sections of the text had been prepared by the Political Committee and the Community sections in the Council framework.

The second case was the adoption of the conclusions of the Council and the representatives of the Governments of the member states on the relations between the European Community and Latin America. This occurred on the occasion of the Council meeting on June 22, 1987. Most of the text had been prepared by the Committee of Permanent Representatives to the European Communities (COREPER), but the section dealing with the political dialogue was taken from an internal EPC paper which had been approved at the Ministerial Meeting on May 25, 1987.

The Single European Act lays down that "the High Contracting Parties shall ensure that the European Parliament is closely associated with European Political Cooperation." But in practice the Parliament does not have a role integral to the functioning of EPC comparable to the one it plays in the Community. It is able to question the Foreign Minister of the Presidency, but can apply no sanctions if it is dissatisfied, as it is likely to be, with the replies he gives on behalf of the Twelve.

Parliament cannot oblige the Foreign Minister of the Presidency to be present at topical debates on foreign policy questions. The resolutions on EPC matters passed by Parliament only rarely have a direct influence on EPC, and the value of the three-monthly *colloque* with the Political Affairs Committee of Parliament depends on the approach and personal commitment of the Foreign Minister of the Presidency, who is the Committee's interlocutor. One *colloque* in two takes place in the capital of the Presidency, the other in Brussels or Strasbourg.

The practice of giving replies to questions asked by Members of the European Parliament was recognized by the Paris Summit in 1974 and referred to again in the Stuttgart Declaration and the Decision of 28 February 1986. The Foreign Minister of the Presidency replies to oral questions on EPC subjects for twenty minutes during question time at each of the Parliament's monthly part-sessions. If several supplementary questions are asked, as they often are, it may well be that only two or three of the questions put down are called. The replies to those not called may be given in writing and printed as an annex to the report of the debate. In theory, the Presidency replies on the basis of "elements" agreed by partners, rather than full texts, and may add comments in a national capacity. In practice, however, the text of the reply, is cleared word for word in advance. The material for replies to supplementary questions is, however, prepared by the EPC Secretariat or the Foreign Ministry of the Presidency and is not seen by partners in advance.

The Twelve also reply to written questions addressed to them. The replies are drafted by the EPC Secretariat and submitted to the Presidency for approval before being cleared by member states over the COREU network and sent to Parliament via the Council Secretariat. Questions addressed to the Council but which in fact refer to EPC topics are transferred to EPC by administrative action. From time to time, a transfer in the reverse direction is made. Very occasionally, a reply is prepared in part by EPC and in part by the Council machinery. There is close practical cooperation between the EPC and Council Secretariats.

Ever since the Luxembourg Report, the Presidency has addressed to the European Parliament an annual report on progress in the field of political unification. The 1976 European Council in The Hague required the Ministers acting in EPC, and the Commission for the Community, to report to it on progress towards European Union. The London Report instituted the procedure whereby the President of the European Council makes a statement to Parliament, including on EPC matters, after each meeting of the European Council. The Stuttgart Declaration confirmed this and also provided that the European Council address a written annual report to the European Parliament on progress towards European Union (replacing the separate reports instituted at The Hague).

The current practice, as summarized in the Ministers' decision of 28 February 1986, is that the Presidency addresses Parliament at the beginning of its period of office and presents its program, including EPC aspects. At the end of the Presidency, it reports on progress. In addition, the President of the European Council reports orally on any EPC discussions the European Council may have had. The Presidency's speeches to Parliament, which are prepared on its own responsibility and not submitted to partners for prior approval, are useful focal points for Parliamentary surveillance of EPC and usually give rise to substantive debate.

The Presidency also sends a written communication to Parliament on progress in the field of EPC. This forms part of the annual report on European Union instituted by the Stuttgart Declaration, and is formally deemed to be approved at the level of the European Council. The EPC section consists of a review of EPC activities in the year in question. It is a bureaucratic exercise which gives little joy to the luckless EPC Secretariat which has to draft it and only mild amusement to the European Correspondents who may, if they choose, pick it to pieces. Parliament does not respond to it and if it is forgotten, nobody notices.

The Stuttgart Declaration recognized that the European Parliament may on its own initiative debate matters relating to European Union, including EPC. This is no more than recognition of the long standing practice whereby Parliament adopts resolutions bearing on EPC questions. Parliament has long complained that insufficient attention is paid to these by EPC. The London Report envisaged the possibility of more frequent references to Parliament's Resolutions and in the Stuttgart Declaration member states undertook to respond to resolutions concerning matters of major importance and general concern, on which Parliament seeks their comments. The latter undertaking was renewed in the decision of 28 February 1986. member states have, however, never been required to honor it, since Parliament has never formally certified that one of its Resolutions falls into this category and requires a response.

The same decision requires the Presidency to ensure that the views of Parliament, as expressed in its resolutions, shall be duly taken into consideration in EPC work. Relevant resolutions are placed in the files of delegations at meetings of the Political Committee and in those of Ministers at Ministerial Meetings.

Parliament feels frustrated at the lack of real content in its association with EPC and regularly produces reports drawing attention to the unsatisfactory situation and putting forward procedural proposals. The reason for this frustration is complex, and lies for a large part in the nature of EPC itself. Parliament is asking for fuller information about EPC policies than actually exists, owing to the limits of consensus. In many cases, a more open relationship between the Presidency and Parliament could only be achieved by revealing the divergences among member states which prevent the adoption of more substantial positions. This would naturally be considered a breach of trust by partners, at any rate so long as the discussions with Parliament are public or semi-public, and would lead to a crisis of confidence internally in EPC as well as on the part of the third countries to which the policy is directed.

A further reason for frustration is Parliament's lack of real powers over EPC and of any power at all over its practitioners (other than the Commission, a fact which has some influence on the Commission's behavior in EPC). There is therefore no reason why EPC should give more than lip-service to the association of Parliament. The situation is unlikely to change as long as decisions on the institutional structure remain in the hands of officials (the Decision of 28 February 1986 was drafted by the European Correspondents), who have a vested interest in remaining free from parliamentary control. An interesting development could be the political use by Parliament of the increased powers it has been given over Community affairs by the SEA.

Interinstitutional Cooperation

The Secretariats

The EPC Secretariat is housed in a wing of the Charlemagne building of the Council in Brussels, which is the headquarters of the Council Secretariat. It maintains its separate identity as responsible to the EPC Presidency, and, so far, does not come under the authority of the Secretary General of the Council. Nevertheless, it relies on the Council Secretariat for infrastructure and services and practical cooperation between them is close.[2]

The existing arrangements seem common sense, and it is difficult to imagine that any others could ever have been envisaged. However, when the Political Directors were discussing how the Secretariat should be set up, they were far from being a foregone conclusion. Several member states, led by Denmark and

---

2   See also the contribution of Giovanni Jannuzzi, head of the EPC Secretariat from its start in 1987 till the summer of 1991, in this volume.

France, insisted that the independence of the Secretariat vis-à-vis the Community framework should be maintained. Denmark in particular was anxious that there should be physical evidence of such separation, for example by housing the Secretariat in a separate building. This was because of criticisms by the Danish opposition that EPC was being assimilated to the Community by the Single European Act. France was also concerned about the need to maintain confidentiality.[3]

The second major concern was the financing of the Secretariat. After long discussions, it was agreed that the capital costs of installing the Secretariat would be met by member states according to a weighted key based on the Community VAT key, as of 24 October 1986. This was an ad hoc decision and did not constitute a precedent; indeed the presumption was that the need for capital expenditure of this type would not arise a second time. (This neglects the possible need to acquire new equipment and the certain removal costs when the Council Secretariat moves to its new building, foreseen for 1992). Recurrent costs are met either by the Presidency or by the enlarged troika partners in relation to their national officials serving in the Secretariat. Other than the costs of the COREU network, which are shared in equal parts by the twelve member states and the Commission, there are no shared recurrent costs, and the Secretariat itself has no budget. A considerable number of services are provided by the Council Secretariat at the symbolic charge of one European Currency Unit (ECU) each Presidency. Care was taken to ensure that no recurrent EPC costs were identifiable as such in the Council budget. The arrangements for administrative cooperation between the EPC and Council Secretariats were set out in an exchange of letters signed by Sir Geoffrey Howe, as President-in-office of EPC, and Mr. Ersboll, the Secretary General of the Council, on 21 July 1986.[4]

---

[3] The possibility of housing the Secretariat in its own building in Brussels was excluded on the grounds of expense. The choice lay therefore between installation in the Charlemagne building and in another building rented by the Council Secretariat. A proposal made was to share with the translation services of the Council a pleasant small building in the Square Frère-Orban, not far from the Quartier Leopold station. The arrangement of the offices was not ideal, however, both from the point of view of security and of convenience, and the choice was made to accept the offer of a complete wing on the thirteenth floor of the Charlemagne. To preserve confidentiality and provide visible evidence of independence, the wing is sealed off by a door with a special security lock. Access can only be gained by members of the Secretariat, who control access by visitors.

[4] This provides for the following:
- Premises: in the Charlemagne building as indicated on the plan annexed to the exchange of letters; to be fitted out at EPC's expense, and provided with the basic utilities.

The cooperation between the EPC Secretariat and the General Secretariat of the Council is with minor exceptions limited to the administrative cooperation described above. At one stage, some member states had envisaged the possibility of the secondment of Council staff to the EPC Secretariat, particularly in the administrative structure. This would have continued the tradition of the former "Troika" support team, in which one of the secretaries was usually seconded by the Council Secretariat or even by the Commission. Such an arrangement for the new EPC Secretariat was not, however, acceptable to all member states. A compromise was reached whereby, in addition to the Head of the Secretariat, the five "diplomatic" members of the Secretariat come from national administrations, whereas the choice of people to fill the infrastructure posts (secretaries, archivist, administration officer, communicators) is left to the member state concerned, who is thus free to ask for secondment of staff from the Community Institutions. So far, this facility has not been availed of.

There is no non-administrative cooperation between the two Secretariats except regarding the handling of parliamentary questions. These are received by the Council Secretariat by telex from the Secretariat of the European Parliament in Luxembourg, regardless of whether they are addressed to the Council or to EPC. In cases of doubt regarding the attribution of parliamentary questions, pragmatic arrangements are made between the Secretariats of EPC and the Council. These can either be the sharing out of questions, their transfer from one forum to another, or an agreement to provide answers to a question partly from EPC and partly by the Council. This pragmatic cooperation does not however extend to mutual consultation on the substance of the reply.

- Office furniture: supplied by the Council Secretariat at the cost of EPC, the furniture to be standard Council Secretariat issue; upkeep to be the responsibility of the Council Secretariat.
- Services: covering translation and reproduction of documents, security of the building, press facilities, meeting rooms, documentation and library service, medical and social service (bar, restaurant), garages, maintenance of office furniture, office supplies, communications including telephone.

Except as otherwise provided, all this is supplied at a half-yearly fee of 1 ECU to be borne by the Presidency. The amount of the fee may be reviewed if the volume of services increases substantially. Entertainment is organized by the Council Secretariat services and the costs reimbursed by the Presidency.

In practice, and in order to reduce capital expenditure, some office equipment is rented by the Presidency and serviced at the expense of the Council Secretariat. This is the case with the word-processors and the photocopy machine, which are the same models as are in use in the Council Secretariat and are covered by the same contracts.

The Commission

The Commission takes part in EPC meetings at all levels. The President of the Commission is a Member of the European Council, assisted by a Member of the Commission at the level of Ministers of Foreign Affairs.[5] Within the Commission, the President of the Commission has overall responsibility for EPC and normally represents the Commission in this forum. He may be accompanied or replaced by one or more of the Commissioners responsible for external relations.

The Commission has until recently been represented in the Political Committee by the Deputy Secretary General, who is also the Commission's representative in the Committee of Permanent Representatives. The increasing workload caused by full association with EPC has meant that the double burden has become too heavy to be carried by one official. Since the end of 1987, a Director in the Secretariat General has had responsibility for all forms of intergovernmental cooperation, including EPC, and is the Commission's representative in the Political Committee. A Head of Specialized Service in the Secretariat General performs the function of European Correspondent of the Commission. He is assisted by a small team of officials who take part in all Working Group meetings together with a representative of the Directorate General principally concerned.

Since 1982 the Commission has been directly linked with the COREU network through a terminal situated in its own cypher office. It receives all COREUs and can send COREUs itself, whereas previously it only received a selection of COREUs in photocopy form via the Belgian Foreign Ministry and had to follow the procedure in reverse if it wished to send a COREU, which happened rarely.

Since the informal meeting of Foreign Ministers at Gymnich in April 1983 it has been agreed that the Commission will normally take part in any EPC activities organized in the Troika format, which has been increasingly used in recent years. This applies in particular to contacts with third countries and to *démarches*. The arrangement is of some importance since it enables the European side to present to its interlocutors an overall picture of EPC and Community policy. The Commission is also represented by its Delegations at coordination meetings of Members States' diplomatic missions in countries outside the Community and takes part in the administrative cooperation set up under Directives from the Political Committee and confirmed by the Decision

---

5   In practice, most EPC discussions at the European Council take place among Foreign Ministers at dinner on the first evening, at which the second representative of the Commission is present. This has traditionally been the senior Vice-President.

adopted by Ministers in connection with the signing of the Single European Act. The agenda for cooperation meetings abroad cover both EPC and Community topics and the distinction between the two is barely, if at all, perceived. A higher degree of integration has been achieved abroad than it has so far been possible to attain centrally.

The Commission's principal role in EPC is to act as a bridge with the Community. This is done in a variety of ways. In the everyday run of work, the Commission must make sure that the participants in EPC are fully aware of relevant activities in the Community framework. It might seem that this ought to be unnecessary, since it is the same member states which participate in Community work as in EPC. However, the structure of many Foreign Ministries, divided into separate political and economic sections, means that information often does not circulate freely enough within a Ministry to ensure perfect consistency and coordination in European policy at national level. There is an information gap which the Commission tries to fill. The fact that the same Commission representatives often participate in EPC Working Groups and in Groups of the Council is helpful, and the central coordinating powers of the Secretariat General of the Commission with regard to other Commission services can also be of assistance. The same process works in the reverse direction. By its presence in EPC the Commission is enabled to propose and to execute Community policies with a fuller knowledge of the broader political framework as it emerges from the EC discussions. Full records are made by the Secretariat General of discussions in EPC and these are circulated to the Cabinets and departments specifically concerned.

It is not so much a question of policy orientations decided in EPC as of the creation of a shared perception within which to work. The process is not without its difficulties: there is a natural tendency on the part of the Working Groups to turn themselves into Management Committees for the execution of policy, a tendency which the Commission is obliged to resist if it is to uphold the Community institutional order and, more practically, if it is not to run into political difficulties with the European Parliament. The positions taken by the Commission in cases like this are frequently misunderstood by member states, which incorrectly interpret them as excessive formalism and a determination to hang on to power.

The search for consistency with Community policies has been a continuing concern of EPC. The responsibility for coordination was awarded to the Presidency in the London Report and concern was again expressed in the Stuttgart Declaration, although no procedures were set out to deal with the question. The Single European Act tackles the problem in a more concrete way. It lays down the principle that the external policies of the European Community and the policies agreed in EPC must be consistent and states that the Presidency and the Commission, each within its own sphere of competence, shall have special responsibility for ensuring that such consistency is sought and maintained.

This is the only aspect of the role of the Commission which is specifically confirmed by Title III of the Single Act. It is interesting in that it awards to the Commission, alone of the Community Institutions, a specific responsibility for ensuring consistency. It would have been possible to revive some of the earlier arrangements for closer contacts with the Council, but this was not done. This is in itself a recognition of the Commission's presence in EPC and the practical work it has been able to do.

Some interpret the passage as signifying that the Commission has an obligation to submit to EPC for prior approval by consensus any action it proposes to take in execution of Community policy which has foreign policy implications. This cannot be correct, since the Single Act itself provides that nothing in Title III can affect the provisions of the Community Treaties, including therefore the respective powers of the Institutions in matters of Community competence. Furthermore, the responsibility for ensuring consistency is laid on the Presidency and the Commission and not on the Twelve collectively. The latter had been envisaged in an earlier draft of the Single Act but rejected as unworkable. That being said, the number of occasions on which there is a risk of inconsistency should not be overestimated. There have been few glaring cases, if any, and it must be obvious that the vast majority of Community policies do not have direct foreign policy implications; similarly, much of the work done in EPC does not impinge on that of the Community.[6]

Dialogue with third countries or groups of countries has from the start been an important means by which Political Cooperation has expressed its personality. A complicated network of contacts has grown up with countries like the United States, Japan, China and many others. The Commission is present on those occasions when the formula of the Troika or of all the Twelve is used, but not when the Presidency conducts the dialogue alone.

The presence of the Commission in the Troika is particularly important. In addition to the advantage, mentioned above, that it is thus possible to present an overall picture of EPC and Community policy and hence the image of a unified political and economic Community, the rules for the rotation of the Presidency have as a side-effect that the Commission is the only permanent dialogue partner on the European side. This prospect caused some member states to have doubts, when the idea was first mooted, of the wisdom of allowing the Commission to participate in the Troika. Experience has shown that the practice is advantageous to all concerned.

---

6   For this assessment see also Eberhard Rhein's contribution in this volume.

In addition to the purely political dialogues with third countries, there are also occasions on which political and economic dialogues are combined, with the Commission playing its normal institutional role with regard to the economic dialogue. This is most often the case with regional groupings and is an approach which has been developing over the years.

The Commission has a specific institutional role to play when Political Cooperation wishes to have recourse to Community instruments in order to achieve foreign policy objectives. There are two broad categories: sanctions and aid. These are described in more detail below. As regards sanctions an unofficial doctrine has grown up whereby the Commission is called on to play its part as a Community Institution although the dynamic of the operation lies entirely within Political Cooperation.[7]

A second category of decisions in which the Commission acts as a Community Institution concerns the grant of aid. Two earlier examples are Central America and South Africa, which again are more fully described below. More recent examples can be found in the Iraq conflict, in relations with Eastern Europe and in the case of the Civil War in Yugoslavia.[8] These examples show how the Commission as the initiator and executant of budgetary expenditure can contribute to the pursuit of foreign policy objectives defined in EPC. The possibilities are unfortunately limited because of the chronic restrictions on Community expenditure and the many competing calls on the Budget.

Diplomatic Representations

In the early day of Political Cooperation member states' bilateral Embassies were seen to play a key role in the process. A section of the Copenhagen Report was specifically devoted to them: in addition to receiving information on a Community basis from the Foreign Ministry of their country of residence, it was foreseen that the Embassies would from time to time be consulted on specific subjects, particularly at the seat of the Presidency. One of their staff

---

7 The sequence of events and what has now become the established pattern for the use of Community instruments to implement sanctions have led the Commission to set out for itself a line of conduct which De Clercq explained to the European Parliament, in connection with the South Africa case, in September 1985. The Commissioner made it plain that the fact that cases of this kind fell within the domain of Political Cooperation had consequences for the Commission's margin of manoeuvre, which meant that the Commission did not have the right of initiative it did in the areas covered by the Treaty and that a Community decision could not be taken without a prior consensus of all the member states.

8 See the contributions of Scott Anderson, David Allen and Geoffrey Edwards in this volume.

was to be appointed for specific contacts with the Foreign Ministry on EPC subjects. It was inevitable that these functions should etiolate as the frequency and range of meetings of national officials increased, the Group of European Correspondents took shape and the COREU network came into being.

Embassies today cannot be said to play an influential role in Political Cooperation. Nevertheless, they retain two important functions. The first is to act as an optional channel for bilateral contacts. The COREU network is intended to serve exclusively for multilateral contacts. A COREU message must be circulated to all partners. The only exceptions are for service messages - either on technical communications questions, or when the Presidency wishes to communicate with a partner which is acting on its behalf in a third country in which the Presidency is not represented, or for administrative messages between the Troika partners - and for emergency messages when individual partners give each other communications assistance, as for example when one member state's communications with its Embassy in a third country are cut off in time of crisis but those of another member state remain open.

It follows that if a partner wishes to discuss EPC business bilaterally with another partner, either to obtain information on the line that partner is taking on a specific issue or to convince it of the merits of a different point of view, the official in the member state must either speak directly on the telephone to his opposite number - and this happens very frequently - or else ask his Embassy in the partner's capital to make the *démarche* on his behalf. The bilateral Embassy's second function is to act as a channel for information on a collective basis. The Foreign Ministry of a member state will, after the visit of an important personality from a third country or following some other important foreign policy event, invite the Embassies of the Twelve to attend a "Community briefing" at which full information about the event is given.

In order to perform these functions correctly, the Embassies must be kept properly informed about what is going on in Political Cooperation. In addition to national telegrams, this is done by providing Embassies collectively with copies of selected COREUs. Formerly there was a complicated system of different distribution markings which controlled the extent of the distribution of COREU telegrams, but this was simplified during the Netherlands Presidency in the first half of 1986. Now, a COREU is marked by the author either for "Copies to EC Embassies" or not. In the former case, the Embassies of the Twelve receive a copy via the Foreign Ministry of their country of residence. The usual system is for the Embassy to be responsible for collecting its copies from the Foreign Ministry on a regular basis. The only exception is the capital of the Presidency, where the Embassies of the Twelve receive copies of all COREUs, regardless of their markings.

Until Working Group meetings moved to Brussels at the beginning of 1987, the Embassies had an important part to play in looking after officials from their national capitals, who came to the capital of the Presidency to take part in meetings. As often as not, a member of the Embassy would take part in the meeting together with his national official and replace him if necessary. This function is now limited to meetings of the Political Committee (and to the two Ministerial Meetings a year which take place in the capital of the Presidency).

Member states' Permanent Representations to the Community in Brussels also play a part in Political Cooperation. They collect from the Belgian Foreign Ministry copies of COREUs on the same basis as the bilateral Embassies to Belgium, i.e. those which are marked "copies to EC Embassies." In addition, they may receive copies of COREUs direct from their home administration: the extent to which this is done varies according to the country concerned. Permanent Representations would also normally receive copies of national reporting on EPC meetings, which may be more or less detailed depending on national practice.

Some member states, like the Netherlands and the United Kingdom, have appointed officials in their Permanent Representation to follow Political Cooperation questions. Inevitably their interest, which is not full time, centers on areas in which there is interaction between EPC and the Community. Other member states, however, have placed responsibility for following EPC activities in Belgium with their bilateral Embassies. An indication of the tendency can be found in the administrative attachment of the members of the Secretariat. Whereas the Head of the Secretariat (G. Jannuzzi) was technically a member of the Italian Permanent Representation, most of the members of the Secretariat have been attached to their country's bilateral Embassy. The reason may in some cases have been a determination to keep EPC as separate as possible from the Community, but may also reflect separation in responsibilities between political and economic affairs in the national capitals.

The role played by Permanent Representations in Political Cooperation is more limited than would seem desirable. One might have thought that the transfer of EPC Working Group meetings to Brussels, and indeed to the Charlemagne building in which most meetings in the Council framework take place, might have encouraged the systematic participation of members of the Permanent Representations alongside their colleagues from national capitals, particularly in areas where there is frequent interaction between EPC and the Community. This has not proved to be the case. Indeed, the relationship between a member state's officials dealing with the Community and those dealing with EPC are as like as not to be characterized by tension as by a spirit of cooperation, reflecting the inmate tensions between the two frameworks resulting from different finalities. This applies both individually and collectively: a Permanent Representative may wonder what in Heaven's name his Political Director can have been thinking of, and vice versa, while Coreper as a body is as determined not to be given political guidelines by the Political

Committee as the Political Committee is not to allow Coreper to take autonomous decisions in areas which impinge on Political Cooperation.

Diplomatic missions of the Twelve abroad engage in intensive cooperation in the framework of EPC. Article 30.9 of the Single European Act provides that "The High Contracting Parties and the Commission, through mutual assistance and information, shall intensify co-operation between their representations accredited to third countries and to international organizations." This disposition is elaborated on in section II of the Ministers' decision of 23 February 1987, which for the most part takes up the existing Political Committee's Directives on cooperation in third countries. The areas of cooperation include the exchange of political and economic information, the pooling of information on administrative and practical problems, mutual assistance in the material and practical sphere, communications, the exchange of information and drawing up of joint plans in case of local crisis, security measures, consular matters, health, particularly in the field of health and medical facilities, educational matters (schooling), information, cultural affairs and development aid.

It is provided that Heads of Mission and the Commission's Representative in third countries shall meet regularly in order to co-ordinate their views and prepare joint reports, either at the request of the Political Committee or on their own initiative when the situation requires.

The Commission's uncontested participation in these meetings and more generally in cooperative activities, which in many countries predates the Commission's full association with Political Cooperation, is of considerable importance for the interaction between EPC and the Community. The agenda for the meetings covers both EPC and Community topics without any separation between the two: indeed, the distinction is barely perceived. Practical cooperation is possible in a more relaxed way than in the formal EPC and Community bodies, particularly in the smaller countries in which not all member states are represented, for example the ACP countries.[9]

The move towards interaction in third countries nevertheless raises some delicate questions which need to be handled carefully. These arise from the fact that, whereas the Missions in a given third country constitute a single forum, the same integration has not taken place between the EPC and Community apparatus back home. Thus, a common report by the Ambassadors and the Head of the Commission Delegation would be forwarded to the Political Committee even if it dealt with a subject which fell more naturally into the Community framework. The difficulty is compounded by the fact that the

---

9 Concrete cooperation under these directives, in which the Commission also participates, for example in the shared provision of medical care, is a further incentive towards interaction.

Commission representative must in certain circumstances also defend the independence of his Institution, even vis-à-vis the Council, let alone vis-à-vis the Twelve; it should be remembered that the Commission, unlike the member states, does not have a right of veto in EPC, so in the long run has no control over reports and recommendations in the formulation of which its representatives abroad have participated. Again, the Commission representative takes part in *démarches* carried out by all the Twelve or by the Troika, in application of the general rule. A delicate situation arises when the *démarche* has been decided by the Twelve against the wishes of the Commission. Should its representative then dissociate himself from the *démarche*. So far, pragmatic solutions have been found, but the possibility of open contradiction one day cannot be excluded.

The situation with regard to international organizations is rather different. Depending on the nature of the organization, the rules for Community coordination are well established. Whether coordination takes on a primarily Community or a primarily Political Cooperation coloring depends to a considerable extent on where it takes place. In Geneva, for example, because of the predominantly economic character of the international organizations there, coordination is Community based. The Commission plays a leading role as spokesman for the Community and the secretariat is provided by the Council Secretariat, even for those parts of coordination which are strictly the concern of EPC. In New York, however, the situation is different. Coordination is most intense during the sessions of the United Nations General Assembly, where items of Community interest are heavily outnumbered by EPC items and where the Commission's observer status leads to a quite different situation in practice from the one in Geneva. This means that the Ambassadors see their coordination through EPC spectacles that conditions them to resistance to interaction between EPC and the Community through the participation of Community Institutions.

The Instruments of Action

EC and EPC use economic diplomacy and foreign policy dialogues to develop consistent and forceful external relations. So far, the record of this instrument-related EC/EPC interaction is mixed.

The Use of Instruments of Economic Foreign Policy

If Political Cooperation wishes to have recourse to Community instruments in order to achieve foreign policy objectives, there are two broad categories: trade policy (sanctions) and aid. The history of Community sanctions over the years is highly instructive and shows member states moving from a refusal to envisage any such possibility to a recognition that acts taken under Community law can be an effective instrument of foreign policy.

At the time of the Security Council sanctions against Southern Rhodesia (1966-1968), member states took the view that implementation was a matter for them alone. By the time of the Iran hostage crisis (1979-1980), the situation had evolved to the extent that the possibility of Community sanctions was at least discussed, if only to be rejected in favour of national action. The Commission's role was restricted to ensuring that national measures did not distort the conditions of competition in the common market (Article 225 of the EEC Treaty).

However, attitudes had changed by the time of the imposition of martial law in Poland. Foreign Ministers meeting in EPC issued a declaration in January 1982 in which they expressed their willingness to envisage economic measures with regard to the Soviet Union. The Council of the Communities then announced that it had instructed the Committee of Permanent Representatives, in conjunction with the Commission, to see what trade policy measures relating to imports would be open to be taken vis-a-vis the USSR. Subsequently, the Council, acting on a proposal from the Commission, adopted a Regulation imposing restrictions on imports (from whose provisions Greece was exempted).

Similarly, when Argentina invaded the Falkland Islands in April of the same year, following a statement by Foreign Ministers in EPC the Council adopted, on a proposal from the Commission, a Regulation suspending imports into the Community of all products originating in Argentina. The Regulation contained a reference to the prior discussions in EPC. Again, the sanctions against South Africa which were decided on by Foreign Ministers in September 1986 were implemented by three Community or quasi-Community measures. The ban on the import of gold coins was put into force by a Council Regulation, based on a proposal from the Commission and with the usual reference to discussions in EPC. The ban on the import of certain iron and steel products and on new investments took the form of decisions of the representatives of the governments of the member states meeting within the Council, so a formal proposal from the Commission was not required. However, the texts had been prepared by the Commission services. (In the case of the ban on new investments the Commission had made a proposal for a Council Regulation, based on Article 235 of the EEC Treaty, which had not been accepted).

These cases have over the course of time made it possible for a recognized framework of action to evolve. A political orientation is defined in EPC, and this is then implemented through Community instruments following normal Community procedures. But the recourse to this form of interaction is not a foregone conclusion; the existence of appropriate Community instruments does not guarantee that they will be used.

Thus, member states were unable in 1984 to agree to have recourse to Community instruments to apply measures agreed in EPC on the export of precursors of chemical weapons. In April 1984, Ministers took the view that it was necessary to control the export of certain chemicals which might be supplied to belligerents, and the Commission made a proposal to the Council based on Article 113. As far as the coverage was concerned, the Commission took up the results of the work done by technical experts in EPC.

Member states were divided on the merits of this proposal, but the negative view prevailed and the measures were applied on a national basis. The reason no doubt lay at least partly in the nature of the products covered, which it was felt were too close to weapons to be allowed to fall into the Community framework. There were fears, too, that an opening here might give the Community a back door into the negotiations on chemical weapons at the Disarmament Conference in Geneva.

Similarly, although a number of the restrictive measures against South Africa adopted in 1986 were implemented in the Community framework, for the first round of restrictive measures adopted by the Twelve in 1985 the member states had not agreed to Community implementation although the instruments were available and the Commission had made the necessary proposals.

A second category of decisions concerns the grant of aid. Central America, South Africa and Afghanistan are examples. In December 1981 the Commission sent to the Council suggestions for an aid programme for Central America, bearing in mind the wish expressed informally by Foreign Ministers in EPC to improve relations with the region. The European Council the following March agreed that aid given by the member states and the Community should be increased within the limits of their possibilities and instructed the Foreign Ministers to work out detailed arrangements for the provision of the Community aid on the basis of proposals by the Commission. The Commission duly forwarded a proposal to the Council for special measures to promote economic and social development in Central America which after much discussion led to a decision by the Council in November to increase the Community's technical and financial aid to the region. With the launching of the Contadora initiative at the beginning of 1983 a new momentum was added to discussions in the Community and EPC on policy towards the region, leading to decisions on a new structure for the political and economic dialogue. It was this new climate which encouraged the Council to include in the draft 1985 Budget additional funds available for use for aid projects in Central America.

When Foreign Ministers in EPC adopted the first series of restrictive measures against South Africa in September 1985, they also decided on a number of positive measures. In this context they asked for the possibility of increasing social and educational assistance from the Community to the non-white population and to political refugees to be examined. The Commission consequently forwarded to the Council proposals for action which might be taken by the Community. In response to this, the European Parliament added a sum of 10 million ECU in commitment and 5 million ECU in payment appropriations to the 1986 Budget. The 1987 Budget contained similar appropriations of 20 million and 15 million ECU respectively. The implementation of the program, which involves some complicated administrative arrangements to ensure that the money is spent on the right purposes and reaches the right people, is the responsibility of the Commission. Ad hoc procedures have been set up for consulting member states.

A further example concerns the provision of aid to Afghanistan following the withdrawal of Soviet troops. In the early months of 1988 it appeared possible that an agreement on Soviet withdrawal was imminent, and indeed an agreement was signed on 14 April in Geneva. This included an agreement between Pakistan and Afghanistan to encourage the voluntary return of refugees to their homes. The Twelve had already discussed before the agreement was signed, at Working Group level, the response of the Twelve and the Community in that event. Two requirements had been identified: aid for the return and resettlement of refugees and longer term reconstruction aid. On 14 April, in a general statement on Afghanistan, the Twelve stated that they would be "ready to contribute, in close coordination with the international organizations concerned and other States prepared to act similarly, to the repatriation of Afghan refugees." On 25 April, following an analysis of the situation presented by the Commission, the Ministers decided in the margins of the General Affairs Council, to set up an ad hoc Group to prepare guidelines for submission to the May meeting of the Political Committee. Meanwhile, the Commission forwarded to the Council a communication on the coordination of Community and member state aid for the repatriation of Afghan refugees. The Commission itself set up an ad hoc Group on Community aid measures. The EPC ad hoc Group duly met and forwarded its proposals to the Political Committee which in turn submitted a set of orientations to the Ministers, who adopted them at their regular EPC meeting on 13 June. These orientations set out the political environment for the grant of aid by the Community and the member states, while providing that existing Community procedures for the management of aid should be respected. The ad hoc Group would continue to meet as required to examine the political aspect of aid to Afghanistan, in the context of close coordination between the competent bodies of the Community and EPC. The European Council at Hanover on 27-28 June declared "the readiness of the Community and its member states to provide humanitarian assistance under the programme to be carried out by the UN coordinator, Non-Governmental Organiszations (NGOs) and the International Committee of the

Red Cross (ICRC) in favour of the voluntary repatriation and resettlement of the refugees and displaced persons. The Community and its member states are also prepared to provide reconstruction assistance for Afghanistan after the formation of a representative government and the establishment of internal peace."

The new approach to coordination of EPC and Community activities regarding aid to Afghanistan, consisting of an EPC ad hoc Group on political aspects and a Commission ad hoc Group on operational aspects, bears some resemblance to the arrangements made in the case of the positive measures programme for the victims of apartheid. The difference lies in the fact that in the case of Afghanistan the "political" group is in the framework of EPC; in the case of South Africa the corresponding group chaired by the Presidency is in the Community framework and is concerned not with the political aspects but with the coordination of Community and member states' actions.

There seems to have been a significant shift in balance towards EPC, with the Commission executing the Community budget in direct implementation of EPC policies.

The Foreign Policy Dialogues

Dialogue with third countries has from the start been an important means by which EPC expressed its personality. The instrument is specifically mentioned in the SEA (Article 30.8). In addition to the purely political dialogues with third countries (United States, Japan, China), EPC sometimes also organizes political dialogue in parallel with the economic dialogue the Community has with its trading and development partners. This may be formal or informal.

Opinions differ about the merits of combining the political and economic dialogues. There are both advantages and disadvantages. On the one hand, a united Community position on both political and economic questions can be put across with more force and effectiveness and may well prove more satisfactory to the dialogue partners, which at least know where they stand. On the other hand, to mix economic and political topics in a single negotiation can lead to increased pressure to make economic concessions because of political considerations or vice versa. Whether this is to the advantage of the Community depends on the circumstances, but there is no guarantee that this will be the case. A further institutional obstacle lies in the different procedures adopted by EPC and the Community. Whereas the Community's spokesman in an economic dialogue is normally the Commission, which should in theory benefit from a strong position agreed through Community procedures, the spokesman in EPC is either the Presidency, which, again in theory, is limited by the consensus, or else the Troika or all Twelve who must either remain mute and let the Presidency do the talking, which is absurd, or else say different things, which is improper. Furthermore, a politico-economic dialogue encourages the trend towards EPC procedures, since diplomatic protocol requires the Commission to play the subsidiary role.

The result of these various considerations, even if they are never systematically exposed, has been that dialogue has taken a variety of forms depending on the conditions and requirements of the case. The impetus for a formal dialogue with the Association of South-East Asian Nations (ASEAN) began on the economic side. Contacts with the Community were initiated in 1972 by ASEAN. Discussions proceeded in the following years as ASEAN's own institutions developed. The breakthrough came following the ASEAN Summit at Bali in 1976, when the ASEAN countries sought to broaden their contacts with both the Community institutions and the nine member states. The idea of joint Ministerial meetings was put forward and it was decided to negotiate a cooperation agreement, which was concluded in March 1980. This Joint Cooperation Agreement, which provides the basis for the relationship between the Community and ASEAN, deals exclusively with economic matters and operates through a Joint Cooperation Committee. It contains no elements of political dialogue, nor is there a separate agreement dealing with this. The practice has grown up, however, of regular Ministerial Meetings at approximately eighteen-month intervals at which both political and economic questions are discussed, the participants being all Foreign Ministers and a representative of the Commission. Political and economic communiqués are issued, each being prepared separately in the appropriate framework. In addition to the Ministerial meetings the Community has also been represented since 1981 at Ministerial level at the annual meeting which ASEAN foreign Ministers hold with their dialogue partners (USA, Japan, Australia, New Zealand, Canada and the Community). The Community as such is represented by the Presidency and the Commission, EPC to begin with by the Presidency alone but since the German Presidency in 1983 by the Troika.

The arrangements made for the dialogue with Central America mark a step forward towards institutionalization.[10] They are set out in the documents agreed at the Luxembourg Conference (San José II) in November 1985. The Final Act of the Conference set out the objectives of the political and economic dialogues with Central America and described how they were to be organized. The economic dialogue would be carried out through the Co-operation Agreement. Regarding the political dialogue, it was agreed that "this political dialogue should be institutionalized, in particular by the holding of annual meetings, in principle at Ministerial level." This was the first time that a political dialogue had been instituted by formal Act. Ministerial meetings have

---

10 See the more extended analysis of the dialogue with Central America in the contribution of Veerle Coignez to this voume.

taken place in accordance with its provisions. At the Guatemala Conference 9-10 February 1987 a joint political declaration and a joint economic communiqué were issued following the model of the ASEAN and of the San José I and II Conferences. In the first case, these were prepared separately, the economic communiqué by the Commission with the group of Central American Ambassadors in Brussels and the political declaration according to the normal EPC procedures. Preparations for the Hamburg Conference 29 February - 1 March 1988 showed more flexibility. They began with an EPC Troika meeting with the Central Americans in New York on 25 September and continued with a further meeting in New York at the beginning of December at which EPC was represented by the Troika (including the Commission) and the Community by the Presidency and the Commission.

Whereas the impetus for the dialogue with ASEAN began on the economic side, that for the dialogue with Central America was political. This may explain why in the latter case member states were willing to accept a formalization of the political dialogue, although not, as the Commission would have liked, as an integral, institutionalized part of a joint politico-economic dialogue.

It was political considerations, deriving from the development of the Iran-Iraq War, which led the Council to adopt in December 1987 negotiating directives to the Commission for an agreement with the Gulf Cooperation Council (GCC), which presented considerable difficulties from the purely trade point of view and on which discussions in the Community framework had been proceeding for some time without a result. These directives include a reminder that a political dialogue should form part of the future relationship. The negotiations were concluded according to the Council's directives and the draft Cooperation Agreement was initialled on 24 March 1988. The resulting texts did not include a reference to the political dialogue; however, the Commission had already circulated in EPC a draft declaration on this to be made by member states at the time of the signature of the agreement. The draft reproduced the terms used in the Council's negotiating directives and was based as to form on the arrangements made in the case of Central America. This draft was subject to intensive discussion in EPC, during which the Presidency and the Commission cooperated closely in extensive redrafting. The resulting declaration was issued on 15 June in Luxembourg, on the occasion of the signature of the Agreement, as a joint declaration of the European Community and its member states and the Cooperation Council for the Arab States of the Gulf and its member states. As regards the political dialogue, the declaration stated that "in accordance with the provisions of the agreement[11] they (both sides) decided to hold one annual meeting with the participation of the member

---

11 There are no specific provisions concerning the political dialogue; the reference is to Article 14.

states of the Community and the Commission on the one hand, and the member states of GCC and the Secretariat General of GCC on the other hand." The European and GCC Troikas had their first meeting in Luxembourg on 15 June 1988.

In addition to the more structured dialogues mentioned above, the machinery of the Community's agreements with third countries provides frequent opportunities for Community Foreign Ministers to exchange views on political subjects with their colleagues in an informal setting. This is particularly the case with the countries of the Mediterranean and, since recent, with East European countries. When a Cooperation or Association Council meets, Ministers usually make use of the dinner which is organized, in the absence of officials, to discuss political topics of particular interest to the country concerned. This can be particularly useful with countries like Israel, Cyprus, or Jordan and the informal and private nature of the discussions can make them extremely productive.

It might be thought that opportunities for political dialogue would arise in the framework of the Lomé Convention. This, however, has on the whole proved not to be the case. In addition to the nervousness felt by ACP countries about engaging in political dialogue, they do not have adequate machinery for working out common positions on a wide range of international political questions; indeed, they are themselves so numerous and disparate that such a task would prove difficult. The one topic on which they are all agreed is the question of South Africa. Indeed, a reference to apartheid is included in the Lomé Convention, and the subject is raised regularly by the ACP countries in all the joint organs of the Convention. The Europeans, however, are reluctant to engage in a dialogue on this question, although isolated meetings have taken place, and respond to the ACP initiatives by reading out statements agreed in EPC on the basis of existing policy of the Twelve.

5

The Core of Decision-Making

Lawrence L. Hamlet

Introduction

The search for a consistent, coherent and forceful foreign policy would be incomplete without a consideration of the issue of voting within the European Political Cooperation (EPC). The "reflection document" from the Foreign Ministers of the Twelve on Political Union confirms this reality as it mentions, among other points, the need to consider the use of "decision procedures including the consensus rule, voting practices involving unanimity with abstentions, and qualified majority voting in specific areas"[1] in the proposed Union. This is not to say that a change in the modes of voting within EPC is the only way to achieve such a truly forceful European foreign policy, but the attention that the Intergovernmental Conference (IGC) will put upon this issue highlights the recognition by the member states that EPC, as it currently functions, is severely hampered by the consensus rule, despite the rule's practical relevance.

It is, nonetheless, the practical relevance of the consensus rule within EPC that is of utmost importance. The existence of such a voting regime testifies to the unwillingness of the Community's member states to give up too much of their national sovereignty in foreign policy to any supranational authority. Consequently, any move that envisions a change in voting procedure to a mode in which member states have less of an opportunity to veto decisions at the European level automatically entails a loss of national sovereignty of historic proportions. In view of this fact, the logical question is: How does one proceed? Does one push for such a change anyway, push for the change in some limited way, or give up the idea entirely?

---

1   See: "Political Union: Subjects for reflection submitted to the European Council in Dublin (25-26 June 1990)," *Europe*, No. 1628, 23 June 1990, p. 4.

Such a question can only be answered by first asking oneself exactly what has been happening with national sovereignty in Western Europe since the founding of the Community. If sovereignty is defined as "supremacy in rule or power" or as "power to govern without external control,"[2] it becomes debatable whether the member states of the European Community (EC) are, in fact, sovereign. Their control over domestic economic policy is limited due to the manifold competences of the EC in this area, and, if present plans for an Economic and Monetary Union (EMU) continue, some of the weapons of their foreign economic policy will be taken out of their hands as well. In many ways, this situation only reflects a reality that inevitably exists in the interconnected, interdependent world of today: that of the permeability of borders and a loss of the "power to govern without external control."

However, power on the national level still exists, and this reality is amply reflected in the Community's institutions and practices. A fundamental dichotomy exists between supranationality (the granting of national sovereignty in certain areas to the EC) and intergovernmentalism (the guarding of sovereignty in sensitive areas through an insistence on keeping EC affairs as relations between sovereign states).[3] This dichotomy is revealed in the history of the link between the European Economic Community (EC) and the EPC, in which the very creation of the EPC, with its intergovernmental format, acted as a counterbalance to the increasing supranationalism inherent in the EC. Likewise, the explicit linking of EPC with the EC, codified in the Single European Act (SEA), and the continued attention given to Political Union today inaugurate a new stage in the "battle" between the supranational and the intergovernmental modes whose outcome is, as yet, undecided.

This battle is amply illustrated by the history of voting practices within the EC. The Luxembourg Compromise, with its focus upon voting in the Council of Ministers, effectively symbolizes the importance of national will in determining the character and functioning of the EC. Consequently, an understanding of the evolution of the use of this compromise can act as a useful tool for understanding the effects of changes in voting procedure within the EPC. Applying the lessons learned in the EC context to the EPC inevitably

---

2 These common definitions are taken from: *The Merriam-Webster Dictionary*, New York: Pocket Books, 1974. More specialized definitions, such as in: *The International Relations Dictionary*, 4th ed., Santa Barbara: ABC-Clio, Inc., 1988, while noting that "supreme power can be modified by consent" and by capability, also emphasize the possession of the final, ultimate power of decision by the sovereign body.

3 One could also describe this dichotomy as being a tension between two tendencies: federal (that is, the establishment of an authority above the nation-state) and confederal (that is, the prevention of the existence of any authority above the nation-state).

leads to one conclusion: any change in voting procedure designed to help achieve a more consistent, coherent and forceful foreign policy must avoid overly threatening national sovereignty.

This chapter will attempt to suggest strategies that can be adopted which would respect the logic of the above conclusion. However, one must begin by dealing with the issue of voting within the context of the EC.

National Will and European Integration

It is a good time for the EC. The so-called "europessimism" of the early eighties has yielded ground to a newfound will among the member states to seriously entertain thoughts of a closer political union and increased economic and monetary union. The SEA of 1987 both spurred on this new optimism and represented a codification of already-existing changes in the attitudes and practices of the national leaders. One of these changes is the less successful use of the "national veto" afforded by the Luxembourg Compromise to the member states. However, to fully understand this evolution, one must return to the Community's past.

The early sixties, like the present times, were also a time of much optimism, and few expected the crisis that soon was to befall the Community. This is not meant to imply that there were not serious tensions in the Community; the debate over British entry, the increasingly strained Franco-German relations worsened by Erhard becoming Chancellor in Germany, and the aborted negotiations over the Fouchet Plan all signalled the existence of a divergence of views among the member states over the role of the United States in Europe and the extent to which power should be given to the Community. However, these differences, while impacting upon the functioning of and the optimism over European integration, did not prevent solid achievements such as the 1960 decision to speed up the application of the Rome Treaty, the continued progress towards a customs union or the setting up of the foundations of the common agricultural policy (CAP) from being realized. As late as December 1964, after an agreement over cereal prices was reached, there was so much optimism among the member states concerning the Community that one scholar, writing in 1966, noted that "although relief that the worst [meaning the collapse of the Community] had not happened was understandable, it is rather surprising that the sky appeared quite so blue and cloudless after the December decisions."[4] This optimism was mirrored in academic circles, in which functionalist and neo-functionalist scholars overoptimistically anticipated the quick decline of the nation-state in Western Europe.

---

4   Miriam Camps, *European Unification in the Sixties: From the Veto to the Crisis*, New York: McGraw Hill Book Company, 1966, p. 27.

In reality, there were two fundamental challenges to the integration process: one arising from the international environment; and the second arising from within the Community. The issue in the international environment was the amount of influence that the United States should have in Western Europe. Much of the reason for France's veto of British entry lay in the risk that De Gaulle felt Britain's entry would pose for a European (and, more significantly, a France-led) Community. Britain's efforts to have a special relationship with the US were taken as omens of a potential increase in American influence through Britain if the British joined the Six. These predominantly French fears of a "creeping Atlanticism" were not fully welcomed by the other member states. Adenauer's desire to strengthen Franco-German cooperation made him partial to France's views, but he was opposed by other powerful political party leaders who had a more pro-US attitude. Other countries differed with the French in an even more pronounced manner. Most of the smaller countries feared the risk of French hegemony that they felt De Gaulle would gladly substitute for American dominance. There also was a general fear in the Benelux countries, Italy and Germany of the implications of France's attitude for NATO, and, by extension, for the protection of Western Europe against a perceived Soviet threat. Consequently, that element of consensus among the member states that is required for significant advances in European integration was in fact under attack during the early sixties.

This lack of consensus was crucial at a time when the Community, due to its rapid progress through its first stage, and its continued momentum in achieving the goals of its second stage, was fast approaching a stage at which significant advances in European integration would be required. The increased supranational control in the third stage, resulting both from the shift in the Council of Ministers from unanimous voting (and thus from a form of decision making that required a consensus among the member states) to qualified majority voting, and from the extension of the Community's authority due to the anticipated intensification of economic integration, heralded the arrival of a real test of the member states' will to proceed with "Europe." This "challenge" arose naturally from the integration process, and has been and will continue to be a constant theme in European integration, thus making the consequent "response" -- the empty chair crisis and the Luxembourg Compromise -- particularly significant.

De Gaulle, in his press conference of September 9, 1965, made it abundantly clear that the real purpose of the crisis was to deal with the increasing power of the supranational institutions of the Community. This view was echoed by Couve De Murville in the first meeting of the Six arranged to deal with the crisis; his "Decalogue" included several proposals designed to limit the Commission's influence and attacked the Rome Treaty's idea of majority voting. The Commission had earned France's ire with its proposals on how to manage the finances of the Community after the end of the transition period for the CAP and the end of the second stage of integration. Not only did the Commission suggest that the Community's "own resources" should be increased by collecting revenue from agricultural levies and customs duties, but it suggested that the powers of the Assembly in determining the budget should be increased. For Hallstein, the President of the Commission at the time, the Commission was simply acting "equally within the framework of the Treaty and its constitutional position"[5] in raising these issues. However, for De Gaulle, "the intervention of [the Assembly] would only aggravate the character of usurpation of that which was demanded [by the Commission]."[6] The Commission further alienated France by choosing to present its proposals to the Assembly before it discussed them with the Council. Thus, France felt that it was confronted by an overzealous Commission whose increasing scope of influence would only further limit national prerogatives.

The aforementioned divergence of views among the Six over the US also played a role in increasing the probability of a crisis. Franco-German relations had become strained over Kennedy's multilateral nuclear force proposal, and they would worsen in 1965 when De Gaulle began to give encouraging signs to the Soviet Union. De Gaulle's moves evinced a growing unwillingness to rely on the Franco-German axis to control the development of the Community. Under these circumstances, the French decided to act unilaterally to preserve their national interests. They found in the inability of the Council to reach a decision on the financing of the CAP by June 30, 1965 -- an understandable occurrence as the French had no intention of compromising on their opposition to the Commission's proposals -- a convenient excuse to break with the Community.

On the one hand, the intransigence of the French, as Miriam Camps notes, had the effect of forcing the remaining five member states to unify around some common theme (the defense of the treaty) and "elect" a common leader (Germany).[7] A unified front of resistance was thus created which, when added to the negative reaction of the French public to their government's policy, produced strong incentives for the French to end their boycott of the Council. However, the French empty-chair policy did achieve its aim. The other member states, out of their desire to prevent a permanent rift in the Community, were forced to negotiate with France. The Commission, by being partially blamed for causing the crisis with its so-called "brash" actions, lost some of its

---

5 This point of view is taken from a book written by Hallstein after the crisis entitled: *Europe in the Making*, trans. Charles Roetter, London: George Allen & Unwin Ltd., 1972, p. 50.

6 The quote is from De Gaulle's 9 September 1965 press conference, included in: André Passeron (ed.), *De Gaulle Parle 1962-1966*, Paris: Fayard, 1966, p. 313.

7 Camps (note 4), p. 94.

legitimacy to propose significant steps forward in European integration. The compromise itself, by providing a method outside of any treaty -- and thus outside of the legal base of the Community -- to combat qualified majority voting in the Council by claiming the violation of vital national interests and thus requiring the search for unanimity, is a testament to the power of the nation-state in the Community. The French action thus proved, for all the world to see, that "there is no iron law of 'spill-over' nor an irresistible internal dynamic that is bound to carry the Six to full economic union and beyond that to some form of political union."[8]

If the lesson of the sixties for the Community and its scholars was not to underestimate the power of the nation-state in determining the course of European integration, the seventies can be seen as having repeatedly confirmed the validity of this observation. The shared view among scholars of the Community is that the seventies were a decade of stagnation for the Community. This view needs to be some what nuanced. One would expect scholars like Michael Burgess, who examine the Community's history from the perspective of federal trends, to conclude that "in the mid-1970s ... federal ideas, influences and strategies ... struggled in a difficult intergovernmental environment."[9] However, even a "gaullist" interpretation of the Community's history still would lead one to conclude that it was a period of great unproductiveness for the Community. A heightened awareness of national priorities among the member states rendered even intergovernmental initiatives difficult to achieve.

The international environment posed many challenges to integration efforts. The oil shocks and the resulting world recessions, coupled with the collapse of the Bretton Woods system, put severe pressure on the national governments to stay afloat in a morass of wildly fluctuating exchange rates and volatile interest rates. European industries were experiencing declining competitiveness. Unemployment and inflation were rising. Thus, even though the member states completed the CAP and decided to allow the British into the Community at the The Hague summit of 1969, and decided in Paris in 1972 to attempt to achieve economic and monetary union along with European Union in 1980, in 1979 at a European Council meeting that one scholar called the "Summit of Euro-optimism,"[10] these achievements were marred by the increased attention to national instead of Community interests. For example, the European Monetary

---

8 Ibid., p. 211.
9 Michael Burgess, *Federalism and European Union: Political Ideas, Influences and Strategies in the European Community, 1972-1987*, New York: Routledge, 1989, p. 81.
10 Christian Franck, "New Ambitions: From the Hague to Paris Summits (1965-1972)" in: Roy Pryce (ed.), *The Dynamics of the European Union*, London: Crom and Helm, 1987, p. 131.

Union was advanced by the Werner Report, which specified the degree to which currencies could fluctuate, but the member states concern over the health of their national economies led to several countries opting out of the system. The British insistence on ensuring that their bill for the CAP would not exceed the benefits that they derived from it facilitated the destruction of consensus in the Community. Even other matters, such as the creation of the European Council in 1974 and the Davignon Report of 1970 that started European Political Cooperation, by virtue of their intergovernmental as opposed to supranational nature, illustrated this trend.

Evidence that this increasing dominance of the national interest over the Community one was mirrored in the increased use of the national veto of the Luxembourg Compromise can be found in the reports of the decade. For example, the Heads of State, meeting in December 1974, made mention in their final report of the need to renounce the Luxembourg Compromise if decision-making in the Council was ever to be ameliorated. The Tindemans report of 1976 also suggested the increased use of qualified majority voting in the Council. More evidence can be found in the number of times, as Paul Taylor has shown, that the forcing of unanimity through the Luxembourg Compromise occurred in the Agricultural Council and in the regular discussions on the Community's budget. As Taylor writes, the voting system of the Council "began to look less like that of consensus building, the traditional image, and more like that which had been known as the *liberum* veto. Each state laid stress upon its right to veto common actions."[11] An interesting example is the British veto on discussions of a common energy policy or monetary union in 1973 due to German resistance to the idea of a regional development fund.[12] The British saw this fund as a way of receiving money from the Community, an issue particularly significant in view of Britain's problems with the budget.[13]

Significantly, Taylor postulates the existence of an anti-integration attitude, independent of the pressures against integration in the international sphere, which he feels is essential in explaining the relative failure of European integration efforts in the seventies. This view is echoed by former British

---

11 Paul Taylor, *The Limits of European Integration*, London: Crom and Helm, 1983, p. 81.
12 A good discussion of this affair and its resolution can be found in: Haig Simonian, *The Privileged Partnership: Franco-German Relations in the European Community 1969-1984*, Oxford: Oxford University Press, 1985, pp. 219-223, 228.
13 An interesting case study of the regional development fund and its significance as part of the debate over "distributional politics" in the EC can be found in: Helen Wallace, "Distributional Politics: Dividing up the Community Cake," in: Helen Wallace, William Wallace and Carole Webb (eds.), *Policy-Making in the European Community*, 2nd ed., Chichester: John Wiley and Sons Ltd., 1983, pp. 81-98.

Permanent Representative Michael Butler, who points out that the enlargement of the Community in the seventies helped to strengthen the Luxembourg Compromise's veto power as it allowed into the EC three states -- Britain, Denmark and Ireland -- that supported the veto's use (especially in the case of Britain). Thus, "in the Community of Nine . . . France and Britain together had a blocking minority and could, by supporting each other if one invoked the Compromise, make it effective against its opponents."[14] This last point suggests that even if some member states, unlike as in 1965 with France, chose to vote down a nation that had invoked its national interests, the distribution of votes would prevent any such qualified majority from being formed.

The tangible pessimism over Europe in the seventies did not herald the new will to advance European integration that materialized in the early eighties both within the Community's institutions and among the member states. William Wallace, in referring to the improvement in the international environment in the eighties, mentions, among other factors, the growing acceptance in Western Europe of the dominance of the West German economy.[15] This acceptance is seen in the Community in the Econonomic Monetary System (EMS), which represents the member states' willingness to be pegged to the Deutschmark and to accept German priorities -- anti-inflation -- as their own for the sake of the system from which they benefit. Consequently, a basis for consensus exists upon which further demands for European integration can rest. This basis is strengthened, as Stanley Hoffman notes, by the perceived failure among national elites of the nation-state to single-handedly solve the problems arising from the financial crises of the seventies and early eighties.[16]

This basis for consensus acts as the seed which, when nurtured by a favorable international environment, an active Community and responsive national leaders, grows into some form of advanced integration. In the eighties, the lessening in East-West tension encouraged the national governments to focus on the consideration of European issues. This reduction in tension was mirrored within the Community both by the resolution of Britain's complaints over the budget and the CAP and by the enlargement of the Community. The political will to revise the treaties arose as a consequence of Mitterrand's fairly pro-European policy, as exemplified in his May 1984 speech before the European Parliament. This tendency was reinforced by France's presidency of the European Council in the first half of 1984. The early eighties were filled with initiatives such as the Genscher-Colombo proposal of 1981-1983 and the

---

14 Michael Butler, *Europe: More than a Continent*, London: Heinemann Ltd., 1986, p. 159.
15 See William Wallace, *The Transformation of Western Europe*, London: Pinter Publishers Ltd. and Royal Institute of International Affairs, 1990, Chapter 3.
16 Stanley Hoffman, "The European Community and 1992," *Foreign Affairs*, Fall 1989, p. 30.

European Parliament's Draft Treaty of European Union which, even if they were whittled down by the member states almost into non-existence in negotiations, still helped to more firmly express some of the concerns and possible compromises that national governments, searching to strengthen the Community, would come to focus on.

The attitudes of the member states towards the Luxembourg Compromise in the early eighties acted as additional proof of the increasing optimism in the European Community. In 1982, the British invoked their vital national interests during the annual agricultural price-fixing in order to apply pressure to a concurrent set of negotiations concerning Britain's contribution to the Community's budget. However, the Belgian president of the Council nonetheless called for a vote by qualified majority. This action reflects the weaker status in the Community that relative latecomers like Britain have, and also hints at the continued importance of the Paris-Bonn axis in Community affairs (France supported the calling of a vote by qualified majority, claiming that linkage between two issues was never intended to be a part of the Luxembourg Compromise, and moreover that the endangering of a common policy was not acceptable). However, as one scholar notes, an important psychological change occurred here, with favorable implications for the practice of majority voting in the Council and for the Council President's power.[17] The importance of the precedent set here must not be underestimated. Germany, in 1985, met similar resistance when it tried to invoke its vital interests over support prices for cereals.[18]

Given the above points, it is not surprising that the Single European Act of 1987, the tangible expression of the national will to move forward with "Europe" in the eighties, would include provisions to deal with the Luxembourg Compromise, even if only in an indirect fashion. The SEA's installation of a cooperation procedure between the Council and the European Parliament which partially operates with a qualified majority vote in the Council, and the replacement in the Council of unanimity by qualified majority voting for all provisions relating to the achievement of the internal market attempts to redress the blockage of decision-making which the easy recourse to unanimity in the Council of Ministers fostered. This is an indirect way of dealing with the compromise because its existence is not challenged by the SEA; in fact, several of the member states supported the continued validity of the Luxembourg Compromise in their ratification debates. Furthermore,

---

17 Guy de Bassompierre, *Changing the Guard in Brussels*, New York: Praeger and Center for Strategic and International Studies, 1988, p. 27.

18 An actual vote was not be taken due to Germany's stance, but the other member states did not object to the Commission's enactment of measures that matched the proposal Germany had vetoed. See Butler (note 14), p. 162.

unanimity is still required in certain sensitive areas such as Value Added Tax (VAT) rates and taxation.

However, this indirect method of dealing with the compromise is not by any means completely ineffective. Qualified majority voting, as several scholars have observed, implies a new need for coalition building -- in order to either achieve or prevent the formation of such a majority in the Council -- and thus can help maintain that "seed" of consensus which helped bring about a *relance européenne* in the eighties. Furthermore, as one scholar notes, the SEA could reduce the recourse to the compromise's national veto by providing an alternative means for the national prerogatives to be safeguarded. Article 100 A(4), by providing within the Single Act a way for member states to escape, if necessary, the consequences of decisions reached by qualified majority, could fulfil this purpose.[19]

How has the Luxembourg Compromise been viewed since the passing of the SEA? In the Agricultural Council, as the study of Martin Vassey shows, recourse to the compromise continues, but at a very moderated pace. For example, Ireland in 1988 forced a unanimous vote on a compensation for its beef producers, but only after it had let itself be outvoted on reductions in milk quotas. Greece's attempt in 1988 to get a larger devaluation rate for the green drachma was unsuccessful; and the delay caused only resulted in the Commission fixing the prices provisionally based upon the view of the other eleven members. Vassey's conclusion, in light of this information, is particularly interesting if one refers back to the way the Luxembourg Compromise was introduced in 1966. He states that the compromise "remains a factor to be reckoned with ... but it no longer offers member states a means of holding up indefinitely an unwelcome decision or of obtaining additional concessions beyond what the Commission and the majority of delegations think reasonable."[20] Outside of the Agricultural Council, the trend towards a reduced use of the Luxembourg Compromise's veto is evident. A study in *European Trends* cited, for 1988 alone, six examples of occasions when countries, over insurance directives, harmonization regulations, or air transport liberalization, were forced to compromise after their attempted use of the Luxembourg Compromise came to naught.[21]

As the Community moves into the nineties, the continued crisis in the Soviet Union, the need to "contain" a reunified Germany within some sort of economic and military structure, and the institutional dynamics towards

---

19 Fiona Hayes-Renshaw, "Decision-Making in the EC Council after the Single European Act," *Economist Intelligence Unit European Trends*, No. 1, 1990, p. 79.
20 Martin Vassey, "Decision-Making in the Agricultural Council and the Luxembourg Compromise," *Common Market Law Review*, Vol. 25, 1988, p. 732.
21 Dick Leonard, "The Single Act and the Parliament: Shifts in the Balance of Power," *Economist Intelligence Unit European Trends*, No. 4, 1988.

integration resulting from the Internal Market project will probably continue to provide the member states with incentive to seek a closer union. In this case, the need to reach decisions quickly and efficiently, as well as to face up to the growing complaints over the Community's "democratic deficit," will more than likely cause the trend towards majority voting in the Council to continue. It is worth noting that many of the proposals that are presently being considered for the intergovernmental conferences, such as the Belgian memorandum or those from the Parliament, state the value in extending the use of majority voting in the EC. However, the lessons of the sixties are applicable today; the reason that the Luxembourg Compromise is so significant and continues to exist is because it plays an indispensable role in representing the desire of the nation-states of the Community to retain as much control over the integration process as they see fit. This control is what makes the Community unique among international organizations, for it is both a supranational and an intergovernmental organization in which the nation-state is both nurtured and transformed. This dual character is perhaps what makes it work, as the reality of the sovereign state is not denied by the Community but incorporated into the very integration process, thus making an eventual transfer of powers to the supranational level more likely. Consequently, the existence of the compromise as a protector of national interests is perhaps, after all, not something to regret, but, rather, a reality that one must accept, and, ironically, a prerequisite for the continued success of European integration.

Consensus and National Control - an EPC Perspective

The analysis in the last section pertaining to the evidence of national control over the integration process anticipated the main point of this section: that the EPC, by definition, is, like the Luxembourg Compromise, a tool for protecting the national interest. This is not meant to say that the EPC's creators did not have other concerns that influenced the shape of the EPC; past experiences with the European Defense Community and the Fouchet Plans probably helped to support the argument for a very gradual approach. However, the intergovernmental, as opposed to supranational, nature of the EPC is enshrined in the Davignon Report, which only required the member states of the EC to consult with each other on a regular basis. There was no creation of elaborate supranational bodies or of supranational jurisdiction over the enterprise. Schoutheete sees this latter characteristic as being very valuable, as it allowed the member states to coordinate their foreign policies without being constrained to do so.[22] However, this point, despite its practical importance, only further

---

22 Philippe de Schoutheete, *La Coopération Politique Européenne*, 2nd ed., Brussels: Editions Labor/RTL, 1986, p. 50.

highlights the fact that Political Cooperation, by not having any treaty basis or any degree of supervision beyond the national level, was the installation of intergovernmentalism on the emerging supranational framework of the EC, just as the Luxembourg Compromise represented the installation of a national "brake" on encroaching supranationalism. The specific interest that was protected by the creation of the EPC thus was national sovereignty in the field of foreign policy decision-making.

Why was it deemed necessary to protect national prerogatives over foreign policy? The answer lies in the significance of foreign policy as a kind of "last frontier" for integration efforts; the strategy of first integrating economically, and then politically, meant that national resistance would tend to be fairly high to any moves in this field. France particularly reflected this attitude. Furthermore, as some scholars suggest, the sensitivity to national goals also resulted from the growing knowledge that the EC's economic authority could have political repercussions, and thus could affect the national determination of foreign policy.[23] This point is particularly salient in light of the aforementioned economic challenges of the early seventies which, while being an impetus towards closer cooperation, also highlighted the member states' national economic priorities. Within the Community, there was a general desire to remove the Community from the stagnation in which the empty chair crisis had pitched it. Germany, in particular, was eager to build the Community to complement its Ostpolitik. However, there also was a tendency away from integration due to the fact that France was also interested in pursuing national goals, a concern to which the Germans, to maintain France's support, had to be receptive.[24] Thus, the international and Community environments complemented the effort to guard national sovereignty. This effort was conducted both by those who wished to see further development of the EPC but were wary of resistance, and by those who explicitly desired to limit the EPC. Thus, "the development of the Political Cooperation machinery served . . . both the interests of those who wished the EC to develop rapidly . . . and those . . . who were unenthusiastic about such progress"[25] as it was both a potential step forward and an actual step nowhere on the road of further integration.

The continued development of European Political Cooperation, from the Paris Communique of 1972 to the Stuttgart Declaration of 1983, is the story of

---

23 Juliet Lodge, "European Political Cooperation: towards the 1990s," in: Juliet Lodge (ed.), *The European Community and the Challenge of the Future*, London: Pinter Publishers, 1989, pp. 225-227.

24 For an excellent analysis of this issue, see: Simonian (note 12), Chapter 4.

25 David Allen and William Wallace, "European Political Cooperation: the historical and contemporary background," in: David Allen, Reinhardt Rummel and Wolfgang Wessels (eds.), *European Political Cooperation: Towards a foreign policy for Western Europe*, Kent: Butterworths, 1982, p. 29.

consolidation and codification, not innovation.[26] During this period, already existing networks of consultation and previously-existing practices such as the participation of the Commission in EPC were officially recognized, and new networks and practices -- such as COREU and the "Troika" arrangement -- were set up primarily to ease difficulties revealed by ongoing attempts at coordination. The words "common" and "security" gradually made their way into reports on EPC. Proposals that were too bold, such as those in the Tindemans report or the Genscher-Colombo proposal, were either ignored or watered down into less binding forms (such as the Stuttgart Declaration of 1983). Thus, even if the will existed among some member states to dramatically advance the EPC, the reality was that the status quo -- an intergovernmental approach -- was maintained, and that many of the member states, while never totally satisfied, were adequately served by it; as one scholar states, "[the EPC] expand[ed] the reach of national foreign policies, without too sharply constraining them; it offer[ed] additional information and the option of common action, but without any binding commitment."[27]

The SEA was the first real innovation in the history of the EPC. While the SEA did not change the non-binding nature of EPC consultation, it did better delineate this consultation's methods, giving due attention to such issues as the formation of consensus and the consistency between EC and EPC. A future integrative factor was created in the form of the Secretariat, which "has the potential to develop into something more than an extra (and closely controlled) arm of the Presidency."[28] More significantly, it was the first act to officially recognize the existence of EPC, thus ending the EPC's extra-legal status and heralding the birth of a new Community.

However, this slight breath of innovation flows within a context of continually guarded national interest, and thus one should not be surprised that the consensus mode of voting remains an integral part of EPC. The fact that the consensus method has been guarded throughout the EPC's history testifies to the fundamentally intergovernmental nature of foreign policy coordination, and thus to a fundamental hesitancy among member states towards establishing a truly "European" foreign policy. This is not to say that the EPC has not had any success in coordinating the foreign policies of the EC member states, but it is to say that the consensus rule can inhibit the formation of a common foreign policy.

---

26 Much of this analysis is drawn from Schoutheete (note 22), Chapter 1.
27 William Wallace, "Introduction: cooperation and convergence in European foreign policy," in: Christopher Hill (ed.), *National Foreign Policies and European Political Cooperation*, London: George Allen & Unwin Ltd., 1983, p. 10.
28 Lodge (note 23), p. 233.

The EPC's efforts in coordinating a response to Southern Africa after 1985 illustrate this point.[29] Before 1985, a consensus was achievable, basically because none of the member states was really interested in having a forceful foreign policy toward South Africa that would run the risk of jeopardizing its economic interests in that country. Thus, a Code of Conduct was produced in the EPC, but with enforcement and monitoring left at the national level. Clearly this policy was not seriously meant to fulfil the stated aim of the EC to end apartheid. However, the situation changed after 1985, when the escalating violence in South Africa prompted several of the member states to consider sanctions. At this point, consensus became difficult to achieve, with some member states like France pushing for strong sanctions and others, like Britain and West Germany, fighting attempts to apply harsh measures. The result was a diluted common foreign policy that nonetheless took a long time to be agreed on. Consequently, many member states adopted bilateral sanctions. This situation contrasted with the EC's move to ban the import of South African gold coins. It is worth noting that Britain's holding of the Presidency during that time forced her to achieve some sort of consensus. If she was freer, it is possible that not even a diluted foreign policy would have been reachable.

A similar situation arose in the eighties with development aid to the countries of the Southern African Development Coordination Conference (SADCC). The EC had chosen as one of its foreign policy aims the encouragement, through aid, of economic independence of other Southern African countries from South Africa. However, Britain, France and West Germany were unwilling to fund industrial development projects for fear of competition, and chose instead to support transportation and telecommunications projects which, though extremely important and beneficial, did nothing about the heavy dependence of many of the SADCC nations on South African manufacturing. Thus, even if a majority of the EC member states had wished to increase aid, and had been firm enough to do so even in the face of Franco-German pressure, this policy still would not have been enacted because unanimity is required. Consequently, the policy adopted encouraged an unfortunate mix of independence and dependence.

The EPC's reaction to the Libyan crisis in 1985 is another good example of the general point concerning consensus.[30] The EC was aware of the US interest in dealing with Gaddafi, and knew that a US military strike was at least a strong possibility. However, the EPC was caught unaware by the US decision to send in its forces. Part of the problem was a fundamental difference of

---

29 The following analysis of the South African situation is based on an excellent study: Martin Holland, *The European Community and South Africa: European Political Cooperation Under Strain*, London: Pinter Publishers, 1988, Chapter 2.

30 This analysis is based on a case study: Anastasia Pardalis, "European Political Cooperation and the US," *Journal of Common Market Studies*, June 1987.

opinion between the allies: many West Europeans, unlike the Americans, felt that a bombing would be pointless. However, the lack of attention paid to the Europeans was also a product of the lack of any discernable unity from the EPC. For example, the EPC would present a common view, such as its condemnation of Libya, but would not follow up with any action because achieving consensus for the action was difficult. Or, the EPC would produce significant measures, but this would only happen 6 days after the attack itself, simply because it took that long to forge a consensus. Consequently, not only were allies like the US disgusted, but EPC members such as Britain, who had incentive to pursue bilateral links with the US instead of coordinated policies, were not encouraged by the system to stay in, and thus opted out to pursue a bilateral route instead. In addition, it is possible that a unified EPC stance could have influenced American policy in a region where the Europeans do have interests, but, by their actions, the West Europeans virtually abandoned their interests to the whims of their ally.

Finally, it is useful to mention an action during the Iran-Iraq crisis and the fairly successful attempt to coordinate foreign policy in the Conference on Security and Cooperation in Europe (CSCE) negotiations of the early seventies to see how and why EPC succeeds in producing common positions. The Iran-Iraq crisis example deals with the quick response of the EPC in rallying behind France after its embassy had been stormed by Iraqi troops. In this case, it is worth noting the perceived need among West Europeans to support France. This move was not only diplomatically wise for bilateral relations with France, but also for European-American relations. A quick, coordinated response involving action in the Gulf would help to ease tension between the US and Western Europe and would promote the view of an EC willing to get involved in defending Western interests. Furthermore, such actions add prestige to the EPC mechanism: the better it works in times of crisis, the more the enterprise will be respected. Lastly, it was in West Europe's interest to become more involved, especially if it wished to give credence to the recent talk about a European pillar of security. Interestingly enough, it was not that difficult on this particular occasion to form a consensus. The CSCE example from the early seventies is also interesting, for the EPC was able to coordinate opinions on security and human rights, and its actions have acted as a base for coordinated policy in this body ever since. The importance of the issue -- East-West cooperation -- probably helped encourage consensus, as well as the fact that, as one scholar notes, the "EPC procedures fit easily in a large multilateral diplomatic exercise."[31] In other words, bloc politics might actually function

---

31 Jean De Ruyt, "European Political Cooperation: Toward a Unified European Foreign Policy," *Occasional Paper, The Atlantic Council*, October 1989, p. 27.

better when consensus rule, and thus a hard search for compromise -- especially in a forum that is valued and will not be abandoned -- is operating.

The Mode of Decision-Making as the Key to an Emerging European Union

Taken together, the history of the use of the Luxembourg Compromise and the EPC eloquently cries out warnings that we should heed in the next decade. For, just like those times of optimism of the early sixties and the beginning of the seventies, we witness in this time an enormous possibility for actual and potential integration in which national prerogatives will come increasingly under attack. Already, the signs are beginning to appear: the national parliaments' call for an involvement in the integration process that could, if it takes the form of a European senate, strengthen the amount of intergovernmental control in the Community;[32] the debate over subsidiarity which could lead to an increase in the powers of the EC, but also could bolster those of national and subnational groups; the Delors line that stresses the need not to go too fast with the integration process for fear of "robbing national states of their fundamental interests";[33] and lastly, Britain who, though recently forced to join the EMS due in part to its weak economy, still pushes the "widening" part of the integration tableau with invitations to many countries to join the EC in order to offset attention from the "deepening" process which is on the horizon.

The rapidly-changing international environment has a lot to do with the quick pace that the Community has established. The sudden collapse of the postwar order, engendered by the changes in the Soviet Union, has released many old specters unto Europe in the form of awaking nationalism, ethnic conflicts, and World War II memories. The very last specter has made an impressive appearance in the form of a reunified Germany, and all across Europe and beyond, the question arises of how to handle this new nation that has much potential power and inspires so much fear. Postwar alliances are in flux or are already fading from the scene. The air is full of new ideas, new plans and new fears.

These global concerns are reflected in the Community environment, and thus this environment also encourages the present quick pace of integration. The pace is a direct response to the following concerns: ensuring the "containment" of Germany within a Western European structure in which it can

---

32 For an excellent discussion of the issue, see: Thierry Bhéhier, "Deux Chambres pour l'Europe?" *Le Monde*, 13 July 1990, p. 1.
33 Mark E. Nelson, "Delors Warns Against Rushing EC Unity," *The Wall Street Journal*, 18 June 1990, p. 2.

peacefully pursue its economic interests and maintain its military forces; ensuring the continued health of the European experiment in the face of the onslaught of hungry cries from Eastern Europe; and ensuring the continued survival of Western Europe in the face of a now certain declining American commitment (a responsibility which many West Europeans seem ready to undertake). Thus, it is not surprising that, in addition to the 1992 project, which alone helped to create a high level of Euro-optimism, we now see plans for Economic and Monetary Union on the table, even though this process will result in much power over foreign economic policy being ceded to the EC (the Council of Ministers, the Commission, and the new Eurofed). It should not be surprising to see, as one newspaper article eloquently expressed, "Europe's cooks fight for the broth,"[34] the broth in this case being the overwhelming need for new security structures, and the cooks being the EC, the Western European Union (WEU), the North Atlantic Treaty Organization (NATO), the Council of Europe, and so on. And in light of this last sentence, it should not be surprising to see the EC bring up the matters of Political Union and a European Foreign Policy in a way that it has never been mentioned before. The Community becomes one of the focal points of the new European order.

The Community's own dynamics help in producing this state of affairs, as the EC, since the SEA, has been on the road of change, thus facilitating further advances in that direction, in the same way that a descent down a slope would be facilitated by a decrease in resistance. This analogy is not a trivial one, for in many ways the present pace of change is like a roller-coaster ride. The motivating power of the Community, the Franco-German axis, is pushed into cooperation both by their own national interests and by the international environment. The aforementioned "formula" for an advance in integration (consensus, a favorable international environment, an active Community, and responsive national leaders) is fulfilled. The question thus is, in view of the potential for change which exists, how does one best proceed, both to get what one wants and to prevent the opportunity from being ruined?

A two-step approach would be useful. First, the optimal goal needs to be defined and established. An EC which conducts a consistent, coherent and forceful foreign policy is the preferred goal. Suspending reality for a time (that is, the presence of national resistance to integration), what does this goal really mean, and what institutional arrangements would carry it out? Once this is done, the second step, the design of appropriate strategies for achieving the goal in light of reality, can be undertaken.

A foreign policy which is consistent would mean one in which there was congruence between EPC decisions and EC actions. This logic or harmony

---

34   Michael Binyon, "Europe's Cooks Fight for the Broth," *The Times*, 26 April 1990, p. 12.

between different branches of the European Union would be paralleled by a harmony within the foreign policy itself; in other words, the member states would, instead of declaring one thing at the European level and then doing the opposite at the national level, pursue a foreign policy which made sense (in its relation of means to a stated end) and which was largely uniform (meaning that a common foreign policy with a minimum of derogations in the name of national interest would be the norm). It is this internal harmony which would make the foreign policy coherent. And finally, making the common foreign policy forceful would mean providing the EC with the means to carry out, monitor and enforce its foreign policy decisions, both vis-à-vis member states of the EC and vis-à-vis the "targets" of the foreign policy.

Establishing such a foreign policy obviously could be done in many ways. Changing the voting procedure in the EPC from unanimity to some sort of majority voting would help to increase the coherence of the foreign policy. We have seen above how the consensus requirement can result in a foreign policy whose means do not match its stated end, or one in which member states pursue alternative policies on the national level. The installation of some form of majority voting would help to prevent the inevitable trend towards what many scholars of the EPC have called "lowest common denominator" decisions, which, while indeed being a consensus, frequently represent diluted or merely declaratory foreign policy. Majority voting would also ensure that there would be a higher probability of actually reaching a decision than in the case of consensus rule, therefore implying that more initiatives could be sought in foreign policy and thus that the present reactive nature of EPC would be altered.

However, such a change in voting procedure would not be enough; consistency and forcefulness would still have to be sought. Consistency could be achieved through tighter linkages between the EC and the EPC in the form of increased consultation between the two and the sharing of certain decisions, shared responsibilities at the national level, and a common authority that overarches both bodies. These tighter linkages would also help make the common foreign policy forceful, as the EPC could conceivably have access to some of the EC's tools for carrying out and enforcing a foreign policy. Alternatively, one could conceive of new bodies and new responsibilities for the EC that would be conducive to forceful common foreign policy.

It is critically important that one would need more than a change in voting procedure to achieve the above defined optimal goal, for this fact suggests the multiplicity of obstacles towards a common foreign policy that national interests produce. Even if decisions in the EPC were taken by some form of majority voting procedure, it still would not guarantee that the decisions would be put into practice by the member states. Part of the reason that the EC has a Court is to deal with those member states which do not enact policies decided at the European level by unanimous or majority vote. Who would enforce foreign policy decisions? Changing the nature of the vote would also not necessarily affect the reality in the EPC that certain national concerns considered too sensitive for the European forum are simply never mentioned. As Michael Butler notes with reference to the EC, "whether the issue is a voting matter or not, quite a lot of effort will be put into securing a compromise if one or two delegations think that the majority position would be damaging to important interests in their country or countries."[35] In short, the disappearance of the Luxembourg Compromise would not mean the end to the search for consensus, and likewise, consensus would continue to be an important concern in EPC even if its voting procedure was changed.

The reality is that consensus is not only necessary, but can function quite well in certain situations, as was illustrated at the end of the last section. The consensus principle forced the EPC members to compromise in the CSCE format, and thus their unity in this forum was strong because everyone agreed. The support given to France was easy to reach because there was overwhelming reason for everyone to do so within the EPC framework; a majority voting procedure could not have achieved a better result. Of course there are a myriad of examples of times when the need for everyone to agree was not beneficial to the formulation of a common foreign policy, as the last section tried to illustrate. However, the desire for greater efficiency in foreign policy decision-making cannot be allowed to overshadow the need for agreement among the member states of the EC. It is only agreement that would allow a foreign policy decided by some fashion of majority vote to be both coherent (in that member states did not derogate from it) and forceful (in that the EC would be allowed by its member states to enforce such a foreign policy). Thus, one comes right back to the lesson learnt in the first section of this chapter dealing with voting in the EC: the national component of European integration should not be trampled in integration efforts. It is worth noting that some writers are already suggesting a lull in the desire to integrate, due to the economic strains resulting from the Gulf crisis and due to an interest in national priorities which some feel is occurring in the new Germany and will come to the surface in France when words concerning European unity must be turned into concrete proposals.[36] Increasing attention to national priorities in Germany could be especially significant for majority voting, as a bigger Germany could

---

35 Butler (note 14), p. 161.
36 These themes can be found in the following articles: Claire Tréan, "Le chancelier Kohl veut hâter l'union politique européenne," *Le Monde*, 30 March 1990, p. 1; Conor Cruise O'Brien, "Thatcher calls their bluff," *The Times*, 30 April 1990, p. 14; Ian Davidson, "Gulf shakes Gaullist taboos," *The Financial Times*, 27 September 1990; William Drozdiak, "Germany's Union Comes as Impetus for United Europe is Flagging," *The Washington Post*, 1 October 1990, p. A22.

carry more numerical weight in qualified majority voting, thus having a greater effect in decision-making.[37] If this is true, it is even more important to devise strategies which, while not strangling all chance for change, proceed in such a way as to not overly attack national sovereignty.

First of all, one could install a system of absolute, as opposed to qualified majority voting. Absolute or simple majority voting in the EPC would, however, have the effect of allowing, in theory, seven of the twelve member states to decide upon a common foreign policy. One could question whether such a foreign policy would truly be representative. Moreover, while the simple majority approach might make for efficient foreign policy decision-making, it could also constitute too much of an attack on national sovereignty -- after all, the Luxembourg Compromise was created in reaction to the introduction of qualified majority voting, which, by virtue of its assigning of votes to member states based on relative size, makes it more difficult for a decision to be reached and easier for a decision to be blocked than in the case of absolute majority voting. A gentler approach towards national sovereignty would thus be embodied by the installation of a qualified majority approach; the lack of national control over integration that comes with absolute majority voting would be mitigated while still rendering the EPC better off than it would be with the consensus principle.

An even more gentle approach, but one which would still improve upon the present voting mode within the EPC, would be the "unanimity with abstentions" idea mentioned in the introduction. This idea spins off of the article in the SEA which suggests that member states should not disturb the formation of a consensus. A similar idea is the installation of a qualified majority regime that allowed any member to opt out of the system. Both of these ideas would have the value of encouraging flexibility in European foreign policy while still allowing it to be utilized as a problem-solving forum for member states.[38] However, one would also run the risk that the changes suggested here would, in reality, not lead to a foreign policy that was any more coherent or forceful than the present one.

Another strategy that could involve less of a risk of stagnation while still "protecting" the national interest would be to situate change within the forum that is, by history, more accustomed to it: the EC. One could make only cosmetic changes in the mode of voting of the EPC, but could compensate for this lack by improving consistency between the EC and the EPC in order to

---

37 The issue of the power of united Germany has interesting implications for the Franco-German relationship. On this subject, see: "A relationship in the balance," *The Economist*, 6 October 1990, pp. 53-54.

38 This aim suggests an approach to integration that stresses problem solving, not integration for its own sake. See: "E pluribus unum," *The Economist*, 22 September 1990, p. 15.

allow the "Community method" to influence the functioning of the EPC. For example, one could install the above idea of majority vote with the option to opt out of the system, but at the same time increase the role of the Commission in the formulation of policy, or allow the ministers to decide foreign policy in their EC capacity. One could put more of the power of implementation and enforcement under the EC rubric. The assumption here is that a move toward supranationality might be more palatable in the EC format than in the EPC, and that the EPC would benefit from the apparent present willingness to see more supranationality in the EC. The fact that the use of the Luxembourg Compromise has decreased in recent years indicates a certain level of comfort with the concept of relinquishing sovereignty which might be lacking in the foreign policy coordination field. However, the risks of this approach are manifold. Firstly, member states created the EPC to avoid precisely such an occurrence -- that is, the assumption by the Community of prerogatives in foreign policy decision-making -- and they may still react adversely to this, depending upon the prevailing will to integrate. Secondly, there is the aforementioned Delors line. Delors feels that "it is too early to create a single EC foreign policy, or even to make foreign-policy questions the subject of weighted majority voting in the Council of Ministers."[39] Influencing this view is the fear of disturbing the balance between supranationality and intergovernmentalism in the EC: if consistency means an overall increase in power for the Council, the EC-EPC relationship on the whole might become more supranational, but the internal EC relationship between the Commission and the Council would be altered in favor of the intergovernmental side. This of course might be a good way to reassure member states that they are not losing too much control over the integration process, but one would have to recognize that, instead of allowing the Community method to influence the EPC, one would be allowing the EPC method to influence the Community.

Another method would be to install a "Luxembourg Compromise" in EPC decision-making: one could use the idea of vital national interests to set up a hierarchy of issues that would be decided by different modes of voting (the most sensitive being decided by unanimity). Shifting national priorities would have to be accommodated, which in practice could prove to be very difficult, and national priorities could conflict if a minimalist approach was not adopted. However, a minimalist approach could end up changing very little. Moreover, as the history of the use of the Luxembourg Compromise in the seventies shows us, such a system could be incapacitated by an upsurge of concern over national goals. Of course, such an upsurge could not be avoided in any case, due to the reality of national power over European integration.

---

39 See Nelson (note 33).

All of the above suggestions do not answer the question raised above of whether or not the important value of consensus needed for integration would still be provided by the proposed changes. Qualified majority voting, while more supranational, does not necessarily impede upon the formation of consensus; as we have seen above, majority vote does not end the search for consensus. Furthermore, coalition-building is encouraged, as the system encourages participants to exchange compromises: a compromise by country A in one particular issue is expected to be rewarded later on by another country compromising to support A. Thus the system of voting in itself does not have to necessarily completely threaten national power.

Conclusion

One has a severe temptation to try to forecast exactly where this process will lead, and what will be accepted in terms of change in the short term, the outcome of the two Intergovernmental Conferences. The very title of the last section indicates that these changes all will affect the possibility of eventually seeing a European Union. These changes will also influence the nature of this union: will it be a beneficent force in international affairs, as scholars like Christopher Hill hope, or will it simply be the nation-state writ large, as Johan Galtung fears? While the long term impact of these questions must not be forgotten, and while the short term possibility for change must be evaluated in order to formulate strategies, this chapter will not seek to answer these questions definitively, but will only raise them for general consideration. The more important task, in view of the potential for change at hand, is to realize that one can seize the initiative in European integration, and produce outcomes which, while always determined by the will of the Community's member states and always an outcome of negotiations between them, are the product of experience, an understanding of reality and a conscious effort to influence the course of events.

6

A Test Case of Consistency: The San José Dialogue

Veerle Coignez

Introduction

In academic literature on European Political Cooperation (EPC), reference is often made to the San José Conferences, which serve as a framework for the economic and political support offered by the European Community (EC) to Central America. The Conferences constitute a welcome example of EPC's ability to go beyond the level of "common information" and even "common perception" to eventually reach the level of "common action." The result -- the dialogue and the subsequent implementation of its conclusions -- is all the more valuable because EPC action takes place in coordination with EC action.

The interest among the five Central American nations, since the mid-1980s, in opening a regular dialogue with the Community has grown out of the particular economic, political and social crises in which Guatemala, Honduras, El Salvador, Nicaragua and Costa Rica found themselves entangled. Their need for help, however, does not explain why they were so keen on getting support specifically from Europe when the US offered a larger and closer market and was, moreover, in a better position to provide financial and military assistance. In fact, it was precisely to escape from the US presence and influence in the region that the Isthmus turned towards the Community.[1] Washington's tendency to interpret regional conflict in terms of East-West antagonism and its willingness to intervene militarily, especially during the Reagan years, were increasingly rejected by the Central Americans. In this context, the Community

---

1 The US influence many aspects of life in Central America, ranging from trade, investments, industrial expansion to culture. From a political and military point of view, they are even more omnipresent. See: Francisco Rojas/Edelberto Torres-Rivas, "Documento base de la reunión: nuevas formas de cooperación Europa-Centroamerica," *Cuadernos Semestrates*, No. 18, Mexico, 1985, p. 32.

appeared to be a particularly attractive alternative. European military intervention in Central America was highly unlikely, not only because of the distance and the fact that no "communautarian army" exists but also because of the Community's disbelief in a military solution for the Central American crisis.[2] The historical and cultural links between the two regions constitute a second factor. In particular, the fact that Europe shares with Central America an intuitive tendency to value the sovereignty and independence of individual countries -- regardless of ideological considerations -- was considered important.[3] Furthermore, the Community provided an encouraging example of regional integration to the nations of the Isthmus, whose own attempt had been less than successful.[4] Last but not least, the EC remained an important trade partner for the Central Americans and their concern over the potentially negative consequences of the 1992 Internal Market program could only add to their efforts to improve relations with Europe.[5] The Community, in turn, no longer considering Central America to be an "exclusive preserve of the US" and was not unwilling to demonstrate its disagreement with the American policy of regional hegemony. The path was thus open to a more pluralist policy in Central America, with all its potential impact on superpower relations.

Theoretical Framework

If one is to test a matter as complex as the consistency of EC and EPC action, a clear definition of the concept and a well considered theoretical framework are indispensable. They constitute the basis of the analysis and the guiding line throughout the argument, upon which the conclusion is based.

An analysis of the European Community role in Central America has to take into consideration a wider context and to relate the Community's actions to their causes and consequences.[6] In general, one can say that the interests

---

2 Santiago Frayle, "Apuntes sobre la presenda de la CEE en Centroamerica en los años ochenta," *Cuadernos Semestrales*, No. 18, 1985, p. 47.
3 Irvinz Kristol, "Deberia preocuparse Europa por Centroamerica?," *Cuadernos Semestrales*, No. 18, 1985, p. 38.
4 Note the creation of the Common Market of Central America on 23 July 1962. The fact that the Community had supported other regional integration attempts -- such as with the ASEAN countries -- stimulated the Central Americans to ask for help from across the Atlantic Ocean.
5 Although the Central American share of total EC imports had decreased since the 1960s, the importance of the EC market for Central American exports had actually increased (the EC becoming Central America's second most important export market). In 1984: imports from EC -- 30% of total; exports to EC -- 40% of total.
6 Indeed, one cannot study the interaction between the EC and EPC in the San José process without understanding why the interaction takes place in the first place. By

involved determine the nature of the interregional relationship. As, in this case, the interests imply action in the economic and the political fields, the Twelve have no choice but to recur to the EC as well as to the EPC framework in order to obtain satisfactory results. It is at this point that the problem of coherence in the Community's foreign relations appears. The Single European Act (SEA) touches upon the matter in Article 30.5, where it states that there should be "consistency" between the external policy of the EC and the EPC.[7] In an attempt to clarify the meaning of "consistency," scholars have opted for the interpretation of "erasing all outward distinguishing marks between EC and EPC."[8] This approach does not, however, explain whether the concept of coherence should apply to the "substance" of the EC and the EPC policy or rather to the "implementation" by the respective frameworks -- or to both. In fact, the SEA is not clear about it either. It seems useful to make a distinction between the "substance and essence" of a policy, on the one hand, and "the way of implementing or enacting" it, on the other, as each implies a specific approach to the relation between EC and EPC.

When economic and political problems are interlinked, it goes without saying that the Community's policy should consist of an economic and a political part in order to be forceful; it is even more obvious that the economic and the political part in that case should not be contradictory but point towards the same goal, which is to say that the two parts should be coherent. "Coherence" takes thus the meaning of "non contradiction" when, in a first step, it is delimited to a question of "substance."

Of course, one cannot talk about the "substance" of a policy, without linking it in a second step to "the mechanisms and procedures that are to enact that substance." "Coherence" has thus to find its corollary in "interaction." Indeed, if the two parts are to be taken care of in different frameworks, then mechanisms and procedures are necessary to ensure their interaction. It is only when a policy is coherent and the interaction occurs accordingly that all outward distinguishing marks between EC and EPC will disappear. It can of course happen that there is an inconsistency between the economic and political part of the policy, in the sense that the action in one part is not as effective as in

---

the same token, you cannot conclude upon its importance, if you do not confront the results obtained with the interests at stake. See: Rojas-Torres Rivas (note 1), p. 33.

7 "Consistency" is the English equivalent of the word "*cohérence*" in the French version of the SEA. As in the SEA, here too, the concept is used in reference to the relationship between the EC and EPC. Consequently, the problem of coherence between the policies of the Community, on the one hand, and the member states, on the other is not delt with.

8 See the conference proceedings of "The European Foreign Policy in the Test," Conference at the College of Europe, Bruges -- Working Group 3, June 1990.

the other. This inconsistency does not call into question the condition of coherence nor the kind of interaction. As long as both parts keep pointing in the same direction, the policy can be considered "of one piece": a product of specific interests, when conceived; a means towards a particular goal, when implemented. Furthermore, results -- whether consistent or not -- only come into consideration afterwards, when, after having been conceived and implemented, the policy is finally evaluated.[9]

The Interests Involved

At the very origin of any policy, one can presume the existence of particular interests. Indeed, a party will not take action so long as he does not perceive it to be in his own interest. The Central American case is a very clear example of this. The five countries of the Isthmus found their calls for assistance unanswered, so long as the Community saw no interest in helping them resolve their crisis. In fact, from the 1960s until mid-1970s, only minimal contact existed between the two regions. From the mid-1970s, there was a degree of rapprochement but it was only in the 1980s that relations were developed and the Community began thinking of the Latin American region as something more than a mere export market.[10]

The first factor responsible for this change was the overall economic decline of the Isthmus, especially the ever increasing debt burden.[11] But the attention

---

9 Mischo's argument that the disposition of Article 30.5 is characterized by an *obligation de faire* rather than an *obligation de resultat*, appears to be in agreement with this line of reasoning. See: Jean Mischo, *Du droit international au droit de l'intégration: Les efforts envue d'organiser sur le plan juridique la coopération des Etats members de la Communauté en matiére de politique étrangère*, 1987, p. 461.

10 The first contacts date back to 1968, when the Consejo Centraamericano sent a mission to Brussels in order to discuss problems concerning the commercialization of basic products. In June 1971 a dialogue with Grula was set up. This did not, however, lead to many results. The Latin Americans complained about European protectionism but did not get much further than complaints. The EC in turn was discouraged by the technical difficulty of the regional negotiations. This was due in particular to the lack of consensus among the extremely diverse Central American governments, the complexity of the institutional networks and the limitations of the instruments at their disposition. See: Rojas-Torres Rivas (note 1), pp. 32-34; Mole Paquet-Soriano, "L'impact de l'adhésion espagnole sur les relations CEE-Amérique Latine," mémoire sous la direction de Wolfgang Wessels, College of Europe, 1988, p. 1.

11 The absence of natural resources in the five Central American countries, their dependence on imports of energy, and particular problems such as the lack of trade diversification, had turned this region into the poorest and least developed of Latin America. Moreover, with a large part of the population being illiterate and political

of the Community was also caught by developments in the political field. In particular, the downfall of the Somoza dictatorship and the subsequent installation of the Sandinista government in Nicaragua was considered a turning point in the regional crisis, and the beginning of its internationalization.[12] The evolution of the guerilla conflict in El Salvador into a real civil war was also an important factor in that respect. The enlargement of the Community by the inclusion of Spain and Portugal should also be taken into consideration, for this brought up again the issue of historical and cultural links between the two continents. Spain was expected to play the role of a bridge and those expectations, whether justified or not, did in some ways create a self-fulfilling prophecy.[13]

However, this does not really explain why the EC suddenly changed its attitude. In other words, those factors would not have succeeded in gaining the Community's attention in the way they did if the Community did not have some interest in responding to them. One can immediately exclude military considerations when trying to define the nature of the particular interests involved; obviously, the region is of no direct geopolitical importance to the EC.[14] Furthermore, it is undeniable that from an economic point of view, the Isthmus cannot represent a considerable weight for the EC in comparison with other regions. This is well illustrated by the decreasing trend in EC trade with Latin America.[15] Consequently, we can conclude that the Community started paying attention to the Isthmus mainly for political reasons. Indeed, after years

---

régimes that served the interests of the élites at the expense of human rights, not many prospects for improvement existed. The Central American countries simply had to acknowledge the fact that they were unable to stop the undermining of their region's economic infrastructure, and even culture, without outside support. See: Rojas-Torres Rivas (note 1), pp. 27-31.

12　Esperanca Duran, "Western Europe's role in the Central American crisis: possibilities and limitations," in: Garcia, Rigoberto (ed.), *Central America: Crisis and Possibilities*, Monograph/Institute of Latinamerica Studies, No. 16, Stockholm: Latinamerika-Institut, 1988, p. 33.

13　See the discussion in: Instituto de Relaciones Europeo-Latinoamericanas (IRELA), *Latin America and Europe in the 90s: toward a new relationship*, Conference Report, No. 3189, 1989.

14　Some argue that the Community does have geopolitical interests in the region, if only in an indirect way. See José Miquel Insulza, "Europa, Centroamerica y la Allianza Atlantica," *Cuadernos Semestrales*, No. 18, 1985, p. 97; Gerd Beinhardt, "El papel de Europa en Centroamerica: desarrollo de là cooperacion de la CEE con Centroamerica," *Cuadernos Semestrales*, No. 18, 1985, p. 65; Duran (note 12), p. 37.

15　EC imports from Central America (million ECU): 1975 - 663; 1980 - 1243; 1985 - 795. EC exports to Central America (million ECU): 1975 - 358; 1980 - 538; 1985 - 518. See: *Neue Zürcher Zeitung*, 13 February 1987.

of formation and preoccupation with procedures and mechanisms to intensify their cooperation, the EPC members felt they needed to prove -- to themselves as well as to the others -- that they were able to speak with one voice and to become a respectful actor in the field of foreign policy. Central America offered them, in addition to earlier established interregional relationships with the Arab League and the Association of South East Asian Nations (ASEAN), a perfect opportunity in this respect. Since no vital economic interests were at stake, consensus would not be that difficult to reach.[16] Moreover, it was a good occasion to show how European foreign policy was not necessarily a mere reflection of US foreign policy. If the game were played carefully, there was little to lose and plenty to gain.

The Community's Central America Policy

The nature of the interests involved influenced the form of action taken. The Twelve sought to improve their political profile while the Isthmus was intent on getting out of its political and economic crisis and becoming less dependent on the US. The only way for EC/EPC to gain credibility as an independent force was to help Central America in an effective fashion. As this implied economic as well as political action, the Twelve established a political and economic dialogue with the Isthmus. More precisely, a political dialogue between EPC and the Central American and Contadora Group countries,[17] and an economic dialogue between the EC and the Common Market of Central America (CMCA) countries and Panama. The fact that the policy of the Community is formed in dialogue with the Central American region implies that, in principle, decisions are made by common agreement.[18] It also implies a degree of flexibility, as the policy can be continuously redefined in light of changing circumstances. The pluralist and non-discriminatory approach of the Community in the process constitutes a third important characteristic. It forms the basis for the regional character of the policy and is appreciated by the nations of the Isthmus. Nicaragua, in particular, has benefitted from the fact that economic decisions are taken independent of the political ideology of a country's government. Last but not least, both components of the dialogue aim at the same goal, namely the stabilization -- economic as well as political -- of

---

16 Duran (note 12), p. 19.
17 Central America: Costa Rica, El Salvador, Guatemala, Honduras, Nicaragua. Contadora Group: Colombia, Mexico, Panama, Venezuela.
18 The political dialogue is indeed presented as "based on equality between sovereign states and mutual respect" (1985 Political Communiqué, Article 3). With regard to the economic dialogue, reference is made to "equity, respect and mutual benefit" as basis of the cooperation activities (1984 Economic Communiqué, Article 13).

the region. Through the dialogues, the EC/EPC want to help Central America in the fight against its interlinked economic, political and social problems.[19]

The political component of the policy can be characterized as consisting of four different aspects. First, the Twelve continuously express their commitment to the principles of independence, self-determination, inviolability of frontiers, fundamental freedoms and respect for human rights.[20] They also hope that the dialogue established on the basis of those principles will lead to a solution to the problems of Central America. Second, they follow political events in the region and comment or express opinions on them. Third, they urge the countries that are part of the Contadora Group, as well as others, to contribute to the peace process in the region. And finally, they officially promise to offer help -- financial, technical and other -- whenever the Central American countries request it.[21] The economic policy consists of discussions and of concrete actions. The discussions concern the general economic situation as well as proposals and programs to cope with particular problems. As to the actions of the Community's Central American policy, the EC focuses on trade, economic cooperation and development assistance. Both the economic and the political part of the Community's Central Athus aim at the stabilization of the region and can therefore be considered coherent.

As mentioned above, the coherence of the political and economic aspects of the Community's policy demands interaction of EC and EPC which are two distructive foreign policy frameworks regarding their legal basis, their decision-making structures and their instruments of action.

It is argued that the differences between the legal bases of the economic and political dialogue may eventually constitute an obstacle for EC/EPC interaction. It is true that the difference between the respective frameworks of EC and EPC was respected at the moment of the San José dialogue's institutionalization in November 1985. With regard to the economic dialogue, this resulted in a concrete five-year non-preferential economic cooperation agreement between the EC and the CMCA countries plus Panama.[22] Being based on Articles 113 and 235 of the EEC Treaty, the Cooperation Agreement is binding for the EC and thus subject to appeal for the Court of Justice. The go-ahead for the negotiation of that agreement had been given on 26 June 1985,

---

19 This is stated in the joint communiqué issued at the end of the first San José conference, September 1984.
20 See: 1985 Political Communiqué, Article 20; 1987 Political Communiqué, Article 12.
21 In particular, the plan to establish a Central American Parliament receives a lot of attention and the offer to assist in its creation is repeated frequently.
22 Elfriede Regelsberger, "The Dialogue of the EC/Twelve with Other Groups of States," *The International Spectator*, Vol. 23, No. 4, October-December 1988 p. 260.

when the Council approved the directives concerning the mandate.[23] It authorized the Commission to start what were to become the first negotiations outside SELA.[24] The negotiations took one month and resulted in a Commission proposal for the conclusion of the first ever EC/Central American Cooperation Agreement. The Council, wanting to prove its readiness to turn economic promises into real actions, finally approved the agreement during its meeting of 22-23 July.[25]

The institutionalization of the political dialogue, on the same occasion, followed a rather different procedure. The negotiations were not conducted by the Commission, but by the Presidency. Consequently, the procedure only required that the Twelve adhere by consensus to what the Presidency had concluded. The San José process did set a precedent in the sense that it was the first time that a political dialogue was initiated by a formal Act, the so-called Final Act of 1985.[26] In this Act, the parties state officially their intention to institutionalize a political dialogue by holding annual meetings at the ministerial or senior official level. The Final Act represents the highest expression of political support, but an expression of support without any binding effect. Indeed, although the text constitutes the legal basis of the political dialogue, it remains a declaration of intent and nothing more.

The Commission would liked to have seen the economic and political dialogue established on the same legal basis. In its original proposal, the Commission defended a cooperation agreement consisting of two interdependent sections; one political and one economic.[27] The inclusion of a political section in the Cooperation Agreement, however, was excluded by the Council. Even a watered down version of the initial proposal could not take away the member states' concern over the political aspect. Germany was especially worried by the fact that an agreement of this kind would have to be ratified by each EC Member State. Consequently, the Council opted for two distinct parts in the Agreement, which explains the separate signing of a Final Act and a Cooperation Agreement. As mentioned above, it is not impossible

---

23 *Bulletin ref. of European Communities*, Vol. 18, No. 7/8, 1985, p. 2.3.85.
24 Sistema Economico Latino Americano (SELA), established in 1975 and adhered to by almost all Latin American countries was intended to promote economic projects but the economic crisis paralyzed it. See: Jean-Pierre Clerc, in *Le Monde*, 18 July 1989, p. 24.
25 The Agreement is an example of what is called an "agreement of the second generation" because it goes well beyond the range of traditional and purely commercial agreements. From a legal point of view, however, the first and second generations are alike as they are both based on EEC Articles 113 and 235. See: Paquet-Soriano (note 10), pp. 53-54.
26 Simon Nuttall, *Yearbook of European Law 1985*, p. 328.
27 *External Relations*, No. 1150.

that the existence of two separate bases could eventually create problems for common EC/EPC actions. However, this does not seem to be the case so far. The political instruments available to EPC for implementation of decisions are in general two: declarations and dialogue. The dialogue is the more complex and important means of EPC action. It entails meetings, visits and declarations. The San José conferences are obviously an example of an institutionalized political and economic dialogue. The first meeting was held in San José in September 1984, at the invitation of the President of Costa Rica. At that first meeting, all Foreign Ministers of the Community were present.[28] This was interpreted as proof of how much importance the Community attached to the improvement of the relations between the two regions. The maximum support that was given to the dialogue at the subsequent European Council in Dublin could only reinforce that impression. Since then, attention has diminished somewhat, as is shown by the decreasing number of ministers present at the annual meetings. In Hamburg, in 1988, for example, only four countries were represented by their Foreign Minister, namely Spain, Denmark, the Netherlands and Belgium (which had the presidency at that moment). However, despite decreasing interest, the San José conferences still constitute the essence of a group-to-group dialogue. The political communiqués issued at the end of each meeting reflect the current state of relations between the two regions.

There are two economic instruments at the Community's disposal: economic sanctions and aid measures. In the case of Central America, it is obviously the latter that the Twelve utilize. The cooperation agreement[29] consists of EC aid on several fronts: trade, economic cooperation and development assistance. Concerning trade, European action is targeted towards the improvement of the General Systems of Preferences (GSP) for products of particular interest, trade promotion, trade related training and technical assistance measures. In the field of economic cooperation, Europe and Central America have both undertaken to provide contacts between firms and branches of industry in the two regions, to encourage and protect European investment and to develop scientific cooperation activities in various economic fields. Finally, with respect to development assistance, the Community provides financial and technical aid to the Isthmus through its program for developing countries outside the Lomé Convention. The Central American countries are encouraged to present projects to the EC; preference is given to those that encourage regional integration --

---

28 The Foreign Ministers of Spain and Portugal, the two countries that were to join the Community in 1986, were present as observers.
29 The non-preferential trade agreement was signed at Luxembourg in 1985, during the second San José conference, and it entered into force in March 1987, after the necessary procedures had been concluded. In 1989, during the San Pedro Sula conference, an "Innovatory Cooperation Agreement" was signed. See: *Europe*, 4 April 1987, p. 7.

such as integrated rural development projects or joint training schemes -- or those with a social content, especially increased food self-sufficiency or improved health care.[30] The San José conferences have the not unimportant advantage of providing an overall economic framework in which the different projects can find their specific place. Consequently, EC assistance is no longer devoted to projects that are independent of one another, as was the case before 1984. The economic framework in turn finds its place in the broader San José context, which gives to the same projects an extra dimension. By the fact that they are used in the context of EPC, they are not merely EC instruments anymore but have in a certain way become EPC instruments as well. In the case of Central America, those extra dimensions have not harmed their efficiency, but have improved it. It is important to note that, from an institutional point of view, the San José Dialogue does not really alter anything. The opportunity for the Foreign Ministers to discuss EC as well as EPC matters in the framework of the European Council, the General Affairs Council and the Gymnich meetings remains unchanged. So does the role of the Commission.[31] This raises the question to what extent the San José process can actually be considered as a "common EC/EPC program" and to what extent September 1984 influenced the Twelve's option to enact the political and economic aspects of their "Central American policy" independently one from the other.

The EPC declaration triggering a concrete proposal by the Commission[32] shows how interaction already took place before the San José conference officially committed the Community to closer engagement in the region. Furthermore, the conference actually illustrated the difference between EC and EPC, as we have seen: preparations took place in separate frameworks and different legal bases were given to the dialogues, in accordance with the different legal quality of EC and EPC action.

---

30 In order to promote and supervise all those activities a joint committee was set up. The funds were targeted to: development projects -- 48.5%; food aid -- 41.5%; emergency assistance -- 5.6%; aid through Non Governmental Organizations (NGOs) -- 2.7%; trade promotion, refugee assistance and training combined -- 1.7%. See: Pierini, p. 4.

31 See Nuttall's article in this volume.

32 At the European Council of 17-19 June 1983 in Stuttgart, the Foreign Ministers express their full support for the efforts of the Contadora Group. The Contadora initiative and the subsequent "Document on peace and cooperation in Central America" of 9 September 1983 indeed provided a strong stimulus for EPC discussion. Ten days later, on an initiative of Germany and the Netherlands, a meeting occurred between some Community Foreign Ministers and their Contadora counterparts on the fringe of the UN General Assembly. In the following twelve months, intensive contacts took place. From the EC as well as from the EPC side, a lot of energy went into the creation of the dialogue.

However, things did change. When interaction did take place before 1984, it was of a somewhat informal character. If signals were passed between the EC and EPC, and reacted upon accordingly, this was considered a "happy coincidence," something which was desirable but not necessarily predictable. After September 1984, this was no longer the case. In essence, the San José conference brought about a qualitative change in decision-making, in the sense that it paved the way for the "orchestration" of interaction between the EC and EPC frameworks. Between 1984 and 1991 *seven* conferences have taken place, alternating between Europe and Central America. At these conferences, the Foreign Ministers of the twelve member states (or their representatives) generally meet with their colleagues on the first day to discuss economic matters in presence of the Commission representative, and on the second day to discuss political matters: the same persons are thus involved in both the economic and political dialogues.[33] These conferences have the merit of setting guidelines for EC and EPC action. EPC needs no longer to express a certain concern in the hopes of triggering a proposal by the Commission; the necessary signals exist in the joint economic and political communiqués. By the same token, there is no need for the Commission to "wait for EPC directions"; it can use its economic instruments in conscious awareness of the broad political framework of the San José Dialogue. Consequently, all proposals by the Commission concerning the Isthmus are almost automatically turned into instruments for economic action in support of political declarations. On the other hand, this does not mean that the EPC Foreign Ministers can decide upon the amount of support to be given. The EC Commission still proposes, the EC Council still decides.

Results and Evaluation

Did the joint EC/EPC action have a particular impact on the outcome of the Community's Central America policy? The first San José conference, in September 1984, was accompanied by great fanfare. The Community pledged to give its "own contribution to peace, democracy, and economic development." A letter from the American Secretary of State, George Shultz, warning against any agreement that could directly or indirectly help Nicaragua, was openly disregarded. This deliberate attempt to keep the US at distance could only delight the Central Americans and further convince them of the Community's intention to follow its own course. The moment of truth came at

---

33 The fact that the preparations can take place in different frameworks does not really change the argument. This also happens on the national level. The separation of the economic and the political departments in the German Foreign Ministry is an often quoted example, in this respect.

the Luxembourg conference, in November 1985 (San José II). Of course, the institutionalization of the dialogue was an important event, but in fact the Cooperation Agreement fell short of Central American hopes. The Costa Rican Foreign Minister spoke for the whole Isthmus when he said: "This Treaty is not all we hoped for."[34] It contained only general and imprecise promises regarding the GSP, no figures on overall financial aid and nothing on a Stabilisation of the Export Revenue STABEX system to support commodity prices, so it could only be characterized as a "minimalist agreement" by the Central Americans.[35] The Guatemala conference, in February 1987 (San José III), brought nothing new. The deadlock in the Contadora process over the differences between Nicaragua and the US allies Honduras, Costa Rica and El Salvador, overshadowed the political dialogue and a common purpose was lacking on the economic front. The Community felt that it could do nothing but wait until circumstances improved.[36] At the Hamburg conference in February and March 1988 (San José IV), the Central American countries presented to the international community an economic action plan, 150 pages in length, containing proposals on food-aid, stimulation of the CMCA, and the scaling-down of the debt burden. As usual, the Community expressed its firm support, but was not willing to make any concrete financial commitments. The laconic answer of the Costa Rican Foreign Minister was, simply, that "We did not expect miracles." Overall, the Hamburg conference gave rise to a sense of qualified optimism, even if harmony had been preserved at expense of controversial issues such as human rights or the verification of the Peace Treaty.[37] At the San Pedro Sula conference in February 1989 (San José V), the submission of a plan to strengthen Central America was met by the Community with the usual expression of support and the usual lack of concrete commitments. Furthermore, the Community once again declined to put pressure on its counterpart concerning human rights. The text in which an increased aid offer was made does not specify any conditions, although an implicit linkage was stressed by some delegations as well as by the Commission.[38] In that respect, the Dublin conference of April 1990 (San José VI) represented more or less the same scenario. The signing of a financial agreement concerning the allocation of 120 million ECU over a period of thirty months was considered as the major event of the meeting. It concerned itself with the establishment of a simplified system of payments and was linked to an agreement to liberalize intra-Central American trade over a period of three

---

34 *The Courier*, January-February 1986.
35 *External Relations*, No. 1168, p. 15.
36 *Neue Zürcher Zeitung*, 13 February 1987. *Christian Science Monitor*, 9 February 1987.
37 *German Tribune*, 13 March 1988.
38 *Europe*, 30/31 October 1989.

years.[39] Not surprisingly, however, there are no conditional clauses of a political nature included. "By its very nature, [economic assistance] requires a peaceful and stable environment" if it is to be successful, so the argument runs.[40] Finally, at the Managua conference of March 1991 (San José VII) an actual debate -- rather than just a lot of speeches -- took place. The EC Foreign Ministers agreed to assess the impact of their recent decision to extend privileged trade status to the Andean nations (in an effort to combat the drug trade) on the Central American countries, and to consider extending the same privileges to the Isthmus itself, despite the effects this might have on the ACP countries. Increased development aid would not be forthcoming until the Central Americans rescheduled their debts with the World Bank.[41]

In day-to-day life, the Central American region is far from peaceful and stable. Human rights violations are still common and problems such as terrorism, narcotics trafficking, inefficient leadership and weak political institutions continue to plague the Isthmus. Overall, however, it is undeniable that fundamental political changes have occurred in the 1980s. In particular the Sapoa agreement and the Esquipulas meetings dealing with the Arias Peace Plan are relevant to the new situation.[42] They represent a desire -- which has grown stronger and stronger over time -- to seek political and diplomatic solutions to the region's problems, instead of military ones. This, in turn, represents a greater independence of attitude vis-a-vis the US, which has seen its relative influence decline. The Central American countries seem to be at less of loss when confronting their many problems, and are thus more responsive to new political initiatives.

It is safe to say that the San José conferences have had some influence on this process. By forcing Central America into a group-to-group dialogue, the Community has in fact created new opportunities for the individual countries to communicate, negotiate and forge compromises among themselves. It has thus promoted mutual understanding. Moreover, by explicitly expressing its continuous support for the peace process through the declarations, meetings, representations and especially the conferences, the Community probably prevented the Central Americans from losing momentum too quickly. In

---

39 The Commission had proposed the elimination of obstacles to regional trade as a condition for the approval of the agreement. *Europe*, 12 April 1990, p. 6.
40 Comment by Mr. Matutes, Commissioner for North-South Relations. See: *Europe*, 9 November 1989.
41 *Frankfurter Allgemeine Zeitung*, 21 March 1991.
42 An agreement was reached on 23 November 1988 between the Sandinista government and the Contras, recognizing that the problems in Nicaragua could not be solved by military means. A ceasefire of 60 days was agreed upon and later prolonged in May 1988.

conclusion, the results might have been different or might not have arrived so soon without the Community's presence in the region.

The economic results are less tangible. The total amount of aid has increased considerably over the years but in that respect the San José process obviously did not meet the expectations of the Central Americans.[43] Substantial aid increases are an annual demand. Trade actually dropped in 1985-86, below the levels prior to the 1983-1984 rise.[44] In response, the Community designed measures to facilitate the import of Central American products, such as customs reductions for tropical products and encouragement of the use of the GSP,[45] but this can only have a limited effect so long as structural problems such as a lack of trade diversification remain basically unsolved. It is likely that the extent of Community support will continue to cause difficulties. Central American demands usually go well beyond what the Community is prepared to give and many are quickly dismissed as unacceptable.[46]

If inconsistency, that is to say the lack of sufficient economic measures in support of political declarations, would normally undermine the credibility of the Community, then this has not been the case in the San José framework. The Central American countries, desperate to end their political and economic instability and to escape from superpower pressure, have been keeping the Community's political profile high, despite their disappointment with the level of its economic support. To conclude, while it does not fully serve Central American interests, the San José process has served the Community's interest perfectly well. The Twelve have indeed been able to play a broker role in the Isthmus, maintaining a moderate stance quite independent of the US.

---

43 Total aid from EC to Central America, under various forms (million ECU): 1976-83 - 180; 1983-88 - 413. The amount of aid attributed for 1988 (122 million ECU) tripled the amount attributed for 1984 (41 million ECU). In 1989 total aid were 92 million ECU, in 1990: 117 million ECU; *Frankfurter Allgemeine Zeitung*, 18 March 1990.

44 CMCA exports to the EC (million ECU): 1983 - 434; 1984 - 758; 1986 - 645. CMCA imports from the EC (million ECU): 1983 - 887; 1984 - 1056; 1986 - 1104.

45 *Europe*, 3/4 July 1989, p. 8.

46 *Europe*, 25 February 1990. Some Central American demands and EC replies: (i) a preferential trade agreement -- this is not acceptable as the Isthmus does not form part of Lomé; (ii) a support mechanism for commodity prices, equivalent to the STABEX system -- again, not acceptable because of Lomé; (iii) a mechanism concerning debt -- the EC cannot contemplate a particular system for a specific group of countries; (iv) the extension of European Investment Bank (EIB) activities to Central America -- the EIB Council of Governors made no provision for such an extension; (v) hard currency resources of up 150 million ECU to support the payment system and the trade of deficit-running countries -- no response.

One can only speculate about the extent to which the coherence and the interaction of EC and EPC have influenced this result. It does seem reasonable to assume that both elements did play a role by bringing about a qualitative improvement in European action. Had the policy of the Community been less coherent and had the interaction not been such that the Community as a whole could be perceived as a partner in the dialogue, then it would probably not have gained credibility as an alternative actor in the region. And certainly not at such a low price.

Conclusions

The Community policy in Central America illustrates how coherence and interaction can be relevant factors in the dynamic interrelation between interests, actions and results. This then becomes an argument for the integration of the EC and EPC -- be it by linking or by merging -- so that all outward distinguishing marks could be erased. However, it is necessary to see everything in perspective. Coherence and interaction are indeed relevant factors, but only in cases where economic and political considerations come into play. As both Nuttall and Rhein point out, an important part of the official relations between the Commission and third governments (i.e. an important part of the Community's foreign policy) has no implications for EPC, or vice versa.[47] Moreover, even in cases where impingement exists, one must proceed with caution. Further integration would be a desirable option only if it would lead to more satisfactory results. Whether or not a policy can be considered satisfactory depends in large part upon the extent to which it serves the original purposes and interests which motivate it, and not upon the extent to which EC/EPC integration takes place. The question of whether or not further integration would make European foreign policy more effective is thus very complex; the Central American case can only shed a little light upon this matter.

---

47 See: Simon Nuttall's and Eberhard Rhein's contributions in this volume.

7

West European Responses to Change in the Soviet Union and Eastern Europe

David Allen

Introduction

Even before the dramatic events of 1989 it had become evident that the states of Western Europe faced major changes both in their collective internal arrangements within the European Community (EC) and European Free Trade Association (EFTA) and, as a result of an improvement in superpower relations, in their individual and collective roles in the evolving international system. In particular, those who saw the Gorbachev detente initiatives and the positive response to them by the United States as the product of superpower decline tended also to anticipate a time when the West Europeans would have to play a fuller role in providing for their own security and seek to exert external political and economic influence more effectively. In the 1980s there had been a series of moves designed both to strengthen internal integration in Western Europe and to reinforce and expand the procedures for collective foreign and security policy. These developments were, however, based on the assumption that European politics would continue to be fundamentally structured by the post-war cleavage between the Eastern and Western Blocs.

From 1988 onwards a series of revolutionary changes took place, first in Poland and Hungary, then in the German Democratic Republic (GDR), Czechoslovakia, Bulgaria and finally Romania. Combined with changes of an equally dramatic nature in the Soviet Union and in its policies towards the outside world, these alterations meant that by the end of 1990, the Cold War and all that went with it had all but disappeared. Germany was united and NATO and the Warsaw Pact had mutually agreed that they no longer represented a threat to each other, a feeling reinforced by their signing of conventional arms agreements. All the members of the Conference on Security and Cooperation in Europe (CSCE) had met in Paris in November 1990 to lay the foundations of a new European order. The European Community was perceived by both superpowers, with apparent enthusiasm, as being the key organization upon which the new Europe would be centered.

The main purpose of this chapter is to examine the individual and collective responses of the West Europeans to the events of 1989 and 1990 and to make some judgements about the extent to which they were able to rise to the leadership challenge that these events posed. On the one hand the changes can be seen to present the West Europeans with a great opportunity to both widen and deepen their integrative experiment in a Europe no longer divided or dominated by the superpower protagonists. This view would see the Cold War as placing definite limits on what is achievable at the collective European level particularly in the foreign and security policy spheres. It would see NATO and the need for the US nuclear umbrella as a restraint on the development of a European security identity, and would consider the continuance of the East-West divide an inhibition to the extension of the European Community (and thus of economic and political integration) to include either the neutral states of Western Europe or the states of Eastern Europe. The end of the Cold War would thus be seen to result in the lifting of a series of restraints on the West Europeans in the pursuit of their collective endeavors.

On the other hand, there is an argument that sees all the current European organizations (Western and Eastern) as being essentially Cold War institutions which were unlikely to survive its peaceful conclusion. This view would have predicted the collapse of the Warsaw Pact and Comecon but would also have anticipated that NATO and the European Community would have problems maintaining internal cohesion once the discipline of the external threat was removed. This view would regard the events of 1989 and 1990 as presenting challenges to the preservation of the achievements of West European integration rather than opportunities for their consolidation and advancement.

Both of these arguments are based on the assumption that the changes result primarily from the reluctance and/or inability of the Soviet Union and the United States to continue in their mutually antagonistic leadership roles. It is possible to see in the recent events a desire by both superpowers to be rid of the problems and responsibilities of their previous roles in Europe and to simply withdraw, leaving the economically successful West Europeans to fend for themselves and to individually and collectively assume responsibility for the economically unsuccessful East Europeans. It is certainly the case that both the United States and the Soviet Union have moved very rapidly from regarding their own relationship as fundamental and their relationship with the West Europeans as marginal to a position where they both see the EC as the key to the new Europe even if their conceptions of that Europe differ. It is also the case that, as well as upgrading the significance of their relationship with the EC, both superpowers now regard their relations with a united Germany as of fundamental importance. This suggests that both the United States and the Soviet Union intended to play a significant role in the new Europe despite all the talk of the "end of their empires" and their mutual withdrawal into relative isolation. In examining the West European responses to the challenges of the past two years this chapter will also try to identify and assess the part played by the two superpowers in conditioning those responses.

Western Europe Prior to 1989

As a result of various budgetary and agricultural reforms, the EC appeared by the mid-1980s to have solved, in the medium term at least, the various problems that had so frustrated it since 1975. One consequence was a revival of the internal integrative process with a commitment to the 1992 program and the subsequent procedural and substantive advances covered within the Single European Act (SEA), which in turn had led to renewed calls for the development of Economic and Monetary Union (EMU). Title 3 of the SEA had given European Political Cooperation (EPC) a treaty base (although not as part of the Treaty of Rome) and had codified all developments so far in the field of collective foreign policy-making. The EC Twelve had also set themselves the target of endeavoring to achieve a common foreign policy in which it was envisaged that the various collective external activities of the EC states in the economic, political and security fields would eventually be gathered together into one coherent whole. EPC now had a decision making mechanism for crises (developed after the debacle of a long delayed response to the Soviet invasion of Afghanistan). Additionally, the Western European Union (WEU) had been semi-revived as part of the search for a framework within which the West Europeans might develop a common security stance. During the 1970s the EC Nine had cut their EPC teeth in the Conference on Cooperation and Security in Europe (CSCE) process, which had proved to be a useful forum in the 1980s where European states from both sides of the ideological divide had been able to preserve and extend detente despite the onset of the Second Cold War. Continuing from the relative success of the Conference on Disarmament in Europe that ended in Stockholm in 1986, and after the Intermediate-range Nuclear Forces (INF) agreements of 1987, NATO and the Warsaw Pact had created a new conventional arms negotiating process "within the framework of the CSCE." This had the effect of fully involving European states and a European process in an aspect of East-West relations that had previously been under the direct and exclusive control of the two superpowers.

Thus it could be argued that the West Europeans were beginning to make their presence felt in a variety of forums, even before the events of 1989. The EPC process, while still lacking the means for significant collective action, had contributed much towards an evolving West European sense of collective identity in international political dealings. The EC itself, while still not fully punching its weight in the international economy, had, with its 1992 program, attracted the attention of Japan and the US (both for a while fearful of the notion of "Fortress Europe") and had forced the non-EC Western states grouped in EFTA to both collectively seek a more structured relationship with the EC and in some cases (Austria and Norway) consider individual applications for full EC membership. Thus, even at the start of 1989 we find all the states of Western Europe contemplating change, in addition to the possibility of the EC widening its membership and deepening its integrative activity. Before the events we are about to consider, the EC seemed able to allow itself the luxury of a relatively relaxed development, with a gradual consideration of the process of EMU and further institutional reform, and a postponement of further enlargement considerations until after the completion of the 1992 targets. One of the immediate effects of the quickly developing changes was to give much greater urgency to all West European decisions, both unilateral and multilateral.

All the West European states had also begun to reconsider their relationship with the Soviet Union and the states of Eastern Europe. Again this was partly inspired by a reaction to the EC's 1992 program but was mainly the result of a Soviet desire, evident from 1985 onward, to forge a new relationship with all the potential inhabitants of Mikhail Gorbachev's celebrated "Common European Home." The EC had already begun to talk to those East European countries that had started to show signs of reform potential. It was also under pressure from Moscow to consider a framework agreement both with the Soviet Union individually and with Comecon. However, until it became impossible to deny that Gorbachev was sincere in his determination to end the Cold War, many West European states, with the United Kingdom (UK) at the forefront, worried that the Soviets were merely pursuing their age-old policy of attempting to divide the Atlantic Alliance and detach the West Europeans from the United States. West Germany was the Western state which had responded most positively to Soviet advances. As a result, France had begun to worry that the West Germans might be considering an "escape" from the restraints of the EC and NATO in favor of neutrality and the possibility of reunification with the GDR.

West European Responses in 1989

At the Rhodes EC Summit at the end of 1988 there had been some consideration about how to respond to the growing signs of reform in Poland and Hungary. At this meeting there was a clear division between those states like Britain who were in favor of a "wait and see" policy and those like the Federal Republic who advocated a more positive and encouraging response.

The Greek government had pushed the idea of an EC-Comecon agreement throughout its presidency (the EC and Comecon had mutually recognized each other at the start of 1988), and they also wanted to concede to Soviet demands for a cooperation agreement rather than a mere trade accord. Most of the rest of the Twelve wanted to find an encouraging and supportive response to Gorbachev but did not want to be seen to prefer the Soviet Union to the rest of Eastern Europe.

At the end of 1988 Gorbachev went to the United Nations and announced major unilateral conventional force cuts in Europe as part of a radical statement of new Soviet foreign policy thinking. The force cuts appeared to be both quantitatively and qualitatively significant in that they supported the Soviet argument that they intended to move from an offensive to a defensive military strategy in Europe. This line of approach was received cautiously by Thatcher who argued that it needed to be "kept in perspective," but with enthusiasm by West German Foreign Minister Genscher who saw it as vindication of his arguments that the Soviets were serious and that there was a need to consider delaying the anticipated update of NATO's short range nuclear weapons. The West Germans were anxious to put off this decision, for both domestic and foreign policy reasons. The rows over cruise missile deployment, followed by the optimism that surrounded the INF agreements, meant that West German public opinion was firmly opposed to any further nuclear modernization and was more inclined to push for the removal of all nuclear weapons from German soil. A general election was scheduled in West Germany for December 1990 and the ruling CDU/FDP coalition was already concerned about growing public support for both left-wing and right-wing radical groupings. On the foreign policy front, the West Germans were opposed to any weapons which were meant primarily to kill other Germans, and were also anxious to build on the new atmosphere created by Gorbachev. At the end of 1988, the British were showing signs of irritation at the German line while the French began to show signs of concern.

This new NATO nuclear row was not confined to the British and the Germans. Although the British line reflected US concerns about the need to maintain the integrity of the flexible response strategy, other West European states joined the Germans in questioning whether the new circumstances might require new NATO thinking. These dilemmas failed to add up to much of a response to Gorbachev's initiatives. Until the June 1989 NATO Summit, the West Europeans were unable to organize themselves collectively because the major West European states continued to stick to their national fetishes. While France was able to use its special relationship with Germany in the EC to seek reassuring German support for speeding up the integration process (and thus more securely "anchoring" the Federal Republic in the West) it was unable to do the same thing in NATO because of its own tenuous relationship with the

Alliance. France certainly hoped to develop WEU as a European defense vehicle which would respond more effectively to French leadership. The real need, however, was for NATO itself to come up with an effective response to the new circumstances. In particular, as the military threat diminished, NATO had to find a way of placing greater emphasis on its political role. Until the Summit in June, a lack of US leadership and Thatcher's determination to do nothing that would challenge the status quo prevented NATO from seriously considering how it might adjust. American policy seemed for a long time incapable of coming up with anything new. The NATO Summit was in the end saved by a last minute initiative from President Bush who came down on the side of the Germans and expressed concern about the UK's growing isolation in the Alliance.

The Bush proposals, which were based on the assumption that "the continentals will go with the Germans and so we can't do anything but go with them too" promised further conventional arms cuts, the revival of the Strategic Arms Reduction Talks (START) and the promise of talks on short range nuclear forces. Just before the Summit, Gorbachev had wrong-footed the Alliance yet again with the promise of unilateral short range nuclear cuts and even more drastic conventional reductions. In effectively pulling the Western response together, Bush talked of the United States and the Federal Republic being "partners in leadership" of "a Europe whole and free." He saw the future task of the more political Alliance as being to provide support for the Gorbachev initiatives and to promote democracy and self determination throughout Europe. Bush had therefore come up with the sort of collective response that the Germans and others were looking for, but which the West Europeans had been unable to put together themselves. Apart from Britain, most of the other West Europeans feared that if NATO proved itself incapable of change, then the Federal Republic might be tempted to respond unilaterally to a Soviet offer of neutralization and reunification for both internal and external reasons. Apart from change within NATO, the other obvious counter to this threat was to bind West Germany more securely into the EC -- an option that was eagerly seized by the French and most other EC states but which was also firmly rejected by Thatcher.

Meanwhile, within the EC the Twelve had decided by April 1989 to adopt a "carrot and stick" strategy towards the Eastern Bloc, approving economic incentives for those governments pursuing reform like Poland and Hungary but suspending all dealings with Romania because of its appalling human rights record. This application of the principle of "conditionality" also placed the emphasis on separate dealings with individual East European governments rather than collective dealings with Comecon as a whole. The EC also decided in April 1989 to begin a political dialogue with the Soviet Union and the EC ambassadors in Moscow started to receive regular briefings from the Soviet foreign ministry. The pursuit of an active and coordinated EC policy towards the East had been strongly advocated by EC Commission President Jacques Delors, partly as a way of gaining German support for his EMU proposals and partly out of a well known desire to advance the competence of the Commission at every opportunity. It was by no means clear at the time that the Commission had the capability to operate conditionality effectively given the inadequacy of its information about the economic and political situation in the Eastern Bloc states.

In July 1989 the G7 met in Paris and once again it was the US in association with the West Germans who took the lead in searching for a coordinated response to developments in Poland and Hungary. Chancellor Kohl, anxious not to stir up more fears about his country's Eastern leanings had suggested that the EC Commission be given the task of coordinating all Western aid to Poland and Hungary and President Bush was able to gain support from the others on this policy. The number of countries involved very soon rose to 24 (all of Western Europe, North America and Oceania and Japan) and the Commission-led program, known as Operation Phare, rapidly started to provide food aid to Poland. In 1989 the Commission organized three meetings of the G24 involved in Phare working on an action plan based on five priorities -- food aid, agricultural restructuring, improved market access, investment promotion and cooperation on the environment. As we shall see, in 1990, Operation Phare was extended to the other Eastern European states and Yugoslavia.

However, just as the West Europeans began to think about the collective management of their aid to Poland and Hungary, events began to escalate with the beginnings of the crisis in the GDR that was to culminate in the fall of the Berlin Wall and the placing of German reunification on the European agenda. As refugees began to stream out of the GDR via a variety of routes, West Germany was once again faced with the need to respond rapidly, preferably with the support of its EC partners. While West European fears that the Germans sought hegemony were groundless, the fact remained that the West Germans did not have the luxury of adopting the preferred British position of "wait and see." If the West Germans could not get their partners to act in harmony in response to this new situation then they would have to act alone, first in providing massive aid to the GDR but eventually in facilitating the reunification process.

The possibility of West Germany acting alone over reunification raised fears among the West Europeans about how the Soviets might react. Those fears were exacerbated by concerns about Gorbachev's own position within the Soviet Union. Indeed the initial Soviet reaction at the time that Gorbachev was due to visit the GDR for its 40th birthday celebrations was to accuse Bonn of undermining the GDR government and encouraging reunification aspirations. However the Soviets did little to prop up the GDR regime and much to encourage the view in Eastern Europe and the West that the Brezhnev doctrine was indeed dead and that the Soviet Union had no intention of militarily intervening to frustrate the reform process anywhere. This tendency in Soviet policy gave rise to a second and contradictory West European fear which was that the Germans would make a deal with the Soviets that would somehow involve the detachment of a united Germany from NATO and a decline in German enthusiasm for further commitments within the EC.

Fears of a declining German enthusiasm for the EC were strongly voiced within the Commission and in France. The solution championed by Delors was to speed up the process of integration and to extend the EC's emergency aid and assistance program. In a speech at Bruges (partly designed to counter that of Thatcher a year earlier), Delors argued that the EC Twelve should move quickly towards establishing the Intergovernmental Conference (IGC) necessary to progress to EMU and that this should be complemented by another IGC on Political Union involving a common foreign and security policy and further reform of the EC institutions. Delors sought to link this with developments in the East by arguing that the Single Market must also be complemented by the Social Charter and by an expanded role for the European Parliament so as to continue to attract those in the East who sought basic rights, prosperity and democracy. In a direct rebuttal of Thatcher's minimalist views Delors said, "Think of the effect in Prague and Warsaw and elsewhere when the EC declares solemnly, by means of a Social Charter, that it will not subordinate fundamental workers rights to economic efficiency."

The German government, under pressure from the French as well as the Commission, was anxious to reconcile its concern about the need to respond positively to events in the East through reassurances to its Western partners. Its hesitation about the timing of the IGC for EMU was exclusively electoral rather than substantive. Chancellor Kohl simply did not want it on the political agenda until after the 1990 German election because he feared that voters might see EC EMU as a potential barrier to, or distraction from, reunification. Foreign Minister Genscher developed the notion of the concentric circles of European cooperation in a bid to meet the demands of many of his EC partners that Germany pushes ahead with integration while at the same time not closing the EC off from the states in the East. The Germans argued that an inner core of EC states, willing and able to create a European Union, should do so and that other European states could associate themselves with such a Union depending on their ability to make various integrative commitments. Thus, the next closest ring would consist of the present EFTA states (and possibly Britain if it continued to show reluctance about EMU and Political Union), which would be more loosely linked to an outer ring of newly democratized Eastern European states. Finally, all three circles might be linked with the US and the Soviet Union in the CSCE process thus giving expression to the Gorbachev notion of a

Common European Home. Genscher's argument was that membership of these circles would be dynamic rather than static, with the possibility of states moving from one circle to another as they became capable of more binding integrative commitments. The implication was then that any European state able to meet the basic conditions of a market economy and a democratic system could begin with a loose form of association but aspire to eventual full membership of the EC.

At an EC foreign ministers meeting in Chartres in September 1989 the Twelve decided both to step up their emergency aid to Poland and Hungary and to examine ways in which the EC might offer longer term structural assistance. As events began to escalate in the Eastern Bloc, there was much talk of the EC and the other members of the G24 collectively organizing a sort of Marshall Plan for Eastern Europe. The problem then as now was that it proved difficult, given the lack of something to unite against, to stimulate multilateral support for the massive program envisaged, while all states were willing to assist in a limited way. In any case many of the EC member states were either reluctant to pour money into Eastern Europe or were concerned about its diversion either from themselves or their own areas of concern. Thus the British although willing to be unilaterally and collectively generous in the short term have been the most cautious about long term assistance preferring, under Thatcher at least, to once again "wait and see" how the reform process develops in the East and eventually in the Soviet Union. Many of the poorer EC members, who in the past have benefitted from EC regional and social funds, have also shown concern about the diversion of funds towards the East. In particular, fears were expressed even before the reunification issue arose, that West Germany, the EC's major net contributor, would seek to redirect its funds from within the EC towards the East. Finally, the EC has of course come under pressure from those outside, such as the Lomé group or the associated Mediterranean states, who also fear that they will lose out as a result of massive funds being sent to Eastern Europe.

By October 1989 the French EC presidency, in close collaboration with the West Germans, was looking to the December Strasbourg summit both to consolidate the acceleration of European Union by fixing a date for the start of the EMU IGC and to extend collective EC aid to the East. The British continued to resist the EMU arguments but showed some enthusiasm for associating both EFTA and East European countries with the EC. While the French and the Commission continued to worry about whether future enlargement was compatible with further integration, the British tended to argue perversely that it was the weakening of integration that made enlargement such a desirable objective.

In the period between the fall of the Berlin Wall and the confirmation that reunification was both feasible and imminent, the West Germans were faced with the tricky task of attempting to pursue a diplomacy designed to reassure its Western partners in both the EC and NATO while at the same time not antagonizing the Soviet Union. The issue was complicated both by divisions within the ruling coalition over tactics and by sensitivities both to the upcoming West German elections (December 1990) and, as events developed, to free elections in the GDR (March 1990).

Although the West Germans constantly encouraged the EC and NATO to adjust rapidly to the changing scene in the East, events moved simply too fast for the relatively cumbersome cooperation procedures even though West European foreign ministers were almost permanently engaged in a constant round of bilateral and multilateral meetings. As events unfolded in the East, a pattern developed whereby the West European states tended to react at first unilaterally, then engage in a round of bilateral diplomacy and finally attempt to coordinate their responses either in the EC or NATO. The major actors were inevitably Britain, France and West Germany with Italy operating on the margins until it assumed the EC presidency in the second half of 1990. Thatcher's standard response to most developments was to reassert the need to preserve the integrity of the Atlantic Alliance and otherwise do nothing hasty. Her statements on German reunification and on the changing military picture in Europe can be best described as Canute-like in their insistence on maintaining the status quo. There was little sympathy for the German dilemma and as a result Anglo-German relations rapidly worsened. Even though the French shared many of Thatcher's concerns about German reunification there was little prospect of Anglo-French cooperation, as Thatcher was also strongly opposed to any acceleration of EC integration, which was the preferred French method of dealing with the problems posed by Germany. The dominant bilateral relationship was that of France and Germany even though the Germans had suddenly become the dominant partner. It was by building on the past strength of the Franco-German relationship that both countries were able to reconcile their instinctual nationalistic reactions to events in the East and to thus preserve a united approach to the development of the EC.

The fall of the Wall in November 1989 led to increased West German involvement in the politics of the GDR and threw both the Alliance and the EC into disarray once the initial jubilation had worn off. While West Germany anticipated reunification with all its attendant political and economic costs and complications, other West European states expressed concern about German power, about the future of the EC and NATO and about the loss of the comforting certainties of the Cold War. In response to the decision of the United States and the Soviet Union to hold a summit in Malta, and perhaps fearful that there might be some truth in the slogan "from Yalta to Malta," the French called an extraordinary EC Summit for 18 November 1989 to discuss the situation in Eastern Europe and to develop an EC line before the superpowers could meet and impose their own views. The French enthusiasm for the special Paris summit was also related to an interest in preventing discussion of events in the East from dominating the normal EC European Council meeting planned for Strasbourg in December at which the French were determined to push the EMU IGC, the Social Charter and their plans for a European Bank for Reconstruction in the East. However the main fear was that the superpowers might cobble a European settlement together (shades of Reykjavik) and even that Gorbachev might give the go ahead for German reunification, provided the US agreed that a united Germany would not be a member of NATO. By then, most West Europeans assumed that self determination in the GDR would lead to a vote for reunification although Thatcher continued to protest that things were moving too fast and that it was necessary to preserve both NATO and the Warsaw Pact in the interests of stability. The implication of this was that it was also necessary to preserve the GDR!

At the Paris emergency Summit the EC achieved an impressive degree of unity in proposing continued conditional support for the now expanded reform process in the East. The political terms for this support were to be democracy, human rights and free and secure elections and the economic terms were to be recognition by the International Monetary Fund (IMF) of a satisfactory movement towards a free market economy. By opting for IMF assistance, the EC both recognized its own lack of expertise in this area and sought to employ a benchmark that was internationally recognized and that would thus be more likely to be acceptable to other potential Western donors. The EC Paris meeting thus showed unity and an impressive sense of history, in sharp contrast to some of the EC's internal debates. There was no discussion of reunification for fear of undermining Gorbachev's position and the only really discordant note was struck by the British Prime Minister in her post-Summit press conference when she somewhat ingeniously urged that the Community should not undermine its unity by embarking on a debate at Strasbourg on EMU. Thatcher also expressed major reservations about French plans for a European Reconstruction Bank and warned that a cautious approach to developments in the East would assist Gorbachev with his internal problems. On reunification Thatcher went out of her way to say that the Helsinki Agreements prevented any questioning of borders in Europe and that all military matters should be conducted through NATO and the Warsaw Pact.

The Franco-German response to Thatcher's caution was a joint address on November 22, 1989 to the European Parliament in which they insisted that EC political integration and democracy in the East must go together, and that the best way to respond to events was to strengthen the EC bonds so that the EC could maintain its magnetic attraction to the East. At the Strasbourg European Council the French by and large got their way on advancing integration at the expense of isolating Thatcher. She left Strasbourg after the EC had decided to hold an IGC on EMU but not until after the 1990 West German election. Thatcher said that Kohl, with French assistance, had fixed a date which "suits his election but not mine." On the German question the Communique talked of unity rather than unification and concern was expressed at indications that the Germans were showing signs (Kohl's 10 Point Plan) of going it alone regardless of the views of either the EC or the two superpowers. Moscow, for its part, had proposed a meeting of the Four Powers (the first since 1971) in order to emphasize the need for the Germans to consider the external as well as the internal ramifications of any movement towards reunification. This move was supported by both Britain and France, anxious to regain some semblance of control of events. In December 1989, there were a number of other meetings in Brussels. The EC chaired a meeting of the G24 at which it was decided to extend aid to Czechoslovakia, the GDR, Bulgaria and Yugoslavia, conditional on the necessary reforms. The EC had earlier agreed to send more food aid to Poland and to provide funds for currency stabilization and bridging loans. NATO foreign ministers met and accepted Secretary of State Baker's proposals for politicizing the Alliance and developing a dialogue within the CSCE. The Soviet foreign minister came to Brussels to sign the first ever, mainly symbolic, EC-Soviet trade and cooperation agreement and also held his first-ever meeting with his NATO opposite numbers. The EC and EFTA ministers met and the Eftans expressed concern that within the Concentric Circles notion EFTA might be seen as a sort of EC kindergarten for potential applicants from Eastern Europe.

There was thus a great deal of multilateral activity at the end of 1989 as the West Europeans sought to make some sense out of the dramatic changes in the East. The EC had succeeded in producing a short term response to the need for aid in the East and had gained much prestige from its management of the overall Western effort within the G24. However, the demands for new aid to those countries recently liberated presented a new set of challenges for 1990, as did the question of German reunification along with methods for approaching and managing that situation. In the short term, the EC agreed on emergency aid to the GDR (but on nothing like the scale that the Germans were providing unilaterally), but in the long term it was becoming clear that the EC would have to confront the rapid admission of the GDR to the EC as part of a united Germany as well as to the demands of both Czechoslovakia and Hungary that their own desire for eventual membership in the EC should not be sidelined by the GDR question. At the same time, most West Europeans had also to contemplate the long term impact of these developments on their security structures and on the fate of Gorbachev in the Soviet Union.

Partly in response to these events, the EC itself was committed not just to completing the internal market, but also to progressing towards EMU and possibly also towards Political Union.

West European Responses in 1990

In 1990, the West Europeans had to face up to the longer term consequences of the transformation in Eastern Europe that was completed with the Romanian revolution at the end of December 1989 as well as to a deteriorating situation in the Soviet Union. In this section we intend to follow four major themes which lead up to the CSCE Summit in Paris in November 1990 and the EC Summit in Rome in December 1990. The four themes are German reunification, EC aid to Eastern Europe and the Soviet Union, developments within the EC and developments within NATO.

German Reunification

There were essentially only three major players in the process that led up to the establishment of a fully sovereign united Germany on October 3, 1990. Although Britain, France and the government of the GDR were given formal roles in the 2+4 procedures that were agreed upon in Ottawa in February 1990 they exerted no significant direct influence on the proceedings. France was indirectly able to extract West German support for accelerated integration because, as in earlier times, the French government was prepared to contemplate the trading of its own sovereignty (for instance with reference to the establishment of a common currency and a European Central Bank) in return for an anchoring of Germany within the EC. France was thus able to seek positive common ground with Germany over the relationship between reunification and integration in a way that the British could never manage. Thatcher came to accept German unity with ill-disguised bad grace and sought to inhibit the process at every opportunity. Her insistence on referring to unification rather than reunification for fear that the Germans would exploit the semantics and insist on a return to 1937 German frontiers, her insistence for a while that only the full CSCE membership could approve a change of frontiers and her obvious support for the views of Ridley made life difficult mainly for her more conciliatory foreign secretary. In Germany, the hostility was treated with open contempt and Thatcher found little support either in Moscow, Washington or among the other members of the EC. The result was that Britain was effectively marginalized from the process.

Among the West Europeans, Ireland prided itself that during its presidency in the early part of the year, it was able to act as an honest broker between West Germany and the rest of the EC. In truth, however, the West Germans appeared essentially to follow their own agenda, constrained only by domestic opinion in East and West Germany and by the need to maintain the support of the two superpowers. In the case of the Soviet Union, this was achieved mainly by the promise of Deutschmarks and a willingness to allow Soviet troops to remain in the GDR for several years after unity. In the case of the United States, Washington was willing to allow the Germans to make their own arrangements, provided they could carry the support of the EC (achieved at the first Dublin summit). The United States even seemed prepared (to Thatcher's dismay) to sanction a looser German "association" with NATO if necessary. In the end, this did not prove to be the outcome, but the Americans must take much of the credit for orchestrating the London NATO Summit in June 1990. There the Alliance was able to agree on a willingness to sign a joint peace declaration with the Warsaw Pact, to invite Gorbachev to address NATO, to get the Soviets to permanently liaise with it and to revise the strategy of flexible response so that nuclear weapons became "weapons of last resort." This movement was enough to satisfy Gorbachev so that he could live with a united Germany in NATO, and he very quickly came to a final arrangement with Kohl in Stavropol just after the NATO Summit. The London Summit was crucial to the German settlement and was illustrative of continued American influence and of a new special relationship between the US and Germany. In the end, the 2+4 talks (which Thatcher had wanted to be only 4 power or at best 4+2) were usurped by a German-US deal and subsequent German-Soviet deal.

Aid to Eastern Europe and the Soviet Union

The West Europeans were faced at the beginning of the year with the problem of extending the support they had already offered to Poland and Hungary, individually and collectively, to the rest of the liberated East. The EC faced a problem in the expansion of food aid (to Romania) in that it was beginning to actually run out of food surpluses (mainly as a result of CAP reform). Once the short term needs were catered for and once basic trade and cooperation agreements had been set in place between the EC and Eastern Europe, the problem of longer-term structural aid and assistance arose. The EC had to decide what sort of second generation agreements to offer those East European countries who continued to meet the reform conditions. The Commission also had to find a level of funding that was compatible with EC budget arrangements and which the member states, many of whom were concerned at the diversion of resources, would accept. In addition, the EC Commission was beginning to experience problems in managing its task as coordinator of both EC aid and G24 aid. The Commission has none of the diplomatic and administrative resources of a state, so that visiting applicant countries and making accurate assessments of their needs and situations, let alone their satisfaction of EC and G24 conditions, became very difficult. Although the EC had the assistance of the IMF and the World Bank, in the early months it was still dealing with ministers from provisional governments whose days were numbered or with ministers who had no previous experience of government responsibility. There was concern inside the Commission that the EC was in danger of being swamped both financially and administratively.

Although the Italians and the Germans have pressed for much larger sums to be allocated to assistance programs for Eastern Europe, such funds have not been forthcoming as yet. Nothing like the much vaunted Marshall Plan for Eastern Europe has emerged. By the middle of the year, the EC had decided that despite requests from Hungary and Czechoslovakia it would not offer full membership, but privileged association, as the next stage in its arrangements with the Eastern states. Towards this end the EC began negotiating in December 1990 some new "European Agreements" with Poland, Hungary and Czechoslovakia. These arrangements would eventually give them the same sort of relationship that EFTA has enjoyed involving free trade, political dialogue, financial support, infrastructure support etc -- all of course conditional on continued progress with economic and political reforms (aid to Romania was suspended by both the EC and the G24 following the government's use of miners to repress demonstrators).

Although the West European states have managed a reasonably well-coordinated political and economic response to the immediate needs of the East Europeans, and although the Commission has gained some prestige from its G24 role, doubts remain about the aid process in the longer-term. Not only are the latest Commission studies of East European long-term prospects fairly grim, the Community, along with its biggest net contributor, must contemplate the cost of absorbing what used to be the GDR as well as responding to the growing crisis in the Soviet economy. Although it was very flattering for the EC to be regarded as "magnetic" because of its relative economic success, this magnetism may well become a burden in the future. It was quite clear at the CSCE Paris meeting that most of the ex-Eastern Bloc countries saw their only route to salvation as being via continued EC assistance and eventual EC membership -- it remains to be seen whether the West Europeans will be able to bear in the long-term the burdens they took on in the short-term in 1989 and 1990.

Regarding the Soviet Union, the German government for obvious reasons has been in the forefront of arguing that the EC countries and the West as a whole have an interest in supporting the Gorbachev reforms with financial assistance. This line of argument was resisted by the United States within G24 and the UK within the EC until the end of 1990, although both then approved considerable aid and credit packages. The EC decided to seek a much closer targeting of aid, to support currency stability (as it had succeeded in doing in

Poland) and to apply maximum conditionality to all aid. The EC threatened to suspend trade and cooperation agreements at the time of the Lithuanian crisis and was forced to carry out that threat for a short time as the Baltic crisis spread and worsened in early 1991. The more cautious EC approach represented a rejection of the desire of the Italian presidency to support the German and French position by massively increasing aid to the Soviet Union. As such, it represents one of the few successes of the "wait and see," "proceed only with caution" approach advocated by the British.

Developments within the EC

Following the Rome Summit, 1990 ended with the successful opening of two Intergovernmental Conferences dealing with Economic and Monetary Union and with Political Union. The initial impetus for this attempted integrative leap did not come in response to developments in Eastern Europe. EMU and further institutional development came onto the agenda as complements to the 1992 Single Market process. As such, they were initially promoted by those anxious to continue the progress towards European Union that had been revived in the mid 1980s. However, it is certainly the case that events in the East and in particular German reunification served to expedite this process, as the Commission and France sought to protect the EC from any German wish to make links with the East easier by toning down integration in the West. The timetable for EMU was therefore accelerated despite some German practical hesitancy based on its experience of concluding monetary union with the GDR. The Political Union IGC was agreed upon between France and Germany as part of a German process of reassuring France about its continued enthusiasm for the EC and further development of European union. The UK certainly tried to argue in 1990 that further integration should be put off in order that the EC be seen as both united and open towards the East. This notion was defeated by those such as Delors who countered that only by fulfilling its potential would the EC be in a position to extend long term support to the East.

The wider question of EC enlargement and its impact on further integration remains, however. The revolutions in the East have given rise to demands for entry from Hungary and Czechoslovakia and these in turn have hastened applications from Sweden, Austria and Norway, who are anxious not to be sidelined by the EC's Eastern policy. The end of the Cold War has also removed the "neutrality barrier" that had previously made Austria and Sweden hesitate about membership (Austria recently agreed to allow forces destined for the Gulf to overfly its territory). Before the changes in the East, the EC already decided that it would not contemplate further enlargement until after the 1992 Single Market process was complete. This line has been maintained, but as negotiations for an European Economic Area with the EFTA countries become bogged down, as the demands for eventual membership from Hungary *et al* become more insistent and as 1993 draws ever nearer, the question of enlargement will become more and more urgent. Nevertheless, both the Intergovernmental Conferences appear to be progressing without regard to these future alterations, and as though the EC is likely to consist of just 12 members for the conceivable future.

The EC has of course already effectively taken on a new member with the integration of the former GDR into the EC in 1990. Although concern has been expressed about the impact on the EC budget and about the long transitional time required for the former GDR to raise itself up to EC standards, the actual process of adjustment in 1990 caused no significant problems between the EC states. All the EC members seemed anxious to ensure that no barriers were placed in the way of reunification and this meant that they were not inclined to argue about the transitional details -- the European Parliament did for a while seek to make some procedural capital out of the need for haste, but this was of no real significance. In return the Germans went out of their way to be reasonable. They did not insist on receiving extra votes in the weighted voting schemes of the Council and they have not as yet claimed any new seats in the European Parliament, although the question of the German representation will need consideration before the next round of direct elections. The Commission took the lead on GDR entry as it had done on the coordination of aid. Its enhanced status was clear by the time of the Houston G7 summit. Throughout the year Jacques Delors never failed to miss an opportunity to get the EC involved in the many forums that were used. Thus the EC requested a seat at the CSCE, liaised directly with NATO, and attended German cabinet meetings for reunification items.

One consequence of the EC's new international status and of the possible demise of NATO has been a constant US call for a more formal process of consultation between the US and the EC. Although the firming up of this new set of procedures was spoiled by the rows over GATT at the end of the year 1990 it nevertheless represents quite an advance from a few years ago when the US exhibited little interest in dealing with either the EC or EPC and preferred to rely on bilateral dealings with the EC member states.

The EC has certainly increased its international stature over the past years and it is now firmly on track on achieve EMU and Political Union in the near future. The EC's star has certainly waxed as that of NATO has waned but it still remains to be seen whether the EC will be able to put any flesh on some of its member's aspirations to give it a much greater security role in the future.

Developments within NATO

In 1990 all the West Europeans achieved their primary objective of keeping a united Germany in NATO even though it seems likely that in the near future both nuclear weapons and possibly foreign troops will be removed from Germany. Inevitably, the ending of the Cold War has led to a questioning of the old security structures, although to date NATO has fared better than the Warsaw Pact. While Britain and France have been anxious to keep their own forces out of conventional force reduction negotiations they have joined all other NATO countries in reviewing their defense arrangements now that the strategy of flexible response and forward defense in Germany is redundant. The possibility of developing multinational forces within NATO has been proposed by the British but rejected by the French. While the UK is anxious to preserve NATO and devise new roles for it, thus maintaining the American connection, other West European countries like France and Italy are keen to seize the opportunity to develop a European security identity either via WEU or possibly even the EC. This particular dispute is currently being carried out within the framework of the IGC on Political Union and the debate here has been confused by a growing US concern that NATO will not be sidelined by any EC developments in the defense sphere. At present, the British and the Dutch would like to see WEU act as bridge between NATO and the EC, while the French, the Commission and a number of other EC states would like to see WEU develop in its own right and become answerable to, and eventually replaced by, the European Council. Hopes that CSCE would provide the framework for the new European security architecture, which were high at the end of 1990, have been dashed both by the events in the Gulf and by the further changes that have occurred in the Soviet Union. The refusal of the Soviets to allow the CSCE to play a role in arbitrating the Baltic crisis was a blow to those who saw a future role for CSCE.

To date little progress has been made on the longer-term adjustment to the impact of change in Eastern Europe and the Soviet Union. In 1990, however, despite the undermining of its *raison d'être*, NATO managed to make the necessary short-term adjustments to reassure the Soviet Union and to thus allow German reunification to take place smoothly. The West Europeans do not have a good track record when it comes to thinking or acting collectively about their security outside the NATO framework. The continued absence of a coherent threat and a declining public support for defense in a number of West European states suggests that this will remain a contentious and undetermined issue for some time to come. In the near future the question of new security arrangements covering all of Europe are bound to be raised. The Warsaw Pact has now effectively been dissolved but it has not been replaced with anything. The Eastern European states have to work out new relationships with the Soviet

Union, with each other and with the states of Western Europe. Requests to join NATO have been rejected and Romania has already made some new arrangements with the Soviet Union, while the EC considers a common foreign and security policy within the Political Union IGC without apparently giving much consideration to developments in the East.

Conclusions

Despite the distractions of the Gulf War at the start of 1991, developments in the East have continued to make major demands on the states of Western Europe and on the European Community. There have been a number of setbacks, most particularly the reverses in the Soviet Union which have thrown Gorbachev onto the defensive, and which have raised doubts about his likely success in realizing political reforms and progress to a market economy with some sort of satisfactory conclusion. Furthermore it is also becoming clear that the Commission and others were overly optimistic about the ease with which the economic problems of the Eastern part of Germany might be overcome. There is a renewed danger that Germany will become distracted from its leadership role within the EC by the problems that are beginning to arise at home. Among the East European states the demands on the West in general, and the EC in particular, are growing and are both political as well as economic. As a result, the EC has recently been forced to readjust its line in the negotiations on the new second phase association agreements it is conducting with Hungary, Poland and Czechoslovakia.

It now seems certain that these three states will be allowed to sign accords that will extend to them freedom of movement of goods, services, labour and capital in the EC's single market by the year 2000, as well as an option on full EC membership. This represents a considerable softening of the EC's negotiating stance. Until recently, reference to possible full membership was being resisted and the EC was holding out for a five year review in the ten year transitional period. The East Europeans are to be given more time to erect tariffs which they will then spend ten years dismantling, and the northern EC states have overcome the objections of the Mediterranean members and made some concessions on both textiles and steel. This softening of the EC stance towards the Eastern states is partly the product of their own political pressure and partly the product of an EC realization that it is very much in the EC's interests to advance the economic revival of the Eastern Bloc. The big fear in the EC is that unless conditions in the East become political and economically acceptable and unless reasonable access to the EC is provided for the states there will be a flood of economic refugees seeking their own individual way of entering the prosperous EC. This is a fear that already exists within the EC as far as the Mediterranean non-members are concerned. One of the conclusions of this study is then that, despite the EC's determination to ignore the issue in the present IGCs, further enlargement of the EC is inevitable as a result of the changes in Eastern Europe. Just as Greece, Spain and Portugal linked EC membership with the creation and preservation of democracy and a free market economy, so now are the newly liberated states of Eastern Europe. The irresistible nature of their demands on the EC are in turn forcing the EFTA states to reconsider the attractions of remaining outside the EC and the result is thus likely to be a considerable enlargement over the next few years.

Despite the problems that lie ahead, the EC's response to the events of the past few years has been quite impressive. As we argued at the start of this paper, the EC has demonstrated that it is more than a Cold War institution, that it is capable of rising to its greatly enhanced role in the European and Global international system and that it is capable of generating ideas at least about its possible future role in the new European security architecture. The future role of the superpowers in the new Europe remains uncertain. It has to be said that for all the talk about their decline, and in particular about their withdrawal from Europe, their role as a catalyst in the events of the past few years was instrumental. Although the success of the EC and its ability to revive itself around the 1992 program did indeed prove to have a magnetic attraction for the states in the East, it was the policies of Gorbachev, not the EC, that made the changes possible. Similarly, the United States played a critical role during 1989 and 1990 in both assisting and stimulating the EC and NATO into an effective collective response. Neither Britain nor France was able to exert significant leadership roles within either the EC or NATO, and Germany required the support and assistance of the United States (and to a lesser extent the Soviet Union) in order to bring about its reunification. Eventually, EC countries may have to manage their collective responses and actions without the assistance and possibly despite the opposition of the United States and/or the Soviet Union.

Since the mid-1980s, as a result of events in the Soviet Union and Eastern Europe, the EC has most definitely moved out of the shadows and into the spotlight of European politics. It is now at the center of all plans or proposals for the construction of the "New Europe," and it will in the near future be required to bring about both its own widening and deepening. Change in Eastern Europe has ensured beyond all doubt that European Union in the medium to long-term is no longer merely about the perfection of economic and political arrangements between the present twelve Member States. European Union now involves all of Europe cooperating on a potentially limitless agenda and the European Community, however it evolves, is the organization upon which all efforts and attention will, in future, be focused.

8

EPC's Performance in Crises

Christopher Hill

Introduction

As the twentieth century moves to its close the peoples of Europe, satiated by collective violence and perhaps anxious to distinguish themselves psychologically from the United States, seem determined to feel badly about any war they become involved in. No matter that in the recent conflicts over the Falklands and Kuwait the outcome was swift and relatively painless (at least for the victors), and that the causes being fought for were more obviously just and more clear-cut in their character than in many past disputes, when outpourings of nationalistic self-righteousness were commonplace. Certainly, a major side-effect of the Gulf War has been a crisis of conscience over the purposes and effectiveness of Europe's would-be foreign policy -- understandably so given that the low profile of European Political Cooperation (EPC) in the crisis contrasted uncomfortably with the ambitious proposals launched during the Italian Presidency of the Community in the second half of 1989 and intended to shape the outcome of the imminent Intergovernmental Conference on Political Union. The failure of EPC to whip (in the British Parliamentary sense) member states into line during the pre-war diplomacy, and the consequent loss of initiative to the United States over coalition policy and to the Soviet Union over efforts at conflict resolution, seemed to have demonstrated conclusively the finite limits of convergence for the national foreign policies of Western Europe.

Those who take a more specialized interest in European international relations know that matters are not quite so straightforward. Not only does EPC, like the rest of the European Community system, exhibit an action-reaction cycle in which setbacks bring forth renewed efforts at cooperation, but any perspective longer than that of the Gulf crisis, from August 1990 to February 1991, shows it in a much more favorable light. Over a twenty year period, there is in fact a pattern of oscillation to be discerned, peaks and troughs along a gradual upward gradient, as the scope of EPC has widened, consensus has become more habit-forming, and the outside world has begun to sit up and take serious notice of what has been happening since the Davignon Report inaugurated a new species of diplomatic association in 1970.

Yet troughs there have been, and in the public eye they tend to be particularly associated with the great dramas of world politics, when the foreign policies of those who aspire to influence the shape of the international system come under the closest scrutiny. Although EPC by its nature tends to be concerned more with quiet, long-term, preventive diplomacy, it is not unfair to judge it according to the test of performance under conditions of extreme strain. For diplomacy cannot be conducted on one's own terms. The international system is intermittently volcanic, and it is as important to be able to deal with the occasional, inevitable eruption as to promote the circumstances in which conflicts can be resolved before they become dangerous. It is therefore necessary to look at the record of EPC in coping with crises, of which there have now been at least a dozen, both because we can often best understand an institution through knowing its deficiencies, and because it is at these times that EPC comes to the notice of the wider public, inside Europe and throughout the world. It must be stressed however, that the focus here is not on "EPC in *crisis*," which would suggest that the system is on the verge of disintegration, but on "EPC in *crises*," where the focus is on how the system has responded to the intermittent onset of highly threatening international developments.

The issue is given particular relevance by the fact that the Conference of Foreign Ministers has in the past addressed precisely the same question. On coming to negative conclusions in 1980-81, they carried through in the London Report the particular reform of instituting "crisis procedures" whereby any three member states can convene at 48 hours notice a meeting of the Political Committee "or, if necessary, a Ministerial meeting" in order to better react in an emergency. Heads of Mission in Third Countries were also to follow these procedures, and Working Groups were "encouraged to analyze areas of potential crisis and to prepare a range of possible reactions by the Ten."[1] How far, then, has EPC lived up to these injunctions, and how bad, indeed, was its record before they were issued?

---

1 "Report on European Political Cooperation issued by the Foreign Ministers of the Ten on 13 October 1981 (London Report)," in: *European Political Cooperation (EPC)*, 5th Ed., Bonn: Press and Information Office of the Federal Government, 1988, pp. 61-69.

The Nature of Crisis[2]

Before the record can be outlined and evaluated, it is important to establish a base-line by clarifying the meaning of "crisis," with particular reference to the EC and its foreign policy activities. In the literature on foreign policy analysis, a consensus has emerged on certain elements of the definition of crisis. In the first place it is necessary to distinguish between an international crisis, involving two or more states, and representing a crisis for either part or whole of the international system, and a foreign policy crisis, which is experienced by individual foreign policy actors according to the incidence of certain conditions. Not every participant in an international crisis will necessarily experience a foreign policy crisis. For example, the United States intervened decisively in the Suez war of 1956, but its foreign policy was not thereby plunged into crisis.

The first of the conditions whose occurrence represents a crisis for the actor concerned is the *threat to fundamental values*. If an entity believes that its core beliefs or principles are in danger, then it will be on the verge of a crisis. But equally important is the *sense of limited time* in which to make a decision about how to react to such a threat. If it seems that there is no particular deadline, and that the danger may not come to a head for a long time to come, then the system concerned will not be on full alert, and it will be difficult to talk about it being in crisis. Lastly, and developing out of the second criterion, there must be *some sense of a compelled choice, or turning-point*. That is, a belief that even if the actor does nothing, things will change. Thus decision-makers come inexorably to a parting of the ways, where they must make a choice. The status quo is no longer an option. If these three criteria are fulfilled for any given entity, whether individual human being or planet earth, its governing system will be in crisis.

It remains to ask what crisis does not mean, what the experience of crisis entails, and in particular what it means for a system like EPC, half state half conference, the centaur of international diplomacy.

Contrary to conventional opinion, at first supported by academic analysis in the guise of Charles Hermann and his followers, a crisis does not necessarily involve the element of surprise. Many thoroughly predictable crises have occurred, such as the Arab-Israel war of 1967. Moreover, once the crisis has begun, even urgency is not a universal characteristic. The reality of operating

---

2 On the problems of defining crises, see: Charles F. Hermann (ed.), *International Crises: Insights from Behavioural Research*, New York: Free Press, 1972; Richard Ned Lebow, *Between Peace and War: the Nature of International Crisis*, Baltimore: Johns Hopkins University Press, 1981; Michael Brecher and Jonathon Wilkenfeld, *Crisis, Conflict and Instability*, Oxford: Pergamon Press, 1989.

under known, finite time constraints is not the same as a sense of urgency, as the slow evaporation of the UN deadline of 15 January must have made clear to Saddam Hussein in 1991.

Equally, despite the weight of Michael Brecher's view, the likelihood of military activity does not seem to be an inherent part of the onset of crisis. Crisis is a state of being which can occur in many entities or organisms, not all of which have the capacity for violence. It does, for example, make perfect sense to talk about a person's life-crisis in terms of the three criteria outlined above, whereas to add the extra condition of the likely resort to violence would simply muddy the conceptual waters. Even in foreign policy crises, the military criterion would rule out the kind of economic crisis that regularly besets European-American relations, or the kind of diplomatic crisis that afflicted the European Community in 1965-66.

Once a crisis has begun, what are the implications for the actors concerned? First, it is always important to ask "a crisis for whom?", given the asymmetrical nature of many international crises. Mussolini's attack on Albania was a trauma for the latter, but a sideshow for the former. China's attack on Vietnam in 1979 can hardly be termed a crisis for EPC -- although it would be revealing to speculate on the reasons why not. In fact those immersed in crises, military or not, are usually all too aware of their condition, for it entails a major increase in stress levels, perceptions of vital interests suddenly at stake, and often major rearrangements of decision-making procedures so as to cope with the new fluidity of events. Pathological changes in behavior will often occur, as individuals and groups reach the edges of trauma. Dean Rusk in the Cuban Missile Crisis, Richard Nixon during Watergate, and half the French population during "la grande peur" of 1789, are all well-documented examples.

The Meaning of Crises for EPC

For EPC, the above definitions and consequences of crisis apply, but with the rider that since "actorness" is a partial and intermittent phenomenon for European foreign policy, it is not possible to assume that what some member states will perceive as a serious challenge will be seen in the same way by all the Twelve. When events in the external environment appear to precipitate a crisis for the Community as a whole, they raise the very issue of whether the separate states do indeed share "fundamental values" in international relations, which when threatened inspire a crisis, or whether -- as in recent dramas -- they in fact rank basic concerns like sovereignty, order, peace and human rights in different ways according to their domestic political culture. Equally, on the other two key attributes of a foreign policy crisis, a sense of finite time in which to act and the existence of an unavoidable turning-point, a group of states like EPC may well display a variety of responses, ill-suppressed by the loose mechanisms of collective decision-making and obligation. Over the Gulf, as there had been over the Falklands, there was considerable disagreement, particularly in private, as to when the chances for a peaceful settlement had become exhausted. Of course, these two cases reveal the other strikingly unusual characteristic of EPC when compared to states-as-actors, namely that not only does it not have the capacity to employ military force, but there even exists great uncertainty as to whether the system should move towards acquiring a defence dimension at all.

Thus it is difficult to predict with confidence that any given crisis in prospect *will* be a crisis for EPC as such, although it is certainly possible to say that it *should* be one. It will depend upon the actual responses of the national governments, in their compulsory consultations (since 1987) but voluntary decisions, as to whether an event becomes a crisis for EPC. Here as elsewhere, the Community's identity is determined by cases, not rules, and by cases which are not even cumulative in their effects.

Looking at the past record, it is nevertheless clear that events have at times imposed themselves on Europe, regardless of its internal differences, so that the existence of a serious crisis could hardly be denied or ignored. At other times the strong concerns of particularly influential member states have effectively imposed a crisis-definition on EPC as a whole. Let us turn, therefore to the actual issues which may be reasonably defined as having been crises for EPC (and by implication to those which may not), given that Europe has so far been more of a "civilian power" than a super-power in the making. What kinds of substantive issues have involved Europe in foreign policy crises, and why? The following preliminary list does no more than give an abbreviated account of the most convincing candidates, of their reasons for inclusion, and of EPC's performance in coping with them. The paper ends with some evaluation, in the hope that the two issues -- the nature of the data-set presented, and its interpretation -- may provoke debate not just on the specific matter of crisis behavior but also on the question of what can be expected of EPC in the current international system.

The Record: a List of the Foreign Policy Crises Experienced by EPC

1973

The October War in the Middle East constituted a crisis for EPC in the sense that it might have led to a major confrontation between the superpowers, and did lead to OPEC targeting all Western states with massive oil price increases, and some with the extra penalty of embargoed supplies. EPC responded to the war with little more than a call for a ceasefire and an eventual reference to the need for Israel to give up its 1967 conquests, while also meeting the rights of the Palestinians. On the energy front, EPC proved incapable of cohesion and initiative, although it did gradually move into the foreground of the Euro-Arab Dialogue, initiated in response to Arab requests at the Copenhagen summit of December 1973.

1974

The coup on 15 July 1974 by which pro-Greek military elements in Cyprus brought down Archbishop Makarios and installed Nikos Sampson as a puppet President was a serious development because of Turkey's fear for the safety of the Turkish Cypriot community. Although the coup was condemned by the Nine, Cyprus only became a crisis for EPC when Turkey invaded part of the island, creating an effective partition. Even then, the fact that for members of the Community this was a regrettable but not fundamentally threatening act explains their lack of strong collective response. It was not perceived (even by Britain) as a major crisis. Intervention was not thought desirable, whether against the Sampson coup or against the Turkish invasion. Perhaps, however, the argument should be reversed. Did the Nine not perceive it as a crisis for the EC partly because they knew they were incapable of action?

1975

The chaotic situation in Portugal, although slow-burning and strictly the internal affair of that country, seems to have represented more of a foreign policy crisis for the EC than the invasion of Cyprus had done. Revolution in this strategically important country, with the possible contamination of Spain, was something of a nightmare scenario. It is well-known how the Nine used positive sanctions through European Investment Bank (EIB) loans to prop up the position of the center in Portugal. Procedurally, however, EPC took second place to the Community institutions proper.

1979

The Soviet invasion of Afghanistan produced a crisis in East-West relations which some have seen as the inauguration of the "Second Cold War." Because the US responded with such hostility, this had to represent a crisis for EPC, although it is arguable that had Washington done nothing the Europeans would have regretted the development and turned to the next business. In the event they did nothing for three weeks, creating an impression of paralysis which brought forth by way of reaction both a neutralization proposal for Afghanistan and the eventual "crisis procedures" themselves of the London Report. The former failed, and US-Soviet relations continued to deteriorate.

1980

The Iranian hostage affair represented a crisis for EPC only insofar as it threatened the United States, Europe's main ally, although it is true that it also endangered the basic principles of diplomatic society upon which the interests of all states depend. Insofar as the Community sought to be pro-active in the matter it was largely in an attempt to defuse the sense of crisis and head off the possibility of violence, whether against the captives by Iran or against the captors by the US. The Nine found it easy to issue statements condemning the hostage-taking, and to support the US in more discreet diplomacy, but when it came to the question of sanctions, they once again fell back on foot-dragging and internal debate. Although later in the crisis the good offices of the Europeans proved useful, EPC had not distinguished itself by effective influence over either Washington or Tehran.

1981

According to Simon Nuttall, during the Polish Crisis of 1981-82, the new crisis mechanism of the London Report "spectacularly failed to function."[3] After General Jaruzelski's proclamation of martial law on 13 December 1981, EPC issued the predictable condemnation but postponed any decision on sanctions. Once again it seems likely that the event itself was less of a crisis for the EC than the American reaction to it -- although Poland was clearly on the verge of a tragedy that could have inflamed the whole continent. Washington's announcement of sanctions -- without prior consultations -- caught EPC napping and as in 1979 it proved difficult to convene meetings, let alone take decisive measures. Greece, in particular, then obstructed the imposition of EC sanctions against the Soviet Union.

1982

In 1982 there were three events which can reasonably be described as actual or potential crises for the EPC system. The first of these was Argentina's invasion of the Falkland Islands, which was a crisis for the Ten simply because

---

3 In Simon Nuttall's forthcoming (1992) book on the history of European Political Cooperation, Chapter 5. In compiling this record of the crises which EPC has had to face, I have drawn liberally on Nuttall's authoritative account. See also the very useful data in: Roy H. Ginsberg, *Foreign Policy Actions of the European Community: The Politics of Scale*, Boulder: Lynne Reinner, 1989.

it involved an attack on the territory of a member state. Although EPC is not a collective security alliance it has to be supposed that any such invasion would ipso facto be regarded as a serious challenge to Europe's solidarity and political will. In the event the Community (i.e. not just the separate states, who also went ahead with an arms embargo) acted quickly to ban imports from Argentina, which was taken aback by its firm response. Solidarity only lasted for a month, however, as both Ireland and Italy found it very difficult domestically to support Britain in what was clearly going to become a shooting war; Denmark also had its problems. Nevertheless, from Britain's viewpoint, the necessary diplomatic message had been sent to the world community by the Europeans, and EPC had responded well enough to the crisis.

The second major event of 1982 was the Israeli invasion of the Lebanon on 6 June, which put paid to the last hopes for European mediation in the Arab-Israel dispute (hopes arising from the Venice Declaration). It was thus a crisis for the EPC line on the Middle East, itself the most important policy area within EPC. At first the Europeans were over-shadowed by the G7 Summit at Versailles in their attempt to coordinate a response. The ten Foreign Ministers met (at the request of Greece and France) on 9 June alongside a NATO meeting in Bonn, but the need for compromise between differing national positions meant that EPC was in no position to take a high profile. All that could be done was to advise the Commission to delay signing the new Financial Protocol of the existing trade agreement with Israel.

In the same month another, if less dramatic, crisis loomed on the scene when President Reagan extended trade sanctions on materials being used to build the Soviet-West European gas pipeline to the European subsidiaries of American companies. This was an assertion of extra-territorial legal rights which the relevant European governments could not accept, and a diplomatic confrontation ensued. It was, of course, primarily a political issue, but since it was a question of restraints on trade, it came under the Community's competence, and a formal EEC protest was issued on 12 August. After various escalatory measures on both sides, the United States backed down on 13 November. This was a distinct, if not very public, triumph for the Europeans' ability to hold together in an intra-alliance politico-economic crisis. Indeed, perhaps it is in such circumstances that the EC is at its strongest, as exchanges in the GATT have often suggested. The latter, however, never involve EPC and are not "foreign policy" actions in the traditional sense.

1983

1983 saw both the Soviet shooting down of a Korean airliner and the American invasion of Grenada loom on the EPC horizon as "mini-crises." The latter, in October, was greeted with a deafening silence from Europe, whose main aim was to pretend that the breach of the principle of sovereignty and independence by the United States did not constitute the same threat to basic values that it would have had any other country perpetrated the deed. The Commission displayed more signs of angst over the invasion than did EPC. The same hesitancy had been evident over the downing of KAL 007, in September, where the obscure circumstances of the affair produced concern lest East-West relations seriously deteriorate. Greek dissent once again prevented unanimity even at the level of declarations.

1985

The developing governmental crisis in the Philippines caught the Ten napping, and possibly divided in their attitudes towards the last days of the Marcos regime. Certainly EPC was not seen at its best in anticipating a change of government and coordinating national positions as events unfolded. On the other hand the Philippines was only likely to become a real crisis for EPC if civil war had erupted and the United States had intervened. That would have put to the test the Europeans' implicit claim to be heard as a distinctive and more moderate western voice in the Third World.

1986

Terrorism dominated 1986. In April the United States bombed Libya in reprisal for suspected Libyan involvement in various acts of terror against US targets in Europe. This was nothing less than a humiliation for EPC, rather similar to the hostage rescue mission of 1980, which came just after the Europeans had agreed to sanctions against Iran as a way of heading off the use of force. The British allowed US F-111s to fly from bases in East Anglia but in doing so deceived their European partners. Sir Geoffrey Howe, wittingly or unwittingly, gave the impression to his fellow foreign ministers just hours before the attack took place that he had no knowledge of any such operation. That this was a crisis for the Europeans was brought home by the immediate execution of two hostages in the Lebanon, in reprisal for the raid, and by the threat of further operations against European interests. The procedures for consultation, however, worked well. No one could complain that the Ministers did not actually meet often enough.

In the autumn came the Hindawi affair, in which a Jordanian-Palestinian was sentenced to a very long prison term in Britain for having plotted to blow up an El-Al jet in mid-air. This time the pattern was reversed, but EPC still ended up looking inadequate, as Britain failed to convince its partners of the virtues of solidarity against Syria, whom it accused of having master-minded the plot, and with whom it broke off diplomatic relations. Several member states refused even to send their Foreign Ministers to attend a meeting on possible sanctions.

1989

The shootings of student demonstrators in Tiananmen Square, Beijing, in June 1989 produced a rupture in the developing relations between the EC and China. The imposition of limited sanctions demonstrated that the Europeans were of one mind on these outrages, and that political dialogue with this potentially important partner would have to come to an end. But Tiananmen was not a crisis for EPC in the same sense that it was for the people of China.

The pattern of dubious actions by great powers taking place during the dead days of late December continued in 1989 with the botched US invasion of Panama. Once again, what might in theory have been a crisis for EPC, involving as it did an intervention in the internal affairs of a sovereign state, turned out to be more of a mere embarrassment. Only if domestic opinion inside Europe had raised a storm about American actions would the issue have to come to a head, and that was unlikely, given the disreputable character of the Noriega regime toppled by the US. EPC could once again get away with barely audible (or even decipherable) expressions of concern.

1990

Clearly, Iraq's invasion of Kuwait on 2 August 1990 represented a crisis for any country or group of countries concerned for the future of international order, in general, and stability in the Middle East, in particular. The Europeans were in fact very quick off the mark in condemning Iraq, and individually active throughout the crisis-slide phase in trying to broker a peaceful solution. Collectively, however, they looked increasingly ragged, and even inept, as the USA and USSR dominated the diplomatic environment. Britain's identification with the Americans, the reluctance shown by a majority of member states to take any high-profile position at all, and the persistence of France in trying to get its erstwhile Iraqi partners off the hook on which they had impaled themselves, all contributed to the image of EPC as superficial and ineffectual. The crisis showed that consultations are not enough; there has to be a common definition of both the problem and of the best means with which to respond to it.

1991

The long-predicted crisis in Yugoslavia finally erupted in June 1991, and the EC could not but be involved. The disintegration of a state on the geographic margins of the Community, with both secessionists and the federal government in Belgrade looking to the Twelve for support, addressed the core values of EPC. Moreover the need for action was urgent, given the willingness of Slovenia and Croatia to back their declarations of independence by force of arms. Thus EPC (to the irritation of countries like Canada and Sweden in the CSCE, whose own new crisis-mechanism was also triggered) monopolized attempts at mediation between the warring parties, and the Troika of Foreign Ministers engaged in frantic shuttle diplomacy. At the time of writing (7 July 1991) the Yugoslav crisis has demonstrated both the strengths and weaknesses of EPC: there is no other actor so widely trusted or so able to respond positively in such circumstances (the US, by contrast, has been almost sidelined here), yet at the same time if diplomacy fails the EC is not in a position to impose order in Yugoslavia. The cards the Twelve do hold, of promises of more aid or even accession to the Community itself, are not enough to stop tanks in their tracks.

Evaluation

It should have been clear from the above recitation of cases -- which may not be comprehensive -- that EPC is not particularly well-suited to handling international crises, even those in which the Europeans are themselves directly involved. There is a distinct tendency not to avoid crises, for that almost by definition cannot be done, but certainly to play down their significance. Of course, this is not uncommon in international relations, but it should be remembered that while in most crises the actors oscillate between wanting to "win" and seeing the crisis itself as the enemy which must be eradicated, the Europeans almost always take the latter view, since they do not have the capacity for games of chicken or compellance.

The "crisis procedures" instituted after the London Report have worked with increasing effectiveness, after a shaky start, in that there have been fewer long gaps between the onset of a crisis and a response from the Political Committee or Foreign Ministers Conference. On the other hand, mere mechanisms of consultation are only one part of the solution, and it is difficult to know whether the Working Groups have in fact managed to anticipate crises by taking a more self-conscious approach towards their prediction or even prevention. EPC is not yet in a position to be able to react firmly, decisively, and dramatically to major international events. It has been able to respond increasingly quickly to such events, but that is a rather different matter.

Thus EPC has tended to try to define crises out of existence by ignoring them or locating them in longer-term patterns of diplomatic exchange. In particular, this has been the case when crises have resulted from American actions, or growing intra-Alliance tensions. Only when a crisis can be contained within self-defined political and economic limits are the Europeans likely to be confident enough to accept the logic of the crisis and consider the possibility of escalation themselves.

Over the twenty years of its life, EPC has got better at engineering consensus, in and out of crisis, and at avoiding the humiliating silence of complete inaction when faced with a new drama or threat. But member states are often still forced into anodyne generalizations by their fundamental lack of the capacity to agree amongst themselves on international questions. This is not, it should be stressed (contrary to popular opinion during the Gulf war) simply a function of the EC's lack of a military dimension, which may eventually be corrected by the convergence of EPC and WEU. Even at the diplomatic or economic levels of civilian power, the collectivity which is the EC is not at its best in a crisis. Its comparative advantage is in the long-term effort to change the environments out of which crises tend to spring -- so as to inoculate against them. Such an approach may seem unnecessarily high-minded to many, and it undoubtedly makes a virtue of current necessity. But it also makes considerable sense when laid alongside, for example, the stumbling failures of crisis-driven policies in the Middle East or Central America.

Yet crises will continue to occur in the short-term, often unexpectedly, and they will continue to exert great pressures on European foreign policy solidarity. It remains to be seen how EPC, now 20 years old and in early adulthood, might cope with another crisis involving a sharp attack on the vital interests of the member states, such as that which when it occurred in 1973 demonstrated so devastatingly the limits of European unity. The many crises of the subsequent years, difficult and embarrassing as they have often been for EPC, have not yet posed the same degree of challenge. The Yugoslavian crisis of 1991 has the potential -- uncontained -- to be Europe's greatest foreign policy test so far.

9

Western Europe and the Gulf War

Scott Anderson

Introduction

It is perhaps fortuitous that the invasion of Kuwait occurred so soon after the European Council's decision, at the June 1990 summit in Dublin, to convene by the end of that year an Intergovernmental Conference on Political Union. The ensuing crisis ensured that the provisions for a Common Foreign and Security Policy, a key aspect of the proposed treaty, remained at the centre of debate. For the nations of the Community, the Persian Gulf experience (just as the civil war in Yugoslavia) has contributed to the proceedings a welcome if somewhat sobering dose of reality; the difficulties encountered and the lessons learned will undoubtedly help determine the final shape of the Union.

How should one evaluate the Twelve's participation in the Gulf conflict -- what are the criteria for "success"? One must consider both the degree of cooperation achieved by the member states and the impact of their collective contribution to the campaign against Iraq. Thus far, the reviews have been decidedly mixed. To many commentators, what seemed a tepid and disjointed response to an obvious and serious challenge demonstrates that deep divisions exist -- and will likely persist -- within the Community. There is some truth to the Belgian Foreign Minister's complaint that Europe was shown to be "an economic giant, a political dwarf, and a military worm" by its inability to influence the course of events.[1] Such disappointment seems, however, to be the product of somewhat unrealistic expectations of the role the EC could potentially have played. One should instead take care to assess its performance solely in terms of existing political and military capabilities, regardless of whether or not these were sufficient to meet the demands of the crisis. Only then can one consider the question of expanding the Twelve's capacity for coordinated action in the future.

---

1   *New York Times*, 25 January 1991.

What are the implications of the Gulf conflict for the development of a European security identity in the context of the Political Union project? The events of the past year can be seen as either discouraging or encouraging the process, depending upon the observer's point of view. For those who believe that a common external policy is neither possible nor desirable, the EC's poor showing is a convincing demonstration of the extent to which differing national interests will remain a barrier to consensus and an obstacle to deeper integration. The obvious consequence is that, for the time being, security and defence matters should remain the responsibility of the national governments, subject only to voluntary cooperation. On the other hand, the champions of unification -- chief among them the EC Commission President Jacques Delors -- claim that this episode provides further proof of the value, if not the necessity, of a single European voice in world affairs. They argue that the obvious "limitations" on the Community's international influence can only be overcome by "moving towards a form of political union embracing a common foreign and security policy," presumably with a high degree of institutional centralization.[2] The problematic aspect of this particular case is that each position has its merits, and may with some justification be supported by the record.

Institutional Framework

Before turning to an account of events in the Gulf, it is worth reviewing the institutional framework within which the Twelve conduct their foreign and defence policies. A variety of organizations -- European Political Cooperation, the European Communiy, the Western European Union, the Atlantic Alliance -- are available to the EC member states as fora for consultation and cooperation. The role and function of each deserves further examination.

The political elements of the Community's external relations have been coordinated through the intergovernmental mechanism of European Political Cooperation (EPC). Under the provisions of the Single European Act (SEA), the member states

> undertake to inform and consult each other on any foreign policy matters of general interest so as to ensure that their combined influence is exercised as effectively as possible through coordination, the convergence of their positions and the implementation of joint action.[3]

---

[2] Jacques Delors, "European Integration and Security," Alastair Buchan Memorial Lecture, London, 7 March 1991, in: *Europe/Documents*, No. 1699, 13 March 1991.
[3] Single European Act, Title III, Article 30.2(a).

As Political Cooperation, the Foreign Ministers and a representative of the Commission meet for regular discussions and, when unanimous consent can be attained, take decisions on the course to be collectively followed. While EPC is itself capable only of making declarations and initiating dialogues, its deliberations provide an overall direction to its members' foreign policies and to the Community's international economic policy. Individual governments are enjoined against actions which might deviate from the common approach, and the EC's external activities are required to be "consistent" with those agreed upon in EPC. This should ensure a high degree of cohesion for those matters which fall within its purview. However, the SEA only mandates cooperation with respect to the "political and economic aspects of security," and the member governments have thus far continued to exclude a defence dimension from EPC's sphere of competence. This restricts Europe's ability to define a common response to crisis situations where the use of military force might be considered.[4]

The economic side of the Twelve's foreign policy is, on the other hand, managed by Community institutions. This rather artificial division of responsibilities has resulted in the curious phenomenon of the Foreign Ministers discussing the economic aspects of a problem while meeting as the EC Council, and the political aspects while meeting as EPC. The distinction has, however, become increasingly less evident: Commission proposals to the Council often reflect EPC conclusions, and ministers have recently begun to address both political and economic issues at the same venue.[5] While such organizational confusion might undermine the Community's overall effectiveness, a more important constraint on its international influence is the nature of the power that it wields. The EC has two main instruments at its disposal: trade sanctions and foreign aid. On numerous occasions over the past decade, Europe has imposed restrictions on trade with certain countries, and has offered financial and technical assistance to others.[6] Nevertheless, such measures have only secondary utility in circumstances such as those encountered in the Gulf.

Security and defence cooperation among the Twelve occurs in the context of both the Western European Union (WEU) and the Atlantic Alliance (NATO). The WEU has enjoyed something of a revival since the mid-Eighties, thanks to the successful coordination under its auspices of the European naval forces deployed to the Persian Gulf during the Iran-Iraq war in 1987 and 1988. All nine members of the WEU belong to the EC, and although there has never existed a formal link, its potential incorporation into the Community is being

---

4   For further examples, see the chapter in this volume by Christopher Hill.
5   *Economist*, 13 October 1990, p. 55.
6   For further examples, see the chapter in this volume by Simon Nuttall.

actively considered.[7] The WEU's principal virtue is that it offers a forum independent of NATO -- and thus of the United States -- for regular ministerial consultation. At present, however, the Atlantic Alliance remains the primary vehicle for military collaboration within Europe. Since the Americans have consistently opposed the formation of a monolithic EC "bloc" in allied councils, it is only in the case of contingencies arising beyond the boundaries of the the NATO area that, through the WEU, the Twelve may attempt to define a distinct Community position.[8] The WEU has therefore acquired a certain value, as its Secretary General has observed:

> The WEU's competence in matters relating to out-of-area threats . . . provides a framework for both concerted action by Europeans and *ad hoc* cooperation between Europeans and their North American allies.[9]

Although it could potentially become the defence arm of the Community, for the moment the WEU has no military capabilities of its own and cannot expect to be more than a politically significant but somewhat peripheral participant in any serious extra-European conflict. The Alliance, on the other hand, possesses the military means necessary for out-of-area operations but will not undertake them. Nevertheless, in spite of these constraints, both organizations have important roles to play in regional crisis management.

Finally, one must not omit reference to the United Nations. The Twelve have obligations not only to defend the interests of the Community, but to support the principles of the UN Charter, particularly Articles 50 and 51. Furthermore, as permanent members of the Security Council, Britain and France have a special responsibility to uphold that body's conclusions.[10] A renewed and

---

7 The WEU members are Belgium, France, Germany, Italy, Luxembourg, the Netherlands, Portugal, Spain and the United Kingdom; Denmark, Greece and Ireland remain outside. Furthermore, all of the EC members save Ireland belong to NATO, although France excludes itself from the integrated military structure.

8 It is an enduring and popular misconception that the NATO Treaty prevents allied action outside of Europe while the WEU Treaty permits the same. In fact, there are no explicit restrictions on such activities in either case, and the geographic limits attached to the mutual assistance clauses are similar for both organizations. Precedent is instead the determining factor: the NATO allies have never agreed to a formal out-of-area role for the Alliance, while the dominant function of the WEU thus far seems to be the provision of political "cover" for joint European military operations in the Middle East.

9 Willem van Eekelen, "WEU and the Gulf Crisis," *Survival*, Vol. 32, No. 6, November/December 1990, p. 523.

10 Lawrence Freedman, "The Gulf War and the New World Order," *Survival*, Vol. 33, No. 3, May/June 1991, p. 199.

effective United Nations would be an obvious complement to an emerging European security identity.

The European Role in the Gulf Conflict

On 2 August 1990, Iraqi forces seized and occupied Kuwait. Within hours, the Twelve issued a statement condemning the invasion; two days later, EPC officials met in Rome to discuss possible sanctions and soon agreed that unless Baghdad were to comply with the Security Council resolution demanding its immediate withdrawal, they would suspend oil imports from Iraq and Kuwait, freeze Iraqi assets and halt all military sales. While the European trade embargo was an important weapon in its own right, it also served to reinforce American calls for UN-sponsored economic action against Iraq. These were realized with the passage of a second resolution on 6 August. The level of consultation increased as the crisis intensified. On the 10th, NATO and EPC ministerial meetings were held in Brussels, helping to facilitate a high degree of cohesion within both the Alliance and the Community, European sanctions entered into effect on this date and were administered by EC bodies. Then, on 21 August, WEU and EPC ministerial meetings were held in Paris. The nine WEU members called for UN authorization of whatever measures might prove necessary to enforce the embargo, including the use of force. Belgium, Italy, the Netherlands and Spain each agreed to send warships to join the British and French naval forces already patrolling the area. Operational coordination of the European flotilla was to be managed by a newly-created WEU military staff group which would draw upon the experience gained in the previous Gulf deployment. The Twelve then reiterated their refusal to close EC diplomatic missions in Kuwait and expressed their concern over the fate of foreign nationals held against their will by Iraq.[11] Commission President Delors proposed that the Community provide humanitarian aid to the refugees fleeing the conflict and financial assistance to Turkey, Jordan and Egypt, the countries most severely affected by the crisis. At this early stage, one may safely say that despite the handicap of some rather cumbersome decision-making procedures, the Twelve responded in a timely and effective fashion. By implementing the trade sanctions, the EC and EPC functioned -- to use the words of the Commission -- as "a single Community instrument" with political and economic measures fully harmonized;[12] furthermore, the WEU took military action in concert with EPC recommendations. American officials even claimed

---

11 The full texts of these early communiques may be found in: *Europe/Documents*, No. 1644, 23 August 1990.
12 *Europe*, No. 5311, 22 August 1990.

to be impressed by Europe's apparent unity of purpose.[13] Such optimism was, however, somewhat premature.

By September it was becoming increasingly clear that a substantial international effort might be required to defend Saudi Arabia and the Gulf states, implement an air and sea blockade and, if all else failed, dislodge the Iraqis. Tensions within the Community rose as the crisis gradually escalated into a massive military confrontation. An obvious sore point was the wide disparity of the various national contributions to Desert Shield. The British government, eager to preserve the "special relationship," offered Washington firm political backing and committed substantial naval, air and ground forces to the Gulf. The French, while reaffirming their traditional independence, were also quick to respond with significant forces, particularly after Iraqi troops had assaulted their embassy in Kuwait City. Of the remaining EC members, most provided support units of one form or another, four participated in the WEU naval operation, and Italy dispatched a squadron of combat aircraft.[14] Germany was something of an exception: the Kohl government found that the constitution -- or, perhaps more accurately, its coalition partner's interpretation of the constitution -- forbade military action beyond European territory. Germany nevertheless sent minesweepers to the Eastern Mediterranean to free other NATO vessels for service in the Gulf, and provided considerable quantities of money and material to assist the coalition effort. On the whole, however, there was frustration on both sides of the Atlantic with the small size of the Community's total contribution.[15] It annoyed both the Americans, who were shouldering a vast military burden, and the Europeans, who realized that they would have virtually no influence over allied policy should fighting break out. Vocal disagreements were heard among the Twelve; Prime Minister Thatcher insisted that, unlike their pusillanimous partners, only Britain and France had "done more than the bare minimum" to assist the build-up. "It is sad that, at this critical time, Europe has not fully measured up to expectations," she said.[16] Yet this could not have been otherwise, for Britain and France (and to a lesser extent Italy and Spain) were the only EC members to possess viable intervention forces and even minimal power projection capabilities. Furthermore, as one NATO official later pointed out, only the British and French "have the mental equipment to use what they've got."[17]

---

13 *International Herald Tribune*, 10 August 1990, *Atlantic News*, No. 2248, 29 August 1990.
14 For a detailed listing of the European forces sent to the Gulf as of mid-October 1990, see: van Eekelen (note 9), Appendix.
15 "European Security and the Gulf Crisis," Report, Western European Union Assembly, 14 November 1990.
16 *Wall Street Journal*, 3 September 1990.
17 *Aviation Week & Space Technology*, 18 March 1991, p. 67.

The problem of commanding the various coalition forces arose at this time, providing another source of friction. There was absolutely no question of utilizing NATO's integrated structures, so ad hoc arrangements would have to suffice. Britain placed its troops under direct American operational control, but France remained aloof, protecting the autonomy of its national command. The hastily assembled WEU naval headquarters did not appear to be particularly effective, partly because of French intransigence.[18] The record of logistical cooperation was considerably better, however, as EC members generally provided a high degree of transport and infrastructure assistance to the coalition. The ridiculous exception came when Belgium, that rhetorical champion of European integration, refused to sell spare ammunition to Britain for fear or retaliation. Despite some characteristic French objections to the use of Alliance facilties for out-of-area contingencies, allied committees helped to coordinate the European contribution to the extensive sealift and airlift requirements of the Desert Shield build-up and made NATO bases readily available to forces and supplies enroute for the Gulf.[19] On the whole, given that defence affairs rest outside the Community's formal jurisdiction -- and that WEU and NATO involvement was somewhat constrained by circumstance -- it is not entirely surprising that the Twelve's military response appeared neither concerted nor forceful.

As time progressed, it proved far easier for the Community to define its political goal, the restoration of Kuwaiti sovereignty, than to maintain a consensus on the best means of acheiving it. Britain, for example, was far less inclined than its fellow EC members to seek further UN permission to use military force against Iraq. France, its Gaullist suspicions of American leadership never far from the surface, adopted a more independent line in its pursuit of a political solution to the crisis. In a speech to the United Nations on 24 September, President Mitterrand suggested that talks on a Middle East peace settlement, which would include the Arab-Israeli dispute, should follow the restoration of Kuwait. Additional problems arose as a result of efforts to secure the release of Europeans held hostage by Baghdad. In particular, Bonn's endorsement of former Chancellor Willy Brandt's mission to Baghdad (after a similar but officially condemned visit by former British Prime Minister Edward Heath) directly contravened the Twelve's decision not to negotiate with Baghdad.[20] The December 1990 release of all captive Westerners soon solved this problem. Lastly, even economic policies could not be implemented without

---

18 Thomas-Durell Young, *Preparing the Western Alliance for the Next Out-of-Area Campaign: Linking NATO and the WEU*, Carlisle, PA: US Army War College, 15 April 1991, p. 10-11.
19 "Problems of European Security," General Report, North Atlantic Assembly Political Committee, November 1990, p. 16.
20 *Europe*, No. 5364, 5/6 November 1990.

embarassment. The trade embargo was a success, but the financial assistance package granted to Egypt, Jordan and Turkey (two thirds from the individual member states and one third from the EC budget) was delayed for months as the governments dithered with their contributions. Worse yet, the Community portion could not be made available until February 1991, thanks to a squabble between the Commission and the European Parliament.[21] From a total EC commitment of $ 3,2 billion, only $ 1.2 billion had been disbursed by the end of May 1991.[22] This was not an impressive performance, particularly in light of the Italian Presidency's insistence that Europe should offer aid to the "frontline" states in place of direct contributions to the Coalition's military costs.

On 29 November, the Security Council authorized the use of "all necessary means" after 15 January 1991 to compel Iraq's compliance with its demands. As the deadline drew near, both Washington and the Community sought to broker a diplomatic settlement. US President Bush offered to send Secretary of State Baker to Baghdad, but the two governments failed to agree on a meeting date (predictably, Saddam Hussein insisted on 17 January). With American encouragement, the Twelve agreed in mid-December not to seek an independent dialogue with Iraq -- which might create the impression of a transatlantic rift -- while hopes of overcoming the impasse remained alive.[23] France, Germany and Italy were still very keen to promote an EC mission, however; the outgoing Council President, Gianni De Michelis, stated that "if by the end of the year direct talks between Washington and Baghdad prove impossible, the Community will have to try an autonomous initiative."[24] The twelve Foreign Ministers met again on 4 January 1991 to consider a French peace plan which linked an Iraqi pullout to the eventual review of unresolved Middle Eastern security issues in the context of an international conference modelled on the Conference of Security and Cooperation in Europe (CSCE). When it was learned that Iraqi Foreign Minister Tariq Aziz had agreed to talks with Baker in Geneva on the 9th, they promptly invited him to meet with the EC Troika in Luxembourg on the 10th.[25] Aziz refused, offered instead an invitation to Baghdad, and then ignored last-minute attempts to fix talks in Algiers; this was all a great disappointment to those who hoped that European

---

21 *Europe*, No. 5368, 12/13 November 1990. *Economist*, 22 December 1990, p. 48.
22 Gary J. Pagliano, "Iraq/Kuwait Crisis: The International Response and Burdensharing Isssues," *CRS Issue Brief*, Washington, DC: Congressional Research Service, 26 June 1991, p. 15.
23 John K. Cooley, "Pre-war Gulf diplomacy," *Survival*, Vol. 33, No. 2, March/April 1991, p. 137.
24 *Europe*, No. 5397, 21 December 1991.
25 The "Troika" is composed of the past, present and future presidents of the Council of Ministers, who in January 1991 were Messrs, De Michelis of Italy, Poos of Luxembourg and Van Den Broek of the Netherlands.

efforts might help avert war. After the Baker-Aziz meeting in Geneva came to naught, the Twelve urged UN Secretary General Perez de Cuellar to carry their proposal to Baghdad, but his mission failed to produce any results. Finally, on 14 January 1991, the EC Council resigned itself to the inevitable and called off all approaches to Iraq. When the UN deadline passed on the following day, there would be no further attempts to resolve the conflict peacefully.

The last weeks leading up to the outbreak of war were the most trying for the Community. It was impossible to preserve even a semblance of unity. The inherent tension between the need to maintain the solidarity of the American-led coalition and the desire for a distinct European stance pulled the member states apart. The ciritical issue was the "linkage" of the Kuwait situation to the Palestinian question through promises of an international conference. On the one hand, the Twelve had implicitly opposed any such connection by their endorsement of UN requirements for an unconditional Iraqi withdrawal. Meanwhile, they had been advocating just such a regional settlement since the Venice Declaration of 1980 (which recognized the Palestinian right to self-determination), in spite of American and Israeli opposition. The EC's troubles did not end there: public opinion on the Continent strongly opposed the initiation of hostilities, putting considerable pressure on several governments, while those nations bordering on the Mediterranean found their large Muslim populations growing restive. Thus the Community became a house divided: an "Atlanticist" minority, primarily the British and Dutch, standing behind the Americans and a "Europeanist" majority desperately seeking a preaceful solution and perhaps willing to allow more time for the economic sanctions to take effect. It was a pointed illustration of just how unrealistic were the expectations that twelve diverse nations could effectively converge differing positions into a single foreign policy. Final confirmation -- the coup de grace, as it were -- was provided by Mitterrand's "freelance" mediation efforts. In early January 1991 a French parliamentarian on an official visit to Baghdad met with Saddam Hussein and repoted that "[Saddam] is ready for concessions if there is a conference on Palestine."[26] Then, on the eve of the UN deadline, Foreign Minister Roland Dumas made a final appeal, once again offering Iraq an international conference. There was no response. So, as Lawrence Freedman writes:

> When France decided at the last minute to go it alone on this initiative, after the Council of Ministers had decided collectively not to do so, it reinforced suspicions that when high national interests are at stake there would be no respect for the discipline of a common policy.[27]

---

26 *The Times*, 7 January 1991.
27 Freedman (note 10), p. 199.

Operation Desert Storm began on 17 January 1991 with massive air attacks against targets in Iraq and Kuwait, and concluded just over a month later following the utter rout of the Iraqi army in a fierce four-day land battle. Once hostilities commenced, those of the Twelve who chose to participate did so in their capacity as individual members of a UN-sanctioned coalition and placed their forces under joint US-Saudi command. Britain, France and Italy joined in the air campaign, British and French ground forces fought alongside their American allies, and the Netherlands even pledged its two frigates to the coalition. (Paris quickly reversed its self-imposed prohibition of attacks on Iraqi soil.) The WEU continued to coordinate blockade enforcement and mine-clearing patrols, but the Belgian, Spanish and Portugese governments insisted that their vessels not take part in any other type of operation. The Atlantic Alliance played no direct role in the conflict other than to ensure adequate levels of logistic support for the coalition, although it had, in a particularly interesting situation, endeavoured to protect the security of southeastern Europe. On 2 January 1991, in response to Ankara's request, NATO ministers agreed to send 42 Belgian, Italian and German fighter-bombers to Turkey as a deterrent against possible Iraqi aggression. The aircraft were little more than a demonstration of political solidarity -- their military value was negligible at best -- but the deployment still provoked controversy. Several smaller nations denied that their treaty obligation to assist Turkey extended as far as the provision of forces before an attack had actually occured, while the German government faced strong domestic opposition to any employment of its forces beyond national boundaries.[28] When American planes began striking Iraq from Turkish bases in late January, however, the allies responded to the increased risk of attacks by sending air defence and chemical detection equipment. By that point, according to NATO Secretary General Manfred Woerner, treaty interpretations no longer differed.[29] With the fighting finally underway, the Community limited to a somewhat peripheral role, and the French safely on side, the Twelve were left with few opportunities for serious disagreement. European governments soon found themselves under less domestic pressure as public support for the war effort rose.[30] The Twelve stood behind the ground attack launched by coalition forces on 23 February 1991, despite having expressed some interest in Soviet President Gorbachev's unexpected attempt to secure an Iraqi pullout. By the 28th, a ceasefire was declared and the war, brief as it was, had ended.

---

28 *Atlantic News*, No. 2292, 25 January 1991.
29 *Atlantic News*, No. 2293, 30 January 1991.
30 Public opinion polls taken in Britain, France, Italy and Germany reveal that the war became surprisingly popular. See: *New York Times*, 29 January 1991.

The Community, perhaps seeking to atone for its poor performance in previous months, was an active and enthusiastic participant in the post-war relief program. Within days of the Iraqi surrender, the Troika set off on a tour of Middle Eastern capitals to renew contacts with Arab states and to promote a regional security conference patterned after the CSCE. A more immediate and compelling concern arose in early April 1991 when the Kurdish and Shiite rebellions failed and refugees by the thousand fled into the mountains along the Turkish and Iranian borders, where many died of exhaustion and exposure. The leaders of the Twelve, meeting at the Luxembourg European Council summit on 8 April 1991, responded quickly to the Kurds' tragic plight by calling for an end to Iraqi repression and approving British Prime Minister Major's notion of "safe havens," protected enclaves for the displaced Kurdish population. Washington was initially wary of any further military internvention, but within a matter of days Americans were working alongside British and French troops setting up a series of relief camps in northern Iraq. A UN police force would eventually arrive to replace the allied soldiers. This relatively minor episode should demonstrate how effective the Community's common foreign policy can in some circumstances be.

Implications and Conclusions

Before turning to the prospects for future collaboration, one should attempt a brief assessment of Europe's overall performance in the Gulf conflict. How effective was the policy coordination process within the Community, and how great an impact did the Twelve have on events? In the initial response to Iraqi aggression, a common position was successfully established. Old inhibitions against mixing EC and EPC affairs to a considerable extent disappeared, enhancing the consistency of economic and political actions, while the timing of EPC and WEU ministerial consultations (both bodies would meet on the same day) de facto afforded the Community some say in the direction of military activities. But when measures short of war -- economic sanctions, naval blockades and diplomatic initiatives -- failed to resolve the crisis, the Community's limited competence in security and defence matters and, more importantly, its member states' divergent views of the need for forceful intervention together ensured that solidarity was not maintained. Collectively, the Twelve could not play a role in the conflict commensurate with their interests in the region; Europe was, to use Jacques Delors' phrase, "ineffectual." The problem has both a political and a military dimension. Disagreement among the Twelve was not overly surprising, given the unprecedented gravity of the challenge and the understandable diversity of national reactions; indeed, one observer characterizes the level of cooperation as "remarkably high" under the circumstances.[31] In military terms, only Britain and France had the capacity (both physical and psychological) to deploy viable ground combat forces to the Gulf, so in that regard little else could have been expected of the Twelve. The reluctance of some EC governments to make even symbolic contributions to the coalition -- despite their providing extensive material and financial aid -- is a greater cause for concern. As François Heisbourg asked, "How can there be a common European policy when the British and French take ground losses in Kuwait and the Germans keep themselves deliberately aloof?"[32] But could it have been otherwise? Again, one must take care to measure the Community's performance against its real capacity for action.

The events in the Gulf will have a considerable impact on the individual Community members, on the institutions within which they interact, and on the future development of a European security identity. First, Germany faces a unique dilemma. The Germans made a truly enormous effort to assist the Coalition, but they were widely criticized for their refusal to send troops -- to be merely the "arsenal of democracy" was not enough. In response, the Kohl government promised a constitutional amendment which would permit the employment of German units outside of the NATO areas, perhaps under UN, EC or WEU auspices. These plans seem to have been quietly dropped, however, so it is difficult to imagine that a significant change in the German attitude will soon occur. For the British, on the other hand, the primary consequence of the war has been the revitalization of the Anglo-American relationship. Britain's willingness to deploy its forces abroad might prove to be of great value to both the Community and the Alliance should "out-of-area" threats to Western security gain in relative importance during the coming years. France drew quite different conclusions from its experience in the Gulf. Desert Storm "painfully exposed the inadequacies" of French forces, which possessed virtually no independent intelligence or airlift capacity and were compelled to rely on US support.[33] France has therefore taken the lead in calling for the creation of a European rapid deployment force, under WEU or EC control, complete with its own command structure, reconnaissance satellites and transport aircraft.[34] Other members of the Community have expressed interest in eventually acquiring these capabilities, while continuing to rely on NATO during the long development process.[35] Some analysts are inclined to greet the whole notion with skepticism: "Franco-British cooperation at Suez in 1956 is

---

31 Freedman (note 10), p. 198.
32 *New York Times*, 25 January 1991.
33 *Newsweek*, 20 May 1991.
34 *Economist*, 1 June 1991.
35 David S. Yost, "France and West European defence identity," *Survival*, Vol. 33, No. 4, July/August 1991, p. 345.

presumably not a suitable precedent for European cooperation out-of-area."[36] Jokes aside, these proposals are currently being given serious consideration.

The Gulf conflict has raised security and defence cooperation to the top of the agenda in Western Europe, forcing the Twelve to treat EC reform and NATO reform as two closely interrelated processes. The Atlantic Alliance, confronting a strategic landscape in which much of its former *raison d'être* has vanished, is struggling to define a valid role for itself -- the new threats to Western security may very well originate beyond the NATO boundaries. The preservation (by past standards, at any rate) of transatlantic solidarity throughout the Gulf crisis and the effectiveness of allied forces and doctrines in Desert Storm have raised the value of NATO stock somewhat, and for the time being it will likely remain the principle organization for military collaboration within Europe. It is as yet unclear whether the WEU will become a "bridge" linking NATO to the EC (the British view) or the defence arm of the Community and thus a cohesive European pillar within NATO (the French and German view).[37] On the basis of its successful naval operations -- not the most demanding of tasks, admittedly -- the WEU will likely acquire a formal "out-of-area" role, perhaps through a "double-hatting" arrangement with NATO's newly-formed Rapid Reaction Corps. This is of course contingent on the Twelve possessing the political will to deploy such a force. Finally, the lessons learned during the Gulf cirisis will undoubtedly influence the outcome of the Intergovernmental Conference on Political Union. The relative ease with which the EC-EPC barrier has been breached suggests that there will be few objections to the formal incorporation of the Political Cooperation mechanism into the Council. Of potentially greater significance will be its effects on the debate surrounding the provisions for a Common Foreign and Security Policy. Under the current proposals, the member states will decide which areas of security policy will be treated by joint action (with decisions taken by majority vote), which will be subject to intergovernmental cooperation (with unanimity required), and which constitute defence matters that fall within the competence of the WEU.[38] If anything, the Gulf experience should encourage caution on the part of the Twelve, for it demonstrates the extent to which individual positions may diverge when basic national interests and traditions are directly at stake. A common defence policy will only become viable when the political and economic integration processes have succeeded in creating sufficient

---

36 Ian Gambles, "Prospects for West European Security Cooperation," *Adelphi Papers*, No. 244, London: IISS, Autumn 1989, p. 37.
37 Catherine Guicherd, "A European Defense Identity: Challenge and Opportunity for NATO," *CRS Report for Congress*, Washington, DC: Congressional Research Service, 12 June 1991, p. 36-37.
38 See ANNEX 1: "Draft Treaty on the Union."

common interests for the member states to willingly relinquish a vital core element of their sovereignty.

To conclude, the Gulf war demonstrates that in such circumstances the Twelve can best defend their collective interests by acting in unison, as the Community, through a common foreign and defence policy. At the same time, it also demonstrates the futility of attempting to pursue such a policy when national differences make agreement impossible, or when the means to take action are absent. In that case, the results are ineffective at best and divisive at worst. The EC members lacked both the political solidarity and the military means to play any more than a secondary part in the conflict. This experience should promote both caution and urgency in their approach to Political Union. At the same time, one should be aware of this particular example's unique features, and not let it serve as a model for all future contingencies:

> The basic problem, . . . in drawing long-term lessons from the Gulf cirisis is that in political terms at least, Iraq's seizure of Kuwait was just about the easiest crisis they could have been presented with. Future out-of-area crises are most unlikely to be so clear cut . . . Trying, therefore, to codify the lessons of the Gulf cirsis might be, at best, pointless and, at worst, dangerously misleading.[39]

One may also argue that the Gulf conflict was an exceedingly anomalous event, and that Europe's poor showing is not as great a source for concern as it may have appeared at the time. As Lawrence Freedman writes:

> The supreme test for the Eurpean Community in its move to a common foreign policy lies in its capacity to cope with the aftermath of the implosion of communism in Europe and this will, in the first instance, require the sorting out of the relationship between its external commercial interests, its external political interests, and its internal development. In this sense, attempting to develop a common capacity to deal with a repetition of the Gulf crisis is a distraction.[40]

---

39 David Buchan, "Whither WEU," *European Affairs*, February/March 1991, p. 70.
40 Freedman (note 10), p. 199.

10

European Responses to the Yugoslav Crisis: An Interim Assessment

*Geoffrey Edwards**

Introduction

No sooner had the Community and its member states begun to assess the lessons of the Gulf conflict than they were faced with an increasingly tense situation in Yugoslavia. If the war in the Gulf had provided an "object lesson" in revealing the limitations of the Community, success in at least ousting Iraq from Kuwait had been achieved through US leadership. In the Yugoslav crisis, the Community and its member states were themselves thrust into the position of leadership, and in a crisis that was far from clearcut as to either its causes or its desired outcome.

While the Gulf war may have been the first "post-Cold War" crisis, it owed little to Cold War issues (though Saddam Hussein may have expected his erstwhile patron, the Soviet Union, to have become involved). The Yugoslav crisis, however, was both a product of indigenous deep-seated national divisions and hatreds and a manifestation of many of the pressures of post-Cold War Europe. It seemed to highlight the tensions that had lain beneath much of the surface of Soviet-dominated Eastern Europe. A great deal was made in the West of the commitment of the newly emancipated countries of Central and Eastern Europe to democratization and marketization and achieving an irreversible movement away from communist and Soviet domination. Rather less was made of the nationalist tensions that had been released.[1] Such tensions, especially over the position of minorities have not always been

---

* The author wishes to acknowledge the considerable help in researching and drafting this chapter provided by Brendan Pearson.
1 See, for example, *The Independent*, 15 April 1991, which reported President Franjo Tudjman of Croatia complaining "that the West talks only of the need for democracy and a free market in Yugoslavia, and ignores the national question."

contained or resolved in the established democracies of the West (indeed, the case of Northern Ireland has been cited as particularly relevant to any discussions of peace-keeping activities in Yugoslavia), but in the East, the combination of democratic experimentation and adverse economic conditions has made it even more difficult.

The divisions between the republics of Yugoslavia, while not new, raised in a particularly acute form the problems of nationalism, national minorities and Europe's territorial boundaries as laid down in 1945. Tensions among the republics had been growing since the death of Tito in 1980, caused in particular by the determination of Serbia to regain control over Yugoslav affairs using both the federal structure to do so and the Communist party. Such division was exacerbated by the moves towards pluralist democracy in Slovenia and Croatia.

But the Yugoslav crisis represented a wider danger, and one that was not easily met. The Conference of Security and Cooperation in Europe (CSCE) or Helsinki process had, for example, emphasized human rights and fundamental freedoms but it had not seriously tackled the question of minorities, at least until the Copenhagen meeting on the Human Dimension in July 1990. The Helsinki Final Act had been based on the inviolability of territorial integrity with boundaries if not immutable, changeable only by peaceful means and not by force. But what had been at issue were the boundaries between the signatories, not internal boundaries, whether merely administrative or representative of different national groupings. At Copenhagen, efforts were made to build further on Helsinki and to address the difficult balance between the rights of individuals and the rights of minority groups, with a more pointed debate on the issue of state allegiance and national loyalties. Ironically, perhaps, Macedonia and non-Yugoslavian Macedonians were an example raised at the meeting which clearly revealed the complexities of the issue and the different interpretations of minorities that were possible. Elsewhere in Eastern Europe, and, of course, the Soviet Union, other cross-cutting national ties and national minorities raised the prospect of disputes and conflicts, whether Czech or Slovak, Hungarian minorities in Romania, the Ukraine or Yugoslavia, Polish minorities in the Ukraine, Lithuania and so on. The problem of Yugoslavia and its constituent republics was therefore one which raised significant questions about peace and security in Europe as a whole as well as giving rise to concern over whether the conflict between them could be contained within Yugoslavia itself.

At the same time, the crisis also raised fundamental questions about the most appropriate and effective institutional structure by which to seek to maintain security in Europe. The Yugoslav conflict revealed almost a plethora of organisations with often overlapping membership, each with a responsibility or potential role in preventing conflict and/or seeking its resolution. They ranged from the pan-European CSCE, via the European Community, NATO, and the

WEU to the Pentagonale, now Hexagonale.[2] To those governments which were members of several (Italy alone being a member of them all), each institution represented a different expression of concern. They signified both an opportunity to promote or reinforce particular interests as well as providing a means of containing or placating different national, domestic pressures. Each body consulted extensively among its membership. Yet the result was largely to assign or delegate primary responsibility to the Community and especially European Political Cooperation (EPC). As Hans-Dietrich Genscher, the German Foreign Minister, had suggested earlier:

> The CSCE process offers the framework of stability within which to establish the peaceful order in Europe from the Atlantic to the Urals which is what we want. The European Community is the anchorage point for the stability of that peaceful view.[3]

If there was a sense of leadership being thrust upon the Community and its member states (EC/12), which obliged them to develop new elements of a common foreign and, indeed, security policy, there was also a sense of relief that, after the Gulf experience, they could adopt and maintain a joint approach. The impact of the Gulf War and the inability of the EC/12 to maintain a common position even before the use of force to oust Iraqi troops from Kuwait had led to different conclusions. Whereas Jacques Delors, the Commission's President, saw the Gulf as an object lesson and therefore a cause for establishing a common foreign and security policy as soon as possible, a view echoed by Chancellor Helmut Kohl, John Major, the British Prime Minister, took the lesson of the Gulf to indicate that a great deal more inter-governmental cooperation was required before a common policy was possible. Given such divergence, President François Mitterrand determined to evaluate the lessons of the Gulf and to consider "Europe's role in all areas" at the highest level.[4] The subsequent summit meeting was to some extent overshadowed by the British initiative to establish Kurdish enclaves in Northern Iraq. Nevertheless, the heads of state and of government as well as others in the Community were clearly aware that the EC/12's performance in the next crisis was fundamental to its credentials as a serious international actor. The test came more quickly than many had anticipated.

Whatever the impact of the EC/12's role on the Yugoslav civil war has been -- and despite some early optimism, the conflict continues at the time of writing

---

2 The Pentagonale of Italy, Austria, Hungary, Czechoslovakia and Yugoslavia, was in 1991 joined by Poland.
3 Quoted by Stanley R. Sloan, "NATO's Future in a New Europe; An American Perspective," *International Affairs*, Vol. 63, No. 3, 1990, pp. 495-511, p. 502.
4 Europe, 11-12 March 1991.

-- common positions have been adopted and have been modified to meet changing circumstances in common, despite great difficulties and pressures. Reactions among the member states have been diverse and assessments of the most appropriate policy instruments to adopt have differed. If, for example, Germany was the most vociferous supporter of early recognition of Slovene and Croatian independence, Spain was among the most determined to continue to treat Yugoslavia as a whole. While France was particularly forward in proposing an "interposition force," the British were adamantly against, and so on. And yet common positions have held. There was and remains a particularly strong sense that the Community could not simply stand aside from a conflict on its doorstep and that despite the risks of becoming involved in an open-ended commitment, positions had to be taken.

The coincidence of the Yugoslav conflict and the Intergovernmental Conference (IGC) on Political Union was not therefore without significance for it has led to a symbiotic relationship between the EC/12's peace efforts and their negotiations on establishing a common foreign and security policy (CFSP) within a European union. The Yugoslav conflict in one sense provides reason for a common policy, indicating a test case for a conflict that while out of the NATO area -- except insofar as it might spill over into Allied territory -- had clear potential repercussions for security in Europe. It also highlights the close interaction between diplomatic, economic and other means, including the possibility of peace-keeping forces, in attempting to resolve such crises, whether in terms of sticks or carrots. Finally, it points to some of the institutional weaknesses and limitations within the existing system and at a rather more practical level than some of the earlier theological debates.

Institutional Responses

This is not the place for either a history of Yugoslavia's descent into civil war[5] or a history of Yugoslavia's relations with the rest of Europe. On the latter, Tito's break with Stalin had allowed Yugoslavia to assume a prized position in relations with the West. Economically, for example, Yugoslavia had a Cooperation Agreement with the European Community under which, by 1991, trade with the Community had reached over 50 per cent of its total (see Appendix I). In addition, it had received significant multilateral as well as bilateral aid under two Financial Protocols. There were also growing expectations that, along with other newly democratizing countries of Central and Eastern Europe, Yugoslavia would be able to negotiate Associate status.

---

5 The reader is referred to Christopher Cviic, *Remaking the Balkans*, London: Pinter, 1991.

Such hopes were tied closely by the Community to the continued unity as well as stability of Yugoslavia. As the Luxembourg Foreign Minister, Jacques F. Poos, then President of the Council, put it, Yugoslavia "could have expectations with respect of its association with the Community if its territorial unity and integrity are safeguarded. Any other attitude could jeopardize internal frontiers in Europe."[6] No hopes were held out for possible membership for breakaway republics, the Italian Foreign Minister, Gianni De Michelis, for example, suggesting that Croatia and Slovenia would receive a cold welcome if they went ahead with and plans for independence.[7] The linkage between unity and closer association was maintained at the end of May 1991 when the bicephelous Presidency of the Community (the President of the Council, the Luxembourg Prime Minister, Jacques Santer, and the President of the Commission, Jacques Delors) visited Belgrade in an attempt to prevent the further development of the crisis over the Serbian refusal to allow the rotating Yugoslav Presidency to fall to Croatia. With the Second Financial Protocol on aid due to expire on 30 June, its successor was also discussed (see Appendix II), as well as the extension of the PHARE programme, coordinated by the Community on behalf of the Group of 24. The linkage between continued benefits, territorial integrity and human rights was also made very directly by the US administration, including President Bush, with US aid frozen from early May.[8]

The deepening crisis was, however, the subject of growing concern with further discussions among the EC/12 and in the CSCE Council which met for the first time in Berlin on 19 June. Whereas the EC/12 were able to insist that the effective functioning of the rotating federal presidency, dialogue between the republics, the improvement of minority rights and continued economic reform were the price of continued aid,[9] the CSCE, which, of course, included the Yugoslav Foreign Minister, Budimir Loncar, could agree only to a rather more anodyne statement that:

> ... Ministers expressed their friendly concern and their support for the democratic development, unity and territorial integrity of Yugoslavia based on economic reforms, full application of human rights in all parts of Yugoslavia, including the rights of minorities, and the peaceful solution of the current crisis in the country.[10]

---

6   *Europe*, 10 April 1991.
7   Christopher Cviic (note 5), p. 95.
8   See *The Independent*, 15 April and again 9 May 1991.
9   *Financial Times*, 3 June 1991.
10 *Europe*, 20 June 1991.

In response, the Luxembourg Presidency of the Community sought a more coherent position for the EC/12 along with the United States, Austria and Hungary. That position included an agreement among the Twelve not to acknowledge any unilateral declarations of independence on the part of any Yugoslav republics as "a unilateral act could not bring any solution."[11] Slovenia and Croatia declared their independence on 25 June.

The declarations and the countermeasures taken by federal forces were discussed at the European Council of 28-29 June. Agreement was reached on a number of options including: the despatch to Belgrade of the Foreign Ministers of the Troika (that is, the present, immediately past and immediately succeeding Presidencies of the Council, which in June 1991 was made up of Luxembourg, Italy and the Netherlands); the suspension of Community aid if the Troika's mission failed to bring about a ceasefire; and a decision to invoke the CSCE's emergency consultations procedure. The visit of the ministerial Troika was seen as important, in part because it meant the inclusion of the Italian Foreign Minister, which lent the visit both greater political weight and expertise. But also, as the Italian Prime Minister, Giulio Andreotti, was reported as saying: "A simple appeal was not enough. The world . . . is full of appeals which are ignored and what is happening on our doorstep requires more than a 'bureaucratic diplomatic' approach."[12] The aim, as an (unnamed) Italian official put it, was as follows:

> What we are saying to the federal leadership is that there must be an immediate ceasefire and that all troops must return to their barracks. As a quid pro quo, the breakaway republics should suspend their application for immediate independence and come to the negotiating table.[13]

The Troika's mission began at 5 pm on Friday 28 June and was completed at 5 am on 29 June. It was, the Luxembourg Foreign Minister, Jacques F. Poos, declared, "the hour of Europe, not the hour of the Americans."[14] However, the fragility of the agreement was revealed when the Yugoslavs failed to agree on what they had signed with the Troika. The three Foreign Ministers therefore returned to Belgrade on Sunday, 30 June, to salvage the agreement and, using the threat of freezing all Community aid, appeared to have been successful.

Slovenia and Croatia thereupon asked the Community to provide observers to supervise the ceasefire and the withdrawal of federal troops. Although

---

11   *Europe*, 24-25 June 1991.
12   *Europe*, 29 June 1991.
13   *The Independent*, 29 June 1991.
14   *Financial Times*, 1 July 1991.

willing, the Community initially preferred to coordinate its action with the CSCE. A meeting of the Conflict Prevention Centre in Vienna agreed only on an immediate ceasefire and a return of troops to their barracks. However, at the Berlin CSCE Council meeting earlier in June, the German Foreign Minister, Hans-Dietrich Genscher, as President of the Council, had won agreement on an emergency consultation procedure whereby if a meeting was requested by at least 12 CSCE participating states no other state could veto it. Although the CSCE's Permanent Secretariat in Prague was scarcely prepared,[15] the Committee of Senior Officials met according to the procedure on 3 July and agreed to two steps: first, to offer their "good offices" to promote dialogue among the parties, though only with the agreement of the Yugoslav authorities; and secondly, on 5 July, after rather more discussion, to ask the Community to organize "a mission to help stabilize a ceasefire," again to operate at the invitation of and in cooperation with the Yugoslav authorities.[16]

At French instigation an emergency meeting of EC Foreign Ministers was also held on 5 July. Again, the Ministers stood back from recognizing the breakaway republics although Hans-Dietrich Genscher was quoted as saying: "If it had been left to me alone, specific mention would have been made of the need to recognize the independence of Slovenia and Croatia in the event of future military action." On the other hand, Roland Dumas, the French Foreign Minister, was reported as talking about the dangers of some republics falling under "foreign influcence" which was taken to refer to Austrian influence, and beyond that, perhaps, the influence of Germany.[17] However, the EC/12 agreed to an arms embargo and to freeze certain elements of Community aid. In addition, the Foreign Ministers took up the task designated to them by the CSCE of preparing a mission of observers, and undertook also to send the Troika back (by now the Netherlands having replaced Luxembourg as President and Portugal displacing Italy) together with the Commissioner responsible for Mediterranean issues, Abel Matutes, to try to broker a further agreement between the republics and the federal authorities.

The result of the Troika's mission was the Brioni agreement of 8 July on the peaceful resolution of the Yugoslav crisis between the Croatian and Slovene republics and the federal authorities. The agreement was immediately sanctioned by the parliaments of the two republics (on 9 and 10 July respectively). It allowed for observers from the Community (and possibly

---

15 Nils Elliassen, head of the Secretariat was reported as saying: "It will take quite a bit of work. We have to get translators, security, photocopiers, tables, whatever. We have done our homework - but I didn't expect only a week after Berlin to be faced with this possibility." *The Independent*, 29 June 1991.
16 *The Independent*, 6 July 1991.
17 Ibid.

elsewhere) to monitor the ceasefire in Slovenia and "if need be" in Croatia.[18] The details were worked out in an EPC meeting on 10 July and were then the subject of a memorandum of understanding signed by the Dutch Presidency and Slovene, Croatian and federal representatives. The monitoring group was to be made up of civilian and military personnel (the latter unarmed and in civilian clothes) from the member states and a small number from the European Commission. Since it was an intergovernmental decision, the British government, among others, insisted that monitors should be paid for by their national governments. An initial group of 20 led by a former Dutch ambassador to Belgrade, Jo van der Valk, left for Yugoslavia and Slovenia on 15 July.

The Brioni agreement was seen by the Dutch Foreign Minister, Hans van den Broek, as "a last chance"[19] and by Hans-Dietrich Genscher as "proof of the European Community's ability to act."[20] The withdrawal of federal forces from Slovenia enabled the monitoring team to fulfill their duties relatively straightforwardly, but they were faced almost immediately with the escalation of violence in Croatia and the question of whether the Brioni agreement included the introduction of monitors there. Despite the lack of an effective ceasefire, EPC officials discussed the possibility of a ministerial decision on extending the monitoring mission on 24 July, the German attitude being that expressed by Hans-Dietrich Genscher that such action "is absolutely necessary to help calm down the situation."[21]

Foreign Ministers of the Twelve met Yugoslav federal ministers and representatives from Bosnia and Macedonia (but not, despite Hans-Dietrich Genscher's criticisms, representatives from Slovenia and Croatia) on 29 July. The EC/12 offered to extend the monitoring mission, increase the numbers involved and include participation from other CSCE states. They also offered to revise the Community's position on aid as soon as negotiations on Yugoslavia's future had begun. As a further incentive to the federal authorities to halt military activities, the Twelve also offered to send the Troika back to Yugoslavia to begin more talks. Because of continued fighting, however, monitors were able to enter Croatia only at the beginning of September.

Peace-Making and Peace-Keeping

Since the Brioni agreement the EC/12 have sought to pursue further the dual aims of peace-making and peace-keeping. On the one hand, the EC/12 offered a further Troika visit, described by the Yugoslav Prime Minister, Ante Markovic

---

18 *Europe*, 15 July 1991.
19 van den Broek to the European Parliament. See: *Europe*, 10 July 1991.
20 *Europe*, 11 July 1991.
21 *Europe*, 25 July 1991.

-- significantly at the Pentagonale/Hexagonale meeting in Dubrovnik in July -- as the Troika going to "a small peace conference . . . in Belgrade."[22] Certainly the Dutch Presidency became increasingly concerned with the idea of such a conference, not least in order to placate growing political pressures especially in Germany to break EC ranks by recognizing Slovenia and Croatia. The French, with German support, had also recommended the idea at the Twelve's meeting on 27 July of arbitration, with a five member committee of Community, Yugoslav and Serbian and Croatian jurists. In order to explore such possibilities, Political Directors of the Twelve had already sent the Dutch ambassador to France to Yugoslavia "to bring together the federal and republican authorities in order to ask them officially their intentions on the opening of negotiations between them and the role they expect the EC to play in the region."[23] However, the visit of the Troika met with little success because of the intransigence of the Serbian authorities. Nevertheless, despite this lack of headway, the EC/12 urged "the collegiate Presidency to convene forthwith negotiations on the future of Yugoslavia. They express their readiness to convene such a conference themselves if necessary."[24]

The withdrawal of the Troika and the growing exasperation in Western Europe over the failure to bring about a ceasefire led to increasing calls, especially in Germany, though also in Italy, for recognition of Slovenia and Croatia. Recognition was (and continues to be) seen as one of the most potent if symbolic of policy instruments, employable, of course, only once and fraught with dangers both as to the expectations of protection then aroused among the republics and as a precedent for others in Europe. At the same time, other member states, including the British were moving towards an acceptance that economic sanctions would have to be introduced as the only means by which to bring pressure on the Serbians, including oil sanctions under United Nations auspices, however long-term their effects on Serbia and costly for some of the Community. Others, notably France, saw the possibilities of taking further action by means of an interposition force. The pressures on the Dutch Presidency to keep the EC/12 together were therefore considerable. It was not perhaps surprising that they and the Twelve took the opportunity of the possibility of another ceasefire to pursue the idea of a peace conference proposal together with the French proposals for arbitration.[25] The Serbian President, Slobodan Milosevic, significantly on a visit to Paris, agreed to look at the proposals, adding: "Europe can help us in solving this problem

---

22 *Europe*, 29-30 July 1991.
23 *Europe*, 22-23 July 1991.
24 *Europe*, 22 August 1991.
25 *Europe*, 29 August 1991.

politically, can help us through economic cooperation but the presence of a foreign army would not contribute to a solution to this problem."[26]

While the Dutch had envisaged the peace conference beginning on 16 September, others pressed the need to exploit Serbian agreement to hold it as soon as possible. The major precondition was that there should be a viable ceasefire in being, verified by EC monitors. However, as one Dutch official put it:

> The whole country is brimming with weapons. Nobody can guarantee that not one single shot will be fired between now and the conference... But equally, you can't have a conference if full-scale fighting is going on. You have to judge where the balance is.[27]

It was a problem that beset the conference throughout. The launch of the Conference, under the chairmanship of Lord Carrington, the former British Foreign Secretary and Secretary General of NATO, was agreed at the EPC meeting of 3 September. Lord Carrington was to be supported by a small secretariat -- which included a Commission representative -- located in the Dutch Foreign Ministry. The aim was to complete the conference by mid-October -- the expiry date for the monitoring missions provided for in the Brioni agreement;[28] it was not expected to continue much longer and it would appear that no provisions were made for it to continue beyond the Dutch Presidency. Working with Lord Carrington would be three working groups, on the constitutional future of Yugoslavia, the question of minorities, and on economic relations among the republics, together with the arbitration committee made up of three eminent Community judges[29] and two further persons to be chosen by the Yugoslavs. The meeting opened on 12 September, the parties having been invited to put their objectives to the chairman beforehand.

At the same time as peace-making efforts were being explored, the Twelve were also giving increased attention to the possibility of a peace-keeping or interposition force. The French had raised the possibility on 29 July, recognizing that it would be an important innovation and that a stage by stage development was necessary but that "it is not forbidden to imagine that the Community could go much further."[30] Although there had been an adverse reaction from several member states, especially the British, Hans van den Broek, the Dutch Foreign Minister, had pointed out immediately before setting

---

26 *Europe*, 30 August 1991.
27 *Financial Times*, 4 September 1991.
28 *Europe*, 4 September 1991.
29 Robert Badinter (France), Roman Herzog (Germany) and Aldo Corrasanti (Italy).
30 *Europe*, 29-30 July 1991.

out for Yugoslavia that if there was no end to the violence "then probably further appeals will be launched in favour of sending something like a peace force to the country, probably through WEU." His views were echoed by Jacques F. Poos, the Luxembourg Foreign Minister and fellow member of the Troika, and also by Hans-Dietrich Genscher.[31] If such statements were designed to encourage Serbia to the negotiating table, they failed. They were nonetheless accurate for, with the collapse of the Troika's initiative, the French urged an emergency meeting of WEU to consider such a force.[32]

The possibility of some form of military intervention in Yugoslavia was discussed in Europe's various institutions against a background of growing concern, exasperation and despair that so little impact was being made on the situation and especially on Serbian intransigence. In early August, Hans-Dietrich Genscher had declared:

> The Serbian government has clearly taken over responsibility for developments in Yugoslavia. The Serbian leadership has not only blocked a ceasefire, it has destroyed the basis for negotiations and for peacefully settling the future of Yugoslavia's people.[33]

But while Germany had long been in favour of recognising the breakaway republics and critical of Serbia, the summer saw the gradual swing of opinion against the Serbian leadership. The Dutch special envoy, Henry Wijnaendts, offered conclusive evidence of the federal army's support for Serbian militants, adding: "We cannot continue to stand idly by . . . It is a war here. If there is one conclusion . . . it is that a ceasefire will not be effective unless there is an impartial foreign presence."[34] It was a view also expressed by the Italian Foreign Minister only a few days earlier, after a meeting with his counterparts from Greece and Bulgaria.[35]

The issue of some form of intervention force was raised in a number of different fora. Germany, for example, raised it in a CSCE framework with a proposal not only for a CSCE defence force but also a CSCE Security Council, which if the model of the United Nations was followed, could authorize such a force.[36] The French raised the possibility in two fora: directly in the context of WEU which was, after all, given a particularly significant place in their proposals for a common foreign and security policy; but they also pursued it more indirectly, through the UN Security Council. The latter, on a joint French,

---

31   *Europe*, 3 August 1991.
32   *Financial Times*, 6 August 1991.
33   *International Herald Tribune*, 6 August 1991.
34   *Financial Times*, 30 August 1991.
35   *Europe*, 28 August 1991.
36   *The Independent*, 12 September 1991.

British and Belgian proposal, gave its full support to the various collective peace efforts being made and also its support for measures to assist and support the monitors of the ceasefire, which was regarded by Roland Dumas, the French Foreign Minister, as going in the same direction as the Security Council Resolution which had allowed for intervention in Iraq.[37]

The bulk of the discussion on peace-keeping roles was carried out in the WEU -- amidst, according to press reports, some acrimony. The Dutch were prepared to raise the issue largely in order to prevent the Germans from recognising Slovenia and Croatia although it also reinforced the sense of purpose that lay behind the peace conference initiative. Others were more cautious, seeing it as possibly undercutting the peace conference. As a last resort and if a ceasefire was in being, it was known that the French, Italians and Belgians were in favour of a peace-keeping force. The Portuguese and the Danes (a non-member of WEU) remained unconvinced. The British were even more reluctant to envisage such a force, the example of Northern Ireland being cited as a situation into which it had been easy to introduce troops and so difficult to get them out. Much was also made of the likely need for substantial and strongly armed forces in the absence of a genuine ceasefire, given the size and sophistication of much of the Yugoslav armoury. As the Foreign Secretary, Douglas Hurd, put it: "I am very anxious that we should not exaggerate what we can do, or pretend that we in Western Europe can substitute for the lack of will for peace in Yugoslavia."[38]

But the key was, as usual perhaps, Germany. The restrictive interpretation placed on the Basic Law by the German government during the Gulf War seemed to many to disbar any German troops from participating in any intervention force since Yugoslavia, strictly speaking, was out of the NATO area in which German forces could operate. As a result, as one "senior British official" suggested: "If the Germans do not intend to participate, they would do better to shut up."[39] On the other hand, even if German forces were made available -- with or without a constitutional amendment -- and the Chancellor and the Foreign Minister had given strong support for such action, others raised the question of whether German participation was actually desirable. While it was argued in Germany that: "The second World War is virtually forgotten . . . The Croatian fascist alliance is forgotten and so is the British alliance with Tito and the British role in creating the Yugoslav state."[40] It was suggested in England that:

---

37 *Europe*, 27 September 1991.
38 *The Times*, 21 September 1991.
39 *Financial Times*, 18 September 1991.
40 Ibid.

So when Genscher argues for a tougher stand against Serbia and (for) EC recognition of Slovenia and Croatia in the Yugoslav civil war, he rekindles memories of when Croatians and Germans fought side by side in the Nazi cause. This debars Germany from participating in any armed intervention, and thus irritates those European partners who would be obliged to implement the policy he advocates.[41]

Divisions over a possible peace-keeping force were clearly deep, but agreement was reached by the EC/12 to give the WEU a mandate to examine ways in which the activities of monitors could be supported so as to make their contribution more effective. An indication of the disagreements that had arisen was suggested by the additional statement that: "It is their understanding that no military intervention is contemplated and that, before a reinforced monitor mission were established, a ceasefire would have to be agreed . . . The Community and its member states would wish to have the opportunity to examine and endorse the conclusions of the study."[42] Nonetheless, there was a consensus that WEU should explore four options: logistic support for EC/12 monitors which might require some 2.000-3.000 personnel; escort and protection of monitors by armed military forces, some 5.000-6.000 men; a lightly-armed peacekeeping force of military personnel and additional monitors to police the ceasefire, some 7.500-10.000 in all; and finally a full scale peace-keeping exercise requiring between 20.000-30.000 personnel. These were discussed at a WEU meeting on 30 September to which non-WEU EC and NATO members had been invited as observers. It was a meeting also that followed almost indistinguishably from that of the EC Foreign Ministers. The results though were clearly a compromise for all that was proposed was that WEU was to be put at the disposal of the Community and Lord Carrington as coordinator of the peace conference.

The Attitudes of the Member States

It was the opinion of one member of the European Parliament that:

> Given the cacophony among the Twelve foreign ministers who refuse to transfer foreign and security policy to a common executive, one cannot expect more from the Community than what it is already doing.[43]

---

41 Professor Lawrence Freedman, in: *The Independent*, 12 September 1991.
42 *The Independent*, 21 September 1991.
43 Klaus Hänsch (Germany, SPD), in: *Europe*, 20 September 1991.

Certainly complaints that the Community were not doing enough were frequent, in the European and in national parliaments and in the media. Whether the EC/12 could have had more impact on the situation in Yugoslavia, by, for example, imposing full economic sanctions, is a moot point. It is clear, though, that there is a difficult balance to be kept between national domestic pressures and the desire, perhaps need, for the EC/12 to stick together to counter in the legacy of the Gulf crisis and to give credibility to the discussions going on within the Intergovernmental Conference on Political Union on a common foreign and security policy.

The impact and the implications of the Yugoslav civil war were and remain different for Community member states. It was significant, for example, that the two EC member states which were geographical neighbours of Yugoslavia, Italy and Greece, were among those who long favoured treating Yugoslavia as a single entity. Many of the problems they faced with the outbreak of hostilities they held in common such as: the possibility that the conflict could spill over into their territories -- with the theoretical possibility of thereby bringing NATO into the conflict; the prospect of a mass of refugees -- the Italians having suffered already in the summer of 1991 from a massive influx of Albanian refugees; and the disruption of trade -- Greece in particular suffering because of the disruption of trade routes. But there were other factors too which could not be ignored including that of national minorities, whether "Yugoslav" minorities (and particularly i.e. Macedonians) or simply the policies being adopted towards minorities -- the Italian position on minorities not being missed by those in the Alto-Adige or Southern Tyrol. Moreover, in the case of Italy, Cviic has suggested that its support for Yugoslavia:

> . . . derived from historical experiences that it is easier to do business with -- and obtain concessions from -- a strong government in Belgrade than those in Zagreb and Ljubljana. It is, of course, easier, when it comes to accommodating Italy's aspirations and interests in the Adriatic region, for the more distant (and therefore also more relaxed) Serbs to be cooperative than for the Croats and the Slovenes who are right next door to Italy . . .[44]

And while such a realpolitik interpretation may seem exaggerated, there was also a further concern that, on the one hand, contributed to Italy's changed position on recognition of Slovenia and Croatia, and, on the other hand, helps to explain the regional initiatives taken by Italy during the crisis, namely, a concern over German leadership. The Pentagonale was after all conceived, at

---

44   Christopher Cviic (note 5), p. 99.

least in part, as a counterweight to German potential dominance in Central Europe.

A similar concern has been discerned in French policy towards the crisis and recognition of Slovenia and Croatia. The very strength of German opinion in favour of early recognition created suspicion, seemingly invoking the prospect of an area from the Rhine to the Croatian border dominated by German economic and political interests. An Austrian official suggested, for example, that: "We have the impression that Paris fears once more a Germanic influence in that part of the world of which we would be the vector."[45] Certainly some sectors of the German press did not always ignore such suspicions, the Frankfurter Allgemeine Zeitung, for example, in an outstandingly hostile article, put French Yugoslav policy into a wider perspective:

> In the new Europe, of which France is no longer the heartland and Germany is no longer the frontline eastern border member of the Community of free democracies, French influence can be sure to decline. That is why the crisis in Yugoslavia is an acid test, much more so than the Gulf War, of the Community's future . . . [46]

The cause of the outburst had been some reported remarks of the former French Gaullist Prime Minister, Michel Debré, to the effect that France's two historic roles were the containment of Germany and the containment of the Arab world in Europe. These were seen as relevant to continuing French support for the unity of Yugoslavia because of German support for Slovenia and the possibility of a Moslem state in Bosnia. But while Michel Debré may have represented certain elements of French political thinking (and one might argue about the motives behind President Mitterrand's call for an Intergovernmental Conference on Political Union as German unification proceeded apace, or about France's long-standing position on Turkey's membership of the Community), few in France were prepared to put French policy in quite such terms. It was, however, the case that until well into the summer of 1991, French policy was to support the Yugoslav federal authorities, President Mitterrand insisting in late June, that the EC "must not be accused of trivialising the territorial integrity of Yugoslavia."[47] And if this set him at odds with the German Chancellor, Helmut Kohl, it was nonetheless regarded as an important factor in restraining Germany from recognising the republics.

French views began to change over the summer in response to events in Yugoslavia, and encouraged by Germany. At his meeting with Chancellor Kohl

---

45 *The Independent*, 1 July 1991.
46 *Frankfurter Allgemeine Zeitung*, 15 August 1991.
47 *The Independent*, 1 July 1991.

in September 1991, for example, President Mitterrand's position had become: "If Croatia wants to secede . . . I don't see any reason why Yugoslavia should prevent it."[48] The question, as Roland Dumas put it on French television, was "no longer to know if these republics were independent but how they will be so."[49] The principle of self-determination had been accepted in the circumstances as over-riding that of the inviolability of frontiers. As part of the Community's contribution, the French had proposed an arbitration panel -- initially, of course, to arbitrate on the internal borders of Yugoslavia, an indication itself of the extent to which the principle of non-interference in domestic affairs had given way to others -- and an interposition force through EPC and WEU. It did so with a reportedly helpful gesture towards Germany that those who could not send troops might send police officers and logistic support.[50] The need to keep Germany in step was considered vital. It was necessary not simply in order to exercise maximum influence in Yugoslavia but also because of the wider perspective of Europe and stability. In that broader view, a European Union with responsibility for a common foreign and security policy was seen as of critical significance in continuing to anchor German policy firmly to that of France.

Since the implications for the Intergovernmental Conference on Political Union could not be overlooked, the British had tended towards caution over EC/12 actions in Yugoslavia. In public at least the British government appeared to favour the continued unity of Yugoslavia, the Prime Minister, John Major, agreeing with his Greek counterpart, Konstantin Mitsotakis, in mid-September that there were dangers in recognising the two republics.[51] There were though suggestions that no strong position was being pressed within EPC or the European Council. As the crisis deepened so sections of the British press became increasingly concerned that not enough was being done by the Community.[52] There was, however, little consensus on what should be done. It was suggested, perhaps only a little unfairly, that it was easier to get the British

---

48 *Le Monde*, 22-23 September 1991.
49 *Europe*, 16-17 September 1991.
50 *Financial Times*, 1 August 1991.
51 *Europe*, 16 September 1991
52 *The Financial Times*, editorial of 1 July 1991, put it as follows: "Clearly the institutional mechanisms of the post-cold war European order are not yet in place. But in real life institutions are more often improvised to deal with specific crises than built from a comprehensive architectural design. The Yugoslav crisis has at least given some tangible reality to the issues discussed recently by the CSCE foreign ministers in Berlin, and by the EC heads of government in Luxembourg. The EC's need for a common foreign and security policy, and the need for Europe as a whole for institutions to manage conflicts and settle disputes peacefully, is being all too graphically demonstrated."

involved in the Middle East or the South Atlantic than it was to win its support in a European crisis.[53] This was seen as especially so when the United States seemed to be playing no part:

> In Britain above all, politicians, officials and journalists -- at least until now -- think it quite normal to take the beat of our foreign policy from Washington, 3000 miles away, and somehow unnatural, even monstrous, to take it from Brussels...[54]

Certainly British involvement in the Gulf had been widely supported as a necessary, practical response to Iraq's invasion (there being little of the jingoism that had characterised previous occasions when British troops had been in action). In the Yugoslav crisis, while there was support for the introduction of EC/12 monitors and for the peace conference initiative with Lord Carrington as chairman, there was little agreement on further measures.

It was the question of expanding the Community's contribution to a peacekeeping role that caused particular problems. There was reluctance on two grounds, one practical, the second, more of principle. The practical problem was that of the sheer scale of activity that might be required given the difficulty of establishing any lasting ceasefire, and the length of time forces might actually be required. The question of principle involved the repercussions of such a force and its organization for Atlantic relations. On the question of Yugoslavia itself, the US had willingly taken a backseat, preferring, while attempting to deal with the Middle East and the Soviet Union, to leave matters to the EC/12 and prepared to be kept informed via normal bilateral channels and by means of the CSCE. However, the British concern was over the implications of EC/12 action for a common foreign and security policy within the IGC negotiations. While the visceral Atlanticism of Margaret Thatcher was being modified by her successor, the British government remained particularly sensitive to US ambivalence over European moves to take on a separate defence identity, especially during a period when NATO itself and the degree of US involvement were under review.

Despite possible problems over the Basic Law, the German government was strongly supportive of French peace-keeping proposals -- as they were of French defence and security proposals within the IGC. The Secretary General of the CDU, Volker Rühe, for example, urged Britain and France to go ahead in establishing a peace-keeping force regardless of Germany's constitutional position. Germany, he suggested, would provide logistical support.[55] The

---

53   Godfrey Hodgson, in: *The Independent*, 8 August 1991.
54   Ibid.
55   *Financial Times*, 1 August 1991.

German press and public opinion appeared overwhelmingly in favour of an early recognition of Slovenia and Croatia, whatever the consequences, a not particularly extreme view being suggested by the Frankfurter Allgemeine Zeitung in July that:

> ... the Western world must recognize Croatia (and equally Slovenia) as a state and then protect it with all means, even armed force if necessary, until it is able to fend off the Serbian aggressors itself.[56]

The groundswell of opinion in favour of the two republics was the result of a belief, as summed up by Volker Rühe, that:

> We won our unity through the right to self-determination ... If we Germans think everything else in Europe can follow a status quo policy and do not recognise the right of self-determination in Slovenia and Croatia, then we have no moral or political credibility.[57]

It was a theme echoed frequently by the Foreign Minister and the Chancellor. Helmut Kohl, for example, declared:

> The peoples of Yugoslavia must be free to choose their own future. Free Europe must stand beside them ... The importance of the principle of self-determination is that much more evident for Germans because by means of self-determination our nation was able to regain its unity.[58]

The strength of political opinion became even greater as the situation worsened in Croatia, making it ever more difficult for the German government to hold to the EC/12 position. The threat of recognition was employed frequently in the hope that it would ensure the implementation of the Brioni agreement, for example, or keep Serbia at the peace conference. At the beginning of September, Hans-Dietrich Genscher declared that: "The hour of recognition of Slovenia and Croatia approaches with each missile fired by your cannons and tanks. We cannot witness these events without taking action."[59] In view of the constant criticism that neither Germany nor the Community were doing enough, it was perhaps not surprising that Genscher sought to explore the possibilities offered by the CSCE, though inevitably the impact was disappointing because of the presence of the Yugoslav authorities with a veto.

---

56 As quoted in *The Independent*, 3. August 1991.
57 *Financial Times*, 4 July 1991.
58 *The Independent*, 5 July 1991.
59 *Europe*, 5 September 1991.

Moreover, Genscher was constrained, if constraint was needed, by Chancellor Kohl who, whether influenced by President Mitterrand or simply reminded by him of the importance of maintaining solidarity during discussions on Political Union, was also prepared to withstand public pressure and maintained the EC/12 line.

As for other member states, their position varied according to the particular issue. Spain very clearly supported the continuation of Yugoslav unity and was as equally clearly concerned with the possible impact on its own provinces if the Community did not. The Greeks too preferred to deal with Belgrade and were anxious that proposals for economic sanctions should be postponed for as long as possible. The Portuguese and the Danes were hostile to a peace-keeping force, as were the Irish unless under UN auspices, though the Belgians were prepared for such a force under WEU control.

The Impact on the European Institutions

In the middle of these divergent pressures, the Luxembourg and then the Dutch Presidencies had to try to hold the ring. At the same time, of course, they were also responsible for moving the various difficult and contentious dossiers involved in the two Intergovernmental Conferences and for dealing with the rest of the business of the Community and EPC -- including, for example, the completion of the Internal Market programme, reactions to the disintegration of the Soviet Union, the coup against President Gorbachev and so on.

The load of the Presidency of the Council has been steadily increasing, creating ever greater burdens especially for the smaller states. Of course, they can rely on the Council Secretariat and, since 1986, the small Political Secretariat, but the political responsibility as well as the work of chairing meetings, mediating among member states, liaising with other Community institutions and representing the EC/12 both in multilateral fora, including the CSCE, and bilateral negotiations continues to rest with the Presidency.[60] They are not always therefore particularly well prepared for managing crises wherever they might occur. As Pijpers[61] has pointed out, some two-thirds of the Dutch Ministry of Foreign Affairs are development specialists. There is little, or at least was little, expertise as far as Balkan politics were concerned; neither the Dutch nor the Luxemburgers before them (nor even the Portugese who follow them on 1 January 1992) have had extensive interests in the area.

---

60   For a discussion of such tasks and national reactions to them see: Colm O'Nuallain (ed.), *The Presidency of the European Council of Ministers*, London: Croom Helm, 1985.
61   Alfred Pijpers (ed.), *The European Community at the Crossroads*, Dordrecht: Martinus Nijhoff, forthcoming 1992.

There has thus been considerable pressure on manpower with a number of diplomats and others with Balkan experience recalled from retirement or switched from other posts.

The greater use of the Troika has in some ways added to the burden of the Presidency. Whereas individual Presidencies have frequently indulged in fact-finding missions in the past -- once condemned as "political tourism" -- the role of the Troika as representing the EC/12 has grown in significance. The Troika's use in the Yugoslav crisis being both indicative of this and a further encouragement of it. Greater use has not simply been because of the greater continuity allowed in EC/12 representation but because, despite occasional slip-ups and disagreements, the representative character of the Troika itself is enhanced, especially when the Presidency is held by one of the smaller member states. Greater weight, in other words, may be given to the position of the EC/12 when represented by the Troika (though perhaps the emphasis should be on "may").

However, it remains the case that the Troika represents the agreed position of the EC/12, even if other member states deviate from it. Such deviation may be more common when the Presidency is held by a series of smaller member states, the incentives for the larger states to put their own individual gloss on a position or even seek to make their own individual contribution is sometimes great. It is a moot point, however, whether the Presidency/Troika would have had any greater impact in the Yugoslav case if it had been held by larger member states. However, the switch in the Presidency/Troika when the Dutch took over from Luxemburg and the Portugese displaced the Italians, may have caused an element of confusion, may even perhaps have suggested the weaknesses of collective leadership, but it hardly affected the outcome. Nonetheless, it raises a serious question in the perspective of an agreed common foreign and security policy within an enlarged European union: should the Presidency/Troika, the formal representative and negotiator of the EC and its member states (whether with or without a representative from the Commission), be left to the vagaries of the alphabet? Should consideration be given to the delegation of specific tasks to individual states or to the Commission or to others? In the Yugoslav case, there was perhaps a sense of relief in the Dutch Foreign Ministry that Lord Carrington was prepared to interpret broadly the role of chairman of the peace conference and so relieve the Presidency of some of the work.

That is not to suggest that either the Luxemburgers or the Dutch provided little leadership. They have, after all, witnessed the introduction of two new policy instruments in addition to the greater use of the Troika -- the ceasefire monitors and the peace conference with its panel of arbitration -- suggesting that there is considerable flexibility within EPC. On the other hand, the fact that the peace conference is run largely from one room with two telephones in the

Dutch Foreign Ministry suggests the pressure on resources for some member states. And yet the smaller countries probably continue to believe that the rotating Presidency is an important antidote to the tendency of the larger member states to attempt to set the agenda -- or at least press home their own positions as the French and German Foreign Ministers attempted to do with an unscheduled press conference against that of the Presidency.[62]

If the introduction of new policy instruments reflects a degree of flexiblility, so too has the organization of business during the crisis. There had already been a considerable blurring of the distinction between the discussion of Community business and that of EPC. The Yugoslav crisis saw a similar blurring of discussions on foreign and security policy. This was particularly noticeable in the movement from General Affairs Council to EPC meeting to WEU Council meeting on 30 September, Denmark, Ireland and Greece being invited to attend the latter as observers. There remain, of course, clear distinctions between the decisions of each institution. However, in the light of the various proposals for a common foreign and security policy, the degree of flexibility in practice in response to a crisis suggests that there is room for compromise.

The European Council has hitherto provided the forum in which such issues, whether Community, EPC or security issues, could be discussed. It was perhaps fortuitous that the European Council was meeting immediately after the declarations of independence by Slovenia and Croatia and the moves by the federal authorities, and that they could despatch the Troika to Belgrade straightaway. Jaques Santer, the Luxemburg Prime Minister, was led to suggest that these actions added up to "a common foreign and security policy even before . . . [it] had found its way into the future treaty on the Union." But he also considered that the decisions represented a "qualitative advance which allows one to affirm that the European Council no longer has the aspect of a classic diplomatic conference."

Such a development had been discernable over the past decade despite the disagreements and differences among Community leaders. It had in some ways been helped by the longevity of many of the leading actors, with the absence of Margaret Thatcher after more than a decade in office highlighting the extent of their consensus. But any greater sense of community rather than of a diplomatic conference was not simply the result of a growing familiarity among the members. It was, too, though in some senses paradoxically, the result of "sub-Community" activity, of increasing bilateral meetings among leaders and their ministers. The significance of the Mitterrand-Kohl meeting in September, for

---

62 Reports of the undignified rush by the French and German Foreign Ministers put their point of view before that of the Presidency after an informal meeting of Foreign Ministers is to be found in *The Independent*, 11 October 1991.

example, lay in part in reconciling France to the independence of the republics and Germany to the common line of non-recognition; the meeting of the German and Italian Foreign Ministers also in September sought to increase the pressure for recognition if the peace process collapsed; the Anglo-Greek summit sought to strengthen those against premature recognition and so on. They and others reflect a qualitative change in the nature of Community politics. They have had their counterparts, too, in the discussions over the formalisation and extension of the embryonic common foreign and security policy that began to emerge during the summer of 1991 along with the myriad of other issues in the IGC framework. They represent at the highest levels the need to find allies and build coalitions across a range of issues that finds an echo less in traditional diplomacy than in domestic politics.

Some Preliminary Conclusions

The EC/12 have had a number of aims in the Yugoslav cirisis above all to contain the conflict within as limited an area as possible, to try to bring about a peaceful solution as quickly as possible and, in attempting to balance the seemingly incompatible principles of self-determination and the inviolability of frontiers, to ensure acceptance of the principle that change cannot be brought about by force. In doing so the EC/12 inevitably revealed their strengths and weaknesses. On the one hand they have developed through the Troika, the use of monitors and the peace conference new instruments of policy. They have shown considerably greater unity in adverse circumstances than during the Gulf cirisis -- even if it has sometimes been a close run thing. For, on the other hand, there has been continuing tension over the recognition of Slovenia and Croatia, especially when several member states had a necessity to look over their shoulders at the possible domestic ramifications of doing so, and when others became alarmed at the possible precedents that might be created elsewhere in Europe. There was tension, too, over moving beyond monitoring to a fuller peace-keeping role, again an issue complicated by wider considerations, in this case, the establishment of a defence identity within a European Union.

But with the worsening of the conflict in Yugoslavia it was not surprising that there was rising criticism that the Community and the member states were not doing enough. With so few exceptions to the peaceful transformation of Eastern Europe, opinion was not prepared for the depth of hatred and the bloodshed in Yugoslavia. There was a widespread belief that given the relative weakness and dependency of Yugoslavia on the West, it could be brought back quickly to peace and rationality. And while there was a recognition that the Community was doing considerably better together than during the Gulf War, the policies of the EC/12 were still seen as determined by the lowest common denominator. What the EC/12 achieved was criticised as too little too late. The arms embargo was seen as a logical necessity, but given Yugoslavia's past defence strategy it was only too clear that all sides (though obviously the federal army especially) had access to plentiful arms. The interruption of aid was again logical but it was clear that it had little impact of the federal and Serbian authorities. Increasingly, therefore, many looked to the implementation of a full economic embargo (including an oil embargo) against those who were not prepared to accept the Community's peace proposals. The threat of an embargo was used but it was doubted in Community circles whether it would have had any great immediate impact for as Freedman suggested:

> Nor should much hope be put in economic sanctions. The economy was in a ruinous state before the fighting and will be in an even more wretched condition now. Sanctions are unlikely to be persuasive when the fundamentals of national identity are believed by all to be at stake.[63]

Moreover, as in the case of recognition, continued use of the threat began to suggest that the Community was incapable of imposing it. To the extent that the Yugoslav and Serbian leaders were thinking about the economic consequences of their actions, it had become clear perhaps during September and October 1991 that they could rely on several states continuing to oppose sanctions while others proposed them merely to distract attention away from other possibilities including the introduction of a peace-keeping force.

With hindsight, of course, more could probably have been done earlier by the EC/12, though it is difficult to disagree strongly with Eyal that:

> Much of what has happened in Yugoslavia was unavoidable. Yet the story of the Community's efforts should serve as a warning. Determination to keep Yugoslavia together merely resulted in the country's violent disintegration. The Community's obsession with handling efforts by consensus did not work. Thus brute force still pays in Europe; Serbia successfully defied an entire continent.[64]

With fighting still continuing, the outcome of the conflict remains unknown. But it is tempting if not necessarily helpful to consider whether such defiance would have lasted so long if a common foreign and security policy had already been in position. Given the differences, say, between Germany and Spain over recognition or France and the UK over a peace-keeping force, it would seem unlikely that the European Council would have been able to have reached any different conclusion. It was the case that the coincidence of negotiations on a

---

63 *The Independent*, 12 September 1991.
64 *Guardian*, 8 August 1991.

possible foreign and security policy acted as a constraint on some member states, and one should not underestimate the influence of institutional structures once established. But such influences are limited; member states may have undertaken not to diverge from the policy once established but the problem remains with establishing the policy in the first place. The prospect of an adhered to common policy may enhance the weight of the EC/12 in international relations, but again that underlines the importance of the policy being acceptable to all first. And even then, there will be those who are not susceptible to rationality and logic, whether in the Gulf or in Yugoslavia.

Moreover, while the existence of a European Union with a common foreign and security policy -- with WEU in some form as its military arm -- may emphasise the key role of the EC/12 in European security, the Union does not necessarily become the exclusive forum for maintaining that security. As in the Yugoslav example, member states have taken recourse to other fora to express their concern over Community policy and to reinforce the leverage they might have; the French through WEU, the Germans through CSCE and Italy through the Hexagonale are cases in point (the almost total non-use of NATO provides an interesting exception). Such recourse may have been as much to do with showing their domestic audiences that their government was doing something as it had with seeking a resolution of the crisis. But they also tended to encourage confusion about the precise commitment member states had to the role of the EC/12, even while the Community invariably provided the major point of coordination.

The implications of the EC/12's responses to the Yugoslav crisis are therefore mixed. The Community showed that it could respond and, even if it was done in an ad hoc and piecemeal fashion, showed that it could explore new instruments of policy. Lord Carrington's peace conference may yet bring about peace and reconstruction. It is arguable that the Community and the member states had to find a greater coherence and consistency if they were to be seen as any sort of credible international actor, especially in view of the nature of the crisis and its potential ramifications elsewhere in Europe. In a limited way they achieved a credible unity. There is, however, danger in assuming that such unity is either an end in itself or that it will always be effective.

Appendix I:

European Community - Yugoslavia Trade Relations (millions ECU)

Year	1981	1982	1983	1984	1985	1986	1987
EC Imports	2210	2763	3586	4361	4815	4893	5073
EC Exports	4365	4278	4605	5123	5914	5853	5342
Balance	+2155	+1515	+1019	+762	+1099	+960	+266
Index of Balance	100	70	47	35	51	45	21

Source: Eurostat

Appendix II:

Principal elements of the three EC-Yugoslavia Financial Protocols

First Financial Protocol
   The First Financial Protocol was an important element of the Cooperation Agreement signed in 1980. The protocol provided loans of up to 200 million ECU over the period 1980-85. These funds were distributed principally to the development of improved infrastructure -- road, rail and electricity projects. In addition the European Investment Bank (EIB) granted loans of 60 million ECU to the Trans Yugoslavia Highway (TYH) project which "is of considerable interest to traffic between Greece and other EC countries." The First Financial Protocol expired on June 30, 1985.

The Second Financial Protocol
   The Second Financial Protocol provided for loans from the EIB totalling 550 million ECU for the period July 1, 1985 to June 30, 1991. The bulk of these loans were devoted to transport infrastructure of common interest, especially the TYH and feeder roads.

The Third Financial Protocol

In December 1990 the Council of Ministers approved the amounts allocated to Yugoslavia under the protocol to be negotiated by the Commission. The Council approved 730 million ECU in the form of EIB loans, of which 580 million ECU would be for transport issues, and 77 million ECU for interest rate subsidies. The provision of these loans would be conditional on the satisfactory outcome of negotiations for the Transport Protocol.

11

West European Cooperation on Nuclear Proliferation

Harald Müller

Introduction

Nuclear proliferation was thrust suddenly into the limelight as a consequence of the revelations on Saddam Hussein's secret nuclear weapons program after the Gulf war. There is unanimous agreement among the twelve EC member states that, after the Soviet threat has lost much of its saliency, nonproliferation policy must be a centerpiece of a common security policy. This is of particular concern to Southern flank member countries which feel the proliferation dangers of the unruly Middle East (and the Maghreb) more than their northern partners.

There is also -- in the light of the various European contributions, wittingly and unwittingly of Iraq's efforts -- a consensus that such a common nonproliferation policy must be stronger and far more effective than in the past. While the Gulf war provided a powerful stimulus for the further development of a common nuclear nonproliferation policy, it did by no means however, start the process. Nonproliferation policy in the Community has undergone a long evolution that has taken only another, important step through the recent upheavals.[1]

---

1 Not much is in the public domain on the proceedings of the Working Group on Nuclear Nonproliferation of the European Political Cooperation (EPC) that embodies the major part of EC nonproliferation policy over the last decade. Most of what is available has been produced by the research projects "New Approaches to Nonproliferation: A European Approach" and "Building Blocks for a European Nonproliferation Policy" which the author has directed at the Centre for European Policy Studies and the Peace Research Institute Frankfurt, respectively. Besides the numerous publications from these projects quoted in this paper, the author has relied on unpublished work by Michael Amory, Julien Goens, and Alain Michel.

Interests and Divergences

The interests of the Twelve in nuclear nonproliferation matters are split along three axes, and these splits are exacerbated by the general dispute about national sovereignty and Community rights.[2]

The first divergence concerns the issue of the safety of civilian nuclear power plants. This dispute, of course, exists within every single country, but it also divides the users of nuclear energy from safety-concerned non-users. Nuclear power supplies more than 70% of French electricity, more than 60% in Belgium, sizable portions in Germany, Great Britain, and Spain. Denmark, Luxembourg, Ireland, Greece, and -- after the 1987 referendum -- Italy are avowedly anti-nuclear and wary of the safety of nuclear power plants in neighboring countries. Discussions about nuclear safety have also occurred between the Netherlands and Belgium, and Spain and Portugal. While nuclear safety is, of course, not directly connected with nuclear proliferation proper, divergent approaches to nuclear energy impede necessarily the formation of a common policy in a field that requires a certain degree of regulation of the nuclear industry.

The second divergence relates to exports of nuclear materials, equipment and technology and of such dual-use items that might be used in nuclear facilities, but have also other plausible industrial and scientific applications. The Community contains two major players on the nuclear world market, France and Germany. The U.K., Spain, and Belgium are also suppliers capable of offering a broad spectrum of nuclear equipment and services. Italy and the Netherlands are minor nuclear exporters, while the rest have no tangible nuclear export interests whatsoever. Naturally, the stronger suppliers have tended in the past to pursue and promote a less restrictive nuclear export policy while small and non-suppliers were rather willing to support stronger restrictions in the interest of nonproliferation. This controversy, as the discussion below will show, is presently loosing much of its previous saliency.

The third divergence concerns nuclear strategy and arms control. The two nuclear weapon states are far less enthusiastic about the "barter" within the nonproliferation regime whereby non-nuclear weapon states renounce nuclear weapons in return for a firm commitment by the nuclear weapon states to engage "in good faith" in talks with a view towards nuclear arms reductions and, finally, disarmament, including a comprehensive ban to all nuclear tests. Anxious to guard their relatively small nuclear arsenals, France and Britain tend to see nonproliferation rather in the narrow sense, as the curb on the

---

2 Harald Müller, "Non-Proliferation Policy in Western Europe: Structural Aspects," in: Müller (ed.), *A European Non-Proliferation Policy. Prospects and Problems*, Oxford: Clarendon Press, 1987, pp. 71-91.

further spread of nuclear weapons to additional countries, with no conditions attached as far as present nuclear weapon states are concerned, while some or all of the non-nuclear weapon states, with varying emphasis and enthusiasm, support or even actively promote this connection, with Ireland and Denmark most active, and Italy and Belgium relatively restrained for reasons of NATO solidarity.

Lastly, the structural contradiction between Community authority and state sovereignty that pervades so many areas of European politics applies to the nuclear field with particular power, since nuclear matters are of a peculiarly sensitive character to security and economic national interests. EC member states -- France and the U.K. in particular -- have carefully protected their prerogatives in the areas they regarded as militarily sensitive (physical protection of nuclear materials, export controls for security) or as police functions under state authority (the enforcement of nuclear safety rules). Attempts by the EC Commission to intrude in those areas have been largely unsuccessful even where the Rome Treaties appeared to convey authority to it (as in the field of the legal possession of nuclear materials). Where a common policy touches this issue of state sovereignty and authority -- as inevitably in the field of export controls -- progress is piecemeal, as states transfer such authority only with the greatest reluctance.[3]

If, despite these considerable obstacles, there has been an evolution towards a more common nonproliferation policy, this must indicate a solid body of converging interests. Indeed there has been no doubt at least since the late sixties that European security would be affected negatively by the spread of nuclear weapons. The southern part of the Community might fall under direct threat by newly emerging nuclear weapon states, a possibility brought into sharp focus by Iraq's achievements. Regions of great commercial and economic interests to Europe such as the Middle East might be severely disrupted by nuclear war. In the past, there was also the fear that a clash of nuclear-armed proxy states could involve the superpowers into a violent conflict, with a strong possibility of escalation into Europe; this fear, of course, has largely receded since the end of the Cold War. Lastly, for the group of European nations which is heavily dependent on foreign trade and international cooperation, the disruption of world order by the sudden spread of nuclear weapons would, in general, augur badly for the welfare and political tranquillity of the European continent that European citizens have come to value so highly. The increasing possibility of terrorists being capable of credibly threatening the use of nuclear

---

3 Julien Goens, "The Limits to Supranational Policy-Making," in: Peter Lomas/Harald Müller (eds.), *Western Europe and the Future of the Non-Proliferation Treaty*, Brussels, Centre for European Policy Studies, 1989, pp. 31-36.

devices is a last exotic possibility, but may become more likely as nuclear weapons or weapon-usable materials are available in countries with lower internal security standards, domestic instability, and ethnic antagonisms. It is this complex of security interests that has motivated the efforts in the EC to achieve some coordination or convergence in the field of nuclear nonproliferation, despite the serious differences discussed above.

Proliferation, Nuclear Energy and the Beginnings of the Community

At the beginning of the Community, however, proliferation meant something else: As the Coal and Steel Community was meant, at least partially, to establish a mild sort of control over a war-essential industry in Germany, so the European Atomic Community (EURATOM) aimed at constraining the uncontrolled development of German nuclear research and industry after the occupation regime had been abolished. Chancellor Adenauer had been persuaded to renounce nuclear weapons in the Protocols to the Brussels Treaty in 1954, but it was felt that more stringent controls than those entrusted in the WEU Agency for the Control of Armaments were needed in a supposedly highly dynamic sector of industry. Moreover, the promising field of nuclear energy, overloaded with wild optimism in the fifties, was seen as an ideal field of common industrial development for the young Community. As a consequence, the Rome Treaties contained rather far-reaching authority for the Commission, including an elaborated system to verify the non-diversion of nuclear materials from declared purposes with far-reaching rights of unlimited access for the EURATOM inspectorate, the ownership of all nuclear material within the Community and the obligation to draw up, and to conduct an ambitious research and development program in all fields of nuclear technology.

Reality, however, fell far short of ambitions. The first reason was the French interest in the military uses of nuclear clauses in the Rome Treaties that permitted the French nuclear establishment to develop and maintain its nuclear arsenal free of EURATOM controls through either inspections or ownership rights. The second reason was the increasing national interest of major member states in the exploitation of nuclear technology for the advantage of one's own industry; the Germans, in particular, began to see unscathed civilian nuclear development as a compensation for their renouncing the military option and became increasingly interested in a national path of nuclear development. As a consequence, the joint nuclear research program became largely irrelevant for the real development of the nuclear industry in EC member states, as the countries followed individually technical paths derived from their military technology (France) or pursued through licenses bought from U.S. companies

(Germany).[4] As the nuclear industry developed, including the fabrication of fuel and the trade in nuclear materials, the ownership rights of EURATOM, initially thought to be the key for control as well as joint development, became mere paper rights, were increasingly ignored in the practice of EC member states and were eventually openly contested by France. At the end of the sixties, thus, of the initial idea of internal proliferation control, only the safeguards system worked reasonably, but not in the military sector in France. For external nonproliferation policy, a field of increasing importance during the negotiations of the Nuclear Nonproliferation Treaty (NPT) in 1967 and 1968, no common EC approach existed at all.[5]

Indeed, the members of the Community approached the negotiations in the 18-nations committee on disarmament with widely different approaches. France practiced a policy of empty chair, partly out of fear that the US-Soviet collaboration on that issue was at least partially directed against the *Force de Frappe*, partly because of principled opposition against the sovereignty denying implications of international arms control, partly just to harrass the US. In the end, France declared its abstention from the NPT but also its willingness to abide by its rules. Of the non-nuclear weapon states, only Italy was a committee member. Italy, Belgium and, with particular emphasis, Germany, fought during the negotiations to protect their national nuclear industries against any competitive disadvantage vis-à-vis those of the nuclear weapon states, and to resist any intrusions in and constraints for their nuclear companies. They were also anxious to maintain the "European option," that is the right of the Community to inherit France's nuclear weapons status if the necessary political and legal degree of political union was ever achieved.

The EC non-nuclear weapon states, in collaboration with other similar-minded countries, extracted major concessions from the nuclear weapon states, for example the limitation of safeguards to nuclear materials in Art. III of the NPT, the granting of the "inalienable right" to nuclear development and the obligation of all parties to engage in the broadest nuclear exchange possible, the 25-year limitation of the Treaty and regular review conferences.[6]

On this basis, however, it still proved difficult enough to find a formula reconciling the requests of the International Atomic Energy Agency (IAEA) -- the agency entrusted with the mandate to verify NPT commitment in non-nuclear weapon states -- and the continued validity of EURATOM safeguards.

---

4   Heinz Kramer, *Nuklearpolitik in Westeuropa und die Forschungspolitik der Euratom*, Köln: Carl Heymans Verlag, 1976.
5   Darryl A. Howlett, *Euratom and Nuclear Safeguards*, Basingstoke: Macmillan, 1990, Chapters 1-5.
6   Mohamed I. Shaker, "The Nuclear Nonproliferation Treaty. Origin and Implementation 1959-1979," London et al., *Oceana 1980*, Vol. I, Chapter 6, and Vol. II, Chapters 10 and 12.

During these negotiations, France extracted a major concession by establishing a new category of nuclear material ("free to use") not included in the then used categories of either military or civilian material and which would be free of safeguards obligations, thereby enhancing considerably the realm of national discretion over nuclear material. The (then) five EC non-nuclear weapon states, after several years of thorough negotiations, finally agreed with the IAEA on a suitable division of labour between the EURATOM and the IAEA inspectorate. With the ratification of the NPT by the EURATOM members in 1975 (meanwhile enhanced by the U.K., Denmark, and Ireland), the lasting dispute over the internal nonproliferation policy within the EC was largely terminated.[7]

New Aspects at the End of the Seventies

Meanwhile, far more attention was focussed on what we understand today as the area of nonproliferation policy, the nuclear relationship of EC countries and the Community to the Third World.

Since the late sixties, and very powerfully in the early seventies, the Europeans entered the nuclear world market as suppliers, thereby effectively finishing the period of a US/Soviet duopoly. The first such exports were largely conducted without great regard for nonproliferation concerns. The most spectacular example, the French supply of technology and equipment for Israel's nuclear weapon program dated back to the fifties. In the late sixties, France followed suit with a power reactor to Spain without safeguards, and the close collaboration in jet-nozzle enrichment technology between Germany and South Africa (terminated in 1974) and the transfer of German heavy water technology to India (1970) did also bear no precautions as to prevent military abuse. In the early seventies, then, France, Germany, and, to a lesser degree, Belgium and Italy emerged as major suppliers, abiding by the letter, but not necessarily the spirit of their nonproliferation commitments. Prototypes of such deals were the French agreement to supply reprocessing technology to Pakistan and South Korea (both cancelled later), its supply of a large research reactor to Iraq, the German-Brazilian deal transferring complete fuel-cycle technology, the Italian export of hot cells usable for plutonium extraction to Iraq, and fuel-cycle consulting of Belgian firms with a couple of Third World countries, notably Pakistan and Libya. While all this was possible under the terms of legal or political commitments entered into by the European states, it was highly dubious in a nonproliferation perspective, and it was criticized not only by the US, but also by the Netherlands and the U.K.[8]

---

7   Howlett (note 5), Chapters 8-11
8   Mans Lönnroth/William Walker, *Nuclear Power Struggles. Industrial Competition and Proliferation Control*, London: Allen and Unwin, 1983.

The serious divergencies on nuclear export policy led to negotiations among the main suppliers between 1974 and 1977. The result, the "London Guidelines," represented a fair compromise between the more liberal French/German and the more restrictive US/Canadian position. The guidelines obliged suppliers to request safeguards on all items listed explicitly in an annex to the guidelines as well as on all material in facilities using similar and thus presumably derived technology in the recipient country (thereby setting up uniform minimum standards for national export regulation), to insist on peaceful-use guarantees, to oblige the recipient to request safeguards on any item reexported or copied for export purposes, to insist on strict physical protection in the recipient country, and to exercise "restraint" (in practice meaning denial) on sensitive materials, equipment and technology directly usable in weapons or for the production of weapon-usable material.[9] While the London Guidelines proved a solid basis for the pursuit of nuclear exports in the legal realm, they created major problems for the Community since some countries were members of the "London Club," and some were not. The stipulations of the guidelines, particularly the "restraint clause," were clearly at odds with the idea of a single civilian nuclear market embodied in the Rome Treaties.

Another difficulty arose in the aftermath of the London negotiations by unilateral changes in US policy concerning the use of plutonium in civilian nuclear fuel cycles. Meant to impede the spread of nuclear weapons in the Third World, the US Nuclear Nonproliferation Act of 1978 made its heaviest negative impact on the most advanced nuclear power programs which, of course, were located in the Western industrialized world. Even European countries which principally agreed with much of the Carter policy felt compelled to dispute the unilateralism by which Congress tried to push this policy down the throat of US allies. The INFCE (International Nuclear Fuel-Cycle Evaluation) conference tried to reconcile the divergent positions, but ended largely with a refusal of most of the American approach.[10]

---

9 Bertran Goldschmidt, "Proliferation and Non-Proliferation in Western Europe: A Historical Survey," in: Müller (ed.), *A European Non-Proliferation Policy*, pp. 3-30, part. pp. 25-30.

10 Karl Kaiser, "Nuclear Energy and Nonproliferation in the 1980s," in: Karl Kaiser/Pierre Lellouche/Erwin Häckel, *Nuclear Policy in Europe, France, Germany and the International Debate*, Bonn: Europa-Union, 1980, pp. 1-30; cf. also Report from the Commission to the Council: International Nuclear Fuel Cycle Evaluation, Document COM(80) 316 Final, 11 June 1980.

From the Foundation of the EPC Working Group to the 1985 NPT Review

At the beginning of the eighties, a new phase of European nonproliferation policy was thus started by four converging impulses:

- The danger of real proliferation in the Third World, exemplified by the Indian explosion in 1974 and the illegal diversion of centrifuge technology by a Pakistani scientist from the URENCO plant in Almelo, Netherlands, forced the Europeans to reconsider and to better coordinate their approaches to developing countries in the nuclear sector.
- The recently experienced unilateralism in US policy proved an important motivation to try to develop joint positions towards the US in order to preserve the integrity of European institutions and to protect European nuclear commercial interests.
- The adoption of the London Guidelines by some members posed the issue of the viability of a common nuclear market.
- Finally, and pointing in the same direction, a longstanding quarrel between France on the one hand and the EC Commission on the other hand had opened the issue of mutual authority in this interwoven field of nuclear policy. The quarrel, which went even to the European Court, started from the request of the EC Commission to cosign, and to obtain certain authorities, under the International Convention for the Physical Protection of Nuclear Materials that obliged signatories to observe precautionary procedures for all transboundary movements of fissile material. The Commission, relating to the trade aspect of this Convention, argued that it had to be involved under the stipulations of the Rome Treaties. The French government, in contrast, argued that the Convention concerned security issues and was thus completely exempted from the Rome Treaties. France thus refused to consider herself in the principal group responsible for nuclear matters, the "Groupe des Questions Atomiques," consisting of experts from the national missions to the EC in Brussels, and representatives of the Commission (Directorate General for Energy, Supply Agency, Safeguards Agency). The Court had largely sided with the Commission, but no political solution had been found. Since this issue converged obviously with the problems created by the partial adoption of the London Guidelines -- both concerned the erection of intra-Community obstacles to the free flow of nuclear material -- a lasting resolution was required.

This solution was found by putting the whole issue under European Political Cooperation rather than under the Rome Treaties. In 1981, on Dutch and British initiative, the Council decided to set up an EPC working group on nuclear nonproliferation policy.[11] Despite its relatively restricted mandate, the installation of this group meant a watershed in the evolution of common policy for three reasons. First, the decision implied that nonproliferation was a common concern in the framework of EPC and thus subject for coordination -- a major inroad in the refusal to include matters of national security in EPC. For this very reason, it took some efforts to overcome French -- and also German -- reluctance to agree to the new body. Second, the continuous collaboration on the issue almost automatically led the group to discussions of an ever wider area connected to its core mandate, and "socialized" national bureaucrats to think about proliferation in terms of coordinated policy. This process took some while, but it prevailed. Third, since this was an EPC body and thus under the supervision of foreign ministries, these ministries received a considerable impulse of enmeshing themselves far more actively in national decision-making on nonproliferation policy. This policy area had been the fiefdom of atomic energy commissions, economics and energy ministries, and ministries of technology in a large number of countries. The new group thus unwittingly affected in the long run the "balance of power" within individual governments and, thereby, the priorities within nonproliferation policies, because foreign offices quite naturally payed more attention to the political and security aspects of this policy than atomic energy commissions or ministries of the economy.

A first remarkable outgrowth of the group's work was the first joint statement issued to the U.N. General Assembly on the occasion of the IAEA's Secretary General's annual report in 1983. Delivered by the presidency, the statement reaffirmed the common interest in nonproliferation and the high value placed by the Ten on international safeguards -- the first traces of a common statement on policy principles had thus been marked.[12]

Then, after three years of intense work, the group achieved its first major success. It prepared for the EC Council meeting in fall 1984 a joint "Declaration of common policy on the consequences of the adoption of the London Guidelines by the ten member states of the Community". It contained the common affirmation that member states "support the objective of the non-proliferation of nuclear weapons" and referred, among other legal obligations, to the NPT. The declaration provided for detailed rules under which sensitive materials, equipment, and technology would be transferred within the Community and retransferred by member states recipient to non-members. Provision was made for notification among the member states of such transfers.

---

11   Julien Goens, "The Opportunities and Limits of European Co-operation in the Area of Non-Proliferation," in: Müller (ed.), *A European Non-Proliferation Policy*, pp. 31-70.

12   Ibid., p. 38

No role was given to the EC Commission. Simultaneously, those countries not yet adhering to the London Guidelines informed the IAEA that from now on they would apply the Guidelines. Readiness to accede to the Guidelines also became a condition for the entrance of Portugal and Spain.[13]

There was, however, no progress possible beyond these limits at the time. The Netherlands pressed hard for obtaining agreement to formulate and publish a more detailed statement on nonproliferation policy prior to the 3rd Review Conference of the Nuclear Nonproliferation Treaty. France agreed to a skeleton statement containing some valuable principles, but stalled completely on the issue of publication, on any connection with the NPT, and also resisted stubbornly a joint preparation for the review conference. As a consequence, the ten participating EC member states (Portugal and Spain had just acceded to the EC, but Spain was not a member of the NPT) gave a thorough impression of complete division on all important issues. Germany, Belgium, and Italy resisted the adoption of "full scope safeguards" as a condition of nuclear supply, in other words, a nuclear embargo against threshold countries not willing to submit all nuclear activities to international safeguards. The Netherlands, Denmark, and Ireland, on the other hand, strongly supported this principle. The majority of EC members supported a Comprehensive Test Ban Treaty (CTBT), while Great Britain objected to it and Italy and Germany gave rather evasive statements. On the issue of International Plutonium Storage, Germany and Belgium were definitely opposed, while Denmark and Ireland lend strong support. In other words, no objective observer would have believed that these countries belonged to the same organization trying to coordinate policies in this field. The appearance of the Europeans was crowned by two hapless young French diplomats walking the corridors around conference rooms and trying to extract some information on the proceedings, since France had decided neither to participate as observer nor to admit an EPC caucus during the conference that could have provided the necessary information to the "outsiders."[14]

From the Chernobyl Accident to the Dublin Declaration

In the period between the 3rd and 4th review conferences, four events helped to improve the climate for a common European nonproliferation policy. First, the accident at Chernobyl intensified the collaborative work; second and third, changes of policy in the two major nuclear exporting nations, France and

---

13 Reprinted in Johan J. Holst et al., *Blocking the Spread of Nuclear Weapons. American and European Perspectives*, Washington: Council on Foreign Relations, 1986, Appendix E.
14 Cf. David Fischer/Harald Müller, "Non-Proliferation Beyond the 1985 Review," Brussels: CEPS Paper, 1985.

Germany, paved the way for a more energetic and effective approach; fourth, the momentum emerging from the Single European Act and the prospects of a Single Market made additional work necessary.

On a purely formal level, the stronger effort was indicated by the rising frequency of working group meetings. Before 1985, the group met once to twice during a presidency on the average. After 1985, the frequency rose to two to three meetings per presidency (with few exceptions). Beyond this, bilateral consultations and the density of COREU communications rose significantly during this five-year period.

The Chernobyl accident necessitated a jump in international collaboration in nuclear safety. In this field, authority is strictly divided between EURATOM and the EC member states, with the enforcement of safety levels resting completely in the realm of the states, while general safety policy is, under the Rome Treaties, also in the purview of the EC Commission. For this reason, the rising activities in international safety policy through the IAEA and the OECD Nuclear Energy Agency -- for example the elaboration of two international conventions dealing with early notification of nuclear accidents and mutual assistance in case of such accidents (1986) -- made it necessary to achieve a new level of political cooperation in this field. Consequently, in 1986 the working group was authorized to deal with issues such as nuclear safety as they affect the international nuclear policy of the Community. While not substantially connected to the subject of nonproliferation, this development fostered closer and more frequent consultations within the EPC Working Group and thus contributed to the above-mentioned effect of "political socialization" of the participants.[15]

One early result of this closer cooperation was a joint statement by the Twelve to the United Nations Conference on the Peaceful Uses of Nuclear Energy in April 1987. This Conference, once requested by the Group of 77 as a response to alleged conspiracies among the nuclear suppliers, proved by and large a failure; it was not able to come up with a final consensus. Part of the reason was the controversy over the relation between guarantees of supplies and nonproliferation commitments. Threshold countries were keen to receive rather unconditional promises of future supplies, while the main suppliers were not willing to give such assurances without reciprocal verifiable guarantees of nonproliferation. The Europeans made it clear in their joint statement from the beginning that they supported such a linkage, and kept a remarkable unity on this issue to the end.[16]

---

15 Julien Goens, "Current Events Related to Non-Proliferation in the EEC," in: Harald Müller (ed.), *A Survey of European Nuclear Policy, 1985-1987*, London: Macmillan, 1989, pp. 11-20, esp. p. 18.

16 Ibid., p. 17/18.

By 1986/87, the agenda of the EPC Working Group contained, on a routine basis, mutual exchange of information on the status of threshold countries, a review of events and forthcoming meetings within the IAEA, and, case-wise, the buying activities of threshold countries and the risks implied by ongoing nuclear trade. Encouraged through these improved consultations, the Dutch attempted to solicit an agreement in 1986 on a "Troika approach" towards threshold countries. However, the major member states were not ready to favor Community diplomacy over their own bilateral relations with important Third World states. However, the members agreed to keep each other informed over diplomatic approaches in individual threshold countries affected through bilateral ties.

Two events marked the higher degree of coordination of nonproliferation diplomacy. In the context of sanctions against South Africa, the 1986 summit decided to embargo all new major nuclear contracts between Community countries and the apartheid state; one year later, late Pakistani president Zia ul-Haq was dismayed by the united denial front he was meeting during a trip through Europe when he sought to persuade the European suppliers to offer a new nuclear power reactor to his country.[17]

The negotiations on the Spanish accession to the EC provoked another interesting debate. The Netherlands (followed by Ireland and Denmark) had attempted to make Spanish accession to the NPT a precondition for the admission to the Community. The French objected, correctly arguing that this was not the subject of the Rome Treaties. During the negotiations on the integration of Spain in EURATOM, however, the EC Commission, supported by the majority of the member states, made the strong point that it would be so much easier to agree on a uniform safeguards regime for the Community if Spain would put itself in the same situation as the other non-nuclear weapon states and ratify the NPT. The difficulties in agreeing on a separate safeguards agreement helped -- apart from other political considerations -- convince the Spanish government, particularly its industrial branches initially skeptical about the merits of NPT membership, that little would be lost and more gained by acceding. Throughout the process, France did not object to the negotiation tactics of either the EC Commission or the other members as long as no formal request for accession was made. Finally, in 1987, Madrid announced it would deposit its documents of NPT ratification.[18]

Toward the end of the eighties, European nonproliferation policy gained momentum. One reason was the coming to power of Prime Minister Rocard,

---

17 Harald Müller, "Introduction: A Summary of Western European Non-Proliferation Policy from 1985 to 1987," in: Müller (ed.), *A Survey of European Nuclear Policy, 1985-1987*, London: Macmillan, 1989, pp. 1-10, esp. p. 6.
18 Katlyn Saba, "Spain and the Nonproliferation Treaty," in: Müller (ed.), *A Survey of European Nuclear Policy, 1985-1987*, pp. 111-130.

one of the few top French politicians to embrace publicly the NPT. While Rocard abstained from any active endorsement in order to avoid intrusion into the French President's prerogative, at least the traditional ideological objections were now absent, and French policy proceeded in a far more pragmatic way.[19] Simultaneously, Germany was shattered by a series of bad scandals concerning nuclear and chemical technology exports. These scandals helped to initiate a major reform process, relating not only to an overhaul of the export control system, but to a major change in political philosophy, away from a predominantly commercial approach to a policy that payed far higher attention to security and political aspects. Moreover, with export controls strengthened, Germany all of a sudden discovered a strong interest in persuading its European partners to follow suit lest its own industry would end up with a competitive disadvantage. The move towards German unification made a higher profile and the proof of "global responsibility" even more urgent, and the field of nonproliferation was well fit for this purpose. As a consequence, the Germans took increasing interest in the working group and, rather than reacting to the initiatives of others, became active themselves.[20]

The "Transnuclear scandal" that had triggered a parlamentarian investigation into the field of nuclear exports in the first place also had consequences at the European level. The European Parliament set up its own investigation that ended with a report asking for higher attention to nonproliferation and obliging EURATOM to submit regular reports on its hitherto rather arcane safeguards activities.

The first result of the new momentum became visible when, in 1989, the Twelve delivered their first joint statement to an IAEA General Conference. It was an additional thrill that it was the French representative -- under the French Presidency -- who explained the common position. It contained a well-balanced account of the EC countries' deep interest in nonproliferation, their appreciation of IAEA safeguards, their support for the further development of nuclear energy (a sentence on which the French, with German, Belgian, and Spanish support, had insisted) and their willingness to foster, in particular, international collaboration to deal with nuclear energy's safety problems (this was included on the insistence of Denmark, Ireland, and Greece). The statement went further than that to PUNE[21] in that it put more political emphasis on the goal of

---

19 Harald Müller, "Falling into Line? France and the Non-Proliferation Treaty," *PPNN Occasional Paper* 6, Southampton, 1990.
20 Wolfgang Kötter/Harald Müller, "Germany and the Bomb. Nuclear Policies in the Two German States and the United Germany's Nonproliferation Commitment," *PRIF Reports* No. 14, Frankfurt, September 1990.
21 United Nations Conference on the Promotion of International Cooperation on Peaceful Uses of Nuclear Energy.

nonproliferation and even mentioned favorably the NPT without committing the non-member (that is, France) to its terms.

In the aftermath of this demonstration of unity, France suggested preparing a statement for the next EC summit, due in December 1989. It added a draft that met some resistance, apparently for two reasons: first, by not mentioning at all the NPT, second, by being too enthusiastic (in the eyes of the antinuclear governments) with regard to the civilian uses of nuclear energy. The controversies prevented the Twelve from finishing the draft in time, but when the Irish took over the presidency, they faced the golden opportunity to have the Twelve pronounce a strong endorsement for nuclear nonproliferation, at the level of heads of state and government, immediately before the 4th NPT Review Conference. Ireland put a great effort into this endeavour, since the NPT is seen in Dublin as sort of an "Irish baby" (Ireland initiated the first resolution asking for an NPT in the General Assembly in 1959). Consequently, when the twelve Community leaders met in Dublin in June 1990, they issued the first top-level statement on nuclear proliferation. The statement emphasized again the security aspect of Europe's interest in nonproliferation, the unanimity of this interest, and went on to emphasize the importance of the nonproliferation regime and the prominent role the NPT was playing within it. That the French had even agreed to express the support of the Twelve for a successful review conference showed an unprecedented degree of unity on an issue that had been so divisive for twenty years. Nuclear energy promotion was balanced, similarly to the IAEA statement, by stronger emphasis on safety issues.[22] The Irish presidency also managed to achieve consensus on forming an "EPC Caucus" during the Review Conference, which the French -- for the first time -- would attend as observers. However, it was not possible to agree on a joint statement before the Conference itself. France deemed it inappropriate to have a joint statement delivered to an event to which it was not a full participant.

Given this improved state of preparation, the performance of the Twelve as a whole during the Conference was disappointing.[23] The high mark was the repeated quoting from the Dublin declaration to which all eleven countries speaking during the general debate referred. On substantial issues, however, there were strong differences, along similar lines as in 1985. The EC countries were divided on the Comprehensive Test Ban, on emphasis on nuclear safety, on the extension of safeguards in nuclear weapon states, and on the question of full-scope safeguards. In a major reversal on this latter issue, Germany emerged

---

22 The declaration has been reprinted in *PPNN Newsbrief* 10, Summer 1990, p. 12.
23 For the following, consult David Fischer/Harald Müller, "A Treaty in Trouble. Europe and the NPT after the Fourth Review Conference," *Frankfurt PRIF Report* No. 17.

as a strong supporter of the concept while Britain, for reasons not well understood, took the lead of those opposing it.

As a group, the EPC countries played no role. One reason was a certain lack of leadership by the Italian presidency. The delegation was well staffed but led in a way that revealed a lack of commitment to the importance of the matter. The caucus met, but was preoccupied more with the preparation of the fall meeting of the IAEA General Conference than with the proceedings of the Review Conference. They thus lost a good opportunity to try to influence the course of a (finally unsuccessful) Conference by putting the weight of the EC members behind some compromise proposal. Greater unity in principle had not yet overcome divisions on the issues, and better coordination had not yet produced more diplomatic effectiveness.

The Impact of the Gulf War

The Gulf War changed the meaning of nuclear proliferation. It became a most tangible and visible threat to global, and, obviously, European security. As a consequence, efforts to improve and to enhance the nonproliferation regime gained an immediacy and a momentum that was unprecedented in the history of efforts to curb the spread of nuclear weapons.

A major effect of the war was to conclude a protracted review of French nonproliferation policy with the decision to join the NPT, thereby removing one major impediment to a smooth cooperation among the Twelve.[24] While this aspect was of diminishing importance as a stumbling block for European unity in nonproliferation matters, it was still cumbersome in procedural terms and required always time-consuming efforts to circumvent French objections to specific language and actions concerning the NPT.

The Gulf War also kept momentum on the German policy change in the field, encouraging a further overhaul of existing export control legislation,[25] since a larger number of German firms were involved in helping Saddam Hussein with his various programs for the production of weapons of mass destruction. High-level attention on matters of proliferation in France and Germany give desk officers a strong incentive to develop new initiatives. As a consequence, the French-German proposal for European security cooperation gave nonproliferation a prominent place (as did the EC Commission's paper on the same subject). In early 1991, the Twelve agreed to consider the possibility of a more sophisticated joint export policy, not excluding a further turn to full-

---

24 Présidence de la République, "Plan de Maîtrise des Armements et des Désarmements," Paris, 3 June 1991.
25 Bundesministerium für Wirtschaft, "Dokumentation zur Reform der Exportpolitik, Bonn, BMWi 1991"; cf. *Nuclear Law Bulletin* 47, June 1991, pp. 48/49.

scope safeguards by those members (France, Belgium, Britain, Italy) that have not yet subscribed to this export principle. This was followed by the first meeting of the "London Suppliers," the group of major nuclear exporters, in The Hague. The Suppliers decided to amend their agreements on export policies, including dual-use items. Significantly, the EC Commission participated, together with all EC member states, in this meeting.[26]

In spring of the same year, the EPC prepared an unprecedented joint initiative for strengthening IAEA safeguards that was submitted to the IAEA Board of Governors in June 1991. Following a British-Dutch initiative during the 1990 NPT Review Conference, the Twelve went for the first time beyond general statements on nonproliferation in an international organization and made more detailed policy proposals. Their proposal included a provision for on-challenge inspections based on paragraphs 73 and 77 of the safeguards document INFCIRC/159, and a plea to rearrange safeguards so as to put more efforts into the "suspect" countries rather than those countries with large civilian fuel cycles.

Finally, the Council meeting in Luxembourg in June 1991 issued another statement on proliferation -- including nuclear, chemical, biological and conventional arms proliferation -- that went beyond the generalities of the Dublin declaration. The Community countries called on all states to join the NPT -- a first consequence of the French decision to accede. It summarized the work done in various EPC working groups, including the one on nuclear nonproliferation, in the field of export policy by formulating a list of criteria to be taken into account when export decisions are made. This list includes, inter alia, the human rights and general internal situation in the recipient country, the degree of regional tension or armed conflict, the security of the member states (obviously aimed at the Southern flank), the general behavior of the recipient, including its stance to terrorism and international law, and, finally, an assessment of the diversion risks concerning the items to be transferred. The Council declared its intention to base, under the condition of Political Union, harmonization of national export policies on these criteria. This statement went beyond the criteria of present international arrangements governing the export of weapons and military-usable technologies and thus presented a genuine initiative of the EC members to improve the existing nonproliferation regimes. It is all the more remarkable because otherwise this summit was not able to agree on the basics of a common security policy; nonproliferation thus became the centerpiece of common activities of the Twelve in the security area.[27]

---

26 Informal Meeting of States Adhering to the Nuclear Supplier Guidelines, Press Statement, The Hague, 7 March 1991.
27 *Atlantic News*, No. 2336, 2 July 1991, p. 2.

Challenges Ahead:
1992, 1995, Eastern Europe and Regional Diplomacy

Four major challenges are before the Community and its member states in the field of nuclear nonproliferation policy: the consequences of the single European market for export controls; the stepwise integration of the new market economies in Eastern Europe; the preparation of the conference in 1995 that is to extend the NPT beyond its 25 year duration; and the development of a consistent diplomacy towards the remaining nuclear threshold countries.

It has been noted since the Single Market was proclaimed that the security aspects of foreign trade policy pose a special difficulty for the Community. Export controls for security purposes have been reserved to individual states, even where intra-community trade was concerned. This practice, however, defies the objectives of the Single Market. On the other hand, it is well acknowledged that the quality of export controls is vastly divergent among the Twelve. Opening up the border gates, without any remaining national precautions, for free-flowing commerce would permit ill-minded exporters to ship weapons-relevant dual use goods, for example, from a country with high-quality controls to a low-quality country in order to transfer it then to the final destination. The Twelve are thus facing an unpleasant choice: either to facilitate large-scale transit transaction with doubtful results for the common security, or to maintain national border controls even for intra-community trade indefinitely, with serious consequences for the "single market," as the lists of militarily relevant technologies, in particular dual-use items, grows consistently.

This dilemma has not escaped the attention of either the EC Commission or the capitals. There are, however, two competing approaches to the dilemma, as was to be expected. The Commission would prefer a centralized solution that gives it enhanced authority -- ideally a kind of central export control office in Brussels with the authority to issue directives to national authorities. The EC member states, most pronouncedly France, would like to develop some extended system of intergovernmental communication to deal with the issue. At the moment, it appears as if a pragmatic interim solution would obtain: national controls in selected fields of security-relevant trade would continue, a system of notification would be developed, and the EC Commission would support efforts in the smaller countries to improve their national systems of control; at a later stage, a more communitarian system could then be brought into being. Already, the EC Commission, on request of the EPC nonproliferation group, has compiled existing national legislation and regulation with a view towards greater harmonization. And it has sent small teams, on request, into smaller member countries in order to review, and to advise upon, the national system of export controls in these host countries.

The same problem is of major importance with regard to the relationship with those Eastern European countries most eager to associate themselves with, and to become in the future members of, the European Community. For Poland, Czechoslovakia, and Hungary, it is even more difficult to avoid becoming the transit stage for illegal transfers during their difficult transitory stage from central to market economies. They are eager to attract investment and to acquire badly needed hard currency. Yet at the same time they are anxious not to damage their reputation by being the source of weapons-related commerce for the Saddam Husseins of this world. And, of course, they lack experience in the intricacies of controlling the external activities of private business, a task that is difficult to accomplish even for seasoned export controllers in Western countries. It falls onto the Community to take the necessary steps to assist these countries in this difficult endeavour and to familiarize and associate them, in one way or the other, with the ongoing developments in West European nonproliferation policy. Apparently, a first step has been taken in informally advising the respective Hungarian ambassador on the proceedings of the EPC working group on nuclear nonproliferation after their regular meetings (except for highly sensitive information concerning individual member states). More must be done, however, if the Community is to play its avowed central role in a European security architecture.

The third major task is to help the NPT survive its critical date of 1995. Art. X of the Treaty requires that a conference be held in this year to decide whether the NPT is to be extended for one or several fixed periods or indefinitely. In other words, this conference will determine the survival of the Treaty. While the chances are not bad at all given recent accessions, the controversies that prevented a consensus at the fourth review conference still cast a shadow over the future of the NPT. In 1995, when the Twelve will all be parties to the Treaty for the first time, it should be possible to make a more visible impact on the course of the conference. A thorough preparation for joint positions, objectives and procedures before and during the conference should now be possible.

Last, but not least, a new effort to deal with the remaining threshold countries would be in order. Much has changed since the Dutch initiative failed in 1986. In the context of a Middle East settlement, the Community countries want to play a visible role. Such a settlement is not conceivable without addressing the issue of nuclear proliferation, as both President Bush and President Mitterrand recognized in their respective arms control plans. Likewise, it is desirable to take steps to address the proliferation issue in the region with the greatest propensity for a nuclear arms race, South Asia. While the presence and importance of the Community is somewhat less there than in the geographically closer Middle East, it, and even more its individual countries, possesses considerable clout as a major donor, market for export goods, source of technology, and supplier of arms. In concert with other major players, mainly the US and the Soviet Union, the Twelve should be ready to develop a joint approach towards this proliferation-ridden region.

Conclusion

Nuclear nonproliferation policy has evolved steadily as a field of a common approach among the six, then nine, then ten and now twelve member states of the European Community. While initially, the focus was more on the Community as an instrument to prevent intra-Community proliferation, it has become an important vehicle now to coordinate the policies of the members towards the spread of nuclear weapons in other parts of the globe.

The decisive, turning event in this evolution has been the creation of the EPC working group in 1981. As analysed in detail in the foregoing paragraphs, this working group fulfilled five essential functions that lie at the heart of the more rapid evolution in recent years.

First, it affected considerably the quality and quantity of information available to all member states in the policy field. Particularly for the smaller countries this has been of invaluable importance. But even for the major countries, the regular meetings and the extensive utilization of the COREU system have accelerated the speed of the circulation of political data and have thus improved the quality of decision-making.

Second, officials responsible for developing and implementing national policy have been exposed regularly and continuously to different points of view. The quite controversial debates within the EPC working group offered the opportunity to better understand the perspectives of the colleagues with a different approach, and to review regularly the validity of one's own position. One main effect of this process was that -- as in other fields of EPC policy -- the European consequences of domestic decisions, or the likely reactions of the partners were frequently reflected before such decisions were made. In other words, the working group "socialized" its members in a more interdependent way of political thinking in the nonproliferation field.

Third, this process also affected the substance of domestic policy-making. This has been documented above in the case of the Spanish accession to the NPT. It is also evident that the exposure to the points of view of eleven NPT members has greatly affected the thinking of those French officials who participated regularly in the proceedings of the working group (Quai d'Orsay and civilian branch of the Commissariat à l'Energie Atomique). The antinuclear rhetoric of some of the smaller countries has also been mitigated by the continuous contact with countries where nuclear power plays a major role in the supply of electricity.

Fourth, in close connection to the integration of different political substances in the domestic nonproliferation discourse, the EPC working group has also affected the structure of the decision making process. EPC is working under the auspices of the foreign ministries. It presented the only regular forum in the nonproliferation field between NPT review conferences where foreign ministries would lead a national delegation. On IAEA Board of Governors' meetings and General Conferences, delegations are normally led by atomic energy commissions, ministries of energy, economy, or research and technology. From 1985 on, the EPC working group was the most frequently meeting forum on nonproliferation, with respective preparations and reporting. The key role of foreign ministries in this proceedings thus strengthened the hands of the nonproliferation desk officers in national decision-making procedures. The necessity of keeping track of the various legal, technical, and political aspects of nonproliferation policy in order to appear well prepared on the EPC working group meetings enhanced the knowledge and competence of foreign ministry officials vis-à-vis their colleagues in the executive who had hitherto possessed privileged knowledge. The enhancement of EPC through the Single Act added to this gain in the position of foreign ministries. As a consequence, political and security aspects -- in contrast to commercial and technological interests -- played a relatively larger role in the policies of several countries in the late eighties, most notably in the case of Germany.[28]

Last, the EPC working group increased the saliency of the nonproliferation issue in the daily work of lower and middle-level bureaucrats. The preparation and reporting process put papers on nonproliferation issues on the desks of department leaders six to eight times a year, and this effect was enhanced through increased COREU correspondence. The effect of this higher frequency of devoting attention cannot be underrated, particularly for the foreign ministries.

In giving due credit to the evolution through EPC, one should not overlook that the nonproliferation policy of the Twelve is still far from being fully integrated. Nuclear nonproliferation policy is a complex of five interwoven policy fields: domestic nuclear energy policy, export policy, regional diplomacy, diplomacy within the institutions of the regime, namely the NPT and the IAEA with its nuclear assistance and safeguards activities, and nuclear arms control with its crucial "climatic" impact on the nonproliferation regime.

Of these five fields, regime policy is now reasonably integrated, and one can hope that over the next one or two years, the same applies to export policy;

---

28 Cf. the discussion on governmental organization and the substance of nonproliferation policy in: Harald Müller, "How Western European Nuclear Policy Is Made: A Comparison," in: Müller (ed.), *How Western European Nuclear Policy Is Made. Deciding on the Atom*, London: Macmillan 1991, pp. 1-24, esp. 19-21.

the Luxembourg declaration gives plenty of hope. In regional diplomacy, the major countries are still weighing their national political interests against the merits of a common approach. In crucial situations, a joint *demarche* may be possible. This field is thus now thoroughly in the middle between pure national and integrated approaches. In nuclear energy issues the Twelve are badly divided; this prevents, for example, the utilization of foreign aid for nonproliferation purposes. And in arms control, the different political profiles of the nuclear weapon states and the non-nuclear weapon states matter increasingly the less France's and Britain's nuclear weapons can be convincingly presented as necessary deterrents against a Soviet threat, and the more their character as instruments of political status becomes visible. Thus, despite the laudable progress made over the last decade, and though more room for convergence exists in the sectors of export policy and regional diplomacy, it is unlikely that in the near future the Community will be capable of producing an all-comprehensive nonproliferation strategy that would cover all five issue areas of the global nuclear nonproliferation regime.

PART THREE

Perceptions and Demands from Outside: What Kind of Political Union?

PART THREE

Economic, Social, Political, Cultural, and Legal Aspects of the European Union

12

View from the United States: Common Foreign and Security Policy as a Centerpiece of U.S. Interest in European Political Union

Christopher W. Murray

Throughout the postwar period, the United States has long looked to the NATO Alliance as the pre-eminent forum for engaging European allies on collective foreign and security policy. Bilateral contacts with the Community's member states have reinforced relations within the Alliance, and addressed issues of specific mutual concern. The postwar era has also found much US interaction with European governments in third countries, as well as in international institutions such as the United Nations, the Organization for Economic Cooperation and Development (OECD), and the Conference on Security and Cooperation in Europe (CSCE) framework.

At the same time, the United States has consistently supported the process of European integration. American policy-makers have seen European integration serving US interests across a spectrum of security, economic and political issues. Trade has doubtless been the most contentious aspect of US-European Community relations. But commercial problems have, on balance, been surpassed by the benefits of political stability and economic prosperity brought about by increasing European integration through the Rome Treaty and other agreements.

A key watershed in US-EC relations came with passage of the 1987 Single European Act. The Single Act's design for a Europe without barriers to the movement of goods, services, capital and people captured both official and private attention in the US. The explanation for this interest was obvious; the Europe of 1992 promised new rules for a game in which the United States had much at stake. The magnitude of US private investment in Europe, and Europe's standing as a major trading partner, prompted keen corporate and financial attention to the changes taking place in Europe. Similarly, the Single Act held out the promise of growing political integration. Not only was European Political Cooperation (EPC) elevated to treaty status, but many Americans inside and outside government sensed that greater economic integration would have a spillover effect on political integration.

President Bush spoke to these trends in May 1989, when he delivered a major address at Boston University. In the company of French President François Mitterrand, he said: "We are ready to develop, with the European Community and its member states, new mechanisms of consultation and cooperation on political and global issues, from strengthening the forces of democracy in the Third World to managing regional tensions, to putting an end to the division of Europe."[1] This commitment by the President provided the basis for subsequent and tangible initiatives.

One such initiative was the joint US-EC declaration, issued in November of 1990.[2] This declaration identified: common goals; principles of US-EC partnership; economic cooperation; education, scientific and cultural cooperation; trans-national challenges; and an institutional framework for consultation. The US-EC declaration recognized the many established points of engagement across the Atlantic. The Declaration also signalled that a panoply of political issues, in addition to trade, would be taken up by the US in its dialogue with the European Community. Many of these political issues may be refined and expanded for joint action by the Twelve in the context of European Political Union. The outcome of Political Union will, therefore, influence greatly the nature and scope of US-EC collaboration on global political issues.

Between the time of President Bush's Boston University speech and publication of the US-EC declaration, Secretary of State James Baker gave a major address in Berlin, entitled *A New Europe, New Atlanticism, Architecture for a New Era*.[3] This speech, delivered in December 1989, set the basis for later American views on European steps toward Political Union, including a Common Foreign and Security Policy. Secretary Baker identified NATO, the European Community, and the CSCE process as major pillars for the United States' continuing engagement in Europe. NATO stands on established foundations and can serve new collective purposes. The EC must be strengthened, in drawing together the West while offering opportunities to the East. And CSCE, Secretary Baker declared, can overcome the division of Europe as it also bridges the Atlantic.

---

1 "The Future of Europe" (21 May 1989), United States Department of State (ed.), *Current Policy*, No. 1177.
2 The US-EC Declaration is repointed in the ANNEX.
3 *U.S. Policy Information and Texts*, No. 175, 12 December 1989.

The American attitudes framed by President Bush and Secretary Baker preceded EC Member State initiatives on Political Union. In the spring of 1990, a succession of documents revealed to US policy-makers an evident will on the part of the Twelve. These initiatives included a paper by the Belgian foreign minister, the Kohl-Mitterrand statement of April, and the conclusions of the two Dublin summits. The United States reacted with a blend of cautious observation and interested concern. There was no retreat from continuing US support for European integration and a political role for the EC. President Bush had just agreed, during a February 1990 visit by Irish prime Minister Charles Haughey, to semi-annual meetings between the US President and the head of government of the EC Member State holding the Presidency of the Council of Ministers. Moreover, the actual content of Political Union remained cloudy.

European Political Union, as it began to take shape following the second Dublin summit, would clearly comprise many issues. Some will be primarily internal to the affairs of the EC member states. Questions such as European citizenship, the alleged "democratic deficit," and relations among the EC Council, EC Commission and European Parliament have been seen by American officials as outside the scope of appropriate US comment. Similarly, the question of expanded EC competences may affect US interests, but its resolution is also seen as a matter for Member State-only determination. Political Union's component of a Common Foreign and Security Policy, however, reaches to the foundations of the postwar order. Common Foreign and Security Policy has become the centerpiece of US interest in Political Union, and with it the subject of intense and continuing exchanges.

US experience with a common European foreign and security policy reaches back twenty years through the process of European Political Cooperation. This experience has been highly positive, with a record of increasingly close contacts and coordination. Recent years have brought a flowering of the US-EPC dialogue, through commitment to semi-annual exchanges between the US Secretary of State and the Twelve's Foreign Ministers, ad hoc sessions on critical world developments such as the Persian Gulf, and dialogue between US officials and EPC Troika working group experts. Secretary of State Baker has not only endorsed, but participated in this richer relationship. Its strength lies in the common values and global outlook shared by the United States and the Twelve.

There is an inherent tension among the channels through which the United States engages its European partners. EPC, and by extension a Common Foreign and Security Policy, develops in sessions closed to direct US participation. By contrast, structures of the NATO Alliance allow the United States direct face-to-face exchanges with eleven of the twelve EC member states, as well as Canada and additional important European countries. Bilateral US contacts with EC Member State foreign ministries allow the frankest of exchanges and render an appreciation of the national views on which EPC consensus is built.

There is no neat resolution to these competing lines of contact. Rather, the United States seeks to maximize the value of each, respecting the will of its European partners and recognizing changes across the continent. It was in this context that Secretary Baker had spoken in Berlin, in December 1989. He proposed, concurrently, an enhanced political role for NATO, strengthened institutional and consultative links between the US and EC, and reinforcement of all three baskets of the CSCE framework.

Secretary Baker's vision of new missions for NATO included political consultative arrangements on arms control agreements and confidence-building measures. He invited consideration of a NATO arms control verification staff. He advocated, with respect to regional conflicts, NATO consultations on non-proliferation of nuclear, chemical and biological weapons. NATO, moreover, should play a role in building economic and political ties to the East, where NATO can also promote human rights and democratic institutions.

Some of Secretary Baker's proposals for an enriched NATO political agenda overlap with ideas subsequently raised by the Twelve as possible elements of a European Common Foreign and Security Policy. He foreshadowed potential overlaps by announcing in Berlin that "We see no conflict between the process of European integration and an expansion of cooperation between the European Community and its neighbors to the East and West."[4] The goal, from an American standpoint, is to ensure that parallel action within NATO, in the European Community, in CSCE, and in other Western fora remains consistent, and promotes our mutual interests. These objectives are being carried out, for example, in the G24 process of assistance to the countries of Eastern and Central Europe. Congruent US and European approaches to changes in the East have been reinforced through coordinated projects that promote democracy and support the evolution of market economies.

Nevertheless, an EC foreign and security policy raises the prospect of competition among Western institutions. Robert Zoellick, Counselor of the Department of State, acknowledged this factor in the course of remarks given in Annapolis, Maryland, in September 1990. He suggested that overlap between NATO and EC processes be managed flexibly and pragmatically. We all, he noted, must bear in mind that NATO is the vehicle for the US defense and security presence in Europe. NATO is also, he continued, "a brilliantly successful expression of how democratic nations sharing common values can work together to maintain their security."[5] He further suggested that a strong

---

4 *U.S. Policy Information and Texts*, No. 175, 12 December 1989.
5 *U.S. Policy Information and Texts*, No. 133, 28 September 1990.

European pillar of NATO can contribute to new Alliance missions while ensuring European stability and the common defense.

Potential EC-NATO overlaps are becoming more apparent as the Twelve define the agenda of a Common Foreign and Security Policy. The Rome EC Summit of December 1990 identified security issues for consideration by the Twelve in the framework of Political Union. These issues are, to varying degrees, also taken up at NATO: arms control and disarmament, CSCE matters, United Nations peace-keeping operations, economic and technological cooperation in the armaments field, coordination of arms export policy, and non-proliferation.

One question confronting the United States is whether its European partners will choose to harmonize their policy on overlapping issues first among the Twelve, and then bring an agreed position to NATO; or whether NATO will be the focus of both primary and conclusive policy formulation among sixteen allies.

This question may be sharper in theory than it is in practice. EPC already has a lengthy record on non-proliferation, arms sales embargoes, CSCE, support for arms control agreements, chemical weapons, and UN disarmament. The EC Council of Ministers approved in early 1990 a regulation on the export of chemical weapons precursors. On balance, the United States has welcomed EPC and Community action that promotes international security. Substantive US and EPC policies are usually quite close. EPC often reinforces Western positions agreed elsewhere. EPC is also well adapted to speak on certain types of issues, such as those outside the NATO area, that cannot be readily addressed by other collective Western institutions.

The debate on a common European foreign and security policy during 1991 has implied the creation of a "super EPC," of many possible formulations. An enhanced EPC process could magnify American concerns with respect to closed policy-making among the Twelve that excludes participation by the US while bearing on issues of US interest. We speak here of the *fait accompli* problem. Issues that straddle EC (or EPC) and NATO competence may arise in either forum. Conclusive consensus positions first agreed by the Twelve and later brought to NATO could leave the non-EC NATO partners without sufficient range for discussion. Should the five non-EC NATO partners face fixed consensus positions, they might have to choose among unsatisfying options: opposing their EC-member NATO partners on a matter in which the Twelve have invested time, thought and commitment -- and thereby incurring the costs that would come when trying to alter the EC position; leaving the issue unresolved in NATO for lack of consensus; or perhaps accepting a position generated by the Twelve but without adequate NATO debate.

The United States, in supporting the evolution of a Common Foreign and Security Policy, views NATO as the paramount institution for Atlantic security.

The *fait accompli* issue is but one of several reasons why NATO must remain the focal point of decisive action on Atlantic security issues. Much of NATO's success rests upon the support that the Atlantic Alliance enjoys among Western publics, national legislative institutions, elected officials, and the executive administrations responsible for carrying out security policy. American support for the Alliance rests in large part on the effectiveness of US participation in deliberations on Atlantic security. Much of NATO's strength also lies in its integrated command structure that successfully ensures Western defense, and deterrence against external threats to the North Atlantic area.

The evolution of Western security policy, in the context of European Political Union, may include new roles for the Western European Union (WEU). Although the United States is not a member of WEU, American officials have applauded its contributions. President Bush did so in May 1989, referring to, "defense cooperation developing in the revitalized Western European Union, whose members worked with us to keep open the sea-lanes of the Persian Gulf."[6] He similarly praised growing military cooperation between West Germany and France. State Department Counselor Robert Zoellick signalled in September 1990 that NATO can usefully promote cooperative operations between the US and WEU in tackling regional security challenges.

The future relationship of WEU to NATO, the EC and the United States presents challenges yet to be resolved. From an American standpoint, new steps involving the WEU should not weaken the role of the NATO alliance. Rather, the US looks toward a Common Foreign and Security Policy that reinforces the Alliance. Accordingly, serious thought must be given to WEU-related questions such as command structures, the political basis for WEU action, and the role of non-WEU European members of NATO. Security problems arising outside the NATO Treaty area, and how they are addressed by Western institutions, will also continue to call for judicious consideration by the Atlantic partners.

The United States recognizes the practical and considered approach that EC member states are taking toward Political Union. This sense of confidence was reflected in the July 1990 NATO summit declaration. The United States, Canada, and the European allies announced that the development of a European security identity will contribute to Atlantic solidarity and lasting peace throughout all of Europe. Similarly, the CSCE process has achieved notable successes, and promises still more, through a widening political dialogue. A Common Foreign and Security Policy on the part of the Twelve would affect this dialogue; the United States would want to work with the Twelve to ensure that new arrangements on their part result in greater stability throughout the continent.

---

6   See note 1.

The June 1991 NATO Ministerial meeting in Copenhagen brought forth a communiqué that tied together the strands of European integration, the EC and North Atlantic security. Foreign Ministers of NATO partners noted that a European security identity and defense role, within the Alliance, could strengthen NATO's effectiveness. At the same time, they recognized that an emerging European foreign and security policy could affect dynamics within the Alliance. Accordingly, Ministers called for links and consultation procedures between the Twelve and the Alliance (of sixteen). A goal at Copenhagen was to ensure that in-house talks at Twelve complement, rather than compromise, the security views and interests of non-EC alliance partners.

In the end, European Political Union including a Common Foreign and Security Policy is a matter that will be resolved by the Twelve. As the Intergovernmental Conference (IGC) on Political Union proceeds, American officials are following a sometimes ambiguous train of events. US responses to IGC proposals, such as the relationship of WEU to the European Council, have been guided by the principles described above. Above all, there is a sense of confidence that Political Union, developed appropriately, will bring a stronger and more secure Atlantic community.

13

View from the Soviet Union: Integration as a Progressive Concept for the Common European Home

Aleksandr Yakovenko

There is no denying that the Europe of today is a complex and fragile phenomenon burdened by the heavy legacy of the past. The Cold War froze the internal development of the Continent, disrupting its natural life processes and piling up mighty icebergs of military confrontation. In the past few years, however, the situation on the European continent has changed beyond recognition. The postwar period that has lasted for decades is now finally drawing to a close. Obsolete notions, instruments and methods of relations between nations and states are rapidly sinking into oblivion. The concept of stability, and not just military stability, but stability in social, economic, political and ethnic terms as well, is becoming the key element of the new world order. The shaping of unprecedented structures based on interaction and confidence has begun. A deep-rooted process of transition from futile and lethal confrontation to multifarious cooperation, blazing the trail to the third millennium of European and world history, is already underway.

By military standards Europe is the area of concentration of an enormous destructive potential, thus placing it in a position of global responsibility. In terms of economics, no matter how large and successful the planned common market of the twelve European Community (EC) countries might be, it will still be just a part of the regional and much greater world economy. From the political point of view, the role of Europe is now indeed inexhaustible, for the Continent now has a chance of overcoming the division between the West and the East, of testing new principles of relations, of developing new and different approaches to security, adequate to the criteria of the new era.

Today, European affairs, as well as world relations, are in transition. This period is characterized by the fact that elements of the nascent alternative pattern of security clash with the realities and mentality of a time that is fading into the past. The very notion of national security is changing. It is assuming new features, due to rapid and profound transformations in human civilization, i.e. an accelerated development of science and technology and closely related production sphere, dramatic growth of commodity exchange, intensified flows of capital and technological ideas: in short, a transformation of the world into a fundamentally new state of political, economic, social and informational interdependence.

As a result of all this, the perception of national security, traditionally defined as the state of being protected from the external threat, is changing. Concurrent with this change, the capability to rebuff and thus prevent attack or military pressure from the outside -- through maintaining armed forces on a certain level, and through the membership in political and military alliances, and the establishment of blocs and coalitions -- as means of guaranteeing national security (as defined above), is becoming increasingly inadequate.

Presently, there emerges a pattern of relations based on a fundamentally different approach, proceeding from a diminished external threat and determined efforts to strengthen all aspects of stability. It is evident that the attempts to strengthen stability by confronting the potential enemy with equal threat alone lead nowhere. Thus, the task of ensuring security seems to be an increasingly political problem. Military might is losing its erstwhile primary role in determining the place of a country in the world. In a situation where everyone recognizes that nuclear weapons can no longer be regarded as a means of war, the military factor is becoming just one of many important elements of foreign policy. A good example of this is Japan, whose might is based on rapid development in science, technology and economics, propelled by achievements in the information revolution rather than by the possession of vast territory, rich sources of various raw materials, or nuclear weapons. Powers of this kind are able to resolve nearly all thinkable rational foreign policy problems by relying on their leading role in technology, economy and finance.

Another element of national security, ever growing in its importance, is the joining of efforts on an international scale, but first and foremost in the economic field. Moreover, integration in Western Europe which has been gaining powerful momentum since the late 1980s has actually extended to external policy where coordination has in fact developed into policies pursued by the EC countries on most of the fundamental issues. Further development of this trend is expected. Not everything is clear in this regard, even to the participants in the European Political Cooperation, not to mention outsiders. For instance, given the existing EC limitations on the extension of the Community's competence to the politico-military aspects of security, the Western European Union (WEU) has come to be regarded by certain West

European countries as a natural instrument of cooperation in this field, complementing the economic cooperation within the EC.

As a result of WEU revitalization, the dialogue of the participating states on politico-military problems has, on the one hand, become more profound, but, on the other hand, some areas of a competition of sorts between EC, WEU and NATO have emerged. In spite of the fact that the political, institutional and financial potential of WEU significantly lags behind that of NATO and the European Community, the Western European Union nevertheless seems to gravitate towards the activation of its functions in terms of ensuring security of its member states. This trend is expressed above all in the desire to expand the relative independence of the West European pillar of NATO, to harmonize activities of European NATO countries outside the North Atlantic Treaty zone, to coordinate their efforts to monitor and verify conventional arms treaties and confidence-building measures, to participate actively in the transition to a new system of security and cooperation in Europe. We could say that the military and economic integration of European NATO members is a strong factor pushing them towards greater independence.

In the present situation, more profound politico-military cooperation against the background of the emerging integrated politico-military economic complex in Western Europe may indeed in the long run become the basis for the development of a kind of "West European defense" which would be relatively independent, although relying on US strategic guarantees. It is as yet unclear, however, at what rate and especially in what form the trend towards military integration will develop in Western Europe. It is possible that at least in the short term the development would be restrained by the apprehensions of the European NATO countries when it comes to major and far-reaching changes in transatlantic relations and Western security structures in this period of uncertainties in the East and general instability of the international situation (meaning, for example, the civial war in Yugoslavia and the war in the Gulf). In short, the long-term position of the West European countries is far from unambiguous. It will be greatly affected by a number of strong elements, of which the principal one is the diminished importance of the military factor in policy and the transition to the development of peaceful cooperation on the scale of the entire European continent. Quite naturally, this will encourage the European countries to use collective forms of security as fully as possible.

It is important to keep in mind that the Paris Charter of November 1990 launched the construction of a system of *pan*-European security, setting its principal reference points. This pattern would be preferable for all who would wish to try it in practice. One of its great advantages is that it will remove the possibility of renewed confrontation in any new forms, while such a possibility cannot be excluded in principle, if the West of Europe started to build one system of security and the East a different one. This possibility should be avoided. The core of transformation in the relations between East and West on the European continent underway now may be found in the idea of the Common European house.

What is the Common European house and what is its essence? Perhaps, it is the problem of whether a convergence between Western and Eastern Europe will be achieved, or whether the situation will develop into a new confrontation. The closer the convergence will be -- without loss of face by either side or by any state -- the greater will be the influence and weight of Europe in world affairs, the greater will be the certainty that all European, but not only the European peoples, will achieve prosperity. It should be emphasized here that the Soviet Union must participate in the Common European house as a whole, that is including of course its Asian part. Besides, the US and Canada should be equal residents of the large European house.

The idea of common European house does not claim to change social systems or eliminate politico-military alliances, not to mention economic groupings, overnight. However, it envisages an accelerated rate of building security and cooperation, of overcoming the division of Europe by removing all types of confrontation. The CSCE process lies at the core of this, and the success of CSCE, as demonstrated at the 1990 Paris summit, proves that it is a reliable and solid core. The idea of the Common European house has struck a sensitive nerve in international politics, as it takes into account the close political, economic and cultural links as well as the growing interdependence of peoples, facing the various challenges and problems with high potential for escalation that we are confronted with today, and that can be resolved only by joint efforts of all states.

We must regard the further evolution of the concept of the Common European House in the context of preparing the Meeting of Representatives of the CSCE Participating States to be held in Helsinki in March 1992. It is necessary to begin drawing up today the principles for the establishment of a Europe of the 21st century, which serve as a basis for the final document of a new Helsinki conference in 1992. Laying a firm legal foundation for the principles of the Final Act is of paramount importance in the area of political aspects of security and cooperation. This would turn them into effective laws for the functioning of an all-European home and would make a substantial contribution to the development of Europe as a community of states ruled by law.

Enhancement of security on the basis of the principle of defense sufficiency must serve as the principal guideline in building the all-European home. Each particular issue still offers a vast field of work. The concept of deep, 40 to 50 percent cuts in conventional armaments proposed by some researchers requires a comprehensive analysis. The problem of military conversion needs to be further elaborated. The outside threat has diminished, turbulent internal developments are taking place in the countries of Eastern Europe, at times, differences between them become acute. Is this a tragic process of collapse? Rather than witnessing a tragic process of collapse we are observing a normal process, where artificial unity is replaced by natural differences of interests, positions and assessments. What is actually meant here is the need to work out a new approach to a possible evolution of East European countries, the need to neutralize possible negative consequences of such an evolution and to safeguard the basic interest of European security and stability.

One of the most pressing tasks is the formation of a large European economic space, the establishment of a single European infrastructure that would embrace environment, energy, transport, standardization, new and innovative technologies, the exploration of outer space, disease control, information systems, etc. The evolution of integration processes must lead to a rational coupling of different levels of development rather than an establishment of separate economic fortresses. Considering the present-day political and psychological atmosphere in Europe, humanitarian cooperation acquires particular importance. The Soviet Union has been thoroughly preparing for the 1991 Moscow conference on human rights, working out not only individual proposals but also a comprehensive concept which would allow the Moscow forum to turn into a significant milestone in the development of European humanitarian cooperation.

Thus, the actual formation of a politico-military, economic, humanitarian, and legal basis for an all-European home has started. This project will be at the heart of Soviet policy in Europe at the turn of the 21st century. The concept and practice of an all-European home provides favorable conditions for radical domestic transformations in the Soviet Union. And it is obvious that it is hardly possible to build an all-European home without ensuring order and normal progressive development in one's own country. Hence the policy of the Soviet Union is based on a desire to orient European security cooperation toward the establishment of new non-confrontational structures to promote the acceleration of positive developments in Europe. To that end, the USSR will develop her ties with various West European organizations.

In practical terms, we expect to further develop our dialogue with the Western European Union, both between its Assembly and the USSR Supreme Soviet, as well as direct contacts with other bodies, in particular with the newly established WEU Institute for Security Studies. That dialogue could address specific practical issues. For instance, we could explore the possibility of promoting cooperation between the USSR and the WEU in the development and practical implementation of measures to verify compliance with treaties. This would not only facilitate the search for mutually acceptable optimal solutions but could also serve as an important element of new all-European security structures.

There are also other promising areas of cooperation which would encourage Western Europe to opt for all-European structures, as opposed to a reliance on NATO alone. They could include mutual transparency in the militaro-economic area, cooperation in the establishment of means of verification, as well as in the development of new technologies for arms destruction, and in the limitation of export of arms and military equipment to third countries. As stated previously, the appeal of all-European initiatives resides in the fact that they are based primarily on the existing realities which, both in the West and in the East, find their reflection in the activities of regional organizations, politico-military alliances and economic groups.

The new political thinking has permitted to look at the integration processes underway in Western Europe in a new way and in a broader context. Reflecting as it does an objective necessity, not only economically but also politically, integration becomes one of the most important trends of today. One can even say that in its political dimension, integration is increasingly asserting itself as a progressive development. This underlies the policy of the USSR aimed at developing active cooperation with the European Community whose contribution to European and also world processes is becoming ever more tangible and constructive. The Twelve are becoming a more and more visible and dynamic factor in international politics and Soviet cooperation with the European Community is becoming a promising channel of mutual adaptation and of overcoming the disunity of the Continent.

The dialogue between the Soviet Union and the European Community as a political entity has been going on for more than two years now. However, it has acquired a high and stable momentum in the form of consultations, held twice a year with the Troika, consisting of representatives from the three countries chairing the European Community (in the previous, current and following six-month periods). The mutual desire of the sides to conduct this dialogue in the spirit of cooperation is a guarantee against any potential serious difficulties that might arise. The current positive changes in Europe serve as a solid basis for raising the political and economic cooperation between the USSR and the European Community to a qualitatively new level.

In terms of a rapprochement between the East and the West of the European continent, the Soviet Union believes it is both feasible and realistic to work towards orienting the political dialogue with the European Community in the direction of a gradual transition from mere exchanges of views and positions to a search for possible areas of common or parallel diplomatic efforts, toward a practical interaction in consolidating favorable changes in Europe and the entire world. To speed up the CSCE process, strengthen stability and security, consolidate the historic shifts on the Continent, and establish a new European Community of the 21st century, represent the most immediate areas for such interaction. The settlement of regional conflicts as well as other transnational problems facing mankind could find an important place in that dialogue.

In this context, the USSR and the Twelve could become co-authors of many ideas and steps. The joint statement on the Gulf crisis and Middle East affairs, adopted in New York on December 26, 1990, serves as a specific example of practical cooperation between the Soviet Union and the European Community in search of solutions to regional conflicts. This provides favorable opportunities for possible joint efforts in the future within the framework of political interaction between the Soviet Union and the European Community. Similar steps could also be taken with respect to other topical international issues as has been done in the case of the Yugoslav conflict. In practical terms, the political dialogue could be promoted by regular consultations at the level of experts on specific international problems and by preparing promising joint studies on issues of mutual interest.

The conclusion between the USSR and the European Community of a general agreement embracing also the sphere of political cooperation, which would reflect the recent changes in relations between the Soviet Union and the Twelve and which would contain guidelines for the future, could become an important stage in that dynamic dialogue. The USSR Ministry of Foreign Affairs has already begun practical preparations for negotiations on the conclusion of a so called "Big agreement" with the European Community. As an intermediate step, a protocol on regular political consultations could be signed.

The Soviet Union is following with attention and interest the ideas that are being expressed with respect to a future Common Foreign and Security Policy of the Community. Naturally, it is the sovereign right of the EC member states to decide themselves how these policies should be implemented. There are good reasons to believe that those policies will be constructive and will seek to finally overcome the division of Europe, and further limit the military factor in European equations. At any rate, it is precisely such policies we would like to deal with.

Most probably, the foreign policies of the twelve states of the European Community will serve as components of that policy. Does this mean that old traditional diplomacy will recede to the past and the Soviet Union instead of contacts with Paris, London and other capitals will hold consultations only with Brussels? Evidently it is still premature to expect that this will be the case. For all the dynamism of the process of political cooperation in the European Community, we are not about to see the establishment or the emergence of the Ministry of Foreign Affairs of the EC in the form that it operates in individual states. However, it is also clear that it will be an institution that will express the maximum that the Twelve states will be ready to yield, in terms of their sovereign foreign policy functions to an adequately established level of interaction between the countries of the European Community.

In conclusion, one has to point out that we are witnessing an unusual period in European politics. Finally the "window of opportunity" has been thrust open through which the warm spring winds of renovation on the European continent have reached us. Politics also knows the time of sowing when it is so important to plant generous handfuls of good ideas. We shall live to see those seeds bear fruit if we do our best now not to lose time which would be at the expense of security and prosperity of the ancient and eternally young Europe.

14

View from Japan: Asymmetries in the Evolving European-Japanese Dialogue

*Kensei Hiwaki**

Introduction

It goes without saying that Japan and the European Community/European Political Cooperation (EC/EPC) have shared similar interests in the same politico-economic camp as important parties of the advanced economies. Thus, as far as political interests are concerned, there have not been many quarrels between them, and, accordingly, Japan-EPC interactions have rapidly developed since the institutionalization of regular meetings between Japan and the EPC Presidency at the level of Foreign Ministers in 1983. In the sphere strictly of economic relations, especially in that of bilateral trade, however, Japan and the EC have long harbored animosity against each other. This is perhaps due to their differing standpoints and conflicting interests, to say nothing of the disparate entities of the negotiating parties (a nation-state versus a supranational organization). The long-standing discrimination of Japanese exports by the EC and its member states and their expanding trade deficits with Japan have overshadowed the course and nature of their dialogue. Probably because of the varying degrees of conflicts with individual member states, Japan has always regarded them as tangible and competent parties in negotiations. Thus, only slowly over the stretch of some thirty years, the EC Commission has gained weight in the eyes of the Japanese policy-makers as an at first additional, and later dominant, party to deal with.[1]

---

* The views expressed in this article do not necessarily reflect those of the Government of Japan.
1 Chihiro Hosoya and Hiroshi Okuma, "EC To Nippon" (literally: EC and Japan), in: C. Hosoya and Y. Minami (eds.), *Oshu Kyodotai (EC) no Kenkyusho -- Seiji*

EC-Japan Perception Gap

It is no exaggeration to say that official Japan-EC contacts have almost exclusively evolved through trade conflicts.[2] The bulk of their negotiations can be uniquely characterized as a tug-of-war over the trade restrictions and imbalances existing between them. From Japan's viewpoint, the Commission and the member states have unfairly maintained a variety of discriminatory measures against their imports from Japan. Thus, Japan's rationale for dealing with the individual member states and/or the Commission has mainly been the removal of the long-standing discrimination, which in essence amounts to an unequal treaty between Japan and the EC.

One important postwar precedence of such inequality goes back to 1955, prior indeed to the establishment of the EEC, when Belgium, France, Luxembourg, the Netherlands and the United Kingdom invoked Article 35 of the GATT against Japan upon its admission to that organization.[3] Paying no heed to the famous GATT principle of nondiscrimination, they refused to grant Japan the most-favored-nation treatment. Their subsequent withdrawal in 1963-1964 (prior to Japan's admission to the OECD) of the invocation after arduous negotiations, however, was followed by introduction of selective safeguards and various other measures, such as quota and voluntary export restrictions, against Japanese products.[4] Therefore, Japan has long tended to perceive the Commission and some of the member states as being protectionist and discriminatory. This perception has imbued the Japanese mind with a suspicion that the EC is tacitly classifying its imports into three general categories for

---

Rikigaku No Bunseki (literally: Studies on the European Community -- Analyses of the Political Dynamics), Tokyo: Shinyu-Do, 1980, Chapter 11, p. 342.

2   Masami Kodama, "Nippon To EC No Boeki Mondai" (literally: Trade Problems between Japan and the EC), in: Teruo Kanamaru (ed.), *EC -- Oshu Togo No Genzai* (literally: The EC -- The Present Stage of the European Integration), Osaka: Sogen-Sha, 1987, Chapter 27, pp. 194-195.

3   Ryutaro Komiya and Motoshige Ito, "Japan's International Trade and Trade Policy, 1955-1984," in: T. Inoguchi and D.I. Okimoto (eds.), *The Political Economy of Japan*, Volume 2: *The Changing International Context*, Stanford: Stanford University Press, 1988, p. 178. Also, see Kenjiro Ishikawa, *Japan and the Challenge of Europe 1992*, London: The Royal Institute of International Affairs, 1990, p. 13; and Endymion Wilkinson, *Japan versus The West: Image and Reality*, London: Penguin Books, 1990, p. 168.

4   Ichiro Shirakawa, "Sainen Suru Hogoshugi" (literally: The Resurgence of Protectionism), in: I. Shirakawa (ed.), *Beika Jiyuboeki-Kyotei -- EC Togo Wo Miru* (literally: Observation on the US-Canada Free-Trade Agreement and the European Integration), Tokyo: Toyo Keizai Shinpo-Sha, 1989, Chapter 1, p. 36-37.

discriminatory treatments, first from Japan, second from the other external GATT members, and third from the non-GATT-members.

Furthermore, Japan has suspected that a solidly unified EC under the leadership of the Commission might work against Japan's interests, despite the Commission's frequent denouncement of Fortress Europe.[5] In other words, it has feared the prospects that the current unfair discrimination of Japanese imports by the individual member states would be mostly reinstituted at the EC supranational level. Such a suspicion has its roots in the EC's politico-economic realities: i.e., judging from a historical perspective as to the EC handling of the so-called "Japan problem," any compromised policy might very well accommodate the strong voices of the weaker and/or protectionist economies among the member states, and of the weaker and/or sensitive sectors among their industries.[6]

Viewed from the EC and the member states, on the other hand, Japan has not conducted itself particularly well as trade partner. To say the least, it has been quite a "disruptive" trader and "trouble-maker" in the EC markets.[7] Japan's "dumping" in the markets and its trading behavior, resembling a "torrential downpour," has incessantly aroused the attention of the EC authorities and caused headaches for the affected industries. And, especially when the member states were struggling with their rampant inflation and/or agonizing unemployment after the first and second oil crises, Japan was seen as aggravating their problems by its recurrent export offensives to the EC markets. Such offensives, as a result, imposed on the EC an added problem of increasing

---

5 Yasuhiro Nakasone, "Japan Should Offer Economic Support to East Europe," *European Affairs*, 2/90, Summer 1990, p. 55. Former Prime Minister Nakasone hints Japan's concern by arguing as follows: "...even if the European Community does not become an exclusive fortress, as it expands it will inevitably come to resemble a convoy of ships. This convoy will be made up of countries which move at different speeds toward free trade and market liberalization. From Japan's perspective, we would hope that the European Community will not adopt a policy towards Japan that is in line with the slower-paced countries, but will adopt a policy that is as open as possible."

6 Shirakawa (note 5), p. 34. Shirakawa, as career bureaucrat at Japan's Economic Planning Agency, argues that the EC Commission with limited power accorded by the member states has to coordinate the interests of these states, often resulting in a compromised policy of maintaining the status quo or a policy leaning toward protectionist interests. For further details, see pp. 34-37.

7 *Keizai Dantai Rengo-Kai, Ho EEC Keizai Shisetsu-dan Hokokusho* (literally: Report of the Economic Mission to the EEC), Tokyo: Keizai Dantai Rengo-Kai, April 1963, pp. 40-42. Even a member of the Mission, Tsunao Okumura -- the then Chairman of the Board of Directors at Nomura Securities -- wrote a report highly critical of Japanese marketing practices overseas, including Shukketsu Yushutsu (below-cost sales abroad).

trade deficits, and also caused the EC authorities to accuse them of causing unemployment.

Under such circumstances, the EC side started to suspect, too, that Japan had resorted to a beggar-thy-neighbor policy only to avoid its own predicament.[8] Besides, its domestic market has been seen by many of those concerned as an impenetrable fortress or, at least a haven only for the domestic businesses, well guarded by the governmental policy and the local business practices. Furthermore, Japan's dealing with the individual member states, on top of its negotiation with the Commission, has often been suspected as a behind-the-curtain maneuver to divide the member states' interests in its favor, against the common cause and solidarity of the EC.[9] More important, perhaps, the lack of transparency or the enigma in Japanese policy-making and implementation may have often left the Commission in a blind alley and made it anxious and frustrated.

Therefore, the views and intentions of the two parties, due probably to their different standpoints and conflicting interests, have often been at odds and hindered their mutual understanding. Indeed, the lack of any common EC external trade policy toward Japan and the absence of an official Japan-EC trade agreement may speak eloquently for the hide-and-seek state of Japan-EC politico-economic realities. Behind the recurrent thaw and the expressed mutual intentions of industrial, scientific and environmental cooperation, as well as that for development of the East European countries, Japan and the EC are still engaged in the tug-of-war over the negative aspects of their economic relations, and, at the same time, they may be struggling in their soul-searching efforts for more positive overall relations beyond 1992.[10]

---

8 Hosoya and Okuma (note 2), p. 346.
9 Ibid., p. 355.
10 See Dries van Agt, "United States-Japan-Europe: The Unholy Trinity," *European Affairs*, 2/90, Summer 1990; and Dries van Agt, "Japan: the Sun in the Afternoon," *European Affairs*, 3/89, Autumn 1989. Also, see Nakasone (note 6), pp. 55-56 and 59. The Japan-EC Ministerial Meeting on 29 May 1990, emphasized enhancement of global cooperation between Japan and the EC both in the bilateral context and within the EC-Japan-US trilateral framework. Confirming a variety of cooperations already underway regarding promotion and development of the East European countries and promotion of European exports to Japan, among other things, both sides expressed earnest desire to "enhance and deepen co-operation in the field of communication and information, development assistance, labor and social affairs and cultural exchange." See Information Centre of the Mission of Japan to the European Community (ed.), *News & Views From Japan*, No. 343, 5 June 1990.

History and Nature of the Community-Japan Dialogue

Reflecting the above skeptic views of the EC and Japan, their typical dialogue has been much tinted with confrontation. Even such dialogue was almost non-existent between the Government of Japan and the Commission until about 1970.[11] Problems of the individual member states with Japan not being uniform, both Japan and the member states perhaps did not want extra shackles in their bilateral negotiations.

Besides, the GATT was considered a more appropriate forum to discuss their trade-related problems, and, after Japan's admission to the OECD in 1964, the latter organization also offered an additional forum for even a broader scope of cooperation and coordination between Japan and the EC member states.[12] Furthermore, their bilateral trade during the period amounted to nothing but small fractions of their worldwide trade volumes.[13]

Early Incidences of Negotiations

This almost total neglect of the Commission by both Japan and the member states regarding their trade negotiations came to an end in 1970. Japan's attitude toward the EC Commission as an important negotiation counterpart evolved gradually in the course of the 1970s.[14] At the time when Japanese exports to the EC started to grow rapidly, the Commission, with the EC common commercial policy coming into effect on January 1, 1970, began to conduct negotiations with Japan on behalf of all the member states. The Commission then wanted to insert a general safeguard clause in a prospective trade agreement with Japan, in accordance with the wishes of the member states.[15]

It was, of course, unacceptable to Japan, especially because it implied an official acknowledgement of discrimination against its products even at the level of the supranational organization. Also, it implied that any Japanese exports to the EC could be restricted. The Japanese negotiators referred the Commission counterparts to Article 19 of the GATT, among other possible compromises, which all together could potentially provide sufficient protection

---

11   Hosoya and Okuma (note 2), p. 353.
12   See a 10-point policy recommendation made public on 30 April 1962 by the Subcommittee for International Economy of the Liberal Democratic Party (Jimin-To Kokusai Keizai Shoiinkai), in: Ministry of Foreign Affairs, *EEC No Hatten To Nippon* (literally: The Development of EEC and Japan), 1962, pp. 102-103.
13   See MITI's White Paper on International Trade for the period between 1959 and 1970.
14   Hosoya and Okuma (note 2), pp. 353-354.
15   Ishikawa (note 4), pp. 20-21.

of the EC markets.[16] As an end result of the negotiations, they could not come up with any concrete trade agreement between them.

Negotiations under the Strain of the First Oil Crisis

After Richard Nixon's announcement of the New Economic Policy in August 1971, Japan started to mount an export drive to the EC. Then the first oil crisis invited Japan to begin a further intensified export offensive, due mainly to the increasing aggravation of Japan's domestic stagflation. Facing the rapidly mounting bilateral trade deficits with Japan, the EC Commission, in the meantime, frequently expressed its grave concern over the expanding imbalance.[17] Visits of a Japanese industrial delegation, the so-called Doko Mission, to the member states and the Commission in October 1976, however, marked a new epoch for Japan-EC relations. The Community with the Commission as a spearhead began to criticize Japan in an emotional pitch, signalling an increasing politicization of trade problems.[18]

The subsequent close contacts and negotiations produced the so-called Yoshino Letter to Commissioner Gundelach, which expressed the views of the Japanese Government, emphasizing the support of the principle of free trade, the desire for improvement of dialogue with the EC and the consideration necessary for third-country benefits.[19] Also involved was the European Council at The Hague in November 1976 and again at Rome in March 1977, which repeated its statements pressing Japan to achieve early results regarding the bilateral-trade imbalance.

Further, the pending issue gave rise to an official visit to Japan of Commission President Roy Jenkins (Jenkins-Fukuda Talk) in October 1977 and an official visit to the Commission by Minister Nobuhiko Ushiba, head of Japan's newly instituted Ministry for External Economic Affairs, to talk with Jenkins in December 1977. Ushiba promised Jenkins an increase of Japan's import from the EC as a measure to reduce the imbalance. Again, Ushiba visited the Commission in January 1978, and the latter stressed the inadequacy of Japan's measures against the trade imbalance and impressed upon him the necessity of strengthened action. This trade dispute centering on the imbalance question came to a tentative conclusion by issuing a joint communiqué at the Japan-EC trade conference in Tokyo of March 1978, only to start a much more embittered dialogue with the recurrence of the oil crisis.[20]

---

16   Ibid., p. 21.
17   Wilkinson (note 4), p. 177.
18   Hosoya and Okuma (note 2), 344-348.
19   Ibid., p. 348.
20   Ibid., pp. 349-50.

Negotiations Stuck in a Bog

Starting in 1979, the EC Commission became more blunt in its criticism of Japan, and a leaked Commission's confidential document which referred to Japan as "a country of workaholics who live in what Westerners would regard as little better than rabbit-hutches" was interpreted at least by the Japanese government as a sharp criticism against the nation.[21] With the growing Japanese exports to the EC, especially the rapid expansion of Japanese car sales, uproarious voices against Japan and its industries came from the leaders of the industries affected and the Member State Governments concerned. The escalating trade dispute even produced a side effect of the EC infighting between France and the United Kingdom over Nissan Motor's plan to set up a factory in the UK.[22]

Japan's Ministry of Foreign Affairs protested strongly against tougher measures since then instituted by the French Government regarding car imports from Japan, referring to no avail to the spirit of the GATT. The Commission, together with the Council and the European Parliament, however, was of the opinion that Japanese car exports to the EC should be subject to self-restraint, similar to the arrangement between Japan and the US, and demanded a concession from Japan in this regard. Without conceding to the Commission itself, however, Japan chose to deal with the member states and made arrangements respectively of its export moderation.[23]

There was still lingering skepticism on the Japanese side about the desirability of dealing with the Commission or, for that matter the Community as such, as its viable counterparts in trade negotiations. Meanwhile, the Commission resorted to a harder-line policy against Japan, introducing monitoring and other restrictive schemes, one after another, against Japanese exports of so-called sensitive products, and, concurrently, attempted to persuade Japan to make its market more accessible to European exports.[24]

The high handedness of the Commission officials dealing with the Japanese counterparts and the skeptic views of the Japanese negotiators over the Commission's viability made the situation only worse. EC allegations of Japan's "traditional and unique" trade barriers were typically met with Japanese denial of such barriers, referring to such allegations as misunderstandings.

---

21   Wilkinson (note 4), pp. 215-216.
22   Ishikawa (note 4), pp. 24-25 and 76-81. Also, see Hosaya and Okuma (note 2), pp. 349-50.
23   Ishikawa (note 4), p. 26.
24   Alastair Sutton, "Relations between the European Community and Japan in 1982 and 1983," in: F.G. Jacobs (ed.), *Yearbook of European Law*, Oxford: Clarendon Press, 1984, p. 285. Also see Ishikawa (note 4), pp. 26-28.

Japan also responded with repeated requests for greater efforts by European businessmen.[25]

Political Breakthrough

During 1982 and thereafter, under the pressure of surging US resentment against Japan's self-righteous protection of its domestic market and the threat of EC policy recourse to dispute-settlement in a multinational forum of the GATT, Japan began to back down on what it had said and adopt a series of package measures to open its market.[26] Also, a breakthrough in the impasse was propelled by an intensified politicization of Japan-EC relations.

In such an effort, Vice-Presidents Haferkamp and Davinion paid a visit to Tokyo early in 1983, and their talks with Prime Minister Nakasone and Foreign Minister Abe, among others, gave momentum to closer ministerial-level contacts on a broader agenda, albeit the fundamental Japanese attitude toward the EC still remaining characteristically pragmatic and self-centered. Their mutual interactions also opened the way to Japan's acceptance of the Commission as the Spokesman of the Community.[27]

Furthermore, on the brighter side of mutual interactions, a series of international politico-economic affairs, such as the hostage question of the US Embassy in Iran, the Soviet incursion on Afghanistan and the internal crises of Poland, offered momentous opportunities to start an official Japan-EPC dialogue, also resulting in positive mutual relations and regular conferences of the foreign ministers.[28] Subsequently, their repeated contacts on and beyond the confinement of economic issues brought forth further channels of regular communication in 1984, such as the conferences of political directors and the high-level consultations. In addition, others followed thereafter to increase the opportunity of their interactions and broaden the scope of their cooperation.

Current State of Bilateral Affairs

Accordingly, Japan and the EC/EPC have, in due course, included for their communication and cooperation the areas ranging from industrial cooperation,

---

25 Sutton (note 25), p. 285.
26 Ibid., p. 286.
27 Ibid., pp. 288-289.
28 As career diplomat well versed in the EC/EPC-Japan relations, Kazuyuki Odaira in: Nippon Kokusai Mondai Kenkyusho (ed.), *Kokusai Nenpo 1983-1984* [literally: Annual International Report], 1990, Chapter 5, emphasizes the favorable change in the atmosphere of EC-Japan economic talks from "confrontation and friction" to "dialogue and co-operation," after the repeated Japan-EPC conferences of the foreign ministers in 1983 and 1984.

science and technology, developmental assistance, environmental problems, and all the way to the question of global security, the last of which has produced important ramifications for both, especially after the fall of the Berlin Wall. Such expansion in their mutual contacts and cooperation has been increasingly seen by both authorities as conducive and necessary to strengthen the Japan-EC side of the Japan-US-EC triangle, not only for a better balance in the trilateral relations, but also for more effective cooperation and coordination regarding any politico-economic questions of global importance.[29]

This does not, however, imply that their trade-related questions have been congenially and/or satisfactorily resolved in an expanding context of mutual cooperation. Though apparent confrontation is well under control, the realities of mutual relations may have indicated many an overhanging cloud, if not have pointed totally in the other direction.[30] The development in the EC after the Single European Act has provided Japan with a looming anxiety over the probable Fortress Europe, especially based on the question of reciprocity.[31] On the other hand, the EC, in view of the ever-growing trade deficits with Japan, has been anxious about ramifications of the Japan-US Structural Impediments Initiative, especially about its range and magnitude of prospective benefits, which would be applicable to and accessible by the Community.[32] A still important problem of mutual concern is that a general Japan-EC bilateral trade agreement is not in sight.

Japanese Perceptions of EC/EPC Foreign Policy

Like other third countries, Japan has, on one hand, watched the evolution of EC/EPC foreign policy, especially its growing overlaps, with bewilderment. On the other hand, it may have regarded the two-tier structure of policy formation a welcome development for broader communication. The latter aspect seems to have assumed a growing importance, ever since the Japan-EC Commission trade negotiations experienced the stalemate of the early 1980s, in their

---

29 Commission of the European Communities, *Japan and the European Communities: A Stocktaking*, Brussels, April 1986, pp. 5-6; *News & Views From Japan* (note 11), pp. 1-3; and Nakasone (note 6), pp. 58-59.

30 Kodama (note 3), p. 199. Kodama views that the mechanism of political dialogue has not produced many EC-desired results in terms of correcting the prevailing trade imbalance. He also views that Japan-EC trade issue has turned into an emotional one, as far as the EC side is concerned.

31 Dries van Agt (in his article "Japan: The Sun In the Afternoon?" (note 11), pp. 97-99) affirms Japanese anxiety stating: "Whether or not the 'misgiving' on the part of the Japanese, their feeling of uncertainty or fears are real."

32 Dries van Agt, "United States-Japan-Europe: The Unholy Trinity" (note 11), p. 65.

bureaucratic bickering over the short-run, dead-end problem of trade imbalance.

To most Japanese, however, EPC itself has been a perplexing institution. Especially when it comes to the Presidency, due to its personnel overlap with the Council of Ministers, its roles and activities have not been easily visualized separate from those of the Council. Even today, EPC scarcely appears in the Japanese news media. When a foreign minister representing both the Presidency and the Council has a talk with the Japanese counterparts, he tends to be simply referred to as President of the EC Council. Likewise, views and policy stances of the two institutions tend to be treated as if they were exactly the same. For that matter, as far as the general public is concerned, often no clear-cut image exists of EPC. When it does, however, its probable image may be quite entangled with those of the EC-proper organizations, such as the Council, the Commission and the European Parliament.

Even to most of Japanese academicians and experts, it has become increasingly difficult to draw a dividing line between the areas of competence belonging to the Commission and EPC. Their information tends to direct attention simply to a growing overlap of competence and/or to the growing visibility of the Commission in international fora, such as the GATT, the OECD, the United Nations, and the Summit.

Perhaps only a limited number of Japanese experts, including some career diplomats and others having direct or indirect experience in dialogue with EPC and the EC Commission, may entertain the view of a growing EPC role in Community-related foreign policy and beyond.[33] Such a view may depend on the degree of importance placed on developments such as a growing role of the European Council and conferences of foreign ministers, the growing prospect of Political Union, the SEA General Provisions defining EPC's important roles for European unity, the establishment of the EPC Secretariat, and EPC's improved continuity with its Troika system.[34]

---

33 Toshiro Tanaka, "Seio No Anzen Hosho Taisei: EC Togo-go Mo Juso-kozo Tsuzuku" (literally: West European Security System: Continuing Multistoried Structure after EC Integration), *Nihon Keizai Shinbun*, 8 December 1988.

34 Asatsugu Tatsumi, "Kameikoku No Gaiko-seisaku Togo E No Doryoku -- Seiji Kyoryoku [EPC]" (literally: Efforts of member states toward Integration of External Policies -- Political Co-operation [EPC]), in: Teruo Kanamaru (ed.) (note 3), Chapter 26, p. 186; and his recent article, "Oshu Seiji Kyoryoku [EPC] No 20 Nen" (literally: European Political Co-operation over the Past 20 Years), *International Relations*, May 1990, p. 140. In the latter, he recognizes the EC-EPC tandem system as "probably the best approach," given the prevailing conditions, but he cautions that success of future EC Common External Policy depends on the will of member states and the political leadership within the European Community.

Especially to those governmental experts and negotiators, the growing EPC/Commission overlap in the realm of foreign policy may be a blessing. In other words, such a development may imply a greater room for maneuver in negotiations with their EC/EPC counterparts. In fact, when the narrowly-defined bilateral dialogue deadlocked in the early 1980s, EPC offered an added communication channel. Furthermore, to governmental officials who have daily encountered cumbersome inter-departmental negotiations and adjustments for policy consensus at home, it may not be an awesome task to handle two-tier or even a multi-tier negotiations with their European counterparts.

Besides, such an institutional overlap in competence can imply non-singular voices of the Community or, perhaps even divided interests between EPC and the Commission in the same policy realm. This ambiguity or counter-uniformity may be more soothing than alarming to the Government of Japan, since it has long observed the widening and deepening development of the EC with a sense of alarm. In other words, Japan has been wary of the growing unification of the EC, primarily concerned that prospective politico-economic unification would be counter to Japan's interest in the free, nondiscriminatory, and multilateral trade arrangements under the GATT.[35] Despite the Commission's repeated assurance of its support of and adherence to the GATT, Japan has long harbored a suspicion about future EC intentions, perhaps based on its historical perspective or rational expectation, that the Commission might lean toward the stronger voices of protectionist member states and stagnant industries.[36]

---

35 Hideaki Kumano, "Japan and the EC should Join Hands," *European Affairs*, 2/88, Summer 1988, p. 117; and Shinji Fukukawa, "The Role of the Japanese Economy in a Changing Western World," *European Affairs*, 4/88, Winter 1988, pp. 148-150. Kumano, the then Director General of MITI, and Fukukawa, a former Vice Minister of MITI, indirectly tried to caution the EC agianst becoming an obstacle to free and multilateral trade. Echoing their concerns, Kazukiyo Higuchi, Director of MITI's International Trade Research Office, was reported to have said "that the EC's trade with Japan is steadily increasing, and that nations should refrain from forming economic blocs and instead stress free trade" (*Japan Economic Journal*, 22 June 1990, p. 4).

36 Hirohide Narusawa, Sekai-keizai Ni Okeru Chiiki-shugi to Gurobarisumu -- EC 1992 To Nippon (literally: Regionalism and Globalism in the World Economy -- EC 1992 and Japan), Sekai-keizai Hyoron, December 1989, pp. 10-11. Narusawa points out three factors which may contribute to "Fortress Europe." First, the existing North-South problems within the EC and the coexistence of strong and weak industries (and firms) may compromise the EC authorities for protection of the weaker. Second, the question of local content, the unsettled definitions and criteria regarding product origins and Community firms, etc., may give rise to unfair discrimination against outsiders. Finally, owing to different historical,

Nevertheless, one can reckon that in this era of increasing politicization of economic matters and "economicization" of political matters, the EC-EPC duplication of competence in the external-policy realm will be conducive, in the long run, to more amicable and positive relations with Japan through its effects on their broader cooperation and policy coordination. It may also become conducive to more balanced EC-Japan-US trilateral relations and more equitably shared leadership and responsibilities of these economic giants in global affairs.

Moreover, based upon Japan's growing interactions with EPC, a new dimension for Japanese international presence is emerging slowly but steadily. That is, Japan is becoming more overtly involved in the political sphere of international relations. Along with this trend, a growing profile of the Ministry of Foreign Affairs vis-à-vis MITI and other economy-oriented government agencies has emerged. Perhaps Japan is well on the way toward a greater balance in its approach to international affairs with both political and economic ramifications.

---

political and economic relations of the Community with Japan and the United States, Japan may receive discriminatory treatments relative to the United States.

15

View from Austria: Preparing for Membership

Manfred Scheich

Austria follows the ongoing efforts to create a European Political Union with particular interest. Having applied for membership in the European Community (EC), it cannot any longer view these developments as an "outsider." Austria is convinced that it shall form part of this Union and thus knows that the present efforts will affect it directly. This prospect does not cause concern. On the contrary: Austria is fully aware that joining the EC does not only have economic implications, but means entering a community of common political values and aims.

The present Austrian government has already made it clear that Austria supports the objective of Political Union. In its inaugural Report to Parliament, the government called Political Union "a valuable contribution to European unity." It is, of course, true that the Austrian debate on EC membership was originally sparked off by the project of the Single European Market. Austria conducts over two thirds of its foreign trade with the Community. Austria's national economy and the Common Market are thus interlinked to an extent exceeding that of any other EFTA country and of many EC member states. Its immediate reaction to the Commission's "White Book" was therefore not surprising. But even then, Austria's analysis transcended simple cost-benefit criteria. The concept of the internal market held a clear political message. Austria saw it as another proof that European integration is a historic process that will shape the future of Europe and thereby also the future of Austria. It has thus decided to participate in this process in a spirit of solidarity, with an equal seat and vote in the organization that determines this process, i.e. the European Community.

It should also be remembered that Austria's application to become a member of the Community was presented in July 1989 -- well before the momentous winds of change that have since swept through Europe. At that time, the

Community's own thinking concentrated on the internal market. Since then, the revolutions of Eastern Europe have turned the European Community into the natural center of gravity of the future "architecture" of Europe. The Community understood that it would have to make rapid progress in political integration and strengthen its internal structures if it wished to deal with this secular challenge. At the same time, Austria realized that it wanted to find its place within this new and deepened Community. Additionally, its traditional links with the countries of Eastern Europe could prove a useful contribution to the Community's new European role. Austria's awareness of the political dimension of European integration has grown throughout these last two years. But in this, Austria has not really differed from the member states of the Community.

A further point to be stressed is that Austria's approach to European integration was never exclusively economic. This became clear as early as 1948 when Austria joined the family of Western European democracies in founding the Organization for European Economic Cooperation -- against marked opposition of the Soviet Union, then still one of the Four Powers occupying Austria. Its recent decision to join the European Community was certainly not taken on the spur of the moment. It is the logical consequence of having participated in the process of European integration for over 40 years. Austria's historical "instincts," its position in the very center of the continent, its political and economic structures make it what I should like to call an "*Etat fondateur manqué*" of the Community. Historical circumstances permitting, it really seems likely that Austria could have become a member of the Community at the very outset. (The issue was, in fact, discussed quite seriously for the first time in the late 1950s.) Now is the chance to join the EC at a moment when it is writing a new chapter of its history. Austria wishes the Community every possible success in its efforts to advance on the path to Political Union, towards European unity -- all the more because Austria knows that a deepened Community will find it easier to admit new members into its midst.

What is Austria's attitude to the various specific aspects of the Community's present day debate on Political Union? Evidently, Austria knows it is not as yet an active partner in this debate. In this sense, it remains an "outsider" until the moment of accession. Austria shall join a Community already moving towards Political Union. At the present stage Austria has one major interest: to remain informed about the development of this debate. President Delors recently told Austria's Federal Chancellor, Franz Vranitzky, that the Intergovernmental Conference would conclude its work by the end of this year (1991), thereby enabling Austria to define its own attitude on this issue. Final negotiations on Austria's inclusion into the future Political Union will have to wait until the latter's concrete shape is known. Yet it appears that intra-Community discussions on Political Union have advanced sufficiently to permit a first Austrian assessment. And this is quite unambiguous. The contours which are progressively emerging lead Austria to conclude that full participation is possible and desirable.

Austria supports the aim of the EC member states to endow the Community with greater democratic legitimacy. It very much shares the general opinion that subsidiarity should be made a basic principle of the Treaties. Austria's experience in federal structures might prove a useful contribution towards the practical realization of this concept. Austria wishes to participate actively and constructively in the framework of the future Common Foreign and Security Policy. In its December 1990 meeting, the European Council described the chief aims of such a policy as to maintain peace and stability, to further the rule of law and human rights, and to favor the economic development of all nations. These have always also been the main priorities of Austria's foreign policy.

Recent developments (Gulf War, civil war in Yugoslavia) have underlined the importance of Europe speaking with one voice. Austria therefore understands and supports the Community's efforts to streamline foreign policy decision-making in a number of fields. Interlinking the structures of classic integration and Common Foreign Policy seems the right way to achieve this result. Austria can also identify itself with the idea of deciding the basic principles of this policy by means of consensus and of foreseeing flexible and operational procedures for their application. The new Europe undoubtedly presents the European Community with specific responsibilities in the field of security. By its very history, the Community has proven the peace-creating force of integration. Robert Schuman was right: through interdependence, war not only becomes unthinkable, it becomes impossible. The international structures of European Communism have been dismantled, the East-West conflict has been overcome. The European Community has thus been granted a historic chance: it can extend its peace-making function to Europe as a whole.

At its December 1990 meeting, the European Council listed a number of issues that a Common Security Policy might deal with. Subjects like disarmament, CSCE matters and peace-keeping operations of the United Nations were mentioned. Austria could make useful contributions to a Common Security Policy in all these fields, but also in many other domains, e.g. in coordinated European action against international terrorism, crime and drug trafficking.

When speaking about the Austrian contribution to European security, the question is often raised about the significance of Austrian neutrality. It is important to stress that by declaring neutrality, Austria never sought to withdraw itself from the Western European community of values. Neutrality was the means to put an end to postwar occupation, to eliminate the risk of division and to regain national sovereignty -- within the fold of Western

Europe's democracies. There has never been the slightest doubt as to where Austria belongs ideologically. Its clear-cut stand in the course of many a European crisis has underlined this fact. This is another reason why Austria can contribute to the future Common Foreign and Security Policy of the Community. Austrian neutrality is self imposed. The concrete obligations enumerated in its Constitutional Law on neutrality are the following: non-participation in military alliances and non-admission of foreign military bases on Austrian territory. During the past decades, Austria has seen this status as its specific contribution to European peace and security. Austrian neutrality retains its significance, at least as long as there is no reliable and proven collective system of European security. Reasoning in this matter is based on one assumption: Europe's security is also Austria's. As the present Austrian government has already stated in its Working Program, neutral Austria will participate in the establishment and the functioning of the future European security system -- in the EC or beyond -- in the spirit of solidarity. In this context, Austria considers "solidarity" a key word. During the Gulf War, the international community has seen that a neutral Austria can exercise solidarity in the framework of a collective security system; Austria was the only neutral country that granted the Allies overflight and transit authorizations for transports to the Gulf region. In the Yugoslav case, too, Austria has been playing a constructive security-related role, especially in the CSCE framework.

The future European security structures are still in the making. For the time being Europe will probably continue to live with a security system that is of "variable geometry." During this phase, national contributions to European security will continue to take varying forms, solidarity thus expressing itself in varying ways. As a candidate for Community membership, Austria has, in any case, always known that accession to the Community means boarding a train on the move. Austria is anxiously awaiting the moment when it can join the common journey towards European unity.

16

The Hungarian View: An EC Associate's Perspective from Central Europe

István Körmendy*

Having made the peaceful and successful transition to multiparty democracy, one of the first major foreign policy initiatives by the new coalition government was to apply for association with the European Communities. The first pronouncements on the reorientation of foreign relations clearly articulated Hungary's intention to become part of an enlarged European/Atlantic community of nations.

I.

The determination to integrate Hungary into the political, economic and security order of the new Europe has become a standard definition of the central objective of foreign policy. This objective has also been reflected in the association agreement under negotiation with the European Communities. Association perceived as a transitory phase towards membership has been regarded as a key instrument of reintegrating Hungary into Europe where Hungarians feel historically, culturally, and intellectually to have always belonged.

With the unnatural and artificial division of Europe behind us, the choice for seeking reintegration through admission to the Council of Europe, association with the Community and rapprochement with security organizations was nearly self-evident. No viable alternatives offered themselves. As for association with the European Communities, there is solid support by all the six parliamentary parties behind government policy. Later on, as the specific implications will

---

* This article contains views of the author which do not necessarily reflect the official positions of the Hungarian Government.

become more clear in the context of economic hardships and social tensions accompanying the transition towards a market economy, feelings in the parliament may become more mixed. Nevertheless, none of the political parties is advocating an alternative to association with and eventual membership in the Community. The same applies to the public. Polls showed that the overwhelming majority of Hungarians, some three quarters or more, supports the policy of joining European integration.

The choice has had a historic context and association is seen as offering a historic chance, probably the only one, to Hungary for making up all the losses caused by the decades of imposed separation from the mainstream of European integration and from the European/Atlantic community of values. Accordingly, association agreement should be perceived as a *par excellence* political instrument. Even if most of its provisions are dealing with issues of trade and economic cooperation the underlying motivations extend well beyond economic considerations.

This is particularly evident if seen in comparison with the European Free Trade Area (EFTA) countries applying for EC membership. Growing interdependence in Western Europe and the economic power of a more deeply integrated European Community gave rise to doubts about the ability of the neutral states to maintain economic independences.

> The rapid abandonment of the traditional neutral view that neutrality is incompatible with EC membership derives from economic realities. It is recognised that national markets have to be open to EC competition if national industries are to compete effectively world-wide. Thus, membership is seen as vital to the survival of national industries. The applications of Austria, Finland and Sweden for EC membership derive from the recognition that it is impossible to secure economic integration with the Community without being involved in the political integration contemplated by the Community; negotiations on the EEA have served only to reinforce this understanding.[1]

For Hungary and the other two Central European states political and security incentives for association are not less strong than economic ones.

In the summer of 1990 Hungarian foreign and security policy began to rapidly dissociate itself from the declaratory allied relationship among Warsaw Treaty member states and from the old patterns of consultation and political cooperation that have become either irrelevant or made disservice to newly defined national interests. Hungarian foreign and security policy needed new

---

1 Richard Latter and Dietrich Schindler, "The Future of Neutrality in Europe", *Wilton Park Papers* 41, June 1991, p. 2, 6.

points of orientation and began to look for like-minded partners. The Community's opening toward cooperation with new and emerging democracies in the Eastern half of Europe and the offer to establish associated relations with the three Central European states coincided with the rearrangement and reorientation in the external relations of Hungary. Some months before the beginning of association negotiations Hungary expressed the intention to take into account the coordinated European foreign policy of the European Community in shaping its foreign policy positions and activities. The initiatives expressed proposed ideas concerning practical forms of exchange of information which would promote effective cooperation between the competent authorities of the European Community and Hungary with a view towards a united European foreign policy. Contacts were also proposed between the Presidency's representatives and Hungarian diplomacy in the Conference on Security and Cooperation in Europe (CSCE) fora, in the United Nations (UN) and other international organizations and on bilateral posts as well in order to mutually inform one another and to harmonize positions and activities to the extent possible.

It was felt that initial experience with informal contacts would facilitate negotiations on the provisions pertaining to institutional foreign policy cooperation. Because no formal status could be given to the evolving contacts and informal cooperation in bilateral posts and in the multilateral field until the entry into force of the association agreement, Hungarian diplomacy has not, of course, sought participation in the Twelve's internal consultations.

II.

As the structure and content of the association agreement was taking shape by the summer of 1991 it reflected a clear recognition by both sides that the political aspect of association was of crucial importance and the chapter dealing with "political dialogue" contains one of the essential integrating elements. In the definition of the objectives of association the first element is to provide an appropriate framework for the political dialogue between the Community and Hungary allowing the development of close political relations. Other elements relate to the gradual establishment of a free trade area making progress towards realizing economic freedoms on which the Community is based, promoting economic, financial and cultural cooperation, etc. The term "political dialogue" appears to be more modest than what it means in practice. It was necessary, however, to differentiate between "political cooperation" among the Twelve in the European Political Cooperation (EPC) framework on the one hand, and the looser but progressively evolving patterns of cooperation between the Community and Hungary.

The political dialogue to be established under the association agreement is expected to accompany and consolidate the approachment between the parties, support the new political order in Hungary and contribute to the establishment of lasting links of solidarity and new forms of cooperation to be specified at later stages of the process of association. The dialogue on political issues is meant by both sides to facilitate Hungary's full integration into the community of democratic nations. Political convergence and economic rapprochement provided for in the agreement are regarded as closely related and mutually complementary parts of the association. Political dialogue should bring about increasing convergence on political issues.

At the ministerial level political dialogue shall take place within the Association Council. Other procedures and mechanisms shall be set up by establishing appropriate contacts, exchanges and consultations including meetings between Hungarian officials and the Presidency and the Commission, regular diplomatic contacts in bilateral and multilateral fields; providing information to Hungary on EPC activities which shall be reciprocated as appropriate.

Conceptually, negotiations have sought for the political equivalent of the associated relationship. Since associated states are not supposed to fully take part in shaping joint positions in the EPC framework, they cannot be expected to automatically submit their national positions on international issues to those of the Twelve.

The brave language of the political objectives of the association agreement and the specific forms and channels established for the dialogue do not tell much about the substance of political dialogue and its evolution towards tangible cooperation. Even if only EC membership enables full participation in policy-making, Hungary and probably the other two Central European associates aspire for more than simply being informed of the net result of EPC consultations on issues of foreign and security policy. In appropriate forms to be agreed upon they intend to contribute, individually and jointly, to shaping common positions. Their specific approach and expertise, particularly on issues more closely related to Central Europe could make a meaningful contribution to the deliberations of the Twelve.

Since there is a large degree of coincidence in foreign and security policies, particularly in a country in transition, it should be noted that the political dialogue envisaged under the provisions of the association agreement may extend to those issues of security policy which are or will be put on the EPC agenda.

III.

Given the perspective of the Political Union and the emerging framework for Common Foreign and Security Policy, Hungary has sought a dialogue with the Western European Union as well. An arrangement similar to the political dialogue, although less formal and with less ambitious objectives, seems now to be possible. The latest meeting of the Western European Union (WEU) Council of Ministers of June 27, 1991, proposed a number of measures to enhance dialogue with the countries of Central and Eastern Europe. These include the possibility of organizing ad hoc contacts at the ministerial level on specific subjects of common interest; the establishment of two-way information links, similar to NATO diplomatic liaison, between the Embassies of the countries concerned and the Secretariat-General, and between the government of each of these countries and the Embassy of the presidency; intensification of exchanges among experts on issues of common interest; scholarships provided to young researchers, etc.

While enhancing dialogue and eventual cooperation with EPC and WEU Hungary has attempted to avoid impairing the development of her relations with NATO. Relying upon NATO's commitment to establishing security partnership with the Central and Eastern European countries, the Soviet Union included, Hungary intends to make full use of the initiatives for further contacts and exchanges included in the Copenhagen statement and in the Genscher-Baker joint communiqué of May 10, 1991.

While it is analytically evident that there is no economic and political integration without integration in terms of security, Central Europeans are aware that in the years to come they have to live under the ambiguous conditions of a transition. The CSCE process is becoming an increasing important framework and institution for assuring security and stability but remains uncapable of providing guarantees. In the next few years of transition Central Europeans cannot expect to obtain membership and commensurate explicit security guarantees in any of the integrated organizations. The possibilities for, and specific conditions of their security integration have not yet taken shape.

Accordingly, what is sought for by Hungary and probably other Central Europeans in setting the right agenda for the dialogue with EC, EPC, WEU and NATO, and in establishing the mechanisms and channels for it is

- to explore the possibilities and prepare for their progressive integration by first familiarizing themselves with these organizations and the processes of reassessment and adaptation to the profound changes that have taken place in the political and military environment in Europe, and possibly to

introduce their own security concerns and positions into the process of rearrangement,
- to seek to manage instabilities during transition in Central and Eastern Europe particularly through cooperation, in appropriate forms, in applying new CSCE institutions and procedures for crisis prevention and resolution and implementing CFE/CSBM agreements.[2]
- to establish cooperative relations and eventual joint actions in meeting new non-military and non-traditional challenges to security in Europe which have not yet found their appropriate place on the agenda for dialogue between Central Europeans and integrated organizations,
- to provide assistance and access to advanced know-how for developing a security and defence policy in Hungary, consistent with the new security order in Europe, aimed at assuring security through progressive integration, while sustaining a stable and cooperative security environment in Central and Eastern Europe.

IV.

During the collapse and demise of the Warsaw Treaty and Council on Mutual Economic Assistance (CMEA) Central Europeans successfully resisted pressures to establish follow-up structures or organizations. The statement of the last Prague meeting of the Political Consultative Committee of July 1, 1990, announcing the common decision to terminate the treaty noted the willingness of the former member states to hold, in case of interest, bilateral or multilateral consultations on an ad hoc basis on topical issues of common interest.

Hungarian, Polish, and Czech-and-Slovak reluctance to establish a political or security organization or institutionalized framework that would embrace former members of the Warsaw Treaty has been motivated by the awareness that any "Eastern" organization would inescapably become a greenhouse for past policies and practices and lead, sooner or later, to a new division in Europe, separating its members again from the process of European integration. Without the Soviet Union it would isolate and antagonize Moscow. Were the Soviet Union incorporated, it would amount to reestablishing the Warsaw Treaty, a vehicle for Soviet overwhelming interests and positions. The Romanian idea of organizing an Eastern version of WEU was ambiguous on this point.

Moreover, the states of the region stretching from the Baltic down to the Black Sea have become too diverse to be organized again into a single entity.

---

2   CFE = Conventional Forces in Europe
    CSBM = Confidence and Security Building Measures

The conditions for Poland's foreign relations and its security are entirely different from those of Bulgaria. Progress in introducing multiparty democracy and market economy has also been fairly uneven. An "Eastern" political or security organization or economic integration could no longer fit into the blueprint of the new Europe as outlined by the Charter of Paris. Its members could only define their common identity and policies in opposition to "Western" organizations, particularly EC/Political Union, WEU and NATO.

A welcome development is the emergence between the Baltic and the Black Sea area of a whole set of frameworks for functional regional cooperation, mainly economic, trade, infrastructural, cultural, etc. These regional arrangements may help to introduce more stability during transition in the region by contributing to stable and cooperative interstate relations, satisfying regional and subregional demands for cooperation and alleviating the sense of isolation in a transforming international environment. It is particularly useful if states other than former Warsaw Treaty members take part in such arrangements. Italian and Austrian participation in the Hexagonale or Germany's admission to the Danube Commission and its interest in enhancing cooperation in the Danube basin helps to link these regional arrangements to the rest of Europe and prevent them from becoming an undeclared alliance of economically less developed or politically unreformed states.

For Hungary, the key aspect for assessing these arrangements is whether they supplement the process of progressive unity and integration in Europe or intend to separate the region concerned from the mainstream of European development by seeking alternatives to European integration.

In the conclusion to his statement at the last meeting of the Political Consultative Committee, Prime Minister Antall said: "Our way to Europe has now become free . . . Europe with its organizations and institutions is open to cooperation with the countries of Central and Eastern Europe that are committed to human rights, democracy and market economy. Each of us is needed in building a united Europe, democratic, stable and prosperous. All of us should embark on the road to Europe, at a pace to be determined individually. None of us can be interested in seeing anyone bog down midway between dismantling old organizations that have outlined themselves and building new structures and relations."

V.

Political pronouncements in the three associates in Central Europe, Poland, Czechoslovakia, and Hungary, often emphasize that they are, and have been for the last thousand years, European states.

> The fact of these states' unquestionably European identity tends to impart certain advantages to the trilateral relationship in its collective

and individual dealings with the rest of the (Western) European community. Some of these advantages . . . are derived from historic traditions while others derive from the events of the last 35 years. 1956, 1968 and 1980-81 are not only road markers, but are powerful symbols of the three central European peoples' commitment to the core values of European civilisation. Finally, the three states' peaceful and successful transition from dictatorship to democracy have served, if additional proof were needed, as clear evidence of Central Europe's willingness and ability to live up to "European norms" and expectations. For these reasons, the three states are natural partners of the rest of European community.[3]

The main thrust of trilateral cooperation, as it appears in the title and language of the Declaration of the Visegrad summit of February 15, 1991 is towards European integration. The Visegrad declaration, a statement of intentions and an ambitious agenda for implementation in the field of regional integration and cooperation in foreign and security policy has had, so far, scarce operational follow-up. While new bilateral treaties are being negotiated in a synchronized fashion, experts and political decisionmakers are still pondering over the unexplored potentials of trilateral cooperation and the structures and patterns of institutionalization.

The three states' coordinated policies have been instrumental in dissolving the obsolete security and economic structures in Eastern Europe. Further coordination of their positions in redefining their bilateral relationship with the Soviet Union in new basic treaties remains an essential source of negotiating power if they are to avoid re-satellization and continue to refuse imposed constraints on their foreign and security policy options, particularly those pertaining to their policy of European integration.

Similar and coinciding features of the three states' evolution toward multiparty democracy and market economy, coupled with parallel and coinciding interests in their foreign and security policy provides ample room for closer cooperation and coordination. Inaction in implementing the Visegrad agenda would result in a mutual loss of important opportunities. The other extreme to be avoided is establishing an institutionalized political and economic entity that may become or be perceived as an alternative to, or replacement for European integration. Moreover, an attempt to establish a security entity or a defensive alliance would only antagonize the Soviet Union, amplify Romanian fears over isolation, and complicate the security aspect of

---

3 Rudolf Tokés, *The Young Democracies of Central Europe -- Cooperation, Rivalry, Co-existence*, Manuscript published in Hungarian by Valóság, September 1991, p. 13.

the three countries' progressive integration in European organizations -- without providing security for them.

Neutrality is neither attractive nor feasible in Central Europe. In Hungary it's felt that traditional neutrality as an option for current Hungarian security and defense policy has become historically disfunctional, financially unaffordable and politically redundant in the process of European integration. For Austria, Sweden and others a period of policy review and adaptation has begun to reconcile their well-established national security and defence policies and positions with the guidelines of Common Foreign and Security Policy and the prospects for a Political Union. Fortunately the pace of integration seems to allow transition without real conflict.

A neutral belt in Central and Eastern Europe may solve some of the real or perceived security problems for the Soviet Union, particularly with a forcefully exercised droit de regard, without providing security to the states concerned in the new politico-military environment. During the security policy debate that preceded and followed last year's change in Hungary neutrality was hardly raised. Apart from a segment of the Socialist Party no political party is advocating neutrality. It is felt that it can only complicate or extend the process of progressive integration, as envisaged in the association agreement, while the intention is the opposite.

Given the range of issues on the agenda of European Political Cooperation and the guidelines for Political Union there does not seem to be major difficulty, apparent conflict in interests, or a risk of heavily compromising national positions that would cast shadow over Hungary's evolving cooperation with EPC.

Secretary-General of the CDU Volker Rühe said in his statement at the foreign policy congress of his party:

> Particularly the Poles, the Hungarians, the Czechs and Slovaks need the certainty already now that they will find their place in the European Community. Therefore it should be our task, not only that of the Germans alone, to look with imagination for further ways of facilitating and shortening the coming home to Europe for these states. Therefore the question which occurs to me is why these countries cannot be involved in the activities of the European Political Cooperation even before they obtain full membership? Isn't there a host of issues which could be addressed together and by which we already speak a common language? Given the security policy vacuum arising from the dissolution

of the Warsaw Treaty, wouldn't such a step be of more than a symbolic value?[4]

From the Community's perspective this proposition undeniably raises a host of complex procedural and conceptual issues that were also implied in Mr. Andriessen' contested idea of "affiliate membership." On the other hand, from the associate's point of view the obvious fact is that unlike the economy, foreign and security policies have less inertia in reorientation and could fit more quickly with that of the Community. For Hungary, the decisive aspect is whether such arrangements would shorten the transitory period of association and of obtaining membership, enabling full participation in all aspects of the Community's activities. Or would this put the country on an orbit around the Community where membership would remain unattainable?

---

4 Helmut Kohl, Volker Rühe, Gerhard Stoltenberg, "Deutschlands Verantwortung in der Welt", *Politik Aktuell*, Bonn: CDU-Bundesgeschäftsstelle, 1991, p. 7 (author's translation).

17

View from Yugoslavia: Political Union to Avoid Nineteenth Century Foreign Policy

Nina Vajic*

Foreign policy is not the central domain of the European integration process. Likewise, foreign policy is not the main reason for Yugoslavia's interest in re-examining its relations with Western Europe in general, and with the European Community in particular. All the same, efforts on the part of member states to improve their cooperation in the sphere of foreign policy, especially since the adoption of the Single European Act (SEA), as well as the impact of this effort on the integrative process have received wide interest in Yugoslavia. In fact, these issues have often been perceived as central to the discussions on the possible future relations between Yugoslavia and the Community. The efforts towards improving European Political Cooperation (EPC) and the prospects for a European Union are naturally viewed in Yugoslavia through the lens of its own foreign policy options. At stake is the question of whether EPC will block the prospects for Yugoslavia's rapprochement and eventual integration within the Community.

Yet, contrary to an attitude once widely held in the country that membership in the non-aligned movement and thus a non-aligned foreign policy represented an obstacle for Yugoslavia's possible membership in the European Community, there is now a growing sentiment that the dilemma of "non-alignment or Europe" is a misleading one. The more appropriate path, according to this evolving view, is that Yugoslavia should try to take advantage of its special status to adapt more rapidly than some other European countries to the changes

---

*   This article was written before the beginning of the civil war in Yugoslavia in the summer of 1991.

of our time.[1] Recognizing this opportunity, Yugoslavia is in fact seeking closer forms of cooperation with the Council of Europe, the European Community, EFTA, etc.

It might be useful to briefly recapitulate the history of Yugoslavia's relationship with the European Community. The initial relations between Yugoslavia and the Community were based on the provisions of Article 113 of the Treaty establishing the European Economic Community (EEC), which provides for the conclusion of tariff and trade agreements with third countries. The first agreement concluded between Yugoslavia and the EEC on 19 March 1970 was a trade agreement of a non-preferential character.[2] It was followed by another trade agreement on 13 March 1973[3] (again of a non-preferential character), in spite of the "global approach" of the EC Mediterranean policy of the EC adopted at the European summit in Paris in 1972, enabling broader fields of cooperation.[4] According to views expressed by some Community officials, Yugoslavia did not want at that time to make use of this new approach towards the Mediterranean countries, fearing that it would compromise its non-aligned foreign policy orientation.[5]

Hence, it was only years later that Yugoslavia succeeded in getting a more favorable position in the EEC market. Thus, on 2 April 1980, a cooperation agreement was concluded following an approach similar to that adopted with other Mediterranean countries.[6] In the event free elections take place in all parts of Yugoslavia in the following months (until now it was the case only in Slovenia and Croatia), it seems possible that a new agreement between Yugoslavia and the EEC could be signed by the end of the year.

By adopting the SEA, the member states of the European Community

---

1 Vladimir Veres, "Perspektive promena u savremenoj Evropi -- mesto i interesi Jugoslavije," *Pregled Centra za strategijske studije*, Beograd (literally: Perspectives of the changes in contemporary Europe -- the place and interests of Yugoslavia, in: *Survey of the Center for Strategic Studies*, Belgrade), 1988/II, p. 660; Zoran Zic, "Savremena kretanja u Zapadnoj Evropi -- polozaj i uloga u medunarodnim odnosima i interesi SFRJ," *Pregled Centra za strategijske studije*, Beograd (literally: Contemporary trends in Western Europe -- the position and role in international relations and the interests of the SFR of Yugoslavia, in: *Survey of the Center for Strategic Studies*, Belgrade), 1987/II, pp. 487-508.
2 *Sluzbeni list SFRJ-MU (Official Gazette of Yugoslavia-Treaties)*, 1970/35, p. 393.
3 *Sluzbeni list SFRJ-MU (Official Gazette of Yugoslavia-Treaties)*, 1976/22, p. 551.
4 See: C.-A. Colliard, *Institutions des relations internationales*, 7th ed., Paris, 1978, p. 551; Louis Cartou, *Communautés européennes*, 8th ed., Paris, 1986, pp. 750-52.
5 See: Charles Caporale, "L'accord de coopération CEE -- Jugoslavie, le dernier-né des accords méditerranéens," in: J. Touscoz (ed.), *La Communauté Economique Européenne élargie et la Méditerranée: quelle coopération?*, Paris: Colloque CEDECE, 1982, p. 189.
6 *Sluzbeni list SFRJ-MU (Official Gazette of Yugoslavia-Treaties)*, 1983/2, p. 15.

proclaimed the will to "transform relations as a whole among their states into a European Union, in accordance with the Solemn Declaration of Stuttgart of 19 June 1983".[7] They were resolved to implement this European Union not only by applying the Community rules, but also on the basis of the Provisions on European Cooperation in the sphere of foreign policy.[8] Part III (Article 30) of the SEA consequently represents a new contractual form of linking more closely member states and their actions in the field of foreign policy, European Political Cooperation. It laid down the principles for such a cooperation and provided for new specialized forms and organs of collaboration in addition to those already existing, the main goal of EPC being the creation and realization of a common foreign policy of the member states. Thus, EPC was established among the member states of the Community under a treaty which at the same time modified the Treaties creating the European Communities. Hence, EPC is closely linked to the European Communities, even if a certain duality and independence of the two structures is still present. This is visible from Paragraph 5 of Article 30 of the SEA under which the external policies of the Community and the policies agreed to in EPC must be consistent.

After a few years of testing EPC's performance in practice, since the coming into force of the SEA, and with the challenge posed by the recent events in Central and Eastern Europe, we are now at a moment when an assessment of EPC is due, and prospects for the future may be suggested. The main question seems to be, however, whether EPC can survive and if so, in what form. At a time when calls for an even closer linking of EPC and the Community are loud, in the effort to achieve a Political Union and to live up to the expectations coming from Eastern and Central Europe, it would be of some interest to discuss and attempt to clarify the relationship between EPC and Yugoslavia's present non-aligned status.

In trying to explain Yugoslavia's ties with non-alignment, one would need to retrace this country's history and development since 1948, which would be beyond the scope of this study. Still, it should be mentioned and borne in mind that Yugoslavia is definitely more than an "ordinary" member of the non-aligned movement. It is in a way its "inventor," certainly one of its founding members. Yugoslavia is still a leading member of the movement, and as such is a symbol of its continuity and vitality. In addition, it presently holds the Presidency which it will keep for another two years. Non-alignment brought many advantages for Yugoslavia at the international level. It helped it to achieve an important position in the United Nations and to attain general recognition and prestige in the international community.

By keeping this in mind while remaining aware of the fact that the

---

7 Preamble, Paragraph 1.
8 Preamble, Paragraph 2.

Community represents the realization of principles and goals fundamentally different from those on which non-alignment is based, it is clear that a true change in Yugoslavia's foreign policy, implying a change in its international status, would represent a radical step. This would be the case not only for Yugoslavia itself, but also for the non-aligned movement. In any case, it would signify a much more significant transformation than in the cases of Malta or Cyprus -- two small states of parliamentary democracy traditionally linked with some members of the Community.[9] Hence, Yugoslavia cannot be expected to automatically accept Community attitudes in foreign policy, in other words, to adhere to EPC. As long as the non-aligned movement and its foreign policy engagements continue to exist, on the one hand, and the purposes set in the SEA persist, on the other, and so long as both commitments are to be taken seriously, then it is hard to perceive how they could be reconciled. The verity in this thinking is proven again and again with each new international crisis.

Yet, notwithstanding its basic commitment towards non-alignment, it is obvious that Yugoslavia is trying to adapt to the ongoing changes of the international environment and that it is becoming more flexible and is ready to make concessions in certain fields; a policy shift is occurring, in a de facto way, by many small and "invisible" moves.

In addition to its foreign policy aspect, for years non-alignment performed an important internal function in Yugoslavia, in the sense of exerting an integrative influence among all parts of the heterogeneous country. Yet, the crisis of the post-Tito era and the processes demanding fundamental changes, i.e. new forms of economic, political and social order as well as a profound crisis in national relations, led with time to a questioning of Yugoslavia's external relations, including its main foreign policy orientation. Even if it is not held directly responsible for the difficulties in which the country found itself, Yugoslavia's foreign policy is still believed to have contributed to the overall situation.[10]

Thus, the new realities which the country is experiencing, the deep transformations within the economic system together with the beginnings of a pluralistic political system, also call for transformations at the international level. Consequently, loud voices are heard demanding changes in foreign policy. New openings, particularly towards Western Europe, are advocated and

---

9 Budislav Vukas, "Pravni aspekti i modaliteti unapredenja odnosa Jugoslavije sa zapadnoevropskim integracionim grupacijama," *Pregled Centra za strategijske studije*, Beograd (literally: Legal aspects and modalities of improving the relations between Yugoslavia and the Western European integration processes, in: *Survey of the Center for Strategic Studies*, Belgrade), 1988/I, p. 143.

10 Radovan Vukadinovic, "Novi izazovi i jugoslavenska vanjska politika," *Medunarodna politika* (literally: New challenges and Yugoslav foreign policy, in: *International politics*), No. 968-9, 1-16 August 1990, p. 10.

perceived in terms of speeding up the process of replacing the old ideological system with a new one. The desire to share the values and aspirations of the democratic countries of Western Europe emerges as the main goal. In this sense, a new foreign policy orientation is seen in the light of such demands for overall and complete transformations. The aspirations which incline towards a confederative type of state, which come mainly from Croatia and Slovenia, also announce the tendency for autonomous foreign policy orientations in these republics. In the meantime, their criticism of non-alignment is based on the approach that it led Yugoslavia into Africa instead of into Europe. At the federal level, Yugoslavia still adheres to its proclaimed foreign policy in international relations. Yet, it is no longer able to find full political support for such a policy within the country itself.[11]

Given the many problems and dilemmas regarding its future internal organization and the serious transformations lying ahead of it, Yugoslavia has to a considerable extent turned towards its domestic problems. Therefore, it is not yet prepared for radical changes in foreign policy, or is not willing to admit so. For the same reason, it is not unduly absorbed by possible changes in EPC itself (as something distinct from the Community), knowing that with time the situation is bound to change on both sides. For the time being, Yugoslavia is engaged in efforts to join the Council of Europe, to sign a new cooperation agreement with the European Community, to develop its relations with EFTA, and to take part in the so-called "Pentagonale" cooperation initiative. A step by step approach towards the Community is under way and seems a sensible path. Given this agenda, questions of foreign policy compatibility or the possible changes in EPC are overshadowed by the priority accorded to the process of forging closer relations with the EC, which is the main goal of the country at this stage. In other words, Yugoslavia is at the present time drawn primarily to the democratic model and economic cooperation which the European Community represents. The years which are to pass while Yugoslavia queues up for admission to the Community (waiting for basic economic and political transformations to actually take place) will probably only lessen the impact of possible foreign policy differences between Yugoslavia and the EC. In other words, once Yugoslavia becomes acceptable for Community membership -- which will not happen overnight -- it is not EPC or a then Common Foreign and Security Policy which will represent a real hindrance to closer links.

Yugoslavia is facing enormous problems in the near future, in which the particular interests of its constituent peoples will surely be the main determinant to which all other demands and goals will be subordinated, even at the international level. At the same time, it should be stated that the Community is also at a critical turning point as it strives to find a way to cope

---

11   Ibid., p. 12.

with the present challenges it faces. To successfully overcome this test, it should strengthen and improve the political mechanism as a superstructure for economic integration. This happens to be a very complex and contradictory process. On the one hand, there is a need and a will for integration and cooperation, a necessity of interconnection. Yet, on the other hand, there is the emergence of a new wave of nationalism, demands for the affirmation of principles such as sovereignty for each of the Yugoslav republics, and the renaissance of deep-seated historic and cultural values of each of the peoples of Yugoslavia. In such a situation, the European Community has to work hard to consolidate itself at a moment when the Eastern European countries are standing at its doorstep, and to prove that it is not confused by its sudden new role brought about by the recent events in Eastern and Central Europe and by the reunification of Germany. Of fundamental importance is the need to prove that the European Community is capable of avoiding the danger of a return to the foreign policies of the nineteenth century. The question therefore is: does an enlarged Community still have the chance of pursuing the goal of Political Union? Or will it be so difficult to achieve a common attitude in an enlarged unified Europe that an inverse process will take place, namely the splitting up into bilateral relations and political unions as in the nineteenth century?

18

View from Turkey: Political Union as a Contribution to the New Europe

Sermet Atacanli

With the process of radical transformation which the international political order underwent during the period of 1989-90, Europe has entered the last decade of the second millennium with reasonable hopes and expectations. Indeed, the 1989-90 period was one of success and achievement. Everywhere in Europe the totalitarian regimes collapsed under the irresistible force coming from the people, and notions like democracy, freedom, pluralism and rule of law have become synonymous with the concept of "the new Europe." For the first time in history, a vision of the continent, whole and free, united around the principle of the primacy of the individual, and ready to work towards peace, friendship and cooperation has appeared within reach. The Berlin Wall has fallen, dragging down with it the most visible symbol of the division of Europe in the post-war era. Germany has become one nation again through a peaceful and democratic process.

Alongside the "Charter of Paris for a New Europe," the heads of state or government of twenty-two states gathered in Paris in November 1990 to put their signatures under two historic documents: the Conventional Forces in Europe (CFE) Treaty and the Declaration of the Twenty-Two States. With the signing of the Paris Charter, the basic principles of the already successful Conference on Security and Cooperation in Europe (CSCE) process were reaffirmed and its future institutionalization was conceived as a means to inject new vitality into the process. With the CFE Treaty, which is the most comprehensive disarmament agreement ever accomplished in the area of conventional weaponry in Europe, the threat of a military conflict in the CSCE area has diminished significantly. We believe that the signing of the CFE Treaty has been a major step in the right direction. Its implementation will irreversibly free European inter-state relations from the dominance of the military factor.

A new approach on the part of the Soviet Union has surfaced vis-a-vis world issues and regional problems, revolving around the "new thinking" advanced by President Gorbachev, while the twenty-two states, all members of NATO and the now dissolved Warsaw Pact, who had bitterly opposed each other for over forty years, formally declared that they no longer regarded themselves as adversaries but as partners. The Cold War has become an episode of the past. As the events in Europe continue to unfold before our eyes with unprecedented pace and significance, efforts are now focused on the political and military components of the future European structure.

One must bear in mind, however, that while the context in which future security decisions will be taken has radically changed, the fundamental need for security remains the same. Even after the successful implementation of the CFE Treaty, military forces will still be maintained on the continent at reduced but substantial levels. The euphoria that was brought about by the winds of change sweeping throughout the continent is now starting to give way to a more cautious and guarded optimism. The war in the Gulf and the civil war in Yugoslavia have brought new dimensions into European security concerns. Although one need not be unduly pessimistic about the prospect of a brighter future for Europe, recent developments and the signals and indications that can be deducted from them refer to the fact that these times of change are fraught with danger and uncertainty. Therefore, the issues at hand must be addressed with utmost care and caution, without ever forgetting that the peace and stability we have achieved in Europe in state systems based on democracy and human rights over forty years are too precious to be put at risk.

On the other hand, of course, it cannot be ignored that things are changing around us, and that we must adapt. As a matter of fact, we have been doing just that. The NATO allies, in keeping with their July 1990 London Declaration and the November 1990 Paris CSCE summit, emphasized the need to adapt the organization to the changing circumstances and have in fact initiated steps toward this end. As part of this wider reviewing exercise, NATO allies are in the process of re-defining their objectives to take into account the evolving European security identity, in terms of sharing of responsibilities, roles and structures. These activities are necessary to maintain the relevance of the Atlantic Alliance and all allies should contribute to them in good faith.

In the changing political and security environment, it is natural that Europe's security identity should be enhanced. Such a process should take place within the North Atlantic Alliance framework, and should strengthen the European pillar of the Alliance. In this respect, the initiatives aimed at developing the security dimension of the European political cooperation within the Community are of interest. The expectation is that these initiatives will not acquire a dynamic incompatible with North Atlantic partnership. As a matter of fact, EC/WEU and NATO partnership are not mutually exclusive entities. It is up to the allies to ensure that all manifestations of the efforts to promote a European security identity proceed in a complementary manner.

NATO will be an essential element of the emerging European security environment because

- it is the only security organization which embodies the transatlantic link;
- it alone has the necessary scope and capability to assure the strategic balance in Europe;
- it constitutes the essential political framework for all allies.

WEU can play an important role in this respect. It can become the European defense pillar of the Alliance. But WEU's military role and missions should not compete with those of NATO. They should be complementary. Furthermore, all European allies of the Atlantic Alliance who wish to do so, should be able to join WEU. In other words, the "European Pillar" should embrace all the European members of NATO. A pillar that excludes some European allies could create divisions in the very organization it is intended to strengthen. There can be a distinct role for WEU outside of Europe. The Gulf War has provided a valuable experience in this respect. It is obvious that this function of WEU will continue to be taken into account by its members.

Turkey has made important contributions to the collective defense efforts of the Alliance and to the security of Europe. Turkey is a secular, democratic country, deeply attached to the common values and ideals that bind together the 16 members of the Alliance. Its important geo-strategic situation at the intersection of three continents, its huge economic potential and choice for democracy make it an element of stability in a highly turbulent region and an indispensable ally for the security of Europe in this new era. As a matter of fact, a European defense without Turkish participation is bound to be vulnerable. Against this background, the accession of Turkey as a full member to WEU will greatly contribute to the strengthening process of the European pillar of the Atlantic Alliance.

On the other hand, transatlantic solidarity and collective allied response can in no way be assured if the EC nations decide to form an exclusive defense club, acting autonomously. Such a development would turn the Alliance into a loose partnership resting on two distinct sub-groupings while leaving NATO's two European members who are yet to join the Community marginalized on the flanks. Hence, a European political and defense identity should be conceived only as the "European security pillar" of the Alliance, in the manner endorsed by the London NATO Declaration. Similarly, a European security organization leaving out Turkey and defined as distinct from North America would not enjoy the same external confidence and the same political influence or prestige. The future of the transatlantic relationship and the developing European dimension of NATO should not be allowed to evolve as conflicting processes. Turkey believes that close contacts between NATO and an enlarged European Community would be a pragmatic method for attaining mutually beneficial harmony.

By applying for full membership to the EC in 1987, Turkey has confirmed the traditional objectives of its foreign policy. These objectives can be defined as becoming part of a Europe which is economically strong, politically pluralist, rich in diversity and strategically situated within the system of defense and security of the Atlantic Alliance. Turkey has shared the political ambitions of the Community since the signing of the Treaty of Rome in 1957. It has opted to join the process of European integration and has voluntarily adopted the political finality of the European ideal. One should not forget that Turkey's relations with Western Europe have always reflected the characteristics of an authentic alliance rather than a simple conciliation of temporary interests. Indeed, the Gulf crisis has demonstrated the deepness of the bonds between Turkey and the EC and the common values and ideals shared by these two partners. The crucial events in Turkish neighbour-hood have underlined the fact that Turkey is well-situated, ready and willing to make a significant contribution to the creating a Community that can affirm its political and economic identity on the international scene for the sake of peace and security.

The founding treaties of the EC have determined the European Union as their final objective. The Political Union is expected to be built on strong and viable economic integration. The security field should also be one of the main elements of the European Union. Thus, European integration will have three major dimensions: economic, political and eventually security, which are the sine qua non of a genuine integration process. Turkey shares all these objectives.

Today's international environment certainly calls for a serious rethinking of Europe's future. In particular, all the dimensions of the European integration process, as well as the structure of the institutions contributing to the construction of Europe, require a profound review. Under the circumstances prevailing in international relations, we believe that Turkey, with its unique geostrategic position as Europe's gateway to Asia and the Middle East, will maintain its role in the future of Europe by contributing to the structure of European integration within a more stable and encompassing framework.

Today, as a country supporting the ultimate objectives of the construction of a new Europe, Turkey would like to see the European Community countries take tangible steps for preparing the ground for further enlargement (at the ongoing Intergovernmental Conferences). The fact that certain specific measures are to be taken within these Conferences to enable the Community to deal with security matters in the future, and the fact that even the fusion between WEU and the EC is progressively envisaged, constitute in our view further reasons for seeking an institutional structure that would permit a new enlargement. We believe that the rather difficult process of reaching a real Political Union should be realized through the common effort of all European countries concerned. Indeed, forty years of experience and the level of integration attained by the EC now enable it to lead the way towards achieving the final objectives of the European ideal as expressed in the founding Treaties of the Community. The success of the EC in its path towards full integration will contribute to the architecture of the new Europe only if it does not exclude other countries of Europe. Otherwise, Political Union will exclude those countries who share the same European ideals and cause a political fragmentation of the fragile European mosaic.

As a concluding remark, we can underline that Turkey's view of a Political Union which would include WEU is based on a global approach which takes into consideration the realities of today's Europe.

How European political unity will affect the question of Cyprus will depend essentially on the extent to which the Turkish Cypriot side is given the opportunity to be part of the process of integration in Europe on an equal footing with the Greek Cypriots. The tendency in Europe is to withhold equal treatment to the Turkish Cypriots under the argument that the Greek Cypriot administration is recognized as the only legitimate government on the island. There is still hesitation, sometimes reluctance to admit the facts of Cyprus for what they are, namely that there are two ethnically different and separate peoples there, each ruled by its own government. Any moves toward European unity which, for whatever reason, include the Greek Cypriots, but fail to include the Turkish Cypriots are bound to make things worse for Cyprus. At each and every step, the political equality of the two sides in Cyprus must be fully respected, if the true goal is to help the two sides establish a new political partnership. By the same token, Europe, united or not, would be well advised to leave the settlement of the problem to the two peoples of the island and in any case refrain from taking initiatives on its own which do not account fully for the political equality of the two parties to the dispute. The same principle applies to the kind of relationship Cyprus might wish to have with a united Europe. That is a decision that can and should only be taken by the two peoples of the island on the basis of their equal status and through the separate exercise of their free will and choice.

PART FOUR

Assessing the Concepts for Political Union: CFSP as a Touchstone

19

From the Draft Treaty of 1984 to the Intergovernmental Conferences of 1991

Rosa Maria Alonso Terme

Introduction

After a period of relative inertia at the beginning of the 1980s labelled by some as "Eurosclerosis," the Twelve resumed their evolution towards Political Union with renewed energy. However, the seven years between 1984 and 1991 do not by any means constitute a regular, unidimensional and linear progression. On the contrary, if anything characterizes them, it is the continual debate (or clash) of two quite diverse approaches to political integration -- intergovernmentalism or supranationalism -- and the policy of small steps versus the policy of grand designs.

Within the aforementioned period, two phases may be distinguished: the first beginning in 1984 with the Draft Treaty (DT) and ending in 1987 with the Single European Act (SEA), and the second covering the debate surrounding the proposals for "European Union" to emerge from the December 1990 Intergovernmental Conferences. There is a striking parallel between these two phases, as far as the institutional debate is concerned. The European Parliament (EP) and the European Council have been talking past one another. The EP hears the voice of supranationalism and envisions a federal Europe, not for the future but for today. The Council, on the other hand, as the representative of the member states expresses their reluctance to bequeath national sovereignty, and refuses to give up intergovernmentalism. In the field of European Political Cooperation (EPC), this means that EP projects are aimed at fusing EPC and the EC, whereas the Council is interested in enhancing EPC, but within the intergovernmental framework.

This chapter will analyze the legal meaning and the immediate political consequences of the foreign policy provisions of the main official documents issued since 1984. The constant theme will be, as noted before, the contrast between supranationalism and intergovernmentalism, between the EP and Council approaches.

Divergent Legal and Political Qualities of the DT and SEA

The main consideration one must keep in mind when analyzing the legal status of the DT and SEA is the political context in which they were approved. The Draft Treaty establishing the European Union is a text of a quasi-constitutional nature which was adopted by the first directly elected European Parliament, on 14 February 1984.[1] In legal terms, it is intended to serve as a substitute for the treaties founding the European Communities. Politically, it would have created a "European Union," whose institutions would "take over the Community Patrimony" (DT Article 7). The Single European Act, on the other hand, is an amendment to the EEC Treaty enacted via the revision process contained in Article 236. It was adopted in its final version by an intergovernmental conference of the EC member states, on 27 January 1986.[2] It consists of two central provisions: one amending the Treaties establishing the European Communities and the other institutionalizing European Political Cooperation and dealing with its foreign policy role.

Why was the second document adopted instead of the first? How do they compare in the field of foreign policy? Was the SEA simply a "watered down" version of the DT, or did it, on the contrary, represent a different and perhaps even more fruitful means of approaching European integration? To answer these questions, one must begin by describing the problems which faced the Community before the adoption of these documents. By so doing, one will better understand the common goals which lie at the heart of both the DT and SEA.

By the early 1970s, it was obvious that not only had progress towards European integration become stagnant but the basic objectives of the EC -- achieving a true free-trade area and smoothly functioning Community institutions -- had not been met. On the other hand, the increasingly complex international situation, when combined with the phenomenon which has been called the "politics of scale," induced the members of the European Community to attempt the renewal of their cooperation. It is in this context that all the documents up to and including the SEA were adopted. A brief reference is necessary because these documents in a sense represent the gestation process of the DT and SEA, and because they already reflect the objectives which underlie

---

1 "Preliminary Draft Treaty Establishing the European Union," *Europe/Documents*, Nos. 1287/1288, 3 January 1984.
2 "Single European Act," *International Legal Materials*, Vol. 25, No. 3, May 1986, pp. 506-518.

both texts. These early steps were initiated by the 1969 Hague Summit, in which the Heads of Government of the EC member states entrusted to their foreign ministers the task of reporting on ways to achieve closer political cooperation. In response to this request, the Luxembourg Report of 1970 created the main structure of what is today European Political Cooperation; the main commitment of the member states being to consult on all major foreign policy issues. The 1972 Paris Summit continued the EC-EPC integration process by according the EC Commission a role in EPC.

In 1973 the Copenhagen Summit adopted a declaration on European identity, elaborating on the growing importance of the EC as a unitary agent in the international arena, and stating the political will of the member states to work towards the achievement of a common foreign policy. It also admitted the Commission to all EPC meetings and invited its participation whenever issues concerning its functions were to be dealt with. The 1974 Paris Summit gave birth to the European Council; from that point on, the Heads of Government would meet three times a year to coordinate their foreign policies and to look into EC matters. Two somewhat more radical documents, the Tindemans Report and the 1981 Genscher-Colombo Proposal, were never adopted as they went too far in their attempts at integrating foreign policy into the EC. And, to conclude, the 1981 London Report created the "Troika" (as a method of reinforcing the negotiating ability of the Council Presidency) and extended the obligation to consult on foreign policy issues to the political aspects of security.

So, by 1984, roughly fifteen years of European Political Cooperation had passed without formal reflection at the legal level; there was no international treaty institutionalizing the cooperation network of the EC member states. At the time, EPC was no more than de facto intergovernmentalism. Thus, the main goal of both the DT and SEA was to overcome the impasse in the EC by institutionalizing EPC and infusing the evolution towards European integration with renovated energy. More specifically, the two concrete conceptions of how member state foreign policy cooperation should be carried out are not very diverse. The documents themselves, however, are of quite different legal and political character. This makes them simultaneously similar and unique; they share common substantive objectives but they are formulated through divergent formal approaches.

Foreign Policy Cooperation: a Comparative Study

The Draft Treaty

The first directly elected European Parliament felt a moral obligation to assume the role of Constituent Assembly and thus formulate a project for European Union. Nevertheless, the EP was sufficiently pragmatic not to elaborate a utopian constitution for an ideal state. It was out of the balance of these two considerations that the Draft Treaty emerged. The DT represents a hybrid, lying between a new international treaty (integrating EPC into the EC) and a truly federal constitution for Europe.

Formally, the DT is structured like a typical state constitution. It begins with a preamble stating the main principles of the Union, and it continues with a section dedicated to such matters as the accession of new members, the citizenship of the Union, fundamental rights and the territory of the Union. The second part is devoted to what are called the objectives, methods of action, and competences of the Union. Part three deals with the institutional set up and part four is concerned with the policies of the Union (With Title III being devoted to the international relations of the Union).

As the essence of federalism consists of the division of sovereignty between two instances of political power and the consequent distribution of actual competences between them, the Union envisaged by the DT qualifies for such a definition. There are certainly two centers of political power, the Union and the member states, and there is a system to distribute competences between them. The system can be outlined in the following way: three types of competences are contemplated -- exclusive, concurrent and a third sort that could be described as potential. Exclusive competences are, according to Article 12.1 of the DT, those in which the institutions of the Union shall have the sole power to act. Concurrent competences are the ones in which the member states can legislate as long as the Union has not yet acted upon them (Article 12.2). "Potential Competences" (the DT does not use a specific term to define them) are those the Union may eventually acquire, although in principle they belong within the sphere of the individual member states.

The Union can act within its area of exclusive or concurrent competence either by common action or by cooperation between the member states. Article 10 defines common action as "all normative, administrative, financial and judicial acts, internal or international and the programs and recommendations issued by the Union itself, originating in its institutions and addressed to those institutions, or to States or to individuals," whereas cooperation refers to "all the commitments which the member states undertake within the European Council." The Treaty establishes the distribution of fields of competence between the Union and the member states, thereby providing for the division of issue areas into those which are to be dealt with by common action and those which are to be dealt with by cooperation. Article 11 allows for transfer of fields originally subject to cooperation to the sphere of common action, while, in an attempt to enhance integration, the opposite is forbidden.

A constant effort to balance supranationalism and intergovernmentalism characterizes the DT. In those areas in which there exists a clear consensus on what should constitute a Community competence (e.g. commercial policy or free movement of persons), the DT accords the Union exclusive or concurrent competence and the power of common action, which implies that decisions will be taken by a majority vote. On the other hand, in those areas where it is felt that the member states would not be willing to renounce their sovereignty, cooperation is the chosen policy instrument and consensus will assure the necessary basis for agreement. The key, however, is the principle of subsidiarity, which is intended to maintain an equilibrium between the respective spheres of power of the Union and the member states. As it is stated in the Preamble to the DT, the aim of subsidiarity is "to entrust common institutions only with those powers required to complete successfully the tasks they may carry out more satisfactorily than the States acting independently."

This represents another compromise between the institutionalists and the functionalists; a new institution is created, but one which will only assume member state competences when the outcome is likely to be of greater benefit to all. Nevertheless, despite the key role the subsidiarity principle should play in the system established by the DT, there is no legal assurance that it would actually do so. Basically, it is left to the Union, in its field of concurrent competence, to decide when it is adequate -- because it would be more efficient -- for it to legislate in the place of the national governments; the member states, as such, would have no say in the Union's decision. This has provoked a major controversy among analysts of the DT, since many feared an uncontrolled overcentralization of the Community as the consequence of an extensive interpretation of the advisability of Union action.

Since foreign policy is a traditional expression of state sovereignty and an area of national competence, the DT adopted a careful approach and included it, for the most part, within the field of cooperation. According to Article 64 of the DT, common action in foreign policy will only be taken by the Union in commercial policy and in those other areas which the Treaties of the European Communities have already conferred to the Community. The only innovation in this matter is a commitment to a common development aid policy, within a period of ten years. It is not specified, however, whether after this transitional period development aid policy will become an exclusive or a concurrent competence of the Union. There is in fact no reason to why it should be considered exclusive, since an extra effort by individual member states would by no means hinder action at the level of the Union. In addition, from the political point of view it is an area in which certain member states (most particularly the Netherlands) desire to maintain national control.

Article 65 elaborates on the conduct of common action. Again, one basically finds a reflection of current EPC practice: the Commission is charged with the representation of the Union in its relations with non-member states or international organizations, while the Council of the Union issues guidelines directed to the Commission for certain international actions. The Parliament must be informed of the actions taken by the competent institutions in the field of foreign policy. The new element in this article lies in the process of Union approval of international treaties; the absolute majority of both the Council of the Union and the Parliament is required. This has led certain observers to point out that, although it constitutes a praiseworthy effort to democratize the institutions of the Union, this policy has been taken too far. In fact, they remark, there is no national Parliament with such far-reaching competences, so there is no reason why they should exist in a polity which is not of a parliamentarian nature. It is also argued that it would be burdensome for the EP to be charged with the responsibility of approving every single treaty, whether essential or of a purely administrative character.

Article 66 endeavors to define the fields in which foreign policy cooperation should be undertaken at the Union level. There are two blocks of issues: political and economic aspects of security; an open field consisting of all foreign policy matters in which the Union would work more efficiently than the member states could alone. In legal terms, therefore, the DT does not attempt to create a "European foreign policy" at one stroke; it simply tries "to constitute a framework or forum for mandatory cooperation."

Two points should be made at this stage. The first is simply that it was the free will of the member states which brought them together under EPC, because of their desire to play a more significant role on the international scene. In Ginsberg's words:

> Foreign policy activity in the EC is a process of integrating policies and actions of the member states towards the outside world . . . [it] is based on the need to protect and defend the common interests of the member governments abroad and to respond adequately to global demands and pressures on the EC . . . This convergence of interests enables the diverse membership to act as one in a number of international issue areas . . . Joint foreign policy activity refers to the process by which EC members and their common bodies coordinate and implement joint civilian foreign policy actions to reap benefits from politics of scale.[3]

The second consideration is that it is precisely this intergovernmental-functionalist approach which has allowed EPC to evolve successfully, while its non-binding, informal idiosyncrasy has permitted the member states to feel at ease with it. EPC has provided them with a framework for cooperation and has thereby strengthened their position in the international world; at the same time,

---

3   Roy Ginsberg, *Foreign Policy Actions of the European Community: The Politics of Scale*, Boulder CO: Lynne Riemer, 1989, pp. 1-2.

it has ensured that no collective decision will be taken without individual acquiescence.

EPC has thrived with the blessing of the member states, but there has also been an enormous effort to keep it separate from the EC. This is why the inclusion of EC and EPC under a single Union is such an innovation (although the 1972 Paris Summit already conferred a role in EPC to the Commission). The motivation behind this step is that experience has taught the member states that in practice it is extremely difficult to discern EC external policy -- especially in the commercial area -- and purely national foreign policy (for example, are economic sanctions to be adopted in the framework of the EEC or in that of the EPC?). Furthermore, as EPC lacked any kind of institutional backing, it was often dependent on EC support for the implementation of its decisions.

Thus, the pragmatic stand adopted in the DT represents a compromise: it reflects the increasing need and desire for unified action while keeping the method of collective policy formulation at the level of intergovernmental cooperation.

The first block of issues mentioned as a potential field for cooperation are those related to the economic and political aspects of security. This was the first time that any defense-related matters had been included in an EC document referring to cooperation. It is obviously a rather sensitive area for the member states, who tend to view it as being a core element of national sovereignty and who usually are only willing to debate these issues in military organizations such as NATO or WEU. The problem is particularly delicate because a number of EC members do not belong to either of these organizations. Notwithstanding such drawbacks, the DT attempts to bring the non-military aspects of security and defense into the EPC arena, which is nothing but a further concession to what is an ineluctable reality, the deep intertwining of foreign and security policy.

Article 68.1 seems somewhat superfluous. It establishes the possibility of extending the field of cooperation to four concrete areas: armaments, sales of arms to non-member states, defense policy and disarmament. The appropriate competence is naturally conferred to the European Council. By virtue of the principle of subsidiarity, the Union shall only act by common action or by cooperation whenever it is deemed to be more efficient than separate member state action. The European Council would therefore only endeavor to bring a field (including of course those mentioned in Article 68.1) under the roof of cooperation if it judged that this complied with the requirements of Article 66, and that the field was one "in which the member states acting individually cannot act as efficiently as the Union." Thus the only true worth of Article 68.1 is in illustrating some "potential" areas for cooperation and, by so doing, expressing the positive attitude of the EP towards their being dealt with in such a way.

A door to closer integration is opened by Article 68.2. This represents a concrete application of Article 11 to the foreign policy sphere, which provides for the possibility of a European Council decision to transfer a particular field from cooperation to common action. To make this a practicable alternative, two derogations from the general principles of common action are permitted: first, the member states will retain their veto power, without any time limit; second, differentiated application of a decision will be allowed in certain cases. Therefore, even if the Union were to enlarge its competence in foreign policy matters, the member states would still retain the ability to prevent any decisions contrary to their national viewpoints from being adopted. Furthermore, Article 68.3 enables the member states to undo the process (which is not possible in other areas) and thereby reacquire competence in fields which had previously been transferred to the Union. Article 68.4 offers yet another method for foreign policy coordination, through the temporary transfer of certain problems to common action for the time necessary to find a solution.

Article 69 deals with the right of representation abroad, and it provides that the Commission, with the approval of the Council of the Union, may set up representations in non-member states and international organizations which will act on behalf of the Union on matters subject to common action.

To conclude, in the foreign policy field the DT offers a variety of options for the member states to select from and utilize. It provides a framework within which cooperation may be enhanced, but it does not impose one single solution. For this reason, one must disagree with statements such as Peter Brückner's:

> By establishing a catalogue and by using a terminology that is so wide and vague that it may embrace any foreign policy issue of concern to more than one member state, the draft has adopted a maximalistic approach. [When Article 66 is] seen in conjunction with Article 68, there seem to be no limits as to what matters might come under cooperation. Under the present system, EPC is governed by declarations of a political nature. According to the draft, EPC will be made the subject of a legal text introduced by the mandatory words, "The Union *shall* conduct..."[4]

---

4 Peter Brückner, "Foreign Affairs Powers and Policy in the Draft Treaty Establishing the European Union," in: R. Bieber, J. Jacque, J. Weiler (eds.), *An Ever-Closer Union: A Critical Analysis of the Draft Treaty Establishing the European Union*, Luxembourg: European Perspectives, 1985, p. 137.

There is undoubtedly a "maximalist" tone to the DT, but this lies in its external form and structure, rather than in its content, particularly with respect to foreign policy issues. The only "legalization" of EPC consists of its institutionalization. Since practically all foreign policy issues are subject to cooperation (unless the member states themselves decide otherwise), it is a *contradictio in terminis* to label this as mandatory; cooperation implies the coordination of policies only as far as the member states deem it appropriate, and only when they believe it to be of greater efficiency -- a subjective concept open to member state interpretation. In fact, one can only speak of the existence of a legal obligation when a given form of behavior is expected from a particular agent in an objectively definable circumstance, and when a method of enforcement is available. None of these elements are to be found in the cooperation procedure envisaged by the DT. First, no concrete form of "behavior" is depicted (the only thing the member states commit themselves to is "cooperation," with no specific outcome required). Second, the circumstances in which cooperation is expected are a matter for member state interpretation (in the case of a legal obligations, the courts determine the correct interpretation of the law). Third, there is no coercive means to enforce cooperation should a member state fail to meet its commitments. Thus, the only value of the word "shall" is to express the strong political determination of the European Parliament, and it should be interpreted in light of the general spirit of the DT. In other words, "shall" should be regarded as an attempt to bridge the gap between the ambitious goals of the document and the deficient legal basis for its effective implementation.

The Single European Act

Although the DT received a high level of support in the European Parliament, it was never ratified by the national legislatures, and thus it never came into force (for reasons to be analyzed). The ideas it expressed could not be discarded and forgotten, however, so the 1984 Fontainebleau European Council charged a committee of government representatives with the task of proposing improvements to EPC and its relationship with the Community. The Dooge Committee, as it was then known, issued a report which devoted one section to a European external identity. The report advocated the maintenance of an intergovernmental EPC with strengthened EPC-Community ties, a formal obligation of prior consultation, and an enhanced consensus with respect to majority opinion; it also recommended the institutionalization of a permanent EPC secretariat. The 1984 Milan European Council was presented with a British Draft Treaty on European Cooperation and a Franco-German Draft Treaty on European Union. It called an intergovernmental conference on political cooperation and it declared these texts to be the basis of its mandate.

The result of the conference was the Single European Act, which was approved in 1986 and came into force in 1987.

The SEA was adopted as an amendment to the Treaties establishing the European Communities, and was drawn up by an intergovernmental conference. In contrast, the DT was meant to be the semi-constitutional foundation of a European Union, and was the work of the European Parliament. In short, the DT was an ambitious and in some respects revolutionary document, while the SEA is the expression of moderate, pragmatic reformism. First of all, the SEA does not establish a European Union, which satisfies both those for whom this notion is deemed undesirable and those whose ideas go beyond mere union. Secondly, the SEA is a "single" document in formal terms, but it encompasses two separate activities -- EC and EPC -- which have developed according to different rules. However, there is a clear attempt not only to bring them under a common legal roof but also to coordinate them as far as possible.

From the structural point of view, the SEA differs greatly from the constitutional format of the DT. Instead, it is a more traditional international treaty, containing a first title describing the common dispositions of both EC and EPC, a second title devoted to the amendment of the Community Treaties, a third title on European Political Cooperation, and a final act of a declarative nature. We will therefore be concerned with Title III of the SEA, "Provisions on European cooperation in the sphere of foreign policy." The fact that the provisions dealing with foreign policy are contained within a single article (Article 30) and the use of the expression "High Contracting Parties" to refer to the member states both reflect the origin of this text as a draft international treaty. Some countries preferred to conserve that wording, to emphasize the point that they were acting as independent states as well as members of the Community.

The first point of Article 30 states the objective of the signatories: they, as members of the European Communities, "shall endeavor jointly to formulate and implement a European foreign policy." The reference to the signatories' condition as members of the Community is significant, since a connection between EC and EPC is thereby made. This provision is a mixture of far-reaching concepts and attenuated commitment. The reference to a "European foreign policy" as the final goal is quite ambitious (this wording does not even appear in the DT), but the extent of the member states' commitment is only an "endeavor" to achieve it. This article contains a curious combination of binding and non-binding wording; the Parties "shall" (i.e. are required to) "endeavor" (i.e. attempt to) formulate and implement a European foreign policy. This seeming paradox must be interpreted in the context of the present stage of EPC evolution; governments can only be "forced" to "do their best" as any further cooperative obligations would likely be rejected.

The second point develops this idea further; the only commitment the member states are willing to undertake is that of consultation with one another prior to the adoption of a national position on "any foreign policy matters of general interest" (Article 30.2.a). The substance of the provision actually coincides with both current EPC practice and the forms of cooperation described by the DT. In technical terms, the absence of a precise definition of "general interest" is perhaps advantageous because it respects the flexible nature of EPC and it recognizes the near impossibility of pinpointing exactly which areas should be subject to cooperation (as opposed to DT Article 66, for instance).

A common element in the DT and the SEA is the reasoning behind the attempt to coordinate European foreign policies. Both share the functionalist approach, viewing cooperation as a function of its goal -- increased efficiency derived from the "politics of scale." In the DT this goal is enshrined in the distribution of competences between the Union and the member states, in the form of the principle of subsidiarity; in the SEA, however, "scale" is simply taken for granted (after an initial reference to efficiency) without regard to the differentiation of common action and cooperation.

Article 30.2.a includes the "implementation of joint action" as an objective of the Community foreign policy; this reflects the political will of the member states to go beyond simple joint declarations and actually carry out collective decisions. Article 30.2.c voices the intention that, through EPC, the "common principles and objectives" of a European foreign policy "are gradually developed and defined" (this is the modest counterpart of DT Article 63, which attempts to synthesize the fundamental principles of the Union's foreign policy). It then continues by establishing that "the determination of common positions shall constitute a point of reference for the policies of the High Contracting Parties." This makes it abundantly clear that the member states have not renounced the sovereign right of determining their own foreign policy -- which is precisely the difference between merely cooperating and, on the other hand, building an effective common policy. The realism of this provision might be praiseworthy, but it should at least have given greater value to the common positions adopted in EPC, rather than relegating them to a mere "point of reference." If the member states freely agree to coordinate their positions on a given issue, their individual actions should only be inspired by the common decision.

Article 30.3.c contains what is left of the "majority consensus" advocated by the Dooge Report. (This corresponds to DT Articles 35 and 68.2, which allow for the differentiated application of decisions). The common goal of these dispositions is their attempt to maintain the "consensus" decision-making process while at the same time providing an escape for those member states who feel that they cannot support a particular policy but who do not wish to block a majority decision. The difference lies in the context in which these provisions are found. In the DT, differentiated application is viewed as an exception to the general rule of majority voting in the Council of the Union on those issues transferred from cooperation to common action. In the SEA, however, it is a general rule applying to all EPC decisions. This brings up another point of divergence between the two documents: unlike the DT, the SEA does not provide for the possible expansion of the field of common action. Of course, it can be argued that since the SEA may be revised after five years, further modifications can then be introduced (according to the terms of Article 30.12). Still, the fact remains that while the DT offers many paths to further integration in the foreign policy field, the SEA limits itself to codifying the present stage in the evolution of EPC practice.

In other words, the point of departure is the same for both documents: the Community acts on behalf of the member states in external commercial policy and other areas contemplated in the Community Treaties; other foreign policy fields are subject to cooperation. But while the SEA does not go any further, the DT envisages the progressive introduction of a common development aid policy, within a 10 year period (DT Article 64.2), and the optional expansion of the fields subject to common action (DT Article 68).

Articles 30.3.a, 30.3.b, 30.4 and 30.5 are concerned with the establishment of a connection between the EC institutions and EPC. Article 30.3.a codifies what was already a reality in EPC working procedures: a member of the Commission is present at EPC meetings and the Ministers of Foreign Affairs may also discuss foreign policy issues when they gather as the Council of the European Communities. Article 30.3.b ensures that the Commission is "fully associated with the proceedings of Political Cooperation."

Article 30.4 specifies that the EP is to be kept informed of EPC affairs and that its views are to be "taken into consideration" (as does DT Article 65.4). The only enforceable duty of the European Council is that of informing the EP; whether or not its opinions are really taken into account will depend upon the political will of the Council. The commitment to keep the Parliament informed is, however, taken quite seriously; a decision taken by the Ministers of Foreign Affairs on the occasion of the SEA's signing elaborates on the modalities of this dialogue.

Article 30.5 represents the key point of intersection between EC and EPC. It entrusts the Presidency of EPC and the Commission, "each within its own sphere of competence," with the responsibility of keeping the external policies of EC and EPC consistent. This provision captures the spirit of the SEA approach to EC-EPC relations, which is one of attempting to achieve the coordination of foreign policy activity by allowing communication between the two institutions while at the same time keeping them apart and maintaining their separate identities. In the DT, despite the fact that both areas are symbolically integrated into the European Union, there is no better guarantee that the foreign policies of the member states will be consistent with the external relations of the Union, since the only provision treating the issue (DT Article 67.2) is purely declarative and could not be effectively enforced.

Article 30.7 of the SEA (corresponding to DT Article 67.4) encourages the coordination of member state positions in international organizations and at international conferences. Once again, in the SEA it is the High Contracting Parties who "shall endeavor" to cooperate, whereas in the DT this is regarded as a function of the Union, which seeks to enhance collaboration by its constituents.

With regard to representation abroad, the SEA only establishes that the member states and the Commission should "intensify cooperation between their representations accredited to third countries and to international organizations" (Article 30.9). The DT, on the other hand, advocates the creation of actual Union representations to international organizations and non-member states. These should be full-fledged representations with an active role "representing the Union in all matters subject to common action." Once again the SEA reinforces existing practice, whereas the DT offers a dynamic alternative. It is not surprising, however, that the "new" political unit envisioned by the DT -- the Union -- should have a means of representing itself, while the more modest non-institutional approach of the SEA should limit itself to existing forms of cooperation and exclude the creation of new structures.

Article 30.10 describes the organization of EPC: the Presidency of EPC (and also of the Council of the European Communities), who shall manage the organizations and act as the representative of the member states with respect to EPC affairs; the Political Committee, a group of Political Directors who meet regularly to prepare the Foreign Ministers' meetings; the European Correspondents' Group, who monitor the implementation of EPC decisions; working groups under the direction of the Political Committee; and, finally, the provision of a permanent EPC Secretariat.

The Secretariat is the main innovation of the SEA. Until that time, EPC had been working without institutional support. The idea had been raised as early as 1971, but it there was some controversy over the matter of its location and whether it should have a purely administrative or more political mandate. In the end, the member states agreed that the Secretariat would be based in Brussels and that it should be, as de Ruyt describes it, "a small administrative organ, coexisting with the Community institutions, neither dominating nor ignoring them, and especially not working against them."[5]

---

5 ". . . un petit organe administratif léger, coexistant avec les institutions communautaires, sans les dominer ni les ignorer, sans non plus se confondre avec elles."

Two pertinent observations are related to the structure of EPC, as it is presented in the SEA. First, it is clear that the leading role in EPC is to be played neither by the Commission nor by the Secretariat but by the Presidency of the European Council, thus promoting intergovernmentalism at the expense of both supranationalism and institutionalism. Second, the creation of an administrative organ to assist in the implementation of EPC decisions is consistent with the overall pragmatism of the document. Article 30.6 (like DT Article 66) includes the political and economic aspects of security as a subject for EPC consideration. No further commitment could be reached as not all members of the European Communities belong to WEU and NATO. Ireland, as a neutral country, wished to ensure that no WEU or NATO-related matters would be included within the EPC framework. To offset this weakness, Article 30.6.c was added to emphasize that closer cooperation within NATO or WEU would not be impeded by EPC.

Recent Progress Toward Political Union

At the Rome Summit in December 1990, the nations of the European Community agreed to convene an Intergovernmental Conference on Political Union, with the intention of devising an acceptable treaty by the end of 1991. The tension between the intergovernmental approach and the supranational or communautarian approach continues to characterize the debate concerning the nature and purpose of the proposed Political Union. The various Community institutions are aligned to their respective positions: the Council, representing the national governments, remains committed to intergovernmental cooperation; the Commission and the European Parliament consistently favor a greater degree of supranationality. The provisions for a Common Foreign and Security Policy, which go well beyond those of the Single European Act, have of course been at the center of the debate. An analysis of 1991 documents should give some evidence of the various institutional positions on Political Union.

The European Parliament

In July 1990, the European Parliament adopted, as a guideline for the upcoming Intergovernmental Conference on Political Union, the Martin report.[6] In very general terms, this envisions a federal polity with competences

---

Jean de Ruyt, *L'Acte Unique Européen*, Bruxelles: Editions de l'Université de Bruxelles, 1987, p. 246.
6 "Resolution on the Intergovernmental Conference in the Context of European Union", *Europe/Documents*, Nos. 1639/40, 19 July 1990.

distributed according to the principle of subsidiarity. Its provisions for a Community foreign policy respresent a significant departure from the terms of the SEA.

The Martin report first calls for an end to the separation of EC and EPC, stating that "the current division between external economic policy handled by Community institutions with the Community's external representative, and political cooperation handled by EPC with the EPC President acting as external representative, is increasingly difficult to maintain in preactice" and should eventually be abolished. The Council, as the representative of the member states, should be given the responsibility for defining a common external policy; the Commission's representational role should be enhanced; the parliament should have the right of scrutiny. Thus the EPC Secretartiat would be absorbed by the Council and the Commission. While this document clearly endorses intergovernmental cooperation in the foreign policy sphere, it insists that "the Community should aim to have common policies on all matters in which the member states share essential interests."

The range of competences outlined by the Martin report greatly expands on those found in the SEA. The Community's foreign policy should "include issues of security, peace and disarmament, with a close coordination of national security policies." It then goes on to suggest that the Community should represent the member states in international organizations in those areas where Community competence has been established.

A proposal for a Draft Treaty on European Union submitted to the Parliament in December 1990 sought to expand the Community competence to include "the field of foreign policy and common security and defense policy, including arms control, in all sectors in which the member states have vital interest; . . . the Constitution shall stipulate the areas in which common action must be taken."[7]

Clearly, the Parliament's proposals are informed by the subsidiarity principle; they envision that areas such as security policy -- once strictly the domain of national governments -- will gradually become Community competences as the integration process generates a greater degree of common interests and cohesion among the member states. However, highly sensitive core elements of national sovereignty such as defense policy will, for the time being, remain subject to cooperation rather than common action.

The Martin report, like other EP projects, continues in the tradition of the DT by advocating a constitutionally-based federal Union with the distinction between fields for common action and for cooperation to be determined by the

---

[7] "A Constitution for European Union: The Basis for a European Parliament Draft Treaty," *Europe/Documents*, No. 1674, 19 December 1990.

subsidiarity principle. It departs from past efforts by the inclusion of security matters within the purview of a common foreign policy.

The Commission

In the Political Union debate, the Commission has endeavord to find something of a middle ground between the supranationalism of the Parliament and the intergovernmentalism of the Council. It also advocates a greatly expanded international role for the Union, and greater coherence between common action and cooperation.

In March 1991, the Commission proposed that the Community external policy, "provided it was based on profound consensus between member states in terms of their common ambition to reinforce the international responsibility of the Union, should encompass the member states' vital common interests and include security and defense."[8] The common external policy envisioned by the Commission would include "the common foreign and security policy, the external economic policy and the development cooperation policy, as well as external relations in the orther areas where the Union has jurisdiction." These new powers are intended to ensure "unity and coherence of Union action on the international scene."

It is clear from the Commission's proposal that "common policy does not mean single policy," and there will be allowances for national differences. The subsidiarity principle will determine which areas should be left to national decision, which will be subject to intergovernmental cooperation, and which will become the preserve of common action. The European Council would be responsible for the allocation of competences. On questions of "vital common interest" (as determined by the European Council), Council decisions would be taken either by unanimity (with abstention permitted) or by qualified majority and would be implemented by common action. member states would be permitted to opt out of decisions with which they disagreed, and would not be obliged to participate in common action; they would, however, be compelled to refrain from pursuing policies contrary to those adopted by the Union.

The Commission also proposes that the mandate of the common security policy go beyond that set out by the Rome Council in December 1990 -- arms control and disarmament; CSCE and UN mattters, including peacekeeping; cooperation in the production, export and non-proliferation of arms -- to include a research and arms production policy. Perhaps of greater significance, it seeks to acquire a defense dimension for the Union either by the adoption of a mutual assistance clause similar to Article Five of the Western European

---

8 Political Union: Commission Proposals at IGC on "Common External Policy", *Europe/Documents*, Nos. 1697/98, 7 March 1991.

Union (WEU) Treaty, or through the gradual integration of the WEU into the Community.

In a speech delivered in March 1991, Commission President Jacques Delors gave clear expression to the objectives of this proposal, and outlined the institutional changes that it would entail:

> The institutional dimension cannot be neglected even if, in the last analysis, progress presupposes strong political will based on consensus.
> That is why the Commission, in its draft Treaty, proposes a single centre provide impetus and a single centre for discussion and action; and why it proposes that all provisions relating to external aspects -- foreign policy, security, economic relations and development cooperation -- should be brought together in one title of the Treaty. Coherence is essential if the pre-eminence of the political aspect is to be highlighted and if disparate, ill-prepared and insufficiently reasoned and considered action is to be avoided.
> Obviously, precautions will have to be taken to avoid a forced march, which would only lead to internal cirises or impotence. It will be for the European Council, consisting of Heads of State and Government who are democratically answerable to their people, to agree on the essential interests they share and which they will agree to defend and promote together.
> Foreign Ministers would work within this framework. They would endeavor to produce a common analysis and then decide on action. In this area and for matters now covered by the Community, qualified majority voting would be an essential stimulant, the leaven of a Community in the making. Everything suggests that Foreign Ministers would use qualified majority voting with prudence and moderation, taking account of everyone's interests and the time needed to bring positions together. This has been the experience since the Single Act came into effect. You cannot ride roughshod over people's hearts of skimp on the time needed for better mutual understanding.
> As the dynamic of vital common interests gathers momentum, people will come to see the need for this missing ingredient -- the means of defense, for the sake of our national integrity, the values which nourish us, the solidarity which unites us and our responsibilities towards the rest of the world.[9]

---

9 Jacques Delors, "European Integration and Security," *Europe/Documents*, No. 1699, 13 March 1991.

Although the responsibility for foreign and security policy would be retained by the member states, through the mechanism of the Council, the Commission envisions that the sphere of common action -- as opposed to mere cooperation-- will gradually expand, eventually to include such sensitive matters as national defense. This, according to the Commission proposal, should take place within the context of a single unified and coherent community, the European Union. Thus one sees again a blend of both supranational and intergovernmental elements in these documents, but with a strong tendency towards centralization.

The Intergovernmental Conference on Political Union

Since the IGC has convened, a number of draft treaties -- commonly known as "non-papers" -- have been submitted to the conference for discussion.[10] The June 1991 paper of the Luxemburg Presidency will form the basis for the Union Treaty which should be approved at the Maastricht Summit in December. An alalysis of its provisions therefore gives some indication of the future direction of the Community's common external policy.

At first glance, the paper appears to advocate a supranational approach to European Union. In rhetorical terms, at least, the document claims to mark "a new stage in a process leading gradually to a Union with a federal goal."[11] The Union, as envisioned by this draft, should aim to "assert its identity on the international scene, in particular through the implementation of a common foreign and security policy which shall include the eventual framing of a defense policy." Furthermore, "the Union shall be served by a single institutional framework which shall ensure the consistency and the continuity of the actions carried out in order to reach its objectives while respecting and developing the acquis communautaire." However, since the European Council "shall provide the Union with the necessary impetus and define the general political guidelines," it remains to be seen to what extent the member states will be willing to transfer competence from national to common action, particularly on security and defense issues.

Other Community institutions will of course play a role. The Commission retains the right of initiative, and may refer questions to the Council; the Parliament will continue to make requests of and recommendations to the Council on matters of external policy.

A closer examination of the proposed institutional arrangements would seem to indicate that significant changes to the provisions of the Single European Act will likely be made. External policy shall be pursued "within a single

---

10 See the reprint of excerpts from these documents in the ANNEX.
11 "Draft Treaty on the Union: Conference of the Representatives of the Governments of the member states," *Europe/Documents*, No. 1722, 5 July 1991.

institutional framework by establishing systematic cooperation between member states in the conduct of policy and by gradually introducing joint action in areas where the member states have essential interests in common." Thus, EPC will be absorbed into the Council and a unified secretariat will be established; one forum will suffice for the discussion of all issues, from development to defense. Foreign and security policy will, however, likely remain a national competence subject to cooperation, rather than common action, so there will be a continuing need for the Commission and the Council to ensure the consistency of intergovernmental and Community measures -- in this respect, the Luxemburg paper does not represent such a great departure from the SEA.

In those areas subject to cooperation, the draft provides that the member states "shall inform and consult with one another" in order to "ensure that their combined influence is exerted as effectively as possible." The individual governments should base their policies upon common positions established in the Council. Furthermore, the member states should support the Union "actively and unreservedly in a spirit of loyalty and mutual solidarity" and refrain from any actions which might prove detrimental to its policies. Also, "member states shall coordinate their action and, wherever necessary, define common positions in international organizations and at international conferences."

On the basis of European Council guidelines, the Council may decide that certain foreign and security policy matters should instead be subject to joint action. In this case, "once the objectives and means of a joint line of action have been defined, each member state shall be bound by the joint line of action in the conduct of its international activity." The Council Presidency will then represent the Union in other international institutions. Again, the member states are enjoined against any form of behavior which might prove detrimental to the common policy.

The draft represents, in one key respect, a significant advance. Where the SEA restricted EPC activity to the "political and economic aspects of security," the Luxemburg draft allows for a much broader range of issues to be included within the Community purview. "The common foreign and security policy includes all questions relating to the security of the Union." After alluding to the role of the Western European Union and the Atlantic Alliance, it goes on to call for the "eventual framing of a defense policy," although few details are given and the immediate prospects for such a development can only be assessed with difficulty.

Much of the common foreign and security policy, and certainly any common defense policy, will remain within the preserve of intergovernmental cooperation. These are highly sensitive matters, core elements of national sovereignty, and it is most unlikely that at any time in the near future the member state governments would renounce their ultimate responsibility for national security in favor of the "pooled sovereignty" represented by the Community. They have nevertheless agreed that certain topics will, once the Treaty enters into force, become subjects for joint action. These are: industrial and technological cooperation in the armaments field; the transfer of military technology to third countries and the control of arms exports; nonproliferation issues; arms control, negotiations on arms reduction and confidence-building measures, particularly in the CSCE context; involvement in peace-keeping operations in the United Nations context; involvement in humanitarian intervention measures; questions relating to the CSCE; relations with the USSR; transatlantic relations. In time, other topics will undoubtedly be added.

As with the Parliament and Commission proposals, the IGC draft on Political Union approaches the problem of a common foreign and security policy in a balanced manner. The mix, between cooperation and joint action, will be determined not by an abstract application of the subsidiarity principle but by the political relations of the member states and by their ability to identify and define common interests and positions during their deliberations within the European Council.

Conclusions

To sum up, the DT and the SEA are two documents which, in spite of sharing some common goals and even a considerable part of their substantive content, embody two different political approaches and two diverse conceptions of what sort of integration is both possible and desirable for Western Europe in the near future.

However, despite the obvious lack of catalytic factors in the SEA, it proved to be the only step that member states were willing to take. The DT experience showed that not even the most "pro-integrationist" European countries were ready for the birth of a "European Union" -- even a balanced and only modestly reformist polity such as that envisaged by the DT. Therefore, without prejudging whether in the long run a structuralist or a functionalist approach will prove more fruitful for Western European integration, the fact remains that the direction and the speed of European Political Cooperation activity is completely in the hands of the member states. For foreign policy issues, under either the DT or the SEA, the evolution of the integration process will depend upon the dynamic combination of several variables, chief among them international pressures, national public opinion and, most important of all, political will.

The same analysis applies to the debate surrounding the Intergovernmental Conference and the plans for Political Union. The same basic tension that characterized the DT and the SEA, between cooperation and common action, will continue to exist in the new Union Treaty. But there will also be significant advances: a more coherent institutional structure should facilitate a greater degree of consistency between the various aspects of the Community's external policy, which will formally include security and defense matters. In the end, however, the success of the Common Foreign and Security Policy will depend not so much on the institutional structure of the Community, but on the political will of its member states.

20

Scope and Structure of the Community's Future Foreign Policy

Giovanni Jannuzzi

According to all evidence, the role of Europe in international affairs does not meet the expectations set in it. The only way to reestablish its role to an acceptable degree is to provide the European Community (EC) with the appropriate structures and means. The EC is the only organized expression of European will and ability in foreign policy. It should be recognized as such and become more and more the focal point for Europe's participation in world affairs. While the world has become increasingly multipolar, with the emergence of a number of new and independent centers of power, the growing size and complexity of the problems to be faced allow only a limited number of "giants" to act effectively in foreign politics, at least on a world scale. Under such conditions, the European Community must emerge -- in the transition from a bipolar to a multipolar world -- as an actual superpower, alongside the US, the Soviet Union and Japan. The four of them are very likely to dominate international affairs in the foreseeable future. Of them, only the US possesses in reality the three constituent elements of superpower status: political, economic and military power. The Soviet Union has clearly lost its economic and political attributes but will essentially remain a European superpower thanks to its nuclear strength. Japan is mainly an economic giant. The EC has all the political and economic attributes of a superpower. Besides the lack of the military component, it is limited in its superpower status by the absence of a "nerve center," a center for political decision-making, comparable to that of nation-states. If the EC succeeds in the coming years in acquiring this center and in expanding its competence to security, then it will be a full superpower, albeit of a specific and somewhat anomalous nature.

The Gulf Crisis clearly showed both the effectiveness of Community action and its limitations. From the beginning of the crisis, the Community acted with total cohesion and in full solidarity with its Western partners in the framework of the United Nations (UN) Charter. Its policy towards the Iraqi aggression and annexation of Kuwait was coherent and unambiguous. A total embargo against Iraq was established by the Community as early as August 4, 1990. All throughout the crisis and conflict, the Twelve stood by the UN resolutions and by those UN and EC members whose forces were engaged in the Gulf. This was made possible not only by a remarkable degree of convergence in the Twelve's objectives, interests, and values, but also by the existence of clear-cut Community competences, structures, and instruments of action in the political and economic fields. In the military field, where the Community still has no competence -- or structures -- the European response was limited and mainly national (albeit with some coordination within WEU). This is an important lesson to be drawn from the Gulf Crisis: a lesson which should apply to a future in which the European presence will be even more necessary than in the past, to ensure peace, stability and progress to the vast Mediterranean and Middle-East area.

The external policy of the Community has indeed been consistently inspired by, and aimed at, objectives of peace, stability and economic and social progress. These goals are evident in the Lomé Agreements but also in the Mediterranean agreements and in the policy in Central America. A specific element of the Community's foreign policy has been the support of human rights, freedom, democracy and justice. These principles inspire EC policy in Eastern Europe, the Middle East, South Africa. The Community is also a strong supporter of the United Nations system and of its principles of independence, non-interference and peaceful solution of disputes. The Twelve, in this context, consistently contribute to the Conference on Security and Cooperation in Europe (CSCE) process and to peace-keeping forces all over the world. The EC and its members are by far the largest donor of aid to development as well as the largest contributor to world trade and of international trade negotiations such as the North-South Dialogue, GATT and the Uruguay Round.

To cope with such a large, and increasing, amount of responsibilities, the Community relies heavily on its dual structures: the Community proper and European Political Cooperation (EPC). They both relate to the same leading structures, the European Council and the Council of Ministers. The substructures, COREPER (Coopération des représentants permanents) and the Political Committee, are still formally separated. This separation however tends to become more and more artificial and obsolete and it is reasonable to expect that it will gradually disappear. What will happen, in my view, is that the present distinction between EC external relations and EPC will be replaced by a different distinction, much less artificial, between internal and external responsibilities of the Community. In its march towards Political Union, the Community is indeed already facing the problem, both political and technical, of improving its ability to formulate and implement a common foreign policy.

This will demand a deep, albeit not radical or overambitious, reform of its rules and structures. This is the aim and the content of the current institutional review, which was primarily launched in 1990 by the Belgian Government and then by a Franco-German initiative contained in a letter by President Mitterrand and Chancellor Kohl addressed jointly to the Irish Prime Minister -- at the time President of the European Council.

These initiatives were discussed at the extraordinary European Council in Dublin and the Heads of State and Government asked their Foreign Ministers to further analyze the propositions and to report to the European Council at the end of June 1990. On the basis of this report, the June Council decided to convene an Intergovernmental Conference (IGC) on Political Union. It also approved a document prepared by the Ministers which, for the part concerning "Unity and coherence of the Community's external actions" reads as follows:

> In accordance with the conclusions reached by the European Council at Dublin on 28 April 1990, the Community will act as a political entity on the international scene.[1]

The proposal for a common foreign and security policy which takes account of the common interests of the member states, acting with consistency and solidarity, and which institutionally goes beyond Political Cooperation as it currently functions, raises a number of questions.

Scope

- the integration of economic, political and security aspects of foreign policy;
- the definition of the security dimension;
- the strengthening of the Community's diplomatic and political action vis-à-vis third countries, in international organizations and in other multilateral fora;
- the evolution of the transfer of competences to the Union, and in particular the definition of priority areas where transfer would take place at an initial stage.

Decision-Making

- the use of the Community method (in full or in adapted form) and/or a *sui generis* method bearing in mind the possibilities offered by the evolution

---

1 "Conclusions of the European Council, Dublin, 25-26 June 1990," *Europe/Documents*, Nos. 1632/1633, 29 June 1990, p. 9.

over time of the degree of transfer of competence to the Union, referred to above;
- the Commission's role, including the faculty of launching initiatives and proposals;
- establishment of a single decision-making structure; central role of the General Affairs Council and the European Council in this context; preparatory bodies; the organization and strengthening of the Secretariat;
- modalities aimed at ensuring the necessary flexibility and efficiency to meet the requirements of formulation of foreign policy in various areas;
- consideration of decision procedures including the consensus rule, voting practices involving unanimity with abstentions, and qualified majority voting in specific areas.

Implementation

There is a recognized need for clear rules and modalities for the implementation of the common foreign policy; the following are to be examined in this context:

- role of the Presidency (and of the Troika), and of the secretariat;
- role of the Commission;
- the role of national diplomatic services in a strengthened collaboration.

The conclusions of the Dublin European Council were re-examined and further elaborated by the European Council in Rome on 14-15 December 1990. As far as the common foreign and security policy is concerned, the Council asked the Intergovernmental Conference (IGC) to define the objectives of the Union, the scope of its policies and the ways to assure their implementation in an institutional framework. According to the Rome conclusions, the institutional framework should be based on the following elements:

- a single decision-making center (the Council);
- harmonization and/or unification of preparatory work; a unified Secretariat;
- a strengthening of the Commission's role through the non-exclusive right of initiative;
- appropriate procedures for consultation and information of the European Parliament;
- modalities enabling the Union to speak effectively with one voice.

Concerning the decision-making process, the Rome conclusions envisage:

- consensus as a rule for defining general orientations;
- possible majority vote for the implementation of agreed policies.

Regarding security, the Rome European Council envisaged the progressive extension of the Union's role to questions discussed in international fora (such as arms control, peace-keeping operations, CSCE items, etc.) as well as industrial and technological cooperation and coordination in the field of arms export and proliferation. The European Council underlined, however, that in the future, the Union should play a role in defense, without prejudice to the existing NATO commitments, and that a commitment for mutual assistance among the Twelve should also be examined.

With the Rome Council and the opening of the IGC on Political Union on 15 December 1990, the actual negotiation has thus started. What will be the main lines of development? It is not likely that there is now, or that there will be in the near future, a consensus to establish a United States of Europe, or of any kind of federation with exclusive competence in security and foreign policy. In other words, the Intergovernmental Conference will not produce a totally supranational structure, absorbing individual countries and national sovereignties. Rather, collective and individual action will have to coexist, albeit in a mix which will be different from the present one in the sense that the focus will be more often shifted to collective - or common - action.

This implies structural adjustments, aimed at strengthening consistency, cohesion, continuity and effectiveness of a common foreign policy and to extend its competence to the field of security. Based on the documents approved at Dublin and Rome and on the discussions at Ministerial level that led to it, a broad outline can be detected. There is a general consensus that the European Council should strengthen its leading role and that the Council of Foreign Ministers should become the operational structure for elaborating and implementing foreign policy. It is questionable whether the possibility of majority vote in foreign policy, envisaged in the Rome conclusions, will be actually accepted. Some countries seem to be ready to accept this "qualitative leap," at least in certain areas, while some will probably oppose it. A possible compromise could be found in limiting majority vote to strictly defined areas and in facilitating the decision-making process by introducing a "consensus with abstentions." A consensus is also emerging on the definition of certain areas of foreign policy (such as Eastern Europe, or Human Rights, or the United Nations) where common positions should prevail over individual ones. A consensus seems to exist also on the need to strengthen the external role of the Presidency and on making it more active. One possibility to that purpose would be the appointment of a President for a given period of time (e.g. two years). Another possibility (not necessarily alternative) could be the appointment of a strong Secretariat, to be put at the disposal of the Presidency. In any case the role of the Secretariat in the formation and formulation of political decisions will have to be reviewed. In this area, the Secretariat has so far interpreted the general provisions of the Single European Act in a restrictive way by refraining both from initiating policies (other than through discreet personal influence on the Presidency) or from drafting and formulating them unless requested by the Presidency or by all partners. In the future it should be possible for the EPC Secretariat to be given more relevant and meaningful functions, modeled according to those performed by the Council Secretariat in Community affairs. The role of the Secretariat could also be enhanced in the field of communication of policies, both to the European Parliament and to the media.

But it is especially in the field of foreign policy implementation that the role of the Secretariat could be usefully enhanced. The task of maintaining the necessary and increasing contacts with the external world lies at present mainly with the Presidency. So does the task of conducting diplomatic action. While this must remain so in principle, there is, in my opinion, a lot that a strengthened Secretariat (and above all a strengthened Head of the Secretariat), placed under the authority of a reinforced and authoritative Presidency, could do to improve the continuity and effectiveness of the Union's external policy in relations with third countries and regional groups.

An additional development under consideration concerns the merging of the EPC Secretariat with the Council Secretariat. It will mean in practice the absorption of the EPC Secretariat by the much larger and stronger Council Secretariat. The Political Secretariat should however remain as distinct identity within the Council Secretariat and be directed by a Deputy-Secretary General for political affairs; endowed with the necessary autonomy and authority.

Political Bodies

From what has been explained above, it is possible to imagine more or less the following structure for the Community external action:

- for the elaboration of policies (with the full participation of, and right of initiative to, the EC Commission): the European Council; the Council of Ministers, assisted by the Secretariat.
- for external implementation: the Presidency or Presidency/Commission or Troika, in any case assisted by the Secretariat; the Commission (for its specific competence).
- for democratic control: the European Parliament.

Security would in principle fit nicely in this structure, given the responsibility attributed in this field to Heads of State and Government and to Foreign Ministers. An appropriate structure (e.g. a Council of Defense Ministers) could however be envisaged, if necessary, to assist the European Council. Or, as a more likely alternative, WEU should be used as the forum to coordinate and implement European security policy. As a matter of fact, there is for the moment no consensus among the Twelve on including in the Political Union defense or strictly military aspects related to it. Rather, a consensus seems possible concerning the extension of the present area of Community competence (political and economic aspects of security) to areas such as disarmament, arms control, confidence building measures and collective security within the CSCE. That would be by all means a serious qualitative leap since it would cover an area which is more and more important for security as such. On this point, there is still some reluctance on the part of those who are afraid of overlapping, and potential conflict, with other existing fora, such as NATO and WEU. Such overlapping is in fact possible and even likely. It should not necessarily mean a conflict. NATO and WEU have coexisted for decades without conflicting. Already, there are areas in which EPC and NATO cooperation overlap. This provokes some problems, but both sides feel a need to harmonize their respective positions and the end result is indeed harmonization. In any case, the existence of NATO and the risk of overlapping should not, and in my view will not, prevent the Community from trying to reach a common position in an area of such vital importance to all the Twelve. This is a fact of life, a fact that the allies in NATO seem to understand and accept. EC member states must understand and accept the fact that beyond Community cooperation there exists the need for a larger Western solidarity. To adjust to these facts is a question of mutual good sense and reason.

To go beyond that kind of competence in the field of defense and security requests focusing on WEU, at least for the next five to six years. In due course, a practice of Community cooperation on security and the progressive enlargement of WEU might bring cooperation in defense matters within the scope of Political Union. In any case, developments should not be seen by the United States, or by the Soviet Union, as a threat but rather as a contribution to common security and stability in Europe.

These are some lines of possible development in the move toward Political Union. Much, of course, remains to be done. How to increase cohesion, how to adequately project collective strength in terms of foreign policy, is the challenge that EC Governments and Parliaments will have to face in the coming months.

21

Beyond Maastricht: Alternative Futures for a Political Union

Reinhardt Rummel

Introduction

It was obvious at the Maastricht European Council meeting in December 1991 that the plans for a European Political Union (EPU) were less mature than those on the Economic and Monetary Union (EMU) in the Community. This was no surprise to anyone, not even to German Chancellor Helmut Kohl, the chief advocat for a linkage of substantial progress in both unions. The asymmetry was an indication for more than just the unequal preparation of two dossiers. It was a hint at the (temporary?) saturation of integration. Unlike the economic and monetary sector, further integration in the field of foreign and security policy simply seems to lack plausibility. Certainly, one can imagine institutional designs for a more complete action center of external relations of the Community, but -- difficult as it may be -- this is not the major question. The central issue seems to be the rationale for a significant centralization of foreign and security policy given the fundamental change in the structure of international relations and specifically in Europe.

While analysts and politicians alike have been quick in assuming that the lessons of the Gulf and the Yugoslav wars strike a convincing cord for the establishment of a unified West European action center, the challenges in Europe at large seem to be of a kind which favors national and sub-national initiatives parallel to those on the West European level. Therefore, the yardstick for Western Europe's external performance has to be rather the range of external influence than the bare degree of unity. The "Community's" success story in foreign and security policy is composed of actions on various levels. All these levels deserve attention when strengthening Western Europe's influence on its international environment. This may not be called "subsidiarity," but it would take account of a differentiation process among ethnic groups, autonomous regions, nations, and states.[1] The orchestration of various levels of external action may be as important as the development of each individual component. To the extent that the Community's external reach can and should be increased, it is determined by its internal texture and potential, which, in turn, depends on national and sub-national identities and interests.

The Internal Fabric: Institutions and Mindsets

There is no way around the definition of a substantial mission for the EPU's Common Foreign and Security Policy (CFSP). The member states have used the Maastricht conference to make a few steps in this direction by mentioning areas of common interest within which to conduct common policies and by reserving for themselves (the Heads of State and Government), the prime decisions on such areas. However, they missed the opportuniy to develop a foreign policy agenda: no contents, no priorities have been given. Thus, a central weakness of the Community system has not yet been overcome. It lacks a set of principles and a central political focus. Too much attention has been attributed to the techniques of decision making and to the implementation of policies. Problems seem to have been multiplied in this regard rather than reduced, while the attitudes of policymakers have remained unchanged: the dominant foreign policy reflex in Western Europe is national, not communitarian, as the conflict management in the Yugoslav civil war has amply demonstrated.

The challenge to West European leadership and the specific demands from partner actors in Europe and beyond are much wider than the individual national perspective of an EC member government. How can the gap be closed? The West Europeans are not the only ones facing such a structural problem. Other international actors are confronted with a similar issue. This is the case of Japan which -- given the scope as well as the nature of the need for change -- requires the innovation of both the institutions and the mindsets of the political leaders.[2]

---

1   For the concept of "subsidiarity" see: Marc Wilk and Ellen Wallace: *Subsidiarity: Approaches to Power-sharing in the EC*, London: Pinter, 1990. Most policy analysts reject the concept of "subsidiarity" for the external relations of the Community. See Christopher Hill, "The European Community: Towards a Common Foreign and Security Policy?", *The World Today*, Vol. 47, No. 11, 1991, pp. 189-192.

2   Hideo Sato, "The Emerging Role of Japan in the World Economy," in: *The International Spectator*, Vol. 26, No. 3, July-September 1991, pp. 75-102. Peter J. Katzenstein and Nobus Okowara, "Japan's Security Policy: Political, Economic and Military Dimensions," in: ibid., pp. 103-118.

Problems of Institutional Innovation

Some half-hearted attempts have been made in the past to establish a planning capacity for the Community. The establishment of the group of planning staff representatives of the twelve foreign ministries was one, Jacques Delors' "cellule prospective" was another. Their momentum, however, is too small. In the end, the European Council (or more specifically the Presidency) will need some institutional substructure, including a group of security and foreign policy advisors. Neither the Political Committee nor the extended secretariat of Political Cooperation or the Commission can alone provide the expertise and operational advice. An active Community Presidency needs a team comparable to the National Security Council of the US President in order to elaborate both proactive risk analyses and impartial (non-national) policy recommendations. To integrate the European Political Cooperation (EPC) and Council secretariats may be regarded as a small step in this direction. The question is: are the member states prepared to strengthen the position of the secretary general by establishing an informed voice on the multilateral level which can effectively contrast national positions? Most international organisations have a problem in this respect, the Community even more so.

The Commission, it is true, has played remarkably well the role of an independent voice in the Community system, and the Parliament has tried its best to help, but their power and expertise remain limited in the field of foreign and security policy, despite the improvements of the Single European Act and the extension of competences in the Maastricht Documents. The only real progress, the wider responsibility of the Commission, will only be effective if it is used in conjunction with the Presidency which in turn will continue to depend on the specific capacity of the respective member government. All co-actors within the Community are in need of non-national, europeanized information and analysis from which they can draw their respective duties of initiative, decision making and political control. In this regard, the creation of a European Institute on Foreign and Security Policy is overdue but can only be part of a solution.[3]

Next to the problem of claiming timely and appropriate initiatives arises the question of how to make decisions. Several issues are unsettled here. The

---

3 A respective report of the EP Political Affairs Committee ends with a wait-and-see strategy. Unfortunately, the major changes and the new security structures are developed now -- not in 1998 when WEU (and its research institute) may be merged with the Community. The report demonstrates, moreover, a revealing misperception of future security priorities. See European Communities. European Parliament, *Report of the Political Affairs Committee on the Creation of an Institute of European Security*, Rapporteur: Edward H.C. McMillan-Scott, Session Documents, 25 September 1991.

Maastricht approach to split political and technical levels of decision making between the European Council and the Council of Ministers will probably not stand the reality test. The formula was invented to make a first step to overcome the consensus rule or, more modestly interpreted, to render two differing decision making procedures compatible, the communitarian and the intergovernmental methods. The solution has not yet been found. Too much emphasis has been put on finding ways to circumvent the need for consensus and to establish the majority rules among member states. If the Community wants to become -- at least in some sectors -- a monolithic international actor like, for instance, the United States, then it cannot avoid developing its federal system. This means developing a politically representative force, the Parliament, in addition to the Council as a representation of the member states and operating on a majority vote basis. The marginal improvements for the European Parliament which the Maastricht Documents suggest are miles away from such an improvement.

Is it worthwhile to ameliorate the implementation side of common foreign and security policy if the capacity for initiative and decision making is underdeveloped?[4] To put all the Community instruments at the disposition of CFSP can certainly be a significant asset for a more forceful external action, but it remains a doubtful progress as long as decisions are taken too late and/or are based on insufficient analysis. The Community has demonstrated some qualities of "learning by doing" during the crisis management in Yugoslavia; but here, too, ad hoc measures will not enable a policy of war prevention. Many observers claim that the Community needs one more instrument, a military reaction force, and then its influence will be assured. However, the Community is already strong on instruments even without the military arm, but it is too weak on action. This may be more of a mental than an institutional question.

Developing New Mindsets

Just as sub-national political leaders have realized that they need foreign policies of their own, Community leaders should be responsible at their level of policy-making. This is not only a task of the Commissioners and the deputies of the European Parliament, it is in the given Community system primarily a duty of the Council members and the Presidency. Most of their decisions obey a national reflex rather than a European one. At best, they operate with two souls, one national, the other European, but more often then not these national Community leaders simply miss the appropriate size of the European dimension. Just as businessmen are obliged to change their mindsets in the

---

4 In this regard see the very valuable suggestions made by Peter Ludlow (ed.), *Setting European Community Priorities in 1991-92*, London: Brassey's, 1991.

perspective of a Single Market from a national to a European space, politicians will have to adjust their mental framework of action.[5] This refers not only to the twelve foreign ministers; it is equally relevant for almost all other ministers and, of course, for the heads of state and government as well. They all participate in European foreign and security policy, some of them in a more indirect, but no less significant, way. Without a change of mindsets, the international actor Community will be confined to an aggregation of national views.[6] A structural solution of this problem can only be achieved via a separation of the national and the European level of responsibility: the creation of a true European executive branch controlled by the EP.

West Europeans need to think more in terms of prevention than conflict management.[7] During the long decades of East-West confrontation, prevention of (armed) conflict in Europe was taken care of by a system mixed of deterrence and cooperation between the two blocs. The end of antagonism did not abolish conflict, but it allows for prevention of major instability or war. Just like the former system, the new structure of extended cooperation is demanding and costly. Most escalations of conflict in Europe can be avoided by economic and social transfer; some conflicts spring from a lack of democratic culture; others could be tamed by an effective judicial system. Investments in these fields are a burden for the well-to-do West Europeans, but preventive renunciation of consumption (i.e. financial transfer) may become the prime-insurance against dangers and burdens of a higher order. This type of preventively stabilizing policy of the Community is an imperative toward the East as well as toward the South of Europe.[8]

Another farewell to mental traditions is required with respect to the goals of integration policy. The Rome Treaty's preamble clause to build an ever closer

---

5 The broadening of minds (*élargissement de perception*) is a widely discussed subject among French geographers and strategists. See the interview with geographer Michel Foucher in *Le Monde*, 7 May 1991, p. 2.

6 This is, in fact, the concern of many analysts. See for example Hans Kastendick, "Convergence or Persistent Diversity of National Politics?" in: Colin Croud and David Marquand (eds.), *The Politics of 1992. Beyond the Single European Market*, Oxford et al.: Basil Blackwell, 1990, p. 68-84. On the other hand, the broadening of minds in Western Europe has been remarkable as compared to before the inception of the Community. See William Wallace (ed.), *The Dynamics of European Integration*, London: Pinter, 1990.

7 Georg Sorensen, "A Revised Paradigm for International Relations: the 'Old' Images and the Postmodernist Challenge," in: *Cooperation and Conflict*, Vol. 26, No. 2, 1991, pp. 85-103.

8 The Community is in the front line of east-west and south-north migration -- and needs to coordinate its response. See Edward Mortimer, "The Immigrants we Need," *Financial Times*, 16 October 1991, p. 15.

community among European nations was forcibly confined for several decades to the non-communist world on the continent. With the end of the bloc structure in Europe this task is naturally widened. The Twelve have to reinterpret the clause accordingly. In demand is not the perfection of integration among a peer group of West European countries, but the development of a Community of all European countries. The present Community cannot persist as an island of stability within a highly unstable and underdeveloped neighborhood.[9] Therefore, the overriding task for Brussels' foreign and security policy has to be the establishment of an all-European Community. The stages toward the realization of this objective need to be spelled out. This is the present Community's new frontier.[10] It has to be accepted, but it cannot be mastered, by the West Europeans alone; they need further Western partners, especially the United States.

The External Reach: the Atlantic and the European Context

In 1991, West European foreign policy and security cooperation has become a prime topic among Atlantic and European policy analysts as well as policy makers. While a war against an aggressor was going on in Iraq with Western allies involved, while a civil war was taking place in Yugoslavia with the European Community trying to mediate and while the disintegration of the Soviet empire continued with the West watching, all relevant security institutions and actors were busy discussing proposals for the future organization of Europe's security and defense structures.[11] All of these efforts

---

9 Patrick R. Ireland, "Facing the True 'Fortress Europe': Immigrant and Politics in the EC," in: *Journal of Common Market Studies*, Vol. 29, No. 5, September 1991, pp. 457-480.

10 Saferworld Foundation (ed.), *Western Security and Soviet Reform. A Programme for Action*, Bristol: Saferworld Foundation, 1991.

11 The European Community's Intergovernmental Conference (IGC) on European Political Union has been elaborating the blueprints for the December 1991 Maastricht treaty, specifying the goals, competences and procedures of Community decision-making in foreign policy and security affairs. Relations with the Western European Union (WEU) were also on the agenda, less so with the North Atlantic Treaty Organization (NATO) and the Conference of Security and Cooperation in Europe (CSCE). The conclusion of the Community-European Free Trade Area (EFTA) agreement in October 1991 to create a large European Economic Area (EEA) and the parallel negotiation of association contracts with East European countries were steps to shape the eastern environment of the Community. With its November 1991 North Atlantic Council meeting in Rome, NATO has almost completed a two year review process of its future role, strategy and force structure. Beyond embryonic interinstitutional contacts, NATO has started to think of more elaborate links with WEU, the Community and the CSCE.

were designed to (re)organize the security structures in Europe. 1991 may well be called the year of institutional competition. So far, none of the major conceptual problems has been settled by this rivalry, and no master plan has emerged except that NATO, WEU and the Community are likely to be interlocked in one way or the other. These three western organizations will then have to be connected with any of the future Eastern European and all-European structures of foreign policy and security, especially the CSCE. The following reflections deal with regional security by analyzing both the new dangers in and for Europe and the old security-related institutions which are now in the process of desperately catching up with a brand-new international environment.

EPU in a Transforming Atlantic Setting

In the immediate future, the division of labor and the interaction of EPU, WEU and NATO need to be spelled out. This raises the question of functional complementarity: which are the specific inputs EPU will be able to add to a concerted foreign policy and security management in the Euro-Atlantic area?[12] According to the Maastricht Documents, all aspects of foreign and security policy will be considered for common activity. Matters of CFSP will be processed in one communitarian body, the Council of Ministers. The EC Commission is acquiring some additional though not exclusive competences of foreign policy initiative, while the European Parliament is suggested to win more information and consultation rights, but no rights of initiative. Beyond this common denominator of the twelve governments, various preferences of how to organize a future CFSP had been discussed before Maastricht.

In February and June of 1991, the Presidency of WEU published statements on the future role of this organization as a bridge between NATO and the Community. In October of 1991, the United Kingdom and Italy as well as France and Germany presented their respective proposals designed to give military substance to WEU and link it to the Community and /or to NATO. In preparation of the 1992 Helsinki II CSCE meeting, a further institutionalization of its agencies in Warsaw, Prague and Vienna was discussed while several Experts Meetings, the first Annual Meeting of the Foreign Ministers in Berlin in June 1991, and a Special Conference on the Human Dimension in Moscow in October 1991 advanced the common all-European norms of cohabitation and cooperation in the CSCE area. Secretary James Baker and Foreign Minister Hans-Dietrich Genscher in October 1991 proposed the creation of a security-oriented Cooperation Council for the CSCE area.

12 German Defense Ministry (ed.), *Managing the Change. European Security Policy and Transatlantic Relationship in a Time of Change in Europe*, Bonn 1991 (Eurogroup-Bonn-Seminar, 9-11 April 1991).

Differing views were held on the transfer of national competences to Brussels. National political leaders have drawn diverse conclusions from external challenges such as the Gulf war or instablilities in Eastern Europe and the former Soviet Union. British Prime Minister John Major's government was not prepared to shift competences on a "wholesale basis" in foreign and security matters from London to the Community. He was in favor of a consensus approach without any majority ruling and believed in an intensified intergovernmental cooperation as the most efficient mode of operation for CFSP. In the British view, the defense of Western Europe has to remain the primary task of NATO. Most of the other member states think that if this model were to guide the evolution of CFSP, the economic giant Community is likely to remain a political dwarf and a military worm (Wim van Eekelen).[13]

These member states regard the transfer of competences from the national to the communitarian level as indispensable and expect more international influence from the introduction of majority rule. Paris (with a certain support from Bonn) favors a prominent role of the European Council in foreign and security policy. According to the French *goût*, the heads of state and government should agree on common priority areas. Once these are established by consensus, it would be the task of the Council of Ministers to implement policies within these priority areas. The Council of Ministers could decide with qualified majority. Belgium, hoping to drag the European Council into the institutional setup and legislation of the Rome Treaty, supported the French approach. The Hague, on the other hand, rejected all moves to strengthen the competences of the European Council without a proportionate elevation of the European Parliament. Therefore, the Netherlands came out quite skeptical on the letter which President François Mitterrand and Chancellor Helmut Kohl addressed to their partners in the Community in December 1990. The Dutch kept their doubts all the way into the second half of 1991 when they held the Community Presidency.[14] The Franco-German tandem clearly proposed to give more influence to the European Council in foreign policy and security affairs.[15]

---

13 Edzard Reuter, "Europe: Still Economic Giant, Political Pygmy?", in: *The World Today*, Vol. 47, No. 10, October 1991, pp. 167-169.

14 The Netherlands were gently forced by the EC member states to withdraw their version of a draft treaty presented to the IGCs in October 1991. The Presidency was advised to go back to the Luxemburg proposal of June 1991 and use it as the basis for finalizing the Maastricht Documents.

15 According to this proposal foreign and security policy areas of "common action" such as relations with the US and USS (Union of Sovereign States) would be decided unanimously by all EC heads of state and government. But the "general rule" would be that the means of implementing a common action would be decided by a qualified majority of at least eight EC states. This does not answer UK

If this model is accepted, and implemented, the Community is likely to resemble more and more the French semi-presidential system, at least in matters of foreign and security policy.

In a relatively short period from 1987 to 1993, and provided the Maastricht Documents are adopted, the Community will have been pushed beyond an economic into a political community. This period is reminiscent of the beginning 1950s when the West European core countries within a couple of years tried to establish a European Political Community, a community which included a defense component with a multinational army. This integration strategy on the basis of a defense-*first* approach failed. The renewed attempt forty years later is a more modest enterprise. This time, defense will only gradually be incorporated into the European Union -- on the basis of a defense-*last* integration strategy. Preparatory defense plans for EPU pose particular problems for some member countries. They state that at a later stage a mutual defense guarantee could well be considered among the Twelve. For the time being, the twelve heads of state and government intend to ameliorate the interrelationship between the Community and the WEU.

This certainly reenforces the relevance of WEU but does not lead to a merger of (parts of) WEU and the Community during the present round of increased integration as the Italian government had originally suggested in the summer of 1990. Many observers regard the ending of the (WEU) Treaty of Brussels in 1998 as a target date for the fusion of both institutions.[16] This leaves many questions unanswered, particularly the problem of how to arrange relations with NATO, especially after 1993 if the Community becomes enlarged by member states which are not members of the Atlantic Alliance.[17] What kind of "bridge" or "channel" function is attributed to WEU in relation to the Community and NATO? Who exactly gives the guidelines to WEU? NATO or the European Council? How are Community member countries (like Greece and Denmark) and European NATO member countries (like Norway and Turkey) connected to WEU? What is Ireland's position, and that of Austria and Sweden once they have joined the Community? How should the Community's East European associates be linked to the club?

---

    complaints about lack of precision between principle foreign policy decisions and implementation.

16 Foreign Ministers Roland Dumas and Hans-Dietrich Genscher in their January 1991 joint proposition for a common security policy mentioned a slightly earlier date (1996).

17 From those who have officially applied for membership in the EC (Turkey, Cyprus, Malta, Austria and Sweden), only Turkey is a NATO member.

Each separate West European security body affects NATO, the US leadership position within it, and the US military presence in Europe.[18] Washington always welcomed closer security and defense cooperation among West European nations, provided it was not to the detriment of the Alliance and on the assumption that there would be an essential Atlantic link. The guiding perception was to remain a part of the same organization across the Atlantic, even if two equal powers should develop over time. Secretary James Baker proposed in his New Atlanticism speech in Berlin in 1989 the development of such an interlocking approach between North America and Western Europe. Pledges to this end were made in two joint US-Community and Canada-Community declarations in November 1990. Once, however, the Europeans start a serious effort to introduce new and -- down the road -- autonomous defense structures in Western Europe, Washington will remind the Europeans that NATO is in its very existence part of the essence of the European integration.[19]

The United States might accept coordinated WEU/EC defense positions in NATO councils, but not on an inflexible basis. The Bush administration has made it clear that it opposes any EC military role that undermines NATO's command structure over allied forces or permits unilateral action in Europe without NATO's consent. Hence the US opposition to a structure where the European Council directs the WEU.[20] To facilitate coordination between WEU and NATO, national permanent representatives in both organizations could be the same and the general secretaries could cooperate intensely. This then is no guarantee against a bloc-voting of the Europeans in NATO but makes it less likely. The issue becomes more sensitive if WEU is assigned forces and

---

[18] Some Europeans, led by France, think that lessening their dependence on the Americans is either a good thing, or else an unavoidable necessity, whether they like it or not. Others, like the British, fear that weakening ties to the Americans could lead to a catastrophe. But even some of them are beginning to worry that the Americans themselves do not really want to stay forever. For an in-depth analysis of repercussions of a West European autonomy in defense of the US see Thomas-Durell Young, *The European Security Calculus: Implications for the U.S. Army*, US Army War College, Carlisle Barracks: Strategic Studies Institute, 1991.

[19] Reinhardt Rummel, "The Transatlantic Link in an all-European Setting: Proposals for an Institutionalised Relationship," in: Armand Clesse and Lothar Rühl (eds.) *Beyond East-West Confrontation. Searding for a New Security Structure in Europe*, Baden Baden: Nomos, 1991, pp. 482-491.

[20] See the Dobbins demarche in the Spring of 1991 as a reaction to the Dumas/Genscher proposals of February 1991. Philippe Moreau Defarges, "Les Etats-Unis et le malentendu européen," in: *Défense Nationale*, Vol. 47, August/September 1991, pp. 87-94.

missions of its own, as proposed by both the Anglo-Italian and the Franco-German initiatives in the fall of 1991.[21]

Despite apparent differences between the Franco-German defense proposals (also backed by Spain) to bring WEU virtually under a Community umbrella, and the British-Italian position (backed by the Dutch) that nothing should be done to undermine NATO, both sides saw room for compromise. Britain has accepted both the idea of an eventual defense role of the Community and the establishment of links between NATO and EPU. In turn, France attributed a primary position to NATO with respect to the defense of Western Europe. The Italian foreign minister, Giovanni De Michelis, said that now "all 12 EC countries agree on the principle of a common defense and security policy, not immediately, but in the second phase."[22] Common ground is also that WEU should be able to operate outside the NATO area. There is also widespread agreement on the need to move the WEU secretariat from London to Brussels, and use it as part of a "European defense identity." The only question is to what extent is it simply a part of NATO. German officials present the plan as a means of binding France more closely into NATO military structures. Bonn claims that in all questions of NATO defense, the proposed European Corps, including French and other European troops, would come under NATO command. But in London and the Hague, it is interpreted as a way of setting up an alternative bilateral (not European) force in which the German NATO forces

---

21 The text of the Anglo-Italian declaration on European security and defense in the context of the IGC on Political Union is reprinted in: *Europe/Documents*, No. 1735, 5 October 1991. The Franco-German Initiative is reprinted in *Europe/Documents*, No. 1738, 18 October 1991. On the eve of the informal meeting of the Community Foreign Ministers, held near Utrecht on 5 and 6 October 1991, and at the center of which was an examination of the chapter on security and defense in the IGC documents, Italy and the United Kingdom issued a joint statement containing specific proposals on this theme. In an effort at synthesis and compromise, this document outlines a conceptual and operational model based on the principle of complementarity between the European security identity and the Atlantic Alliance, attributing to the WEU an essential bridging role which could be effective in the creation of a "European Reaction Force." This force would be assigned to out-of-area missions only where NATO cannot operate. The Franco-German initiative which came only ten days after the Anglo-Italian one proposes decisions on the most contentious issues involving future military arrangements in Europe until the mid-1990s, after the United States, its European allies and the former Soviet Union have had time to absorb the consequences of the collapse of communism. The immediate aim of the proposals is to prompt EC leaders to agree to start military cooperation via WEU and to plan for a European army based initially on a combined unit of German and French troops but politically guided by the European Council.

22 *The International Herald Tribune*, 17 October 1991, p. 1.

would be "double-hatted," expected to be acting simultaneously within and outside the Alliance. They point to the inherent conflict of having German troops under NATO command, and French troops outside NATO command, serving alongside each other.[23]

Either way, under a firm American-European umbrella, the reorganization of military cooperation between Western Europe and the US would depend on the contingency in a given situation and on the level of West European institutional development in the long run. Many details have to be spelled out before the European Pillar inside NATO is a compatible element to both the North Atlantic Alliance and the European Union. At that point the present state of trilateral links between EPU, WEU and NATO will have been mutated to a bilateral relationship.

EPU as an Actor in an All-European Security Structure

EPU could, as of 1993, strengthen the Community internally and externally. Its decision-making capacity could grow, and its democratic foundations could be enhanced. This does not lead to a clarification regarding the type of a union or state which would finally emerge from the overall integration process. The principal of subsidiarity is likely to play a more important role, though, than in the past. Taken together, the Maastricht results of the IGCs on EMU and EPU are likely to restructure significantly the West European entity. The Community has reached a state of development where the appropriate distribution of power and authority between the center, the member states, and sub-national actors has to be raised in a fundamental, maybe final, way.

Member countries are confronted with irreversible decisions concerning the authority in foreign, security and defense policy. National prerogatives in these sensitive areas are at stake, and the main ideological orientation of the Community as an international power is still an open question. The nation-state in Western Europe could undergo considerable reform via more elaborate subnational as well as supranational competences and structures. Yet the EPU of 1993 is not likely to include the decision for a constituent assembly which would be asked to elaborate the constitution of the European Union (EU). In Maastricht, the European Parliament's aspirations in this respect were again

---

23 In an unofficial interpretation (see: an anonymous article of a highranking German officer: "Hochspannung in der NATO, weil Deutschland die europäische Karte spielt", *Welt am Sonntag*, 27 October 1991), the Franco-German plans for a European Corps are regarded as a reaction to the British move earlier in the year to claim and get the command of the newly established NATO Reaction Force. In the view of Paris and Bonn, the creation of this force itself was seen as a preemptive political stike of London.

external policies to the background and, thus, emerge as a more unified international actor which presumably shows some attitudes of a political giant in international relations, particularly in the United Nations, in the trans-European network, in the transatlantic partnership, and in connection with specific regions in the world.[24] When it comes to projecting military power, the Community will probably remain in the background. NATO member countries will, all things considered, continue to form the appropriate grouping for major military challenges. It is also needed as the supportive military infrastructure for Community/WEU led military missions (peace-keeping operations). This would tie in with the view of NATO's Secretary General, Manfred Wörner:

> The Atlantic Alliance of the future will continue to be first and foremost an institution that provides its members with the most cost-effective security insurance on the market. Yet more and more it will address the concerns of non-members as well. It will do this by interlocking with other institutions which will contribute to security in Europe, like the CSCE, Community, WEU and even possibly the UN.[25]

Concerning the all-European order, the European Political Union will help developing it as well as forming a constituent part of it. These two functions remain to be specified, using the Charter of Paris for a New Europe[26] as a framework of orientation. As far as EPU is regarded as a constituent element of a transeuropean order, reference should be made to the last forty years of integration policy in Western Europe. During this period, a Community was built up which can be regarded as a security system per se. The evolution of interdependences in almost all policy areas among formerly hostile nation-states and the quality of their transnational cooperation have reached a point of no return. The system has a number of remarkable characteristics as it has coped fairly well with all those types of conflict (socio-economic asymmetries, cultural clashes, mass migration, border disputes, territorial claims, differing size and status) which are also found on the present crisis agenda of Eastern Europe. Could this model of "security-via-integration" be a solution for the East European problems as well? The Community can either export its particular security concept or include East European states in the system by

---

24 For future alternative internal constellations of the EC see Philippe C. Schmitter, "Possible Political Configurations of the European Community After 1992," in: Armand Clesse and Raymond Vernon (eds.), *The European Community After 1992: A New Role in World Politics?* Baden-Baden: Nomos, 1991, p. 98-110.

25 Manfred Wörner, Address to the North Atlantic Assembly in Madrid on 21 October 1991, Brussels: NATO Press Service, p. 10.

26 The Charter of Paris for a New Europe is reprinted *in: Europe/Documents*, No. 1672, 14 December 1990, pp. 1-8.

no return. The system has a number of remarkable characteristics as it has coped fairly well with all those types of conflict (socio-economic asymmetries, cultural clashes, mass migration, border disputes, territorial claims, differing size and status) which are also found on the present crisis agenda of Eastern Europe. Could this model of "security-via-integration" be a solution for the East European problems as well? The Community can either export its particular security concept or include East European states in the system by enlargement. Either way, East European countries would have to comply with the highly elaborate rules of the integration game in Western Europe which is not easy. The Community and its member states have decided to continue their integration efforts despite the restructuring of the postwar order in Europe. Trends toward renationalization are so far rather weak. The Twelve seem determined to intensify their cooperation and to contribute an element of stability to the all-European order.

The policy of security-via-integration produces security inside the Community but is no guarantee against risks and dangers outside of it. The Twelve alone can not control events on the Continent and in critical regions of the world, but they can add to a stabilization of their external environment. With the successful inception of EPU (and its future CFSP including WEU), the Community is likely to contribute particularly to stable structures in Europe. It will do so with a variety of instruments, each endowed with its specific mode of operation for foreign and security policy as well as for security and defense policy:

(1) Foreign and Security Policy

Conflict management. Once the Maastricht Documents are ratified by the twelve parliaments, this type of external policy needs to be turned into practice. The first issues for a test of the new CFSP will most likely be conflicts in Eastern Europe and the former Soviet Union. Concepts to deal with them effectively will be in demand and CFSP will both mobilize relevant coactors and set the agendas for successful conflict management. It will also be the driving force for extending the Council of Europe to host all European states and in adapting CSCE norms and instruments to the new imperatives in Europe.

Economic diplomacy. The European Community will extend its traditional trade and cooperation agreements as well as the new associations with East European countries (European Agreements).[27] This network of economic contracts with post-socialist countries on the Continent is supplemented by

---

27 Three of these agreements were signed in Brussels, 16 December 1991, with Poland, Czechoslovakia and Hungary.

most difficult partner to be hired will be Japan.[28]

European Political Cooperation. EPC is likely to extend its network of bilateral dialogues with the former Soviet Union as well as with East European countries.[29] Will the EFTA and Community countries contemplate the creation of a common "Political European Area" in addition to the European Economic Area? If this is the case, the European Union would be the center of a diplomatic cobweb cast over all of Europe. The European Union will use this system to strengthen democracy and human rights in all countries of the Continent and to develop the normative code of conduct among its nations.

Development policy. Foreign aid policy has not yet been connected with all-European relations, but will certainly become part of the contemplations on new ways of supporting reform and liberal economy in the East, especially for countries which do not qualify for an association agreement with the Community. Would a system of stabilizing export income be helpful for some East European and former Soviet republics? The Community will have to find a balance between the new clients in the East and the traditional partners in the South (Mediterranean rim and African, Carribean and Pacific countries).

(2) Security and Defense Policy

Arms control. A future EPU will most likely represent the West Europeans' view in negotiations on arms reductions, in talks on ceilings and, even more important, on bottom lines of national and regional armed forces. This will become particularly relevant at the start of a Conventional Forces in Europe (CFE) II round of disarmament talks after the Helsinki 1992 CSCE meeting. Until then, NATO remains the main forum of West European consensus building on arms control. Afterwards, EPU will be used to reach consensus between Western Europe and North America.

Military technology. The EPU may develop roles for virtually all major issues connected with military technology: production, cooperation, transfer, export, export control, proliferation, conversion. Particularly important might be questions of how to control the export of military knowhow and the technological capacity for military reconstitution. Is the creation of a West

---

28 Eric Grove (ed.), *Global Security. North America, European and Japanese Interdependence in the 1990s*, London: Brassey's, 1991.

29 EPC has held calendar meetings with the Soviet Foreign Minister twice a year as well as ad hoc meetings such as the Kremlin visit of the Troika on the Iraq war 18 February 1991. Since their turn to autonomy, several former Soviet republics have asked for a regular political dialogue with EPC. The Twelve will have to multilateralize their formerly unilateral relations with Moscow. All of the association agreements with East European countries include a "political dialogue" section alongside the economic and financial parts of the agreement.

building on arms control. Afterwards, EPU will be used to reach consensus between Western Europe and North America.

Military technology. The EPU may develop roles for virtually all major issues connected with military technology: production, cooperation, transfer, export, export control, proliferation, conversion. Particularly important might be questions of how to control the export of military knowhow and the technological capacity for military reconstitution. Is the creation of a West European agency (i.e. modeled after EURATOM) a solution to the problem or should such an agency be designed for transatlantic countries or for Europe as a whole?[30] No such agency has been developed yet, and it must remain an open question whether the size of the CSCE is the best framework for the development of control regimes, or whether it should rather be the Western Economic Summit, or a new northern hemisphere grouping if not the UN, or a combination of all of these bodies.[31]

Peace keeping. Here, too, a body on the European level is missing, as the new Conflict Prevention Center in Vienna does not have the quality of a conflict management agency with a strong authority and instruments for sanctions as suggested by a minority of CSCE delegations. Any conflict management capacity in Europe will have to be connected in one way or the other to the UN Security Council for reasons of division of labor. Four of the five Security Council members are part of the CSCE area. EPU's eventual peace keeping forces could base its missions on a mandate of either the CSCE, or the UN, or both.

Defense relations. With the Warsaw Treaty Organization (WTO) dissolved in 1991, East European countries are in need of bilateral and multilateral connections to fill an obvious vacuum for both software and hardware military assistance. EPU will not provide military operational support nor defense guarantees, but it can establish a defense dialogue that helps to overcome some isolation problems of East European countries, or helps them to balance their continued dependence on the former Soviet Union in terms of military equipment. Moreover, the close connection between EPU (CFSP and WEU) and NATO will constitute the main counterweight to the remaining Soviet

---

30 The Single Market in 1993 will press for a clarification of relations between the Community and NATO with respect to defense acquisitions. See Simon Webb, *NATO and 1992*, Santa Monica: RAND, 1989.

31 In the fall of 1991, the five permanent members of the UN Security Council started talks on a regime for weapons' exports. Ethan A. Nadelmann, "Global Prohibition Regimes: The Evolution of Norms In International Society," in: *International Organization*, Vol. 44, No. 4, Autumn 1990, pp. 479-526. Charles Lipson, "Why Are Some International Agreements Informal?" in: *International Organization*, Vol. 45, No. 4, Autumn 1991, pp. 495-538.

military power and will assure the central strategic axis of military stability in Europe.

Alternative Futures of EPU

The above outlined structure and scope of the future foreign, security and defense, policy of the Twelve is just one possible scenario of Community development.[32] The intergovernmental road to Maastricht and the parallel "management" of the Gulf and the Yugoslav wars have reaffirmed that various alternatives of the development of EPU remain conceivable. The choice will depend on whether the Community is enlarged and/or deepened,[33] whether it includes a substantial security component or not, and whether it establishes a full-fledged executive branch for foreign and security policy. Each mix of these

---

[32] Federal Trust for Education and Research (ed.), *Europe's Future: Four Scenarios*, London: Federal Trust, 1991. Based on six major driving forces (technological change, financial integration, environmental pressures, social trend, democratic aspiration, interdependence among states), the study sorts out four alternative scenarios for the future process of integration (a multitier Europe, a wide and strong EC, a wide but weak EC, a disintegrating Europe) by extrapolating the present state of affairs over the next 10-20 years.

[33] The extension of the Community alone will cause a major restructuring. Five states -- Austria, Sweden, Turkey, Cyprus and Malta -- have applied for EC membership and at least five more -- Poland, Czechoslovakia, Hungary and with some reservations, Finland and Switzerland -- have indicated their interest in doing so. This plethora of candidates has led to growing acceptance, in Brussels and EC capitals, that enlargement is inevitable and that, for the first time, an overall approach needs to be taken. When looking into the options, the majority of Commissioners discussing the issue in November 1991 rejected the idea of taking all applicant countries in at the same time. Such a "big bang" approach has had some proponents in Brussels, who say that it would force the EC into radical institutional reform, including an extension of majority voting beyond that foreseen in the Maastricht Treaty. However, the applicant countries' interests and problems are too diverse to be accommodated all together. It seems obvious that the applicants should be organized into different groups, and admitted into the EC in successive waves -- members of EFTA first, and others later. There were mixed reactions to Andriessen's idea of a European Political Area, which would serve as a sort of "holding pen", particularly for central European states worried about their security, in the same way that the recently negotiated European Economic Area is to serve as a halfway house for EFTA countries on their road to EC membership. Some Commissioners felt that the European Political Area might simply whet central European states' appetite for full EC membership. Bernard Cassen, "How Large is 'Europe'?", in: *European Affairs*, Vol. 5, No. 4, August/September 1991, pp. 18-21.

parameters leads to alternative EPUs, with differing abilities of performance in international relations. Which of these combinations is the most likely to cope best with the main future external challenges to the Community: the transformation of Eastern Europe and the former Soviet Union, the establishment of common rules of cohabitation of all European nations, and the insurance against dangers at Europe's periphery and beyond?

EC Enlargement Options

Deepening without Major Enlargement

The Maastricht Documents are declared a success and shortly afterwards EFTA countries join the Community which remains, however, under 20 member states. The Community (or at least a majority of its members) increasingly develops a statehood (union) in all political areas including security policy, and establishes an autonomous executive branch as well as a substantial parliamentary control. The union is part of the European Economic Area comprising the EC and the EFTA countries. The East European states and the former republics of the Soviet Union are not becoming members, but can be associates of the Community. The stabilization of Europe is attempted by an economically strong and politically autonomous union of the West Europeans. From a politico-economic point of view, the European Union holds a dominant position in Europe, security-wise it is a decisive coactor. Is it fair to assume that this constellation is prepared to cope successfully with the pressing main challenges inside and outside Europe?

Enlargement with Minor Deepening

Maastricht is a failure in the sense that the Draft Treaties do not lead to progress in integration, either because the Heads of State and Government can only agree on generalities or because the member Parliaments refuse to follow the bold step of their governments. The pressure of the EFTA and some East European countries for membership is accepted; Malta and Cyprus enter as well. The transition periods for East European countries are quite long, but nevertheless requires harsh adaptation with massive socio-economic difficulties. The Community takes over a heavy financial burden which leads to respectively disruptive processes among the old member states ("import of nationalism"). The consensus on security policy has declined in this grouping of now more then twenty countries, also because the congruity of economic and security integration has not been achieved. Can a European confederation guaranteeing a minimum of stability still be reached, even if the ability to address challenges outside the area can hardly be expected?

Serious Deepening and Extended Enlargement

Maastricht is swiftly implemented and soon thereafter, as already proposed by Jacques Delors, a third Intergovernmental Conference on enlargement is launched. A catalog of priorities is established which enables Sweden, Switzerland and Austria to become members by the mid-90s, while the remaining EFTA countries are members of the European Economic Area anyhow and East European countries are associated. Also in the mid-90s, the economic partial members are enjoying full membership in the common foreign and security policy of the European Union. The Union is becoming the predominant power on the Continent and is seeking a common understanding with the United States, Russia and the Ukraine on key questions of security. The Council of Europe, NATO, and CSCE are additional building blocs for the formation of a cooperative order in Europe. They assist in integrating those states which do not adhere to the European Union. Does this constellation engender sufficient stability in Europe? Can it create management power for conflicts outside of Europe?

Minor Deepening and Postponed Enlargement

The Maastricht package has not been ratified in some of the member states. No need is felt to bring the EFTA states into the Community; rather the Community avoids giving up options of deepening because of premature enlargement. The European Union ends up as a clearly multitier enterprise, in the economic as well as political field, with the Franco-German tandem forming the leading team. In addition, Germany is taking on a bridging function in Europe between the Community and the other actors. It is accepted in this role by the US, Russia and the Ukraine. Is it possible to generate adequate potential for a stabilization of the transformation process in Eastern Europe and the former USSR without neglecting the Mediterranean area? How should appropriate norms be introduced into the CSCE area? How can such a stagnating Community take global challenges into account?

Continuation of the EC but Growing Renationalization

After Westminster and the *Bundestag/Bundesrat* have rejected the Draft Treaty for the European Union, one reason being that the treaty was too far-reaching and the other because it did not go far enough, a growing tendency to go it alone pops up among the participating states. The EC remains on the nominal and institutional level of development of 1991, but increasingly slides toward the level of a mere Internal Market. The EEA becomes the true actor of the West Europeans and is opened up to the East European states, too. The

EEA has only a very little political and almost no security related profile. WEU remains negligeable, while NATO is "europeanized" such that it takes in further European states. The individual states in Western and Eastern Europe are moving more to the foreground. They look for frameworks of consultation on a supranational (though not communitarian) level in order to assure their interests. Germany and Russia move to leading positions in Europe, complemented in leadership by France and the Ukraine. Does this constellation allow for a stable Europe which is strong on norms? How much of a formative power can be dispatched for tasks outside Europe?

Options of EC Security Policy

Multi-Institutional Organization of Security in Europe

Western Europe does not reach a decision on the inception of a common security policy. The mediating effort in Yugoslavia is a failure and is regarded as a deterring exception to autonomous Community security policy. The European contribution during the Gulf conflict is regarded a success. None of the actors in Europe can achieve a dominant position throughout the Continent. The conclusion therefore is that each emerging conflict has to be dealt with on an ad hoc basis, bringing together those actors who can offer inputs (principal actors approach). Preventive conflict control is practically excluded. The West European partners develop a routine in forging temporary and varying coalitions for each contingency. This renders a high degree of flexibility for action and allows alternative formations of the West European actor. Are the Community and its member states on these grounds able to make an optimal contribution to the stabilization of their international environment?

European Union with a Security Policy of its Own

The Community develops a broadly based security policy in which all instruments needed for a comprehensive crisis management are used, preventive nonmilitary measures as well as military means of intervention. Not all member states participate in the security council of the union, but those which stay out do not obstruct and deliver their eventual contribution in multilateral frameworks such as NATO or the CSCE. This security minded European Union takes on the duty of stabilizing the processes of reform in the CSCE area and of implementing the principles of the Paris Charter. Does this context breed enough momentum for the West Europeans to provide a maximum contribution to the stabilization of Europe and beyond?

Community with a Military Security Policy of its Own

An autonomous military component in the Community does not materialize, not even in WEU, partly because of the successful implementation of the European Economic Area plans instead. Military tasks continue to be taken care of, on a national level or in NATO, where the individual member state contributes its share. On the other hand, the Community is participating as an organization in stabilizing Europe via its association links to the East European countries, although this is only a selective participation, concentrated on preventive nonmilitary measures and the application of norms. Is this the setup where the West Europeans have found an effective avenue of joining in the task of assuring security inside and outside Europe?

Renationalization of Security Policy

The surprising Franco-German initiative for a European Corps has destroyed all plans for a common West European security policy. Thus, even the British-Italian proposal to transform WEU into a European out-of-area instrument for NATO has been rendered obsolete. It is crystal clear: Germans and Frenchmen do not want to abandon their respective obsession with either America or Europe. Consequently, no European autonomy is conceivable. Besides, there is the objective difficulty for all the other EC member states to engage in an unequivocal, alliance oriented security policy. Therefore, a largely nationally based security policy seems a natural solution. Within this policy it seems wise to engage only in limited permanent commitments in Europe and the world. On the other hand, the dedication to the establishment of a stability zone in Europe is nevertheless vivid and is demonstrated on the individual national scale. Is this the "king's path" to a fairly stable process of adaptation in Europe after the Cold War? Can an additional potential be extracted from this constellation to tackle tasks outside Europe?

Options for Community Development, Due to Alternative Modes of Foreign Policy Decision-Making

The choice of alternative futures of EPU will not only depend on whether the Community is enlarged or deepened and whether it includes a substantial security component or not, but also on the question of how far it elaborates its executive branch for foreign and security policy. Reflections on this aspect lead to three more options of Community development.

Consensual Foreign and Security Policy (Veto Accepted)

Purely consensual external relations are a step backwards from the status quo as the Community has been practicing a procedure of majority voting in its trade and cooperation policy with third countries for a long time. A wave of renationalization in a considerably enlarged Community may lead to a halt of any further communitarization ambitions. Especially new areas of the Community's economic policy, such as monetary and ecological questions, the policy of conversion and the policy of economic support for third countries are handled in a consensual fashion. Such a policy may well be based on common analysis and may also allow for common action, but it usually requires a clumsy process of finding a consensus and ends up with some of the member states going it alone anyway. The executive center of the West European foreign and security policy is poorly developed in this case, without any relevant parliamentary support. Policy is emanating from this center in a way which cannot be calculated from outside. Does such a fabric enable the formation of an adequate foreign and security policy for Western Europe?

Majority Rule (No Individual Veto)

Core countries of the Community have settled with the principle of majority voting, with some significant exceptions, however, concerning sensitive domains of military matters and foreign policy. The principle of "vital interest", known as the Luxemburg Compromise, and practiced in the EC, is extended to foreign and security policy at large. Yet normally an early, comprehensive, and operation oriented analysis is followed by establishing common positions and actions of the European Union. Third countries can rely on the outcome of such a decision making procedure. The foreign and security policy-making apparatus in Brussels has been significantly expanded. The European Parliament is a co-decisionmaker. A disadvantage of this development is that the union is confined to areas which may not be the primary ones (for instance the collaboration within the UN, but not within the UN-Security Council) and that, as a sort of compensation, those activities remaining in the national competence are handled in a cooperative way. Can such a partially unitarian actor cope effectively with the regional and global tasks of Western Europe?

Consensual-Majoritarian Option

The West Europeans have made the decision that the area of foreign and security policy will not be transfered as a whole under Community jurisdiction. It is intended to form an area where both levels of interest, national and unitarian, are brought to bear, depending on the context or the issue at hand.

Thus, on international trade and monetary questions unitarian procedures are the rule. With respect to international development policy and concerning multilateral security policy at the CSCE and in the UN, a procedural mix of national and communitarian elements applies. Military policy in NATO and WEU is handled via national representation. Such a flexible, issue oriented regime for the conduct of foreign and security policy meets the interest of the peoples of the Community, but it is doubtful whether this is a good basis for a productive management of Europe's major external challenges.

Tasks and Productivities

To what extent do these options correspond with the three main tasks of a future Common Foreign and Security Policy: to foster the Eastern processes of politico-economic transformation, to impose norms of cohabitation in Europe, to defend dangers outside Europe?

The *transformation challenge* comprises the shift from a largely militarily based to a mainly political-economic order in Eastern Europe and the former Soviet Union. The requirement of buiding up democracy and social market economy is met best by a Western Europe which allows a collaboration of East European and formerly Soviet societies as soon as possible within "Western" networks and organisations. This is to be expected of all enlargement options and of a confederalized Community. The best results can be reached with the creation of a "superpower", emerging from a substantial deepening and an extended widening of the Community. This option is preferable, if it hosts a foreign and security policy of its own and a consensual decision making system. A framework containing majority voting in foreign and security policy would create a rather repulsive effect, as the systemic political and economic unification is already hitting the ceiling of what East Europeans can take. As far as military transformation processes are concerned, they seem to be largely independent of the kind of Community development; of relevance in this case is the participation of the United States.

The *imposition of norms* in Europe makes reference to a common agreement on and an individual observance of a broad code of conduct for cohabitation and handling conflicts of ethnic groups, nations, and states in Europe. The adherence to such norms presupposes a political culture of a certain degree of sophistication and a willingness to yield to sanctions, including military pressure. This task can best be met by an intensified Community as it can both accomplish a high degree of observation of norms at home and gather momentum to persuade partners in Europe to adhere to the house rules. A European Union with a foreign and security policy of its own would be a particularly credible promoter of a code of conduct if it were to admit majority voting in these matters at home.

The *challenges outside* Europe include a wide spectrum of escalatory conflicts at the borders of Europe (South-North migration) via the containment of regional aggression to a worldwide proliferation of technology for weapons of mass destruction. This large field is best covered by a Community which either has a communitarian foreign and security policy or leaves the core responsibility with the national actor. A massively enlarged or a halfway deepened Community could only make minor contributions to deal with the core challenges, as the given heterogeneity of interests of European states would only permit a very conservative behavior. These are responsibilities which demand a certain amount of risk taking and dynamic which most likely can be expected from a West European actor operating on a mix of consensual and majoritarian structure of decision making, depending on the nature of the challenge at hand.

Taken together, Western Europe's stakes in the pan-European stability seem to outnumber all other concerns, particularly the ambition to introduce a common code of conduct in Europe and to meet the dangers from outside the Continent. Under these assumptions the Community and its member states should be interested primarily in building an enlarged or confederated political union. This type of union can deal best with the task of transformation in Europe and the duty of absorbing dangers from outside. In this constellation, an autonomous foreign and security policy will only be helpful, however, if it is not based on a strict majority rule. The West Europeans should concentrate on this task combination for and option of Community development while running the risk of a lower priority for the European code of conduct.

In summing up, it has to be repeated that these reflections on alternative futures of EPU are of a highly abstract nature, intended to demonstrate theoretical developments in the years ahead. They show, however, that almost all alternatives will lead the Community into a new quality of external activity. The central conclusion of these reflections is that the Community is inevitably on the way to become a superpower (Delors); however, neither a superpower in the sense of a civilian nor a hegemonic power. Rather, the Community is likely to evolve as a cooptive power, forceful enough to insert its contribution into the international network of contributors and to organize collaboration among principal international actors. The Community could be a driving force to set agendas for both conflict prevention and management. Its main innovation would be to coopt partners for the multiinstitutional response to the new set of foreign and security policy problems, having emerged since the tumbling of the Cold-War order and especially since the disintegration process in Eastern Europe and the former Soviet Union.

ANNEX

Extracts of Selected Documents on Political Union in 1991

ANNEX 1: European Council

Treaty on Political Union[1]

COMMON PROVISIONS

Article A
By this Treaty, the High Contracting Parties establish among themselves a European Union, hereinafter called the "Union".

This Treaty marks a new stage in the process leading gradually to a Union with a federal goal.
This Treaty marks a new stage in the process creating an ever closer Union among the peoples of Europe, where decisions are taken as closely as possible to the citizens.

The Union shall be founded on the European Communities, supplemented by the policies and forms of co-operation established by this Treaty. Its task shall be to organize, in a manner demonstrating consistency and solidarity, relations between the Member States and between their peoples.
The Union shall be founded on the European Communities, supplemented by the policies and forms of co-operation established by this Treaty. Its task shall be to organize, in a manner demonstrating consistency and solidarity, relations between the Member States and between their peoples.

---

1 Source: *Europe/Documents*, Nos. 1750/1751, 13 December 1991. This is an extract of the final draft prepared by the Dutch Presidency (in the light of the work of the second conclave of Foreign Ministers on 2 and 3 December 1991), with the changes made during the European Council meeting on 9 and 10 December 1991. The passages proposed by the Presidency and then changed are printed in bold characters; the revisions finally approved by the Heads of State and Government are printed in italics.

Article B
The Union shall set itself the following objectives:

- to promote economic and social progress which is balanced and sustainable, in particular through the creation of an area without internal frontiers, through the strengthening of economic and social cohesion and the establishment of economic and monetary union ultimately including a single currency,
- *to promote economic and social progress which is balanced and sustainable, in particular through the creation of an area without internal frontiers, through the strengthening of economic and social cohesion and the establishment of economic and monetary union ultimately including a single currency in accordance with the provisions of the present Treaty,*

- to assert its identity on the international scene, in particular through the implementation of a common foreign and security policy which shall include the eventual framing of a common defence policy,
- to strengthen the protection of the rights and interests of the nationals of its Member States through the introduction of a citizenship of the Union,
- to develop close co-operation on justice and home affairs,

- to maintain in full the "acquis communautaire" and build on it in order to subject the policies and forms of co-operation which it introduces to Community mechanisms and institutions, in accordance with the procedure referred to in Article W(2).
- *to maintain in full the "acquis communautaire" and build on it with a view to considering through the procedure referred to in Article W 2 to what extent the policies and forms of co-operation introduced by this Treaty may need to be revised with the aim of ensuring the effectiveness of the mechanisms and the Institutions of the Community.*

The Union shall respect the principle of subsidiarity as defined in Article 3b of the Treaty establishing the European Community.
The objectives of the Union shall be achieved as provided in this Treaty and in accordance with the conditions and the timetable set out therein while respecting the principle of subsidiarity as defined in Article 3b of the Treaty establishing the European Community.

Article C
The Union shall be served by a single institutional framework which shall ensure the consistency and the continuity of the actions carried out in order to

attain its objectives while observing and building upon the "acquis communautaire".

The Union shall in particular ensure the consistency of its external actions as a whole in the context of its external relations, security, economic and development policies. The Council and the Commission shall be responsible for ensuring this consistency. They shall ensure the implementation of these policies, each in accordance with its respective powers.

Article D

The European Council shall provide the Union with the necessary impetus for its development and shall define the general political guidelines thereof.

The European Council shall bring together the Heads of State or of Government of the Member States and the President of the Commission. They shall be assisted by the Ministers for Foreign Affairs of the Member States and by a Member of the Commission.

The European Council shall meet at least twice a year under the chairmanship of the Head of State or of Government of the Member State which holds the Presidency of the Council.

The European Council shall submit to the European Parliament a report after each of its meetings and a yearly written report on the progress achieved by the Union.

Article E

The European Parliament, the Council, the Commission and the Court of Justice shall exercise their powers under the conditions and for the purposes provided for, on the one hand, by the provisions of the Treaties establishing the European Communities, the subsequent Treaties and Acts modifying and supplementing them and, on the other hand, by the specific provisions of this Treaty.

The European Parliament, the Council, the Commission and the Court of Justice shall exercise their powers under the conditions and for the purposes provided for, on the one hand, by the provisions of the Treaties establishing the European Communities, the subsequent Treaties and Acts modifying and supplementing them and, on the other hand, by the other provisions of this Treaty.

Article F

1. The Union shall have due regard to the national identity of its Member States, whose systems of government are founded on the principles of democracy.

2. The Union shall respect fundamental rights as guaranteed by the European Convention for the Protection of Human Rights and Fundamental Freedoms

and as they result from the constitutional traditions common to the Member States as general principles of Community law.
3. The Union shall provide itself with the resources necessary to attain its objectives and carry through its policies.

. . . . .

PROVISIONS ON A COMMON FOREIGN AND SECURITY POLICY

Article A
1. The Union and its Member States shall define and implement a common foreign and security policy, governed by the provisions of this Title and covering all areas of foreign and security policy.
2. The objectives of the common foreign and security policy shall be:

- to safeguard the common values, fundamental interests and independence of the European Union;
- to strengthen the security of the Union and its Member States in all ways;
- to preserve peace and strengthen international security, in accordance with the principles of the United Nations Charter as well as the principles of the Helsinki Act and the objectives of the Paris Charter;
- to promote international co-operation;
- to develop and consolidate democracy and the rule of law, and respect for human rights and fundamental freedoms.

3. The Union shall pursue these objectives:

- by establishing systematic co-operation between Member States in the conduct of policy, in accordance with Article B;
- by gradually implementing, in acccordance with Articel C, joint action in the areas in which the Member States have essential interests in common.

4. The Member States shall support the Union's external and security policy actively and unreservedly in a spirit of loyalty and mutual solidarity. They shall refrain from any action which is contrary to the interests of the Union or likely to impair its effectiveness as a cohesive force in international relations. The Council shall ensure that these principles are complied with.

Article B
1. Member States shall inform and consult one another within the Council on any matter of foreign and security policy of general interest in order to ensure

that their combined influence is exerted as effectively as possible by means of concerted and convergent action.
2. Whenever it deems it necessary, the Council shall define a common position.
Member States shall ensure that their national policies conform to the common positions.
3. Member States shall co-ordinate their action in international organizations and at international conferences. They shall uphold the common positions in such fora.
In international organizations and at international conferences where not all the Member States participate, those which do take part shall uphold the common positions.

Article C
The procedure for adopting joint action in matters covered by the foreign and security policy shall be the following:
1. The Council decides, on the basis of general guidelines from the European Council, that a matter should be the subject of joint action.
Whenever the Council decides on the principle of joint action, it shall lay down the specific scope, the Union's general and specific objectives in carrying out such action, if necessary its duration, and the means, procedures and conditions for its implementation.

2. The Council shall stipulate as a general rule that the detailed arrangements for carrying out joint action shall be adopted by a qualified majority.
The Council shall, when adopting the joint action and at any stage during its development, define those matters on which decisions are to be taken by a qualified majority.

Declaration of the Conference:
Member States will, with regard to Council decisions requiring unanimity, to the extent possible avoid to prevent a unanimous decision where a qualified majority exists in favour of that decision.

Where the Council is required to act by a qualified majority pursuant to the preceding subparagraph, the votes of its members shall be weighted in accordance with Article 148(2) of the Treaty establishing the European Community, and for their adoption, acts of the Council shall require at least fifty-four votes in favour, cast by at least eight members.
3. If there is a change in circumstances having a substantial effect on a question subject to joint action, the Council shall review the principles and

objectives of that action and take the necessary decisions. As long as the Council has not acted, the joint action shall stand.

4. Joint actions shall commit the Member States in the positions they adopt and in the conduct of their activity.

5. Whenever there is any plan to adopt a national position or take national action pursuant to a joint action, information shall be provided in time to allow, if necessary, for prior consultations within the Council. The obligation to provide prior information shall not apply to measures which are merely a national transposition of Council decisions.

6. In cases of imperative need arising from changes in the situation, and failing a Council decision, Member States may take the necessary measures as a matter of urgency, in accordance with the objectives of the joint action. They shall inform the Council immediately of any such decisions.

In cases of imperative need arising from changes in the situation and failing a Council decision, Member States may take the necessary measures as a matter of urgency having regard to the general objectives of the joint action. The Member State concerned shall inform the Council immediately of any such action.

7. Should there be any major difficulties in implementing a joint action, a Member States shall refer them to the Council which shall discuss them and seek appropriate solutions. Such solutions shall not run counter to the objectives of the joint action nor impair its effectiveness.

Article D

1. The common foreign and security policy shall include all questions related to the security of the European Union, including the eventual framing of a common defence policy.

The common foreign and security policy shall include all questions related to the security of the European Union, including the eventual framing of a common defence policy, which might in time lead to a common defence.

2. The Union shall request the Western European Union, which is an integral part of the development of the European Union, to elaborate and implement decisions and actions of the Union which have defence implications. The Council shall, in agreement with the institutions of the WEU, adopt the necessary practical arrangements.

3. Issues having defence implications dealt with under this Article shall not be subject to the procedures set out in Article C.

4. The policy of the Union in accordance with the present Title shall respect the obligations of certain Member States under the North Atlantic Treaty and be compatible with the common security and defence policy established within that framework. It shall not affect the specific character of the security and defency policy of certain Member States.

4. *The policy of the Union in accordance with th present Article shall not prejudice the specific character of the security and defence policy of certain Member States and shall respect the obligations of certain Member States and shall respect the obligations of certain Member States under the North Atlantic Treaty and be compatible with the common security and defence policy established within that framework.*

5. The provisions of this Article shall not prevent development of closer co-operation between two or more Member States on a bilateral level, in the framework of the WEU and the Atlantic Alliance provided such co-operation does not run counter to or impede that provided for in this Title.

6. With a view to furthering the objective of this Treaty, and having in view the date of 1998 in the context of Article 12 of the Brussels Treaty, the provisions of this article may be revised as provided for in Article W (2) on the basis of a report to be presented in 1996 by the Council to the European Council, which shall include an evalution of the progress made and the experience gained until then.

Article E

1. The Presidency shall represent the Union for matters coming within the common foreign and security policy.

2. The Presidency shall be responsible for the implementation of common measures; in that capacity it shall in principle express the position of the Union in international organizations and international conferences.

3. In the tasks referred to in the preceding paragraphs, the Presidency shall be assisted if need be by the previous and next Member State to hold the Presidency. The Commission shall be fully associated in these tasks.

4. Without prejudice to the provisions of Article B(3) and Article C(2), Member States represented in international organizations or international conferences where not all the Member States participate shall keep the latter informed of any matter of common interest. Member States which are also members of the United Nations Security Council will concert and keep the other Member States fully informed. Member States which are permanent members of the Security Council will, in the execution of their functions, ensure the defence of the positions and the interests of the Union, without prejudice to their responsibilities under the provisions of the United Nations Charter.

Article F
The diplomatic and consular missions of the Member States and the Commission Delegations in third countries and international conferences, and their representations to international organizations, shall co-operate in ensuring that the common positions and common measures adopted by the Council are complied with and implemented. They shall step up co-operation by exchanging information, carring out joint assessments and contributing to the implementation of the provisions referred to in Article D of the Chapter on citizenship of the Union in the Treaty establishing the European Community.

Article G
The European Parliament shall be kept regularly informed by the Presidency and the Commission of the basic choices made in the Union's foreign and security policy. The Presidency shall consult the European Parliament on the main aspects of the common foreign and security policy and shall ensure that the views of the European Parliament are duly taken into consideration.

The Presidency shall consult the European Parliament on the main aspects and the basic choices of the common foreign and security policy and shall ensure that the views of the European Parliament are duly taken into consideration. The European Parliament shall be kept regularly informed by the Presidency and the Commission of the development of the Union's foreign and security policy.

The European Parliament may put questions or make recommendations to the Council. It shall hold an annual debate on progress in implementing the common foreign and security policy.

Article H
"The Council shall adopt the measures necessary to guarantee the secrecy of all work done by the Council pursuant to the provisions of the Treaty on European Union concerning the common foreign and security policy and co-operation in the spheres of justice and home affairs."

1. The European Council shall define the principles of and general guidelines for the common foreign and security policy.
2. The Council shall take the decisions necessary for defining and implementing common foreign and security policy on the basis of the general guidelines adopted by the European Council. It shall ensure the unity, consistency and effectiveness of action by the Union. The Council shall act unanimously, except for procedural questions and in the case referred in Article C(2).

3. Any Member State or the Commission may refer to the Council any question relating to the common foreign and security policy and may submit proposals to the Council.

4. In cases requiring a rapid decision, the Presidency, of its own motion, or at the request of the Commission or a Member State, shall convene an extraordinary Council meeting within forty-eight hours or, in an emergency, within a shorter period.

5. Without prejudice to Article 151 of the Treaty establishing the European Community, a Political Committee consisting of Political Directors of the Member States shall monitor the international situation in the areas covered by CFSP and contribute to the definition of policies by delivering opinions to the Council at the request of the Council or on its own initiative. It shall also monitor the implementation of agreed policies, without prejudice to the responsibility of the Presidency and the Commission.

Article I
The Commission shall be fully associated with the work carried out in the common foreign and security policy field.

Article J
On the occasion of any review of the security provisions under Article D, the Conference which is convened to that effect shall also examine whether any other amendments need to be made to provisions relating to the common foreign and security policy.

Article K
1. The provisions referred to in Articles 137, 138 to 142, 146, 147, 150 to 153, 157 to 163 and 217 of the Treaty establishing the European Community shall apply to the provisions relating to common foreign and security policy.

Declaration by the Conference:
"Use of languages will be in accordance with the rules of the European Communities. For meetings of officials and COREU communications, the current practice of European political co-operation will serve as a guide for the time being."
"Use of languages shall be in accordance with the rules of the European Community.

For COREU communications, the current practice of European Political Co-operation will serve as a guide for the time being.

All Common Foreign and Security Policy texts which are submitted to or adopted at meetings of the European Council and of the Council as well as all texts which are to be published are immediately and simultaneously translated into all the official Community languages."
2. The administrative expenditure incurred by the Institutions through the provisions concerning the common foreign and security policy shall be charged to the budget of the European Community.

The Council may also:

- either decide unanimously that the operational expenditure involved in the implementation of the said provisions is to be charged to the budget of the European Community; in this case, the budgetary procedures provided for in the Treaty establishing the European Community shall apply;
- or find that such expenditure should be charged to the Member States, possibly in accordance with a scale to be determined.

Declaration by the Member States which are members of the WEU on co-operation between the WEU and the Union

(for the record)

(See Annex V)

. . . . .

ANNEX V

Declaration of the Member States of Western European Union which are also members of the European Union on the role of WEU and its relations with the European Union and with the Atlantic Alliance

INTRODUCTION

1. WEU Member States agree on the need to develop a genuine European security and defence identity and a greater European responsibility on defence matters. This identity will be pursued through a gradual process involving successive phases. WEU will form an integral part of the process of the development of the European Union and will enhance its contribution to solidarity within the Atlantic Alliance. WEU Member States agree to strengthen

the role of WEU, in the longer term perspective of a common defence policy within the European Union which might in time lead to a common defence, compatible with that of the Atlantic Alliance.
2. WEU will be developed as the defence component of the European Union and as the means to strengthen the European pillar of the Atlantic Alliance. To this end, it will formulate common European defence policy and carry forward its concrete implementation through the further development of its own operational role.
WEU Member States take note of Article D relating to the common foreign and security policy of the Treaty on European Union which reads as follows:
"1. The common foreign and security policy shall include all questions related to the security of the European Union, including the eventual framing of a common defence policy, which might in time lead to a common defence.
2. The Union requests the Western European Union, which is an integral part of the development of the European Union, to elaborate and implement decisions and actions of the Union which have defence implications. The Council shall, in agreement with the institutions of the WEU, adopt the necessary practical arrangements.
3. Issues having defence implications dealt with under this Article shall not be subject to the procedures set out in Article C.
4. The policy of the Union in accordance with the present Article shall not prejudice the specific character of the security and defence policy of certain Member States and shall respect the obligations of certain Member States under the North Atlantic Treaty and be compatible with the common security and defence policy established within that framework.
5. The provisions of this Article shall not prevent development of closer co-operation between two or more Member States on a bilateral level, in the framework of the WEU and the Atlantic Alliance provided such co-operation does not run counter to or impede that provided for in this Title.
6. With a view to furthering the objective of this Treaty, and having in view the date of 1998 in the context of Article XII of the Brussels Treaty, the provisions of this article may be revised as provided for in Article W(2) on the basis of a report to be presented in 1996 by the Council to the European Council, which shall include an evaluation of the progress made and the experience gained until then."

A. *WEU's relations with European Union*

3. *The objective is to build up WEU in stages as the defence component of the European Union. To this end, WEU is prepared, at the request of the European Union, to elaborate and implement decisions and actions of the Union which have defence implications.*

To this end, WEU will take the following measures to develop a close working relationship with the Union:

- *as appropriate, synchronization of the dates and venues of meetings and harmonization of working methods;*
- *establishment of close cooperation between the Council and Secretariat-General of WEU on the one hand, and the Council of the Union and Secretariat-General of the Council on the other;*
- *consideration of the harmonization of the sequence and duration of the respective Presidencies;*
- *arranging for appropriate modalities so as to ensure that the Commission of the European Community is regularly informed and, as appropriate, consulted on WEU activities in accordance with the role of the Commission in the Common Foreign and Security Policy as defined in the European Union Treaty;*
- *encouragement of closer cooperation between the Parliamentary Assembly of WEU and the European Parliament.*

The WEU Council shall, in agreement with the competent bodies of the European Union, adopt the necessary practical arrangements.

B. WEU's relations with the Atlantic Alliance

4. The objective is to develop WEU as a means to strengthen the European pillar of the Atlantic Alliance. Accordingly WEU is prepared to develop further the close working links between WEU and the Alliance and to strengthen the role, responsibilities and contributions of WEU Member States in the Alliance. This will be undertaken on the basis of the necessary transparency and complementarity between the emerging European security and defence identity and the Alliance. WEU will act in conformity with the positions adopted in the Atlantic Alliance.

- *WEU Member States will intensify their coordination on Alliance issues which represent an important common interest with the aim of introducing joint positions agreed in WEU into the process of consultation in the Alliance which will remain the essential forum for consultation among its members and the venue for agreement on policies bearing on the security and defence commitments of Allies under the Washington Treaty.*
- *Where necessary, dates and venues of meetings will be sychronized and working methods harmonized.*
- *Close cooperation will be established between the Secretariats-General of WEU and NATO.*

C. Operational role of WEU

5. WEU's operational role will be strengthened by examining and defining appropriate missions, structures and means covering in particular;

- *WEU planning cell;*
- *closer military cooperation complementary to the Alliance in particular in the fields of logistics, transport, training and strategic surveillance;*
- *meetings of WEU Chiefs of Defence Staff;*
- *military units answerable to WEU.*

Other proposals will be examined further, including:

- *enhanced cooperation in the field of armaments with the aim of creating a European armaments agency;*
- *development of the WEU Institute into a European Security and Defence Academy.*

Arrangements aimed at giving WEU a stronger operational role will be fully compatible with the military dispositions necessary to ensure the collective defence of all Allies.

D. Other measures
6. As a consequence of the measures set out above, and in order to facilitate the strengthening of WEU's role, the seat of the WEU Council and Secretariat will be transferred to Brussels.
7. Representation on the WEU Council must be such that the Council is able to exercise its functions continously in accordance with Article VIII of the modified Brussels Treaty. Member States may draw on a double-hatting formula, to be worked out, consisting of their representatives to the Alliance and to the European Union.
8. WEU notes that, in accordance with the provisions of Article D(6) concerning the common foreign and security policy of the Treaty on European Union, the Union will decide to review the provisions of this Article with a view to furthering the objective to be set by it in accordance with the procedure defined. The WEU will re-examine the present provisions in 1996.
This re-examination will take account of the progress and experience acquired and will extend to relations between WEU and the Atlantic Alliance.

. . . . .

ANNEX 2: EC Commission

Political Union: Commission Proposals at IGC on "Common External Policy"[1]

OBJECT: EUROPEAN UNION: THE COMMON EXTERNAL POLICY

In its Opinion of 21 October 1990 the Commission identified among the most important elements necessary for the creation of European Union the emergence of an external policy in osmosis with economic, social, financial and monetary policy to ensure the unity and coherency of Community action on the international scene.

It expressed the belief that this policy, provided that it was based on profound consensus between Member States in terms of their common ambitions to reinforce the international responsibility of the Union, should encompass the Member States' vital common interests and include security and defence.

The European Council of Rome on 14 and 15 December 1990 stressed the Union's vocation to treat aspects of the policy on external relations and security according to a constantly evolving unified process. It entrusted the Intergovernmental Conference with the task of defining the Union's objectives, the scope of its policies and means . . . to ensure their implementation . . . in an institutional framework. The Commission's Opinion and the European Council's Conclusions speak of a single decision-making center (the Council); a harmonized preparation of decisions; a non-exclusive right of initiative by the Commission; the informing and as a general rule consulting of the European Parliament -- replaced by a preliminary authorization (that is to say assent) for the conclusion of the most important agreements and unity of the Union's position in international organizations and relations with third countries.

Hence, in addition to the amendments of Articles 2 and 3 pertaining to the objectives and areas of application of the Treaty; establishment of EMU;

---

1 Source: *Europe/Documents*, Nos. 1697/98, 7 March 1991.

expansion of certain powers and reinforcement of democratic legitimacy and effectiveness of the institutions, revision of the Treaty with a view to European Union means the adoption of a new heading entitled "the common external policy."

A. GENERAL PRESENTATION OF THE COMMON EXTERNAL POLICY

The rules applicable to this common policy include the material provisions concerning three sets of proposals:

- common foreign and security policy (point B),
- external economic policy (point C),
- development cooperation policy (point D).

These rules also include procedure provisions for conclusion by the Union of international agreements (point E) in these areas and in all other matters where the Union already has (e.g. transport, environment, research), or would have as a result of revision of the Treaty, internal powers, and within the limit of these. In substance, it is explicitly stated that for every internal power of the Union there exists an external power, and this becomes exclusive in a determined matter when the Union has used it internally, constituting the expression in the Treaty of Jurisprudence of "AETR," which is part of Community achievements to date. The general balance of provisions with regard to the common external policy rests on two complementary and indissociable steps.

On the one hand, specific decision-making procedures recognizing namely the fundamental role of the European Council in defining the Union's powers and the decision-making role of the (General Affairs) Council in their implementation are among the areas being added to the EC's current powers, i.e. common foreign and security policy. On the other hand, the Union's powers, resting now on clear legal bases and expressly stated in the Treaty, are asserted in the other areas, in particular that of economic integration. Generalized recourse to the qualified majority in decision-making is also a guarantee for efficiency.

B. THE COMMON FOREIGN AND SECURITY POLICY

1. Fundamental principles:

Insertion of common foreign and security policy rules complies with a fundamental objective of ensuring unity and coherency of Union action on the international scene by adding to its powers elements of external relations not present in the current Treaty.

This common policy would be based on the notion of progressiveness; the European Council would be responsible for establishing or enhancing the Union's powers so far as necessary. This approach constitutes an application of the principle of subsidiarity, leaving Member States full powers in matters which have not been deemed necessary for the Union, subject to recourse to intergovernmental cooperation for questions of general interest.

It is therefore clear that common policy does not mean single policy. To the extent that Member States have privileged relations with certain parts of the world or occupy positions inherited from their history, it would be more a question of coordinating national actions in a common framework than replacing them with a single manner of action. There too subsidiarity must play a role. What is important is that Member States comply with an obligation of result. The common policy would be implemented in the existing institutional framework in order to guarantee the Union's unity replacing the current Community, while taking into account adaptations of the institutions' roles justified by the matters in question and the state of progress, at this stage, of European construction.

Finally, contrary to European political cooperation, the common foreign and security policy would involve adoption and implementation of decisions that are binding for Member States, and agreed on, depending on the case, either unanimously or by a reinforced qualified majority, leaving some room for the so-called opting out formula.

2. Applicable rules:

Chapter I on the common foreign and security policy contains general provisions covering both foreign and security policy (section one) and specific provisions on security, including defence (section two):

a) foreign policy, whose objectives are defined in Article Y 1, is based for its implementation on a distinction between:

- questions considered "of vital common interest" by the European Council for which the principles and implementation of common actions are, with regard to deciding actions to be undertaken, the responsibility of the Council deciding by a qualified majority and reinforced by the favorable

vote of at least 8 Member States. However, the European Council would determine the conditions in which a Member State would, at its request, be freed of the obligations of a common action;
- the other questions whereby, as is the case at present, joint action results from intergovernmental cooperation, reinforced with regard to the provisions of Article 30 of the Single Act; the understanding is that abstention by a Member State must not be an obstacle to joint action and the coherency of national actions and those of the Union must be guaranteed.

In case of particular, serious or exceptional circumstances, provision is also made that all Member States must refer to the Council with a view to obtaining rapid decision on possible common action.

b) For questions of vital common interest, i.e. the scope of application of the common foreign policy, the decision-making initiative to be agreed by the Council would be shared between Member States and the Commission. Preparation and follow-up of these decisions would be ensured, through COREPER, by the Secretariat General of the Council in organized cooperation with the Commission. The European Parliament would be closely involved in the definition and implementation of the common policy in order to ensure democratic control. The acts adopted would not come under the jurisdictional control of the Court of Justice. Likewise, the Union would be represented outside its borders, and namely in international organizations, jointly by the Presidency of the Council and the Commission, the main importance being that the Union speak with one voice.

c) the common security policy, whose objectives are stated in Article Y 11, would include certain specific provisions (section two). Its scope of application would be defined in the Treaty itself and would include:
- guarantee of automatic assistance by including Article 5 of the WEU which would give concrete form to the will of Member States to link together their security and defence; should one of the Union's Member States be the subject of armed aggression, the others would provide aid and assistance, using all means in their power, whether military or other;
- a list of questions of vital common interest in security and defence, as defined by the December 1990 European Council of Rome, which the European Council could then complement;
- arms control and disarmament;
- matters of security under the CSCE and the UN;
- cooperation in the production, export and non-proliferation of arms;
- the Commission proposes adding the definition of a research and arms production policy, which is not foreseen as such by any other provision of the current Treaty, with the understanding that aspects dealing, for

example, with rules of competition or the common trade policy are already covered;
- a mechanism for regular meetings of the Ministers of Foreign Affairs and Defence, with a view to developing collaboration and enabling the immediate convening of a meeting, if necessary, that is to say in the presence of a threat or danger to the Union.

Contrary to matters of common foreign policy, definition of principles and actions to be implemented in the framework of the common security policy would result from decisions of the Council voting unanimously. However, the Council could decide to resort to other means of decision-making for implementation of certain actions. For binding reasons, i.e. deriving from national constitutional provisions or obligations resulting from international commitments previously entered into, a Member State would not, if it so requests, have to abide by certain obligations in these decisions; exemptions would be regularly re-examined by the Council.

In addition, some of these decisions, and namely those concerning cooperation in the area of defence, could be implemented in compliance with commitments of the Atlantic Alliance through specific arrangements with the WEU, which could act on behalf of the Union, in light of gradual integration of this organization in the Union.

The introduction of a common security policy shall result in abrogation of Articles 223 and 224, whose scope of application is henceforth covered by this policy. Finally, the general provisions in point b) above would apply in the area of security and foreign policy.

. . . . .

HEADING Y: THE COMMON EXTERNAL POLICY

Article Y 0

The common external policy includes the common foreign and security policy, the external economic policy and the development cooperation policy, as well as external relations in the other areas where the Union has jurisdiction. In the conduct of this policy, the Union aims to promote democracy, the State of law and respect of human rights.

Chapter I: The Common Foreign and Security Policy

Article Y 1

The Union conducts a common foreign and security policy which aims to maintain peace and international stability, to develop friendly relations with all countries, by taking into account also the particular relations with all countries, by taking into account also the particular relations of the different member States. This policy is regulated by general provisions and by particular provisions on defence and security.

First Section: General Provisions

Article Y 2

For its implementation, the common foreign and security policy is based on a distinction between questions considered of vital interest to the Union and the other questions of this area.

Article Y 3

1. In order to ensure the effectiveness of the Union's common action in common foreign policy and the establishment of principles and common objectives, and without prejudice to powers deriving from the other provisions of the Treaties, the European Council, at the initiative of either its Presidency, the Commission or a simple majority of Member States, determines, after hearing the European Parliament, questions of vital common interest.

When determining vital common interests, the European Council foresees the conditions in which a member State, at its request, does not have to abide by the obligations of the common action. This member State shall refrain from any measures likely to affect execution of the decisions of the Union.

2. For questions declared of vital common interest, in the absence of other provisions of the Treaty, the Council acting by the majority foreseen in Article 148, par. 2, second line [This is a reinforced qualified majority when the Treaty does not foresee any Commission proposal and which requires the favorable vote af at least 8 ember States], at the initiative of either the Presidency, the Commission or a simple majority of Member States:

- defines the principles of the common policy;
- defines actions to be conducted whether implemented by the Union or Member States.
- When Council decisions are adopted pursuant to the present Article, Article 149, par. 1 is not applicable.

Article Y 4

1. For questions which have not yet been declared of vital interest, the Member States and the Commission coordinate their efforts within the Council on any question of external policy of general interest in order to ensure that their combined influence is exercised in the most effective manner through consultation, alignment of positions and the carrying-out of common actions.

For this purpose, Member States shall consult one another mutually and with the Commission on all actions foreseen in the framework of national external policies.

2. In order to increase their capacity of joint action, Member States shall ensure the gradual development and definition of principles and common objectives.

3. Member States shall refrain from preventing formation of the consensus and the joint action which might result.

4. Each Member State, in its positions and national actions, shall fully take into account the positions of the other partners, shall duly take into consideration the interest of adopting and implementing common positions and shall avoid harming the effectiveness of the Union as a coherent force in international relations or within international organizations. The definition of common positions is a point of reference for national policies.

5. If a member State is of the view that a situation of particular seriousness or exceptional circumstances requires action on its part, it shall, before acting, refer to the Council, which acts without delay, under the conditions foreseen in Article Y 3 paragraph 2 on the timeliness of Union action.

Article Y 5

The European Parliament shall be closely associated with the definition and conduct of the common foreign and security policy. For this purpose, the council and Commission shall regularly inform the European Parliament of the themes dealt with in the framework of this policy and ensure that the European Parliament's views are duly taken into consideration.

Each year, the Parliament shall discuss the common foreign and security policy. It shall hear on this occasion the explanations of the Council and the Commission. Moreover, at the request of the European Parliament or on their own initiative, the council and Commission can be heard by the parliamentary committees.

Article Y 6

Preparation of council work and decisions and follow-up of their application shall be carried out within the General Secretariat of the Council in organized cooperation with the Commission.

The Committee of Permanent Representatives of the Member States shall have the task of preparing Council work on common foreign and security policy and executing the mandates entrusted with it by the Council for this purpose.

Article Y 7

1. In matters of common foreign and security policy, the Unions is represented by the Presidency of the Council and by the Commission, and if necessary assisted by the Member State which ensured the previous Presidency and by the Sate which will ensure the following Presidency (According to the Troika formula which is in reality made up of four members on account of Commission participation) in relations with third countries, within international organizations and in the framework of international conferences.

The Council, acting by the majority foreseen in Article 148, par. 2 line 2, on proposal from the Commission or a member State, can entrust one or several member States with presentation of the Union's position in particular cases such as that of the United Nations' Security Council, bodies of the Atlantic Alliance and the WEU.

2. In order to ensure better representation of the Union Member Sates and the Commission, thanks to mutual assistance and information, shall step up cooperation between their accredited representations in third countries or with international organizations.

Article Y 8

The Member States' external policies and the action of the Union under the other provisions of the Treaty must be coherent with the common foreign and security policy.

In the case where there is a risk of incoherence, the Commission or any other Member State can ask for convening of the Council which shall deliberate in view of a decision according to the procedure foreseen in Article Y 3, paragraph 2.

Article Y 9

Each time that it deems it useful, the Union shall organize political dialogue with third countries and regional groups.

Article Y 10

Articles 164 to 188 of the Treaty are not applicable to the provisions of the present chapter (This provision aims at excluding the jurisdictional competence of the Court of Justice).

Second Section: The Common Security Policy

Article Y 11

The common security policy is an integral part of the Union's foreign policy. It aims to reinforce the security of Europe and maintain peace in the world in compliance with the Charter of the United Nations. For this purpose, it relies on cooperation undertaken in the framework of the WEU. It must enable establishing in the end a common European defence in full compliance with commitments within the Atlantic Alliance.

Article Y 12

Should a Member State be the subject of armed aggression in Europe, the others will lend, in compliance with the provisions of Article 51 of the United Nations Charter, aid and assistance by all the means in their power, military and other.

Article Y 13

1. Without prejudice to powers deriving from the other provisions of the Treaty, the Union considers of vital common interest in the area of security and defence according to Article Y 3 arms control, disarmament and related questions, questions of security regarding the CSCE or debated at the United Nations, including peacekeeping operations, economic and technological cooperation in the field of arms, the coordination of the policy on the export and non-proliferation of arms (list of the European Council of Rome II). In the framework of the common security policy, the Union shall formulate a research and arms production policy.

2. Other questions of vital common interest can be identified by the European Council.

3. For questions declared of vital common interest, in the absence of other provisions of the Treaty, the Council:
   - shall define, by acting unanimously (abstention is not an obstacle to adoption of the decision) the principles of common policy and decision-making procedures applicable to determining actions to be conducted;
   - shall decide actions to be conducted, whether they be implemented by the Union or by Member States.

4. The decisions foreseen in paragraphs 2 and 3 free a Member State, at its request for binding reasons, from some of the stated obligations. This member State shall refrain from any measures liable to affect execution of the Union's decisions. In the case such an exemption is decided, the Council shall proceed regularly in its examination according to common policy developments, in order to decide to what extent maintaining the exemption is compatible with the common interest.

The Member State benefitting from the exemption shall not participate in Council discussions on this item or in those aiming to define, to complement or to apply the obligations from which it is exempted.

Article Y 14

The Ministries of Foreign Affairs and Defence and the Commission shall hold a joint meeting at least twice yearly with a view to developing collaboration between Member States in the area of defence. If necessary, they shall meet immediately at the request of a Member State.

Article Y 15

1. By deciding actions to be conducted, in line with paragraph 3 of Article Y 13, the Council shall decide if the Council of the WEU should be referred to for implementation of the guidelines which it has set.

2. In view of application of paragraph one, the Union shall pursue with the WEU the necessary arrangements enabling the presence of Member States which are not members of the WEU and the Commission at meetings of WEU bodies.

3. For questions declared of vital common interest or for questions dealt with in the framework of the WEU, Member States which are part of the Atlantic Alliance shall express the position of the Union.

4. The Union shall strive to use the provisions of Article XII of the Treaty of Brussels of 17 March 1948 with a view to favouring the WEU's gradual integration into the Union.

. . . . .

Political Union: The Structure of the Draft Treaty[2]

CONTRIBUTION BY THE EUROPEAN COMMISSION TO THE INTERGOVERNMENTAL CONFERENCE

1. The Dublin and Rome European Councils, responding among other things to initiatives by Mr. Kohl and Mr. Mitterand, declared the intention of transforming the Community into a European Union, and of developing its political dimension, notably on the international scene. The Commission considers that the intergovernmental Conference should be guided by the basic thinking which has been behind the construction of Europe for 40 years now, namely that all progress made towards economic, monetary, social or political integration should gradually be brought together in a single community as the precursor of a European Union.

This being so, it is somewhat paradoxical that the current trend in the intergovernmental Conference favours a kind of revision of the Treaty of Rome that would depart from this general unification process and keep the Community no longer as the focal point but simply as one entity among others in a political union with ill-defined objectives and a variety of institutional schemes.

True enough, the intergovernmental Conference is faced with the difficult task of generating a consensus on a common foreign and security policy at a time when the twelve Member States are faced with a series of challenges on the world scene.

It is equally true that the foreign and security policy will undoubtedly involve adjustments to the way in which common decisions are prepared and implemented and confer an eminent role on the European Council.

But in this area, as with EMU, where a new institution is also to be established, this adjustment to the Community approach cannot be allowed to go so far as to break up the existing model, which has demonstrated its dynamism and efficiency.

---

2 Source: *Europe/Documents*, No. 1715, 31 May 1991.

2. In its instructions to the Intergovernmental Conference, the Rome European Council laid emphasis on "the vocation of the Union to deal with aspects of foreign and security policy, in accordance with a sustained evolutive process and in a unitary manner, on the basis of general objectives laid down in the Treaty" as a fundamental principle. It was on this basis that the Commission supported a single Treaty. Yet the structure of the draft Articles presented by the Luxembourg Presidency on 15 April highlights the risk that the Conference will depart from this basic orientation.

In that draft foreign and security policy is conceived and defined as standing alone as a separate pillar of the general structure. It is fully separated from all other policies, described as Community policies. A third pillar, also to be set up alongside the Community, is also envisaged as consisting of "home affairs and judicial cooperation". These new entities are attached to the Community only artificially and only under the heading of a political union which, in Article B(2), gives equal but separate status to the Community, foreign and security policy and cooperation. This jeopardizes the Rome European Council's avowed objective of securing "coherence of the overall external action of the Community in the framework of its foreign, security, economic and development policies".

3. Following the guidelines set by the European Council, the Commission stands by the view set out in its Opinion of 21 October 1990 that the main, indeed the central, objective of transforming the Community into a European Union should be to ensure the unity, the consistency and, as a result, the efficiency of its international activities. It is, of course, clear that a common foreign and security policy is a sui generis policy that can be implemented only gradually; but it is not possible to affirm the identity of the Union and the consistency of its international personality simply by adding a foreign and security policy to existing policies. The reality of international life makes clear how closely political relations, extending from external security to compliance with human rights, are related to economic policies. This consistency can be guaranteed in full only if the construction of the Community is conceived on a unitary base. Consequently, there can be no question of grafting the Union concept onto the existing Treaty; the Union must absorb the Community and all that it has achieved.

4. The Commission accordingly proposes that the Presidency draft be amended on a number of points which are essential if objectives defined by the European Council are to be achieved. In particular:

(a) the external policy of the Union can be made efficient and coherent by:

- the existence of institutional machinery for the preparation and implementation of Union decisions in the common foreign and security policy area;
- strengthening the existing external policies -- a redefined common commercial policy; cooperation with European countries to be written into the Treaties; likewise for developing countries;
- a clear statement of the Union's international identity in terms of its treaty-making power in areas within its general jurisdiction, particularly, of course, in relation to its common foreign and security policy and its presence on the international scene;

(b) the unitary character of the European construction should be reflected in the structure of the Treaty:

- by combining in the introductory articles all the foundations and objectives of the Union, both those already covered by the existing Community, including the single market, and those of Economic and Monetary Union and of the new foreign and security policy;
- placing in this first part of the Treaty both the provisions for the Union institutions and the concept of Union citizenship, with the rights and obligations pertaining to it.

The few proposed amendments to the Presidency draft annexed to this paper chiefly concern the structure of certain parts of the Treaty and affect the texts of the relevant articles only in so far as is strictly necessary.

. . . . .

ANNEX 3: European Parliament

Resolution on the Intergovernmental Conference in the Context of the European Union (Martin report, Soc., UK) adopted by 204 votes to 26, with 4 abstentions[1]

COMMUNITY FOREIGN POLICY

. . . . .

8. Considers that Article 30 of the Single European Act should be revised in order to provide for matters currently dealt with under EPC to be dealt with in the Community framework with appropriate procedures; believes that the current division between external economic relations handled by the Community institutions with the Commission acting as the Community's external representative, and political cooperation handled by EPC with the EPC President acting as external representative, is increasingly difficult to maintain in practice; considers that any genuine attempt "to assure unity and coherence in the Community's international action" must abolish this increasingly artificial distinction;

9. Calls therefore for the Council (rather than a separate framework of foreign ministers) to be given the prime responsibility for defining policy; for the Commission to have a right of initiative in proposing policies to Council and to have a role in representing the Community externally, including appropriate use of its external missions in third countries; and for the functions of the EPC secretariat to be absorbed by the Commission and Council; and for the Community's foreign policy to be subject to scrutiny by the Community's elected Parliament;

10. Calls for the scope of the Community's foreign policy to include issues of security, peace and disarmament, with a close coordination of national security

---

1 Source: *Europe/Documents*, Nos. 1639/40, 19 July 1990.

policies, and to respect the principle of solidarity and the inviolability of the external borders of Member States;

11. Considers that in all these areas, the Community should aim to have common policies on all matters in which the Member States share essential interests;

12. Considers that membership of international organizations should adjusted accordingly, with the Community as such seeking membership and representing the Member States in those areas where Community competence has been established, and it should therefore belong notably to the Council of Europe;

. . . . .

A Constitution for European Union: The Basis for a European Parliament Draft Treaty[2]

. . . . .

61. The Union shall have competence in the field of foreign policy and common security and defence policy, including arms control, in all sectors in which the Member States share vital interests; the Community's foreign and security policies shall be founded on respect for international law and the principles of solidarity between Member States and the inviolability of their borders; the Constitution shall stipulate the areas in which common action must be taken;

. . . . .

---

2 Source: *Europe/Documents*, No. 1674, 19 December 1990.

Resolution on the Intergovernmental Conference on Political Union
(10 October 1991)[3]

The European Parliament,

- having regard to its proposals and positions adopted on Political Union,
- having regard to the Interinstitutional Conference of 1 October 1991,

A. recalling the events and suggestions which led to the Intergovernmental Conference on Political Union, in particular President Mitterrand's request to Chancellor Kohl to proceed with the transformation of the entire complex of relations between the Member States of the Community into a genuine European Union with a view to defining the foundations and structures of a strong and united Europe, accessible to the individual citizen and moving along the path marked out by its federal aspirations;

B. having regard to the process of democratisation in Central and Eastern Europe, the desire expressed by the leaders of those countries and their citizens to participate fully in the political, economic and social integration of the Community, and the need to take due account of the economic and institutional difficulties deriving from the accession of those countries to the Community,

1. Duly reminds the Community institutions and the Member States of their responsibilities in relation to the deepening of Community integration so that sufficient resources are available for this to constitute a nucleus of stability contributing to peace and respect for fundamental rights throughout Europe;

2. Hopes that the necessary reforms to achieve this objective are adopted at the European Council at Maastricht on 9 and 10 December 1991;

3. Points out that these changes are desired by the overwhelming majority of Community citizens and also correspond to the expectations of a very broad section of public opinion in the other European countries;

4. Considers that, at this stage of the proceedings, the method chosen by the Presidency of tackling problems piecemeal is rational, provided that the result is an integral structure;

5. As regards foreign policy, calls for the following procedures to be applied:
   - the European Council shall define the essential common interests which shall be submitted to the European Parliament for approval,

---

3 Source: *Europe/Documents*, No. 1737, 17 October 1991.

- the Commission, together with the Member states, shall have a right of initiative,
- the Council shall decide on the implementation of foreign policy by qualified majority in accordance with Article 148(2), second indent (with the possibility of derogation decided by the same majority),
- the Member States and the Commission shall be responsible for implementing this policy and for the Community's external representation in accordance with their respective spheres of competence,
- the European Parliament shall be associated with the formulation of foreign policy and scrutiny of its implementation;

6. As regards security and defence policy, calls for the application of these procedures and for:

- the phased implementation of security and defence policy with a precise and binding timetable, taking into account the time limits laid down in the WEU Treaty,
- the possibility of certain executive powers over Community decisions to be conferred on the WEU until 1996,
- the powers of the WEU to be transferred to the Community after that date,
- the formulation of security and defence policy to be regarded as falling with the Community's sphere of competence, taking due account of the various Member States' international commitments, particularly within NATO,
- any Member State which cannot take part in a defence operation to be exempted therefrom without this impeding joint action,
- the European Parliament to have the power to oppose by a majority of its Members any resort to the use of force;

7. Confirms the need for the Community's external policy to group together a common foreign and security policy, trade policy, development cooperation policy and external monetary policy within a single Community structure;

8. Points out that it will not approve a draft treaty which falls short of its demands regarding citizenship, the participation of the European Parliament in the legislative process on an equal footing with the Council, qualified majority voting in the Council -- with particular regard to social, environment, energy and taxation policies -- and regarding revision of the Treaties;

9. Reaffirms that the ultimate objective remains the building of a European Union of a federal nature on the basis of a constitution to be drawn up by the European Parliament;

10. Instructs its President to forward this resolution to the Intergovernmental Conferences on Political Union and Economic and Monetary Union, the

Council, the Commission and the governments and parliaments of the Member States.

ANNEX 4: Western European Union

Council of Ministers, Brussels, 23 April 1990: Communiqué[1]

. . . . .

4. It was with this new prospect in view that Ministers recalled the importance they attach to building a European Union consistent with the Single European Act which they have signed as members of the European Community. They also reaffirmed the importance of the Atlantic Alliance and Western European Union as essential instruments for the security of the member countries and as factors for stability throughout Europe.

The continued presence of the forces of the United States and of Canada stationed in Europe provides a necessary contribution to our common security and overall stability, together with the contribution of WEU countries and their other European partners. Ministers reaffirmed the importance of The Hague Platform and the Comprehensive Concept of arms control and disarmament of the Atlantic Alliance.

. . . . .

6. European stability continued to be based on the collective and individual Commitment of all partners in the Alliance. It is also an essential matter for the Europeans themselves. For the Europeans to enhance their contribution to stability on the European continent and to the protection of their legitimate security interests, a greater degree of cooperation will be fundamental.

Ministers therefore recognized the need to continue working to strengthen the European identity and to promote the process of European integration including the security dimension. This growing identity is destined to be given concrete expression in the form of close, and even new cooperation between the member countries.

In the field of verification of the CFE Treaty and "Open Skies," Ministers welcomed the specific measures which had been adopted by WEU member

---

1 Source: *Europe/Documents*, No. 1613, 25 April 1990.

countries particularly as regards the opening of national inspection teams to include inspectors from other WEU member countries.

On the subject of the computerized processing of verification data, Ministers welcomed the fact that a WEU group of experts had jointly defined realistic parameters for a system of interconnected data bases, and that this common WEU viewpoint had been taken into account by the Atlantic Alliance.

Ministers also noted the progress which had been made in studying the possibilities for European cooperation in the field of space-based observation systems for the purposes of arms control verification, and also for crisis and environmental monitoring. They called for concrete proposals to be submitted to them at their next meeting, inter alia with a view to examining the possibility of establishing a satellite verification agency.

. . . . .

Council of Ministers - Vianden (Luxembourg), 27 June 1991: Communiqué[2]

INTRODUCTION

At their meeting in Luxembourg on 27 June 1991, the Foreign and Defence Ministers of WEU member States reaffirmed the central position now occupied in the debate on the emergence of a European security and defence identity.

Ministers reviewed the efforts being made to promote a security architecture to guarantee all European States the peace and security to which they aspire. They pointed to the complementary role of the three levels around which the security of their countries should be organized in the years to come: a European level: the Western European Union and the Twelve; an Atlantic level: the Atlantic Alliance; a pan-European level: the CSCE.

1. Role and Place of WEU in the Security Architecture

Ministers recalled that the European security and defence identity was emerging within the Twelve and WEU. In this connection, Ministers confirmed their desire that WEU be fully part of the process of European integration while enhancing its contribution to solidarity within the Atlantic Alliance.

---

2 Source: *Europe/Documents*, No. 5523, 29 June 1991.

They stated that the role of the WEU should be strengthened in the context of the European construction process, which is leading the Twelve to a Political Union having a common foreign and security policy. They agreed that European Political Union implies a genuine European security and defence identity and thus greater European responsibility for defence matters. This is in accordance with the Hague platform which makes clear that the construction of an integrated Europe will remain incomplete as long as it does not include security and defence. Ministers therefore agreed that the WEU should be developed in this phase of the European integration process as its defence component.

They also agreed that the development of a genuine European security and defence identity will be reflected in the strengthening of the European pillar within the Atlantic Alliance. This will reinforce the integrity and effectiveness of the Alliance and will require, at each stage, appropriate practical arrangements to ensure transparency and complementarity. This will call for appropriate procedures for cooperation with other Allies.

Ministers noted the need for the European and Atlantic debates to proceed in parallel.

. . . . .

ANNEX 5: North Atlantic Treaty Organization

London Declaration on a Transformed North Atlantic Alliance (Issued by the Heads of State and Government participating in the meeting of the North Atlantic Council in London on 5th-6th July 1990)[1]

. . . . .

3. The unification of Germany means that the division of Europe is also being overcome. A united Germany in the Atlantic Alliance of free democracies and part of the growing political and economic integration of the European Community will be an indispensable factor of stability, which is needed in the heart of Europe. The move within the European Community towards political union, including the development of a European identity in the domain of security, will also contribute to Atlantic solidarity and to the establishment of a just and lasting order of peace throughout the whole of Europe.

. . . . .

Ministerial Meeting of the North Atlantic Council in Copenhagen, Denmark, on 6th-7th June 1991 (Final Communiqué)[2]

. . . . .

1. A transformed Atlantic Alliance constitutes an essential element in the new architecture of an undivided Europe; we are agreed that the Alliance must have

---

1 Source: *Atlantic News*, No. 2240, 7 July 1990.
2 Source: *Atlantic News*, No. 2329, 8 June 1991.

the flexibility to continue to develop and evolve as the security situation dictates. An important basis for this transformation is the agreement of all Allies to enhance the role and responsibility of the European members. We welcome efforts further to strengthen the security dimension in the process of European integration and recognize the significance of the progress made by the countries of the European Community towards the goal of political union, including the development of a common foreign and security policy. These two positive processes are mutually reinforcing. The development of a European security identity and defence role, reflected in the strengthening of the European pillar within the Alliance, will reinforce the integrity and effectiveness of the Atlantic Alliance.

2. We are agreed, in parallel with the emergence and development of a European security identity and defence role, to enhance the essential transatlantic link that the Alliance guarantees and fully to maintain the strategic unity and indivisibility of security of all our members. We will continue, in particular, to ensure the Alliance's capability to fulfil its essential functions. The Alliance is the essential forum for consultation among its members and the venue for agreement on policies bearing on the security and defence commitments of Allies under the Washington Treaty, as expressed in the Statement on NATO's Core Security Functions accompanying this Communique. We all agree that the military dispositions necessary to ensure the collective defence of the Allies must be maintained. This applies in particular to the integrated military structure for the Allied countries that participate in it.

3. Recognizing that it is for the European Allies concerned to decide what arrangements are needed for the expression of a common European foreign and security policy and defence role, we further agree that, as the two processes advance, we will develop practical arrangements to ensure the necessary transparency and complementarity between the European security and defence identity as it emerges in the Twelve and the WEU, and the Alliance. There will be a need, in particular, to establish appropriate links and consultation procedures between them in order to ensure that the Allies that are not currently participating in the development of a European identity in foreign and security policy and defence should be adequately involved in decisions that may affect their security.

. . . . .

NATO's Core Security Functions in the New Europe
(Statement issued by the North Atlantic Council meeting in Ministerial Session in Copenhagen, on 6th and 7th June 1991)[3]

The Fundamental Tasks of the Alliance

. . . . .

7. Other European institutions such as the EC, WEU and CSCE also have roles to play, in accordance with their respective responsibilities and purposes, in these fields. The creation of a European identity in security and defence will underline the preparedness of the Europeans to take a greater share of responsibility for their security and will help to reinforce transatlantic solidarity. However the extent of its membership and of its capabilities gives NATO a particular position in that it can perform all four core security functions. NATO is the essential forum for consultation among the Allies and the forum for agreement on policies bearing on the security and defence commitments of its members under the Washington Treaty.

. . . . .

---

3   Source: *Atlantic News*, No. 2329, 8 June 1991, pp. 4-5.

ANNEX 6: Bilateral Initiatives

Franco-German Proposal at the Intergovernmental Conference of the Twelve on Political Union (updated edition)[1]

SECURITY POLICY COOPERATION IN THE FRAMEWORK OF THE COMMON FOREIGN AND SECURITY POLICY OF POLITICAL UNION

1. General aims and concepts

a. Political Union and its Member States are to develop a Common Foreign and Security Policy (CFSP). The mission of the CFSP will be to extend to all areas of external relations.

b. CFSP will have as its objective the defence of the fundamental interests and common values of political Union in its external relations. It should in particular reinforce the security of Member States, contribute to maintaining peace and international stability, develop friendly relations with other countries, and promote democracy, primacy of law and human rights as well as the economic development of all nations.

c. A common security policy implies the following:

1. Within the framework of CFSP, political Union should implement a common security policy in the aim of setting up a common European defence system in due course without which the construction of European Union would remain incomplete.

2. This implies suppression of the restrictive indication "political and economic aspects of security" under Article 30, paragraph 6(a) of the Single European Act.

---

1 Source: *Europe/Documents*, No. 1690bis, 21 February 1991.

3. The validity of the commitments that the partners have undertaken in the framework of the Atlantic Alliance and the objectives connected to them should not be questioned.

4. The Atlantic Alliance, and notably a permanent US military presence in Europe, remains indispensable for European security and stability.

5. The possibilities given by the Western European Union should be put to use. WEU would become the cooperation channel between Political Union and NATO with a view to ensuring mutual reinforcement of European or trans-Atlantic security structures. As common European security policy develops, the formal link established between the WEU Treaty and the Alliance should be adapted in accordance.

6. WEU acquisitions should be preserved: WEU is founded on a treaty which includes a specific commitment for mutual defence and institutes an adequate organization which associates foreign affairs and defence representatives. The 1987 Platform underscores the fact that WEU activities, as a European defence organization, are carried out in the perspective of European Union.

7. The Atlantic Alliance as such should be strengthened by a more important role and greater responsibilities for Europeans as regards security and defence policies. In this perspective, a European identity for security and defence should be reflected in the development of a European pillar within the Alliance. It is hence necessary to take into account the interaction between the development of the security factor of the Union and the transformation that the Alliance undertakes further to political changes in Europe.

2. Proposals

a. On these bases, the provisions relating to cooperation as regards security policy within political Union should be progressively established. To this end, the European Council should have the jurisdiction to decide what areas of security policy should be the subject of a common policy.

b. As an example, the following elements could already be listed which should be tackled within the Union framework:

1. Disarmament and control of armaments in Europe. Work in this field will take on particular importance after the CSCE Summit in 1992. Cooperation between the Twelve should make it possible for Europeans to put forward common positions as a contribution to the coordination taking place within NATO.

2. Security questions, including peace-keeping measures in the context of the United Nations. This should include the definition of common positions in the debates on disarmament and the control of arms within the United Nations.

3. Nuclear non-proliferation. The decision should be taken, on the base of results obtained in this field in the EPC context, to intensify efforts to implement a common nonproliferation policy dealing with all the aspects examined in the general debate on non-proliferation policy.

4. Economic aspects of security, namely cooperation concerning armaments (including questions relating to the arms market and competition) as well as the control of arms exports (notably for dual-purpose products, precursors of chemical and biological arms, installations and equipment, and ballistic technology) should, because of their link with external policy, be dealt with in the context of CFSP. The question of knowing to what extent these subjects should also come into the areas of Community policy in the framework of Community responsibilities, in relation to the achievement of the European Internal Market and Common Commercial Policy, should also be examined. Adequate coordination with the work of international bodies having jurisdiction in this field, and in particular the GEIP, should be studied.

c. As regards the role of the WEU, it could be stipulated that the WEU makes up an integral part of the European unification process. The following points could be approved concerning this:

1. The work of WEU should be organized in order to establish organizational relations between Political Union and WEU, thus enabling the WEU, with a view to being part of Political Union in course, to progressively develop the European common security policy on behalf of the Union.

2. The obligation of aid and assistance in accordance with the Treaty of Brussels should be maintained for as long as no other equivalent commitment exists between Political Union Member States.

3. The different forms of cooperation which exist within WEU on security and defence matters will be continued. After a certain period of time -- during which it will be possible to put the link between the Union and WEU to the test -- it will be possible to examine, by 1996 at the latest, while taking into account the development of the European security structure, to what extent the pertinent stipulations of the Treaty should be revised.

4. Cooperation within the WEU will be made more operational in the politico-military area as well as in the purely military field, and the appropriate operational and institutional consequences will be drawn.

d. In order to progressively bring WEU closer to Political Union, a cooperation in the sense of coordination of work and complementarity in the distribution of tasks between the Union (CFSP) and WEU should be sought by using the following methods:

1. European Council decisions on the principles and guidelines of common foreign and security policy should serve as a guideline for cooperation in the framework of the Treaty of Brussels.

2. The order and duration of the terms of office for presidents of Political Union and Western European Union will be harmonized as far as possible (by adjusting the transitional provisions in the case of Denmark, Greece and Ireland).

3. The dates and places of Political Union Council and Western European Union meetings at ministerial level, as well as certain meetings of high-ranking officials will be synchronized.

4. The Secretariat General of the Council and the Secretariat General of the Western European Union will finalize appropriate provisions in order to ensure mutual information.

5. Links should be established between the European Parliament and the WEU Assembly.

e. The modified Treaty of Brussels should be revised in due course in order to take into account the changes that have occurred in the European security structures, mentioned in the present document.

f. In order to promote cooperation between the various bodies of the Union and WEU, and given the links between WEU and NATO, it could be desirable to transfer WEU administrative divisions to Brussels.

3. Relations with the European states which are not WEU members

a. Relations between the WEU and the EC Member States which are not members of WEU will be progressively strengthened with a view to possible WEU membership of the above States.

b. Cooperation between WEU and the European members of the Alliance which are not EC members should also be increased. Specific contacts or specific forms of cooperation could also be approved with European members of the Alliance not belonging to Political Union.

British-Italian Initiative
(London, Rome, 5 October 1991)[2]

AN ANGLO-ITALIAN DECLARATION ON EUROPEAN SECURITY AND DEFENCE IN THE CONTEXT OF THE INTERGOVERNMENTAL CONFERENCE ON POLITICAL UNION

1. Italy and United Kingdom are fully aware of the challenge that Europe will have to face in the new political and strategic environment of the 90s. For this reason, they wish to contribute -- in close association with other partners -- to the definition of the framework in which Europe will be able to play a fuller role on the international scene by establishing a political Union.

I. The European identity in the field of security and defence

2. Political union implies the gradual elaboration and implementation of a common foreign and security policy and a stronger European defence identity with the longer term perspective of a common defence policy compatible with the common defence policy we already have with all our allies in NATO.

3. The development of a European identity in the field of security and defence shall be pursued through an evolutionary process involving successive phases.

4. The special relationship between Western Europe and North America, resting on shared values and interests and expressed through the Alliance, is a key element of the European identity. Our mutual defence commitment in the Alliance and the presence of North American forces in Europe as part of a collective structure, are therefore essential to the common defence of Europe.

5. The revision of the Alliance's tasks and strategy and the development of a common foreign and security policy in the context of the political union are complementary. They must proceed in parallel and reach mutually satisfactory results. NATO's reform should imply a reinforced European contribution as part of a changed and rebalanced relationship between North America and a more cohesive Europe.

6. The transatlantic relationship is an integral part of the broader idea of Europe which is reflected in the CSCE process. A reformed NATO embodying the transatlantic relationship will therefore be the key component in the development of a system of security including the whole of Europe.

---

2 Source: *Europe/Documents*, No. 1735, 5 October 1991.

II. The European defence identity and the Alliance

7. The development of a European identity in the field of defence should be construed in such a way as to reinforce the Atlantic Alliance. Such a process will not be contradictory but compatible with a strengthened and reformed NATO.

8. WEU should be entrusted with the task of developing the European dimension in the field of defence, it will develop its role in two complementary directions: as the defence component of the Union and as the means to strengthen the European pillar of the Alliance.

9. In order to perform these functions better, WEU ministerial organs should be transferred to Brussels. The role of WEU and its relationship with the Alliance and the Union should be reviewed by 1998 in the context of article XII of the Brussels Treaty. In order to ensure a better coordination of the activities of WEU, meetings should be synchronized: links appropriate to the different institutions should be established between Secretariats as well as between Presidencies and Parliamentary Assemblies.

10. Consistant with the above, the WEU will take into account in its activities the decisions of the European Council in the context of the common foreign and security policy and positions adopted in the context of the Alliance, bearing in mind the different nature of its relations with each body.

11. In order to achieve complementarity between the European defence identity and the Alliance two principles should apply:

(a) Intensified coordination among Europeans on security and defence issues will respect the principle of openness in consultations, in accordance with the Rome Declaration of 1984 on the contribution of all European allies to NATO and The Hague platform of 1987 on the need to keep all Allies informed of WEU activities.

(b) Complementarity to the decisional process. The Alliance remains the essential forum for agreements on policies which refer to the commitments of their Members in matters of security and defence according to the Washington Treaty. Members of WEU will consult with the allies in a spirit of openness based on concerted positions. On other questions related to the European security identity (for instance collective actions to defend the European interests outside of the NATO area) decisions will be made by WEU in close consultation with the other allies.

12. A special relationship of association should be envisaged for other European partners and Allies. Liaison arrangements will be made for other European countries where appropriate.

III. The European defence identity: operational role

13. In order to give a first practical content to the European defence identity, members of WEU should develop a European reaction force. This would be capable of responding flexibly in a range of possible circumstances outside the NATO area, for example in response to threats to the interests of WEU members or in peacekeeping operations. It would thereby make a new contribution to the Common defence.

14. Such a force would be autonomous, separate from the NATO structure, and would have its own peacetime planning cell to develop contingency plans and organise exercises. Political control would be exercised by WEU Ministers.

15. There should be co-ordination with other members of the Alliance, so that such a force could deploy alongside forces of other allies.

Franco-German Initiative on Foreign, Security, and Defence Policy
(Bonn, Paris, 11 October 1991) [3]

TREATY ON POLITICAL UNION: COMMON FOREIGN AND SECURITY POLICY

I. Article ... of the draft Treaty on Political Union on basic objectives:

The objectives of the Union are ... :

- .....
- to affirm its identity on the international scene, particularly with regard to the implementation of a common foreign and security policy which, in the long term, would include a common defence."

---

3 Source: *Europe/Documents*, No. 1738, 18 October 1991.

II. Article ... of the draft Treaty on Political Union on security and defence

1) The common foreign and security policy will include questions relative to the security and defence of the Union.

2) The decisions and measures taken by the Union in this area may be developed and implemented entirely or in part by the WEU, which is an integral part of the process of European Union, in the context of the areas of competence of this organisation and in conformity with the orientations established by the Union.

3) The Council shall oversee relations between the Union and the WEU in agreement with the institutions of the WEU, and shall ensure the progressive development of the Union's common security policy.

4) For some Member States of the Union, the obligations arising from the Treaties bearing upon the creation of the WEU and the Atlantic Alliance are not affected by the provisions of this present chapter, nor are the specific points of the defence policy of some of the Member States.

In addition, the provisions of this present chapter shall present no obstacle to closer bilateral cooperation between two or several Member States of the Union, within the WEU and the Atlantic Alliance.

5) The provisions of this present article will be revised on the basis of a report presented by the Council to the European Council in 1996 at the latest, in cooperation with the competent institutions of the WEU and in light of progress and experience up to that point.

In conformity with the orientations established by the European Council, the Council shall establish all provisions necessary for the subsequent development of the process.

III. Statement of the Member States on the priority areas of a common foreign and security policy

The Member States agree that the following topics in particular are likely to be the subject of joint action, in conformity with Article ...

- political and economic relations and cooperation with the Soviet Union,
- political and economic relations and cooperation with the countries of Central and Eastern Europe,
- the CSCE process, including the implementation of the results of the Paris CSCE summit of November 1990,

- relations with the United States of America and Canada on the basis of joint declarations of November 1990,
- political and economic relations with the Mediterranean region and with the Middle East,
- policy and cooperation within the United Nations and other international organisations,
- participation in humanitarian measures.

With regard to Article . . ., the following areas are taken into consideration:

- disarmament policy and arms control in Europe, including confidence-building measures,
- participation in peace-keeping measures, especially within the framework of the United Nations,
- nuclear non-proliferation,
- the economic aspects of security, i.e., cooperation regarding arms exports and the control of arms exports.

IV. Essential points of the statement by the WEU Member States on Article . . . regarding the foundations for cooperation between the WEU and the Union, and between the WEU and the Atlantic Alliance

1. The WEU's objectives:
   - In conformity with the WEU Treaty, the Hague "Platform" of 1986, and the Vianden communique of 27 June 1991:
     . strengthening the role of the WEU, which is a full partner in the process of European unification and whose goal is union,
     . the necessity to develop a genuine European defence and security identity and to assume increasing responsibility in the area of defence,
     . the subsequent step-by-step building up of the WEU as a component of the Union's defence.
   - an invitation to the members of the Community which also belong to the Alliance to become part of the WEU, and for those which do not belong to the Alliance, the granting of observer status within the WEU,
   - consultation of the Commission: in accordance with its competencies, the Commission will be kept informed by the Presidency of the WEU.

2. Creation of an organic link between the WEU and the Union:

- Development of a clear organic relationship between the WEU and the Union, and the operational organisation of the WEU, which shall act in conformity with the Directives of the Union, and to this end:

  . harmonisation of the sequence and length of Presidencies,
  . synchronisation of sessions and working methods,
  . closer cooperation between the General Secretariat of the WEU and the Council of Ministers, on the one hand, and between the General Secretariat of the Council and the Council of Ministers of the Union on the other hand, and between the WEU Parliamentary Assembly and the European Parliament,
  . creation of a military planning and coordination group within the WEU which will be in charge of the following tasks:

  - planning of joint actions, including in cases of crisis,
  - operational planning for cooperation in the case of natural disasters,
  - coordination of needs studies in all areas of cooperation,
  - organisation of joint maneuvers.

  . closer military cooperation with the Alliance, especially in the areas of logistics, transport, training, and information,
  . increased cooperation in the area of armaments, with a view to creating a European armaments agency,
  . regular meetings between Joint Chiefs of Staff,
  . transformation of the WEU Institute into a European security and defence academy.

- As a consequence of the above measures to strengthen the WEU, transfer of the WEU's General Secretariat to Brussels,
- The setting up of military units under the WEU.

3. WEU-NATO cooperation:

- This is a matter of strengthening the Atlantic Alliance as a whole "by increasing the role and responsibility of Europe and by establishing a European pillar." (joint letter of 6 December 1990),
- in conformity with NATO's Copenhagen communique and the WEU's Vianden communique, the establishment of practical provisions ensuring transparency and complementarity between the WEU and NATO,

- development of cooperation between the WEU General Secretariat and that of NATO,
- regulation coordination of the WEU Member States with a view to developing common positions on all essential questions within the Alliance,
- for representation to the WEU, the development of a "two-hat" formula to include representatives to the Alliance and to the Community,
- association with the countries of the Alliance which are not part of the Community through consultations when the interests of these countries are affected.

4. Relations with the other States of Europe, in particular those in Central, Eastern, and Southeastern, Europe (developments corresponding to the Copenhagen communique for the Alliance and to the Vianden communique for the WEU).

For the record:

Franco-German military cooperation will be strengthened beyond the present Brigade.

Thus, the reinformed Franco-German units could serve as the core of a European corps, including the forces of other WEU Member States. This new structure could also become the model for closer military cooperation between the WEU Member States.

ANNEX 7: EC and United States

Declaration on EC-US Relations[1]

The United States of America on one side and, on the other, the European Community and its member States,
- mindful of their common heritage and of their close historical, political, economic and cultural ties,
- guided by their faith in the values of human dignity, intellectual freedom and civil liberties, and in the democratic institutions which have evolved on both sides of the Atlantic over the centuries,
- recognizing that the transatlantic solidarity has been essential for the preservation of peace and freedom and for the development of free and prosperous economies as well as for the recent developments which have restored unity in Europe,
- determined to help consolidate the new Europe, undivided and democratic,
- resolved to strengthen security, economic cooperation and human rights in Europe in the framework of the CSCE, and in other fora,
- noting the firm commitment of the United States and the EC member States concerned to the North Atlantic Alliance and to its principles and purposes,
- acting on the basis of a pattern of cooperation proven over many decades, and convinced that by strengthening and expanding this partnership on an equal footing they will greatly contribute to continued stability, as well as to polical and economic progress in Europe and in the world,
- aware of their shared responsibility, not only to further common interests but also to face transnational challenges affecting the well-being of all mankind,
- bearing in mind the accelerating process by which the European Community is acquiring its own identity in economic and monetary matters, in foreign policy and in the domain of security,

---

[1] Source: *Europe/Documents*, No. 1622, 23 November 1990.

- determined further to strengthen transatlantic solidarity, through the variety of their international relations,

have decided to endow their relationship with long-term perspectives.

Common goals

The United States of America and the European Community and its member States solemnly reaffirm their determination further to strengthen their partnership in order to:

- support democracy, the rule of law and respect for human rights and individual liberty, and promote prosperity and social progress world-wide;
- safeguard peace and promote international security, by cooperating with other nations against aggression and coercion, by contributing to the settlement of conflicts in the world and by reinforcing the role of the United Nations and other international organisations;
- pursue policies aimed at achieving a sound world economy marked by sustained economic growth with low inflation, a high level of employment, equitable social conditions, in a framework of international stability;
- promote market principles, reject protectionism and expand, strengthen and further open the multilateral trading system;
- carry out their resolve to help developing countries by all appropriate means in their efforts towards political and economic reforms;
- provide adequate support, in cooperation with other states and organisations, to the nations of Eastern and Central Europe undertaking economic and political reforms and encourage their participation in the multilateral institutions of international trade and finance.

Principles of US-EC partnership

To achieve their common goals, the European Community and its member States and the United States of America will inform and consult each other on important matters of common interest, both political and economic, with a view to bringing their positions as close as possible, without prejudice to their respective independence. In appropriate international bodies, in particular, they will seek close cooperation.

The EC-US partnership will, moreover, greatly benefit from the mutual knowledge and understanding acquired through regular consultations as described in this Declaration.

Economic cooperation

Both sides recognize the importance of strengthening the multilateral trading system. They will support further steps towards liberalization, transparency, and the implementation of GATT and OECD principles concerning both trade in goods and services and investment.

They will further develop their dialogue, which is already underway, on other matters such as technical and non-tariff barriers to industrial and agricultural trade, services, competition policy, transportation policy, standards, telecommunications, high technology and other relevant areas.

Education, scientific and cultural cooperation

The partnership between the European Community and its member States on the one hand, and the United States on the other, will be based on continuous efforts to strengthen mutual cooperation in various other fields which directly affect the present and future well-being of their citizens, such as exchanges and joint projects in science and technology, including, inter alia, research in medicine, environment protection, pollution prevention, energy, space, high-energy physics, and the safety of nuclear and other installations, as well as in education and culture, including academic and youth exchanges.

Trans-national challenges

The Unites States of America and the European Community and its member States will fulfil their responsibility to address trans-national challenges, in the interest of their own peoples and of the rest of the world. In particular, they will join their efforts in the following fields:

- combatting and preventing terrorism;
- putting an end to the illegal production, trafficking and consumption of narcotics and related criminal activities, such as the laundering of money;
- cooperating in the fight against international crime;
- protecting the environment, both internationally and domestically, by integrating environmental and economic goals;
- preventing the proliferation of nuclear armaments, chemical and biological weapons, and missile technology.

Institutional framework for consultation

Both sides agree that a framework is required for regular and intensive consultation. They will make full use of and further strengthen existing procedures, including those established by the President of the European Council and the President of the United States on 27th February 1990, namely:

- bi-annual consultations to be arranged in the United States and in Europe between, on the one side, the President of the European Council and the President of the Commission, and on the other side, the President of the United States;
- bi-annual consultations between the European Community Foreign Ministers, with the Commission, and the US Secretary of State, alternately on either side of the Atlantic;
- ad hoc consultations between the Presidency Foreign Minister or the Troika and the US Secretary of State;
- bi-annual consultations between the Commission and the US Government at Cabinet level;
- briefings, as currently exist, by the Presidency to US Representatives on European Political Cooperation (EPC) meetings at the Ministerial level.

Both sides are resolved to develop and deepen these procedures for consultation so as to reflect the evolution of the European Community and of its relationship with the United States.

They welcome the actions taken by the European Parliament and the Congress of the United States in order to improve their dialogue and thereby bring closer together the peoples on both sides of the Atlantic.

Abbreviations

ASEAN	Association of South East Asian Nations
ACP	African, Caribbean and Pacific Countries
CAP	Common Agricultural Policy
CET	Common External Tariff
CFE	Conventional Forces in Europe
CMCA	Common Market of Central America
COREPER	Committee of Permanent Representatives to the European Communities
COREU	Correspondence Européenne
CSCE	Conference on Security and Cooperation in Europe
DPC	Defense Planning Committee (NATO)
EC	European Communities
EEC	European Economic Community
EDC	European Defense Community
EIB	European Investment Bank
EFTA	European Free Trade Area
EMS	European Monetary System
EMU	Economic and Monetary Union
EP	European Parliament
EPC	European Political Cooperation
EPU	European Political Union
EUREKA	European Research Cooperation Agency
GAC	General Affairs Council
GATT	General Agreement on Tariffs and Trade
GCC	Gulf Cooperation Council
IGC	Intergovernmental Conference
IMF	International Monetary Fund
LDC	Less Developed Country
NAC	North Atlantic Council (NATO)
NATO	North Atlantic Treaty Organization
NGO	Non-governmental Organization
NPT	Nuclear Nonproliferation Treaty
OEEC	Organization for European Economic Cooperation
OECD	Organization for Economic Cooperation and Development
PU	Political Union
SEA	Single European Act
UN	United Nations
VAT	Value Added Tax
WEU	Western European Union

Contributors

Allen, David, University of Loughborough, England

Alonso Terme, Rosa Maria, Central University of Barcelona

Anderson, Scott, School of Advanced International Studies, Washington, D.C.

Atacanli, Sermet, Ministry of Foreign Affairs of Turkey, Ankara

Coignez, Veerle, School of Advanced International Studies, Washington, D.C.

Edwards, Geoffrey, University of Cambridge, England

Hamlet, Lawrence L., Council on Foreign Relations, New York

Hill, Christopher W., London School of Economics and Political Science

Hiwaki, Kensei, Tokyo International University

Jannuzzi, Giovanni, Secretariat of European Political Cooperation, Brussels

Körmendy, István, Ministry of Foreign Affairs of Hungary, Budapest

Lak, Maarten W. J., The Netherlands' Ministry of Foreign Affairs, The Hague

Müller, Harald, Peace Research Institute Frankfurt

Murray, Christopher W., United States Mission to the EC, Brussels

Nuttall, Simon, Commission of the European Community, Brussels

Rhein, Eberhard, Commission of the European Communtiy, Brussels

Rummel, Reinhardt, Stiftung Wissenschaft und Politik, Ebenhausen

Scheich, Manfred, Ministry of Foreign Affairs of Austria, Vienna

Vajic, Nina, University of Zagreb

Yakovenko, Aleksandr, Ministry of Foreign Affairs of the USSR, Moscow

Editorial Staff:
Scott Anderson, Sylvia M. Schwaag and Ellen Thalman,
Paul H. Nitze School of Advanced International Studies, The Johns Hopkins University, Bologna, Italy and Washington, D.C.

TOWARD POLITICAL UNION
Planning a Common Foreign and Security Policy in the European Community
edited by
Reinhardt Rummel

At a time when a major effort is being made in Europe to turn the previous, largely *economic* Community into a *political* union, this book provides insight into both the present state of European Community foreign policy and the plans for the future development of foreign and security policy within the Community.

The contributors, representing major Community institutions and member states, offer their assessments of the political and institutional issues influencing the formation of a common foreign and security policy for the twelve member states. Representatives of non-EC countries (particularly the United States, the former Soviet Union, and Japan) provide perspectives on the status and potential functions of a European political union within the context of a broader European and global network of actors.

Reinhardt Rummel is a senior research fellow at the Stiftung Wissenschaft und Politik in Ebenhausen, Germany.

For order and other information, please write to:

WESTVIEW PRESS
5500 Central Avenue • Boulder, Colorado 80301-2847
36 Lonsdale Road • Summertown • Oxford OX2 7EW

ISBN 0-8133-8518-0